CONGRESS

Process and Policy

Second Edition

CONGRESS

PROCESS AND POLICY

by

RANDALL B. RIPLEY

THE OHIO STATE UNIVERSITY

SECOND EDITION

W·W·NORTON & COMPANY

New York • *London*

Library of Congress Cataloging in Publication Data

Ripley, Randall B
Congress: process and policy, 2nd ed.

Bibliography: p.
Includes index.
1. United States. Congress. I. Title.
JK1061.R55   1978   328.73   78–16055
ISBN 0–393–09004–3

Book designed by Jacques Chazaud
Type set in Baskerville by Fuller Typesetting of Lancaster

1 2 3 4 5 6 7 8 9 0

To: G.A.F.

TABLE OF CONTENTS

LIST OF TABLES

LIST OF FIGURES

PREFACE

As a basic text on the Congress of the United States, this volume portrays the institution and its principal activities. An effort has been made to take the reader beyond description to an analysis of the way in which Congress makes public policy. The concern with policy has been used to help guide the judgments about what to include and what to exclude in this treatment of our national legislature.

Congress is the most systematically studied of all American governing institutions. I have mined the rich literature on Congress in order to offer empirical support for a variety of general points. Congress is a very complex institution; there is no pretense in this volume that it is simple. However, what follows provides an interpretation of Congress as well as a description.

There is more of an interpretive theme in this second edition than there was in the first. Part of the reason is that I have thought about Congress in some different ways in the intervening years. Part of the reason is that Congress itself has been in a continuing state of ferment even in the few years between the time I prepared the first edition and the time I prepared this edition. The post-Watergate Congress has evolved rather rapidly in some regards, and those short-term evolutions are reflected in the present volume.

The viewpoint adopted in this volume can be summarized very briefly. First, fragmentation is a more "natural" state of affairs in Congress than integration, although it is not inevitable. Second, Congress is important in helping to determine the nature of public policy in the United States no matter where it falls on the spectrum between extreme fragmentation at one end and extreme integration at the other end. Third, the substance of congressional policy impact is affected by where Congress falls on the fragmentation-integration spectrum at any given time. Fourth, different values and interests are served best by different degrees of fragmentation or integration—there is no single "right" way for Congress to conduct its business. Debate over congressional processes is simultaneously debate over substantive outcomes. Process and policy are intricately interwoven.

Congress can be observed from many perspectives. In this volume the focus is on two related aspects—the characteristics and performance of Congress as an institution; and the disparate and often fragmented membership of Congress, whose individual behavior determine a great deal about how the institution performs and is perceived.

A reader of this volume should come away with a good sense of Congress as an institution, of congressional relations with key portions of its environment, and of the importance of Congress as a policy-maker. Above all, he or she should come away with a sense that the members of Congress are not caught up in some ritual with inevitable endings but instead that they have a number of options open to them in relation both to personal behavior and the collective behavior of the institution. Congress is neither immutable nor is it moribund. Like many institutions, it appears conservative much of the time. But it is also important and influential as a policy-maker even in its most conservative mood and can enlarge that influence in periods of aggressiveness.

Although the author has worked in Congress and continues to be fascinated by some of the trivia of its workings, there is no aspiration to present this book as an "insider's" look at the daily routine of Congress. Gossipy details that do not have much utility beyond whatever intrinsic interest they possess are omitted. Nor is there a lengthy guide to parliamentary procedure as used in Congress or technical discussion of "how a bill becomes law."

In general, writing on Congress has been of two types. The first type is the scholarly study that focuses on the details of some rather minute portion of Congress (for example, the whip organizations, single committees, the behavior of new congressmen in one year). Such studies usually fail to pose broader questions about the meaning of the scrap of behavior investigated. The second type consists of attacks or defenses that betray rather great ignorance about the details of the institution. This book has an empirical focus rather than a normative one, although questions of "should" and "ought" are not ignored. The empirical treatment in this volume is essential to posing important normative questions; it is even more important in answering those questions.

The data for this study of Congress come from many sources. An attempt has been made to summarize the major relevant data-based literature on Congress. Not everything in the literature was found useful, however, and less useful items have been excluded as there seemed to be no obligation to summarize everything just for its own sake (some of these omissions are referred to in the footnotes). In addition to published studies, some original empirical work is presented. Where summaries of empirical studies do appear, they are presented in a non-technical manner that should make them accessible to all readers.

It is good form to state an author's overriding biases before the reader plunges into a book: I have long taken Congress seriously as a maker of public policy and continue to do so. Long before Watergate highlighted the dangers of allowing all important decisions to be made in the White House I was anxious for Congress to contribute vigorously to the solution of the most important public problems.

I also harbor the prejudice that before meaningful discussion of "reform" can occur, the discussants must have a thorough knowledge of how Congress works, and this can come only from serious study. The literature of reform is too often marked by a great deal of emotion and not enough attention to reality. I believe systematic analysis must precede prescriptions for change. This prejudice does not mean that I am an apologist for all that Congress is and does. There is much in congressional practice and performance that distresses me as a citizen and as a political scientist, but that makes me even more eager to analyze it as objectively as possible as a necessary prelude to making sound normative judgments.

The organization of the book is straightforward. In part I Congress is presented in broad strokes. Chapter 1 paints a general picture of Congress in its environment and discusses the position of Congress in relation to policy-making. Chapter 2 summarizes the development of Congress. Chapter 3 deals with the elections that provide the members of the House and Senate.

Part II investigates the internal environment for policy-making by Congress. Chapter 4 presents an overview of how members of Congress are socialized into certain patterns of making decisions and how those decisions get made. Chapter 5 focuses on committees and subcommittees; Chapter 6 examines the party leadership; and Chapter 7 deals with a variety of other internal influences such as state delegations, ideologically based groups, personal and committee staffs, and support agencies for Congress as a whole.

Part III focuses on the external relations of Congress that are critical to determining both the nature and the scope of its policy impact. Chapter 8 explores congressional relations with interest groups and constituents. Chapter 9 discusses congressional relations with the president and the institutional presidency. Chapter 10 examines congressional relations with the bureaucracy.

Part IV draws together the policy-related themes introduced in earlier chapters and focuses on two broad facets of congressional influence over American public policy: congressional access to policy-making (in Chapter 11) and congressional impact on policy (in Chapter 12).

Like anyone who studies a subject for a long time, I owe many debts to many people. A number of those are acknowledged in the footnotes and selected bibliography. A few individuals deserve special mention, however. Over the years three friends and fellow students of Congress have proved to be particularly stimulating as I have thought about Congress and public policy: D.B. Hardeman, Charles O. Jones, and Theodore J. Lowi. I am hopeful that a number of their insights they have shared with me in a variety of ways are reflected in this book. John F. Bibby and John F. Manley helped concretely in my labors to transform a first edition into a second edition by providing very thoughtful reviews of the first edition and suggestions for how to improve it.

Above all, I am grateful to my friend Grace A. Franklin for being a superb and sharing colleague in a number of explorations of American institutions and policies, including this one. I am pleased to dedicate this book to her.

PART I

CONGRESS
IN THE
AMERICAN
POLITICAL
SYSTEM

CHAPTER 1

THE NATURE OF
CONGRESS

C ONGRESS, UNLIKE MOST OTHER NATIONAL LEGISLATURES IN THE TWEN-
tieth century, is at the heart of public policy-making.[1] Although
some details of its structure and practices have changed since its creation in 1789, it has always played a vital part in determining the scope
and character of American governmental activity. It shares its policy-
making powers principally with the executive branch—both the president and the vast bureaucracy that has developed—and the interaction
between Congress and the executive, often with spokespersons for private interests also involved, is responsible for most of the detailed
decisions about what specific policies to pursue and what specific
programs to implement.

Paradoxically, perhaps, the natural tendency is for Congress to go
about its important business in a highly fragmented, nonintegrated,
almost chaotic manner. Some argue that this central fact of fragmentation prevents Congress from being truly important in terms of shaping public policy in the United States. Others argue that this fragmentation supports other important values, particularly the value of
allowing a great many different interests to be heard in the policy
process.

---

1. Other societies, of course, have very different traditions. Some legislatures are
principally window dressing (as in the Soviet Union) with power lodged in a
combination of party and administrative bodies. Some societies operate without
national representative assemblies at all. This was true of Czarist Russia and Nazi
Germany. It is also true of a number of nations in the contemporary world. For
example, in the mid-1970's just in Latin America alone Cuba, Peru, Chile, Ecua-
dor, and Bolivia had no national representative assemblies that actually met
(some of them had constitutions providing for legislatures but the constitutions
were all in a state of suspension). In modern Great Britain, Parliament is largely
subservient to the policies announced by the executive part of the government.
In other Western European nations a similar situation exists.

This chapter sketches the basic nature of Congress by introducing the theme of fragmentation vs. integration (a theme that will reappear throughout the volume), by beginning to explore the relations between Congress and the executive branch, and by discussing the principal functions performed by Congress.

FRAGMENTATION VS. INTEGRATION

There are two principal dimensions to fragmentation and integration as they are defined in this volume. One involves the organizational state of Congress. The second involves the degree of coherence or coordination between individual policies and programs contained in legislation. Fragmentation is characterized by a decentralized organization and by a lack of planned coherence (and only limited random coherence) between individual policies. Integration is characterized by a centralized organization and by the potential (although not the certainty) for planned coherence between individual policies.

In a highly fragmented situation there are no forces and mechanisms that allow for the planned achievement of policy coherence and integration. Thus the results stemming from such a situation usually include specific policies and programs that have no planned relationship to one another. In fact, they may be inconsistent and flatly contradictory when viewed together. Different specific goals are articulated or at least implicit for individual policies, and there are no overriding goals that bind the individual policies together.

In a highly integrated situation there are forces and mechanisms that at least provide Congress with the opportunity of producing policies and programs characterized by a high degree of coherence and coordination. Collectively, individual policies can be linked in a broad program aimed at achieving some concrete overriding goals. Naturally, Congress may not grasp the opportunity or make the most of it.

Note that policy coherence is impossible when the organization is highly decentralized. Policy coherence is not guaranteed when the organization is highly centralized, but at least it is possible.

As with most facets of American politics, including Congress, the two situations described above are really representative of a whole range of possibilities that lie along a spectrum from fragmentation to complete integration. Most of the time Congress falls somewhere between the extremes. Exactly where it falls makes some important differences in what policies emerge.

Conditions Favorable to Fragmentation

There are eight major facts of congressional life that push primarily in the direction of greater fragmentation. Each will be discussed in some detail after an initial listing:

—members are popularly elected from specific geographical constituencies in which they must reside.

—there are two separate, and quite different, houses of Congress.

—the federal government has a very large and diverse substantive agenda.

—Congress shares powers with a very large and disaggregated bureaucracy.

—Congress is open to the activities and influence of a large number of diverse organized interest groups.

—Congress organizes itself into a very large number of committees and subcommittees in order to process its business (the 95th Congress in 1977–78 had a total of 323 committees and subcommittees).

—the national political parties are very weak and have almost no impact on Congress.

—many members are ambitious primarily in terms of personal influence, re-election, and/or advancement to more prestigious elective office.

Popular Election. Members of the Senate are popularly elected from individual states in which they must reside. Members of the House of Representatives are popularly elected from individual districts in which they must reside. The consequences of these simple facts for both the individual members and for the institution are enormous.[2] Of necessity, members are concerned much of the time with the locally-oriented interests of their constituents. This necessity in turn helps shape the general policy orientation of Congress. Because members attend to the needs of 435 districts and 50 states there are only rare incentives or opportunities to assert congressional primacy in

---

2. For an argument that virtually everything about Congress can be explained by the fact of popular election see David R. Mayhew, *Congress: The Electoral Connection* (New Haven: Yale University Press, 1974). For my own views on both the strengths and limits of Mayhew's argument see my review of the book in *Capitol Studies* 4 (1976): 85–87. My basic criticism is that his argument oversimplifies the nature of Congress' policy impact and does not satisfactorily account for many of its facets.

large national policy areas. The constituency focus has a centrifugal effect that makes presidential-bureaucratic primacy easier to achieve than congressional primacy.

Also, given the diversity of interests in the various districts and states, natural impetus is given to a bargaining and compromising style of decision-making by the members of Congress. Many major bills are aggregates of specific provisions designed to benefit specific constituency interests. Bills are thus constructed inductively rather than deductively on the basis of national goals and standards.

Another result of constituency focus is that the diversity of interests to be satisfied prevents any single voice emerging as "the" congressional spokesman except very rarely. The internal organization of Congress reflects this fact.

Two Houses. The House and Senate have some important similarities. They also have some important differences. The fact of having two houses that must agree on every detail before legislation can emerge is a force favoring fragmentation (and relatively slow action) much of the time. The fact that the two houses differ compounds the contribution of bicameralism to fragmentation. It must also be noted that, unlike the situation in some countries where there are two houses in name but only one has much power (the United Kingdom, for example), both the House and Senate are powerful and the members of each are jealous of their power and their prerogatives.

Most of the major differences between House and Senate stem from the basic facts of size and constituency: a Senate of 100 persons each representing an entire state and a House of 435 persons each representing a district of about 500,000 people.[3] This basic difference leads to additional differences that often complicate the process of getting agreement between the two houses in timely fashion:

—Senators are more visible than representatives and so are often more concerned with a national audience and with broad policy pronouncements than with the details of legislation that is often not very glamorous.

—Representatives concentrate much more than senators on the details of committee and subcommittee work, both because they are more concerned with the fine points of legislation and because they have fewer assignments and fewer outlets for their energies.

---

3. This discussion of House-Senate differences is based, in part, on David J. Vogler, *The Politics of Congress,* 2nd ed. (Boston: Allyn and Bacon, 1977), 207–213.

—the House is more tightly organized to conduct business on the floor than the Senate.

—the party leaders in the House, although far from omnipotent, are usually in a stronger position to produce procedural order and efficiency than are the party leaders in the Senate.

Large Substantive Agenda. Through the years the agenda of the entire federal government, and therefore the agenda of Congress, has increased enormously in size and complexity. Thus the congressional workload has also increased dramatically. This has had a number of results, such as reinforcing a highly developed specialization of labor for individual members in committees and subcommittees and making necessary the increasing use of staff, both for individual members and for committees, to help with the heavy workload.

The increasing workload has also contributed to the development of elaborate rules that facilitate the processing of a large amount of business in reasonably good order. The rules are not impartial. They facilitate the legislative process but can also be used to substantive advantage by one side or the other. They also allow for relative invisibility in handling issues if visibility is not demanded by a sizeable group of members. And the rules in no way promote stronger or more disciplined political parties in Congress that might tamper with the freedom of individual members to follow their own policy preferences.

In general, the rules protect the status of the committee system by making it difficult for members outside committees or dissidents within committees to challenge successfully the legislative products of those committees. The rules ensure that any piece of legislation must go through several committee and floor processes in both houses. This means that the opportunities for defeating or amending proposals are numerous. Typically, a given bill will be considered by two subcommittees (one in each house), two full committees (one in each house), the House Rules Committee, a conference committee to iron out differences between the versions passed in the two houses, and a meeting of both houses (perhaps two—once for initial passage and once to consider the handiwork of the conference committee). Given this complexity and the protection offered committee and subcommittee decisions and members, the necessity of bargaining and compromise between members representing differing points of view and perhaps competing interests is underscored.

Power-sharing with the Bureaucracy. The federal bureaucracy is divided into a seemingly infinite numbers of bureaus, administrations, offices, divisions, and branches, each with its own piece of the policy world as its turf. The numerous congressional subcommittees parallel the turf division of the bureaucracy in most instances. Thus a situation is created whereby a few individuals in each house with their counterparts "downtown" (that is, in the bureaucratic offices scattered around Washington) are at the center of policy-making in each of numerous small—but often important—substantive areas.

Openness to Organized Interest Groups. Both Congress and the bureaucracy are permeable. They are open to representations and influence from outside interests and individuals. Organized interest groups are able to be particularly effective in representing their points of view both in Congress and in the bureaucracy. Thus the opportunity is created for the emergence of "subgovernments"—small groups composed of a few key bureaucrats, interest group members, and senior members of subcommittees who, in effect, make policy by themselves in specific substantive areas with very little input by anyone else such as rank-and-file members of the two chambers, congressional party leaders, or the president or institutional presidency.[4]

The widespread occurrence of these semi-autonomous subgovernments makes coordinated policy very difficult, if not impossible, to achieve in many instances.

Committees and Subcommittees. The establishment, growth, and entrenchment of congressional committees and subcommittees has been primarily a response to a strong executive branch and to a growing workload. Congress, with many of its members intent on retaining important influence over policy, hit on a strong committee system as the device for retaining influence in the face of a growing substantive workload (both in amount and in scope) and a growing bureaucracy. The device has worked to achieve that purpose. But it has also become the cornerstone of both organizational and policy fragmentation in Congress. Each committee and particularly each subcommittee has its own niche in the policy world and is rarely challenged in it. More to the point, there is little coordination on the sub-

---

4. The term "subgovernment" comes from Douglass Cater, *Power in Washington* (New York: Random House, 1964). Ernest S. Griffith uses the term "whirlpools" for the same phenomenon in *Congress: Its Contemporary Role,* 3rd ed. (New York: New York University Press, 1961). Other terms in the literature include "iron triangle" and "unholy trinity." In addition to some examples in Cater, see J. Leiper Freeman, *The Political Process,* rev. ed. (New York: Random House, 1965) and Randall B. Ripley and Grace A. Franklin, *Congress, the Bureaucracy, and Public Policy* (Homewood, Ill.: Dorsey, 1976) for empirical examples of subgovernments at work.

stance of legislation between committees in the two houses, between committees in the same house, or even between subcommittees of the same committee. There are occasional readjustments of jurisdictions (usually to reflect changes in the structure of the bureaucracy), but the general fragmenting thrust of the committee and subcommittee system remains the same.

Weak National Parties. National political parties in the United States are wraithlike. Primarily, they are constructs in the minds of people who think of themselves as Democrats or Republicans. Organizationally their main function is to prepare for a national convention every four years (and occasionally a meeting between presidential elections) in order to nominate candidates for president and vice-president and adopt a party platform. They have virtually nothing to do with congressional nominations and elections. This situation also lends itself to helping create policy fragmentation in Congress. In some countries, the United Kingdom being the best-known example, national parties help frame national policy and enforce support of that policy in the legislature through active and authoritative participation in nominations and elections. That potential source of policy integration or centralization is missing in the United States.

Personal Ambition of Members. Most of the time most members of the House and Senate are concerned with their own careers. This means that they are primarily interested in re-election to their seats. In order to enhance their chances of re-election they are very interested in receiving credit in their constituencies for their work in Congress. This means that they are likely to concentrate on helping their constituents who are having trouble with parts of the bureaucracy ("casework") or with getting credit for constituency-oriented legislation or actions by the bureaucracy. Concern with broad, integrated national policies is likely to be secondary.

If the members are not interested primarily in re-election to their present seats, they may well have their eyes on other elective offices: governorships or Senate seats or even the presidency in the case of House members; governorships or the presidency in the case of senators. Those aspiring to the presidency may take more interest in broad, integrated policy, but those individuals are relatively few in number (despite the occasional feeling just before a presidential election year that virtually all senators want to be president).

These concerns mean that individual members have a stake both in organizational decentralization—so they are relatively free to pursue

their interests without interference—and in low coordination between policies—so that their pet interests will not be held up by the
necessity of considering other policies simultaneously.

Conditions Favorable to Integration

Although not as numerous or as compelling, there are also some
major aspects of congressional life that can push in the direction of
greater integration:

—members take pride in Congress as an institution and are ambitious for the policy impact of the institutions compared to the
   impact of the executive branch.
—there are well-developed party organizations within the House and
   Senate that have potential for providing centralized leadership.
—some members have strong, broad substantive policy commitments.
—Congress shares power with a strong president, who is buttressed
   by a well-developed institutional presidency; the president and
   presidency have the potential for providing centralized leadership.

Institutional Pride and Ambition. Although personal ambition tends
to predominate, there are also members who worry about the institutional place of Congress in the American governing scheme. These individuals want to make sure that Congress as an institution is important. In seeking to make their case they can appeal to the pride in
being a member of Congress that many of the members exhibit, even
if personal ambition governs most of their actions.

Party Organization in Congress. Party leaders may not be very effective in bringing a degree of integration to Congress both organizationally and in terms of policy results at any given time, but the
important fact is that party leaders and party machinery exist continuously and represent a constant potential for increased integration,
especially organizationally. This is particularly true in the House and
less true in the Senate, given the differences between the two chambers
outlined above. Given the weakness of national parties and even constituency parties, the parties in the House and Senate are the only
political parties that matter in any concrete sense for most senators
and representatives.

Broad Substantive Policy Commitments by Members. Despite the
strength of personal ambition and the various forces pulling members

to consider mainly bits and scraps of policy, much of it constituency-oriented, there are a number of members that have broad policy commitments. This number, naturally, varies from time to time. As the number grows the chances for integration are enhanced.

Power-sharing with the President. The fact that the president is constitutionally an important legislative actor provides a possible location for some integrating leadership both organizationally and in terms of policy coherence. In much consideration of the relationship between Congress and the president, the assumption seems to be that the two institutions are competing for a fixed amount of power or influence over legislation and policy. Necessarily, if this were true, as one gained the other one would lose. When Congress was thought to be "strong," the president would be "weak," and vice versa.

This view of zero-sum competition for influence between Congress and the president is, however, misleading. By virtue of the constitutional structure in which they both must work, Congress and the president are more realistically viewed as "partners" who share power —power that, in fact, has grown over time and is not limited to a fixed sum.[5] To be sure, they compete with each other on some matters, but they also cooperate with each other on a large number of other matters. And at some points in history both have seemed weak and ineffectual; at other points both have seemed strong and aggressive.

The presence of an aggressive legislative leader in the presidency does not guarantee integration. But such a leader in that office, working with aggressive congressional leaders of his own party, can bring considerable organizational integration to Congress and can create conditions allowing a fair amount of programmatic integration.

Policy Consequences of Fragmentation and Integration

Fragmentation pushes toward the following policy consequences:
—stability of policy content; changes that occur are slow and small.
—a tendency to define most domestic policy as distributive (providing only subsidy and support for private activity).
—a low degree of concern in Congress with the oversight of bureaucratic performance and with the evaluation of the impact of policies and programs.
—a generally passive stance toward the policy role of Congress on the part of the members.

---

5. See Ralph K. Huitt, "Congress: Retrospect and Prospect," *Journal of Politics* 38 (1976): 209–227.

Integration pushes toward the following policy consequences:

—a willingness to change some existing policies, including some major changes.

—a willingness to define some domestic policy as protective regulatory or redistributive (with some sanctions for prohibited private activity and perceived attempts to shift tangible benefits in the direction of greater social equality).

—a higher degree of concern in Congress with the oversight of bureaucratic performance and with evaluation of policy impact.

—a more aggressive stance toward the policy role of Congress on the part of the members.

Stability of Policy. Change in policies is difficult in a highly fragmented situation. Each policy tends to be produced within its own subgovernment and by and large those subgovernments are happy with what they have wrought. There is no impetus to change very much or very fast.

When there is organizational centralization and more concern with policy coherence, there are more forces pushing for more change. Greater integration does not guarantee that such change will occur, but the conditions are present to allow it.

Type of Policy. There are four major types of domestic policy: distributive; competitive regulatory; protective regulatory; and redistributive.[6]

Distributive policies and programs are aimed at promoting private activity that, in theory, would not or could not otherwise be undertaken and are thought to be desirable for society as a whole. These policies and programs provide subsidies for those private activities. Examples include land grants for railroad companies in the nineteenth century to build western railroads; direct cash payments for agricultural commodity purchases; tax benefits for home owners; and grants to companies and inventors. Much defense policy also involves heavy subsidies to defense contractors and to localities through decisions about where to locate military facilities in the United States.

---

6. This categorization is adapted from work that has been going on in political science since 1964. See Theodore J. Lowi, "American Business, Public Policy, Case-Studies, and Political Theory," *World Politics* 16 (1964): 677–715; Lowi, "Four Systems of Policy, Politics, and Choice," *Public Administration Review* 32 (1972): 298–310; Robert H. Salisbury, "The Analysis of Public Policy: a Search for Theories and Roles," in Austin Ranney (ed.), *Political Science and Public Policy* (Chicago: Markham, 1968); and Ripley and Franklin, *Congress, the Bureaucracy, and Public Policy.*

Competitive regulatory policies and programs are aimed at limiting the provision of specific goods and services to only one or a few designated deliverers chosen from a larger number of competing potential deliverers. In a sense this policy is a hybrid with elements of subsidy for the winning competitors and of regulation in the public interest. Examples include the granting and review of licenses to operate television and radio stations; authorization for specific trucking companies to haul specified commodities over specified routes; and authorization for specific airlines to operate specific routes.

Protective regulatory policies and programs are designed to protect the public in some sense by setting the conditions under which various private activities can be undertaken. Some conditions are prohibited; others are required. Examples of such policies include requirements that banks, stores, and other grantors of credit disclose true interest rates, prohibitions of unfair business and labor practices, prohibition of harmful additives to food, and licensing of medical drugs before they can be put on the market.

Redistributive policies and programs are intended to alter the allocation of wealth, property, rights, or some other value among broad classes or groups in society (such as socioeconomic classes or racial groups). The redistributive feature enters because a number of actors perceive that there are "winners" and "losers" in the policies and some value is being transferred from one group to another group *at the expense of* the first group. The perceptions of redistribution are such that, although many policies may redistribute items of value from the less well off to the more well off, the relatively disadvantaged persons and groups in society are the presumed beneficiaries. Examples of redistributive policies include setting progressive income tax rates so that affluent people pay a higher percentage in taxes than less affluent people, requirements that housing, public accomodations, and public education be available without racial discrimination, provision of food stamps for the disadvantaged, and government-sponsored health insurance to help the elderly meet the costs of medical care.

The easiest of these four types of policy for Congress to work with is distributive because it threatens no one. In principle, all claimants for support in the form of one or more subsidies can be satisfied. The policies are disaggregated and resources to satisfy requests are not perceived to be tightly limited.

The most difficult issues are those perceived to be protective regulatory or redistributive. In both of these instances some actors' interests are directly threatened. There are "losers" in the cases of these decisions, as well as "winners"—and even the "winners" might not know it or be particularly happy or particularly grateful to individual members of the House and Senate.

Competitive regulatory issues are simply delegated to executive branch agencies and independent regulatory commissions such as the Interstate Commerce Commission or the Federal Communications Commission to administer. Congress sets the framework for decision by those agencies, and individual members of Congress may attempt to intervene privately in specific decisions, but Congress as a deliberative body does not make the specific decisions.

Fragmentation in Congress lends itself to supporting a situation in which almost all issues are considered to be distributive and are handled as such. Integration does not guarantee that protective regulatory and redistributive issues will be handled in a straightforward fashion, but it increases the chances that will happen.

Concern with Oversight and Evaluation. In a fragmented situation, in which most policy is distributive and in which most decisions are made by subgovernments, few members of Congress see any necessity of much oversight of the bureaucracy. Members and bureaucrats and beneficiaries have all agreed ahead of time what should be done. It is in the bureaucrats' self-interest to follow through with implementing policies in the ways that all parties find congenial. Similarly, policies in this fragmented situation are usually simply assumed to be effective and to be having the desired impact. Even if systematic evaluation of impact showed little or no impact, that finding would be perceived mainly as a threat to an entrenched set of interests rather than as a cue to scrap the policy or alter it in a major way.

Integration does not guarantee systematic attention to oversight or evaluation but does enhance the chances that both will be taken seriously, since there is more chance that some significant policies will not be distributive and will not simply be the product of subgovernments with a stake in maintaining existing policies without the implicit threats contained in both systematic oversight and evaluation.

Passiveness vs. Aggressiveness. Members of Congress have two particularly important general choices they are free to make: (1) how vigorously to assert substantive policy preferences, and (2) whether to support the institutional status quo in Congress or whether to advocate and pursue institutional change. These choices are separate, but they are both important in helping determine the policy importance of Congress at any given time.

In many ways the easiest choice for individual members to make is to adopt a rather passive stance in terms of pushing for specific policy preferences on broad issues and a conservative role in terms of supporting the institutional status quo. Members making such choices do not renounce all impact on public policy—rather they opt for highly specific, marginal impact most of the time. Such an option is attractive in general terms because it is immediately workable within the highly complex process by which legislation makes its way through Congress. It also allows many members to maximize their interests in such things as re-election, projects and services for their constituencies, and amicable relations with the bureaucracy. Likewise, it helps members process the vast array of information potentially available to them by simply ignoring much of it and thus saving time to be used for other purposes.[7]

Members who opt for a more aggressive stance with regard to their personal impact and the collective congressional impact on the substance of policy and for a more change-oriented position toward the institutions of Congress take a difficult route. They are likely to run head-on into frustrations generated by the slowness and complexity of the legislative process and may also jeopardize amicable relations with the bureaucracy and interest groups and thereby lessen their ability to produce projects and services for their constituencies.

A passive member of Congress tends to be principally interested only in the work of his or her committee and of a few subcommittees. Within that province the member usually supports the policies advocated by the bureaucrats and the leading interest groups appearing before the committee or subcommittee and will suggest only small changes from those proposals. His focus is narrow and his manner is accommodating.

An aggressive member of Congress tends to have interests beyond the jurisdiction of his or her particular committee and subcommittee assignments. He is more willing to question the judgments of the bureaucrats and interest group representatives with whom he comes in contact. He will work for the adoption of wide changes from exist-

---

7. The workload of Congress is so enormous it is impossible for any individual member to know anything about many matters on which he or she must act. Thus members look for shortcuts as they make up their minds—"cues" they can trust. An important study of this process of decision-making is reported in John W. Kingdon, *Congressmen's Voting Decisions* (New York: Harper and Row, 1973). This study will be discussed in more detail in Chapter 4, below. The central point here is that the pressing necessity of managing limited time and potentially overwhelming amount of information pushes members in the direction of relative policy passivity.

ing statutes when he thinks them necessary and useful. He is not willing to compromise on those issues about which he feels strongly.

A relatively passive congressional stance offers numerous benefits to members. It maximizes committee autonomy and thus the influence of committee members. The nature of most issues before Congress is likely to be non-controversial, which enhances members' perceptions of electoral safety. Proceedings can be relatively invisible, especially if the agenda contains few controversial items. Available time for members to spend on constituency-oriented business, including frequent trips to the state or district, is maximized by a passive congressional stance. Likewise, good relations with the bureaucracy, which facilitate servicing constituency interests, are more likely. Good relations with the president are valuable, at least for members of the president's party, because White House good will can influence the allocation of tangible benefits to members' states or districts, and good relations with the president are more likely to occur with a Congress that is relatively passive. Finally, members benefit from a low-profile, passive congressional stance because, given the fact of weak congressional parties, they are free to take policy stances of their own different from the majority of their party without fear of meaningful sanctions.

The costs of passivity are that Congress as an institution has little unified impact on national policy. Members who envision broad national policy goals have little opportunity to see their goals realized in a passive Congress. And consequently there is not likely to be any feeling of pride among members toward the institution they serve. But perhaps the most costly disadvantage of congressional passivity is that Congress leaves itself open to domination by the executive branch, a development that not only further weakens Congress but that may make passivity an entrenched characteristic, difficult to overcome.

Relative aggressiveness, on the other hand, presents a mirror image of the costs and benefits of relative passivity. The major benefits are that members increase their potential for seeing the adoption and implementation of national policy important to them and that they can take pride in the institution as an important participant in policymaking. By exercising its power, an aggressive Congress is much more likely to resist domination by the executive branch.

If a large number of members pursue policy aggressiveness, the possibility of diminished committee and subcommittee autonomy exists because members will rather freely cross jurisdictional lines in terms of their interests and proposals. Such a situation also enhances the possibility that more controversial issues will come before Congress in a more visible way because of the lessened importance of usually quiet and unreported committee meetings. This may pose a threat to perceived electoral safety on the part of a number of members.

If members increase the scope of their legislative interests and their willingness to pursue ends different from those proposed by bureaucrats and interest group representatives, they may also reduce the time they have available to spend on constituency matters or in the constituency. They may antagonize parts of the bureaucracy, thereby reducing the desire of the bureaucrats to respond favorably to constituency-oriented requests. They run an increased risk of antagonizing the president, thereby reducing the desire of the White House to cooperate in providing a variety of tangible benefits for specific states, districts, and constituents.

Finally, if the desire to be aggressive about policy preferences spreads to the party leaders in Congress, they may begin to work to strengthen party mechanisms that will allow the imposition of greater "discipline" on members, thereby reducing the freedom of those members to take whatever policy positions they choose without much regard for a party position.

It is clear that the average member of Congress is likely to find passivity more attractive than aggressiveness. However, this is not an inevitable and unchangeable situation. At given points in the past Congress has, for a variety of reasons, opted for an aggressive stance. This option is still very much alive. Thus, although there is considerable pressure to be relatively passive, conditions emerge that produce quite a different response. One central argument in this book is that Congress is free to choose various courses of action. Pressures will be described that push more strongly in one direction than in another, but the ability of the men and women who constitute Congress to do something in the face of these prevailing pressures is specifically and vigorously affirmed.

Principal Values Served by Fragmentation and Integration

Several observers of Congress have commented on the potential conflict between two of the primary functions Congress was created and is structured to perform: lawmaking and representation.[8] Lawmaking implies action, decision-making, and choice. Representation implies full consideration, widespread consent, and ample opportunity for various interests to be heard. The two sets of values are not com-

---

8. See, for example, Vogler, *The Politics of Congress,* Chapter 1; and the introduction to Theodore J. Lowi and Randall B. Ripley (eds.), *Legislative Politics, U.S.A.* 3rd ed. (Boston: Little, Brown, 1973).

pletely exclusive, but the two central thrusts are different. If law-making receives primary attention, consideration, consent-building, and the solicitation of statements from all interests will be attentuated in the interest of making a decision. If representation receives primary attention, decision will be deferred—perhaps forever—in order to max-imize full consideration, consent, and the opportunities for differing interests to make their cases.

A summary of some of the most important differences that flow from whether representation or lawmaking is given primacy in view-ing Congress is contained in Table 1–1. Given the content of that table and the discussion of fragmentation and integration thus far, it is clear that fragmentation in Congress is most compatible with a primary stress on representation and that integration in Congress is most compatible with a primary stress on lawmaking.

Institutional Stability, Change, and "Reform"

Members of the House and Senate are faced with a choice that in-volves their desire to support institutional stability in Congress or to strive for institutional change. This differs from the choice of change or stability in the substance of specific governmental policies. Yet there are ties between degree of institutional stability, degree of policy stability, and relative impact of Congress on the substance of policy. Unfortunately for the members, however, increased institutional sta-bility can both strengthen and weaken the ability of Congress to have important substantive effects.

Thus, members of Congress interested in maximizing the policy im-pact of the institution face a dilemma. On the one hand, the institu-tional stability and organization possible under relatively stable con-ditions are likely to be necessary if Congress is to have major policy input of its own rather than depending on the executive branch for all direction and details. But on the other hand, stability also breeds substantive policy conservatism and tends to stifle innovation. Thus, in theory, a stable organization may be the most likely to have a large policy impact but in fact may become moribund, allowing com-peting organizations such as the Executive Office of the President or various parts of the bureaucracy to acquire policy initiative by default. Despite the claim that "reform" can cure congressional ineffectiveness, there is no pat answer to this dilemma. Both change and stability may promote either congressional potency or impotence. The advan-tages and disadvantages of either course have to be weighed again and again in specific situations.

"Reform" can push in many different directions. Some changes

Table 1–1
Views Associated with Valuation of
Two Principal Congressional Functions

If Representation Is Most Valued:	*If Lawmaking Is Most Valued:*
1. Congress is a forum for articulating group interests.	1. Congress is a decision-maker that translates popular mandates into law.
2. Emphasis is put on representation of minorities.	2. Emphasis is put on majority rule.
3. Decentralized legislative structure is favored.	3. Centralized legislative system under party presidential leadership is favored.
4. Legislative coalitions are formed after elections—likely to be shifting pattern of dissimilar groups brought together through logrolling.	4. Legislative coalitions are formed at elections. Congressmen are expected to follow party and presidential mandates reflected in elections
5. *Public interest* is defined as the sum of the many constituency interests.	5. *Public interest* is defined in national terms as being more than just the sum of constituency interests.
6. Constituency casework is considered an important part of an individual legislator's role.	6. Casework is relegated largely to staff so as to free the congressman for important work.
7. Administrative oversight is regarded as a process for advancing ideas and information and for representing interests of constituent groups.	7. Administrative oversight is regarded as a process of insuring that mandates of earlier legislation are being carried out.
8. Chief criterion for evaluating legislative performance is the number of groups and interests considered in the legislative process.	8. Chief criterion for evaluating legislative performance is the efficiency with which electoral mandates are translated into policies.

Source: The content of the two columns from David J. Vogler, The Politics of Congress *(Boston: Allyn and Bacon, 1977, 2nd ed.): 14. The title of the table and the column headings have been altered somewhat.*

labeled as reforms can serve fragmentation. Some changes can serve integration. There is no simple correspondence between being a "reformer" and promoting specific policy values. The relationship is complex and needs to be assessed with respect to specific proposed or actual changes. And it also needs to be remembered that the same "reform" may serve different values at different times. For example, depriving the Speaker of the House of a number of powers in 1910–11 was supposed to be serving "liberal" policy values. Creating some additional powers for the Speaker in the 1970s was also supposed to serve "liberal" values. Ralph Huitt, a long-time and highly perceptive student of Congress, provides the best summary statement about the links between institutional "reform" and policy values: "Structural and procedural devices give little assurance of permanent rectitude." [9]

In the last several years there have been contradictory strains of deliberate change in both the House and Senate, particularly the former. One strain has served primarily to disperse power among individual members—what might be called a "democratizing" strain. The other strain has served primarily to centralize power in order to enhance the power of Congress as an institution. Examples of the former are changes enhancing the power of subcommittees in relation to parent committees, dispersing subcommittee chairmanships more widely, and ensuring virtually all members of having at least some highly desirable committee and subcommittee assignments. Examples of the latter include the creation of a new budgetary process in a 1974 statute, the passage of the War Powers Act in 1973, and strengthening the hand of the Speaker. Some changes have pushed in both directions simultaneously. For example, moves to make the House Democratic caucus (composed of all Democratic members of the House) more powerful were democratizing in that they gave individual members a vote over party policy but also had some centralizing potential to the extent that the caucus could be dominated by the party leaders. These changes and a number of others will be considered in some detail in subsequent chapters.[10]

Summary: An Overview of Fragmentation and Integration in the Contemporary Congress

Table 1–2 contains a summary of much of the foregoing discussion of fragmentation and integration in terms of the organizational state within Congress, the degree of policy coherence, supporting conditions within Congress, principal policy consequences, principal values served, and the likelihood of occurrence.

---

9. Huitt, "Congress: Retrospect and Prospect," 227.

10. For useful overviews of change and reforms in Congress in early and mid-1970's—a particularly active and successful time for those favoring change—see Leroy N. Rieselbach, *Congressional Reform in the Seventies* (Morristown, N.J.: General Learning Press, 1977); Malcolm E. Jewell, "New Perspectives on the U.S. Congress: A Review Article," *Legislative Studies Quarterly* 2 (1977): 77–91; and Michael J. Malbin, "House Reforms—The Emphasis Is On Productivity, Not Power," *National Journal* (December 4, 1976): 1731–1737.

Table 1-2
Fragmentation vs. Integration in Congress: A Summary

	High Degree of Fragmentation	High Degree of Integration
Organizational State	Decentralized	Centralized
Degree of Policy Coherence	No Possibility of Planned Coherence; Limited Random Coherence at Most	Possibility of Planned Coherence; No Guaranteed Coherence
Supporting Conditions	Popular Election Two Houses Large Substantive Agenda Power-sharing with the Bureaucracy Openness to Organized Interest Groups Well-developed Committee System Weak National Parties Personal Ambition of Members	Institutional Pride and Ambition Party Organization in Congress Broad Substantive Policy Commitments by Members Power-sharing with the President
Principal Policy Consequences	Stable Policy Policy Primarily Defined as Distributive Low Concern with Oversight of Bureaucracy Low Concern with Evaluation of Policy Results Policy Passiveness on Part of Members	Chance of Important Policy Change Some Policy Defined as Protective Regulatory or Redistributive More Concern with Oversight of Bureaucracy More Concern with Evaluation of Policy Results More Policy Aggressiveness on Part of Members
Principal Function Emphasized	Maximizes Representation	Maximizes Lawmaking
Likelihood of Occurrence	Most Likely; The "Natural" State of Congress; Requires Little or No Deliberate Action to Create or Sustain	Difficult, but Not Impossible to Achieve; an "Unnatural" State; Requires Considerable Deliberate Action

On the last point it is argued that fragmentation is the "natural" condition of Congress. Unless there are forces working to the contrary, Congress naturally gravitates toward a state of fragmentation. Most of the supporting conditions for fragmentation are simply givens, a number of them contained in the Constitution. It requires no act of will to promote fragmentation. Even in periods of relatively high integration, elements of fragmentation remain.

Integration, on the other hand, is difficult to achieve and requires deliberate choice and acts of will. Important aspects of integration can, however, be achieved. There is nothing "inevitable" about fragmentation as all-encompassing. Its "naturalness" does not mean that "unnatural" elements of integration cannot be introduced and maintained for considerable periods of time, even though they are likely to be under continual attack.

RELATIONS WITH THE EXECUTIVE BRANCH: A BROAD PERSPECTIVE

Regardless of whether Congress appears to be pursuing a more aggressive or a more passive policy course, it must choose a direction of interaction regarding the executive branch—the president, the insti-

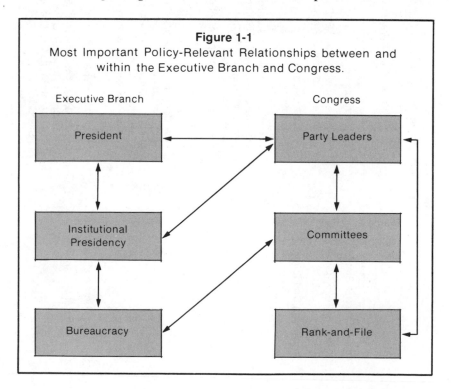

Figure 1-1
Most Important Policy-Relevant Relationships between and within the Executive Branch and Congress.

tutional presidency (that is, those offices that exist primarily to serve the president in an immediate sense), and the bureaucracy. This interaction is at the center of national policy-making.

Both the executive branch and Congress can be conceptualized as three-level institutions. The executive branch has the president, the institutional presidency, and the vast bureaucracy (peopled mostly by civil servants). Congress has party leaders, a committee structure, and rank-and-file senators and representatives. Eight two-way relationships between these six institutional participants are especially important. They are summarized in Figure 1–1.

Within the executive branch, relationships are relatively hierarchical in that the direct relationship between the president and the bureaucracy is not very strong. Instead, the institutional presidency —particularly the White House office, the Office of Management and Budget, and cabinet and sub-cabinet officials appointed by the president—plays a critical mediating role between the president and his policy preferences and the various parts of the bureaucracy. The president often experiences a great deal of difficulty in getting what he wants from the bureaucracy. Within Congress all of the possible relationships are consistently important in determining the legislative results emerging from the institution as a whole.

The relationship between the two branches has two levels. The president and institutional presidency relate mostly to the party leaders of the president's party. They rely on the leaders to relay their preferences both to committees and to rank-and-file members. Conversely, members of the House and Senate look to the leaders to carry information and preferences back to the president and presidency. Individual organizations within the bureaucracy, however, primarily relate directly to the committees and subcommittees responsible for substantive decisions involving them. The reason that central direction of policy is so difficult to achieve is the weakness of the link between the party leaders and the committees. The committees tend to be much more responsive to the parts of the bueraucracy than to the party leaders. Given that the parts of the bureaucracy are also imperfectly responsive to the president and institutional presidency there is often little central direction to policy decisions.

Policy-Relevant Relationships: Cooperation or Conflict?

The relationship between the president and Congress is relatively visible and its visibility is fully justified by its importance. The Constitution created a governmental scheme in which virtually nothing new can be started unless Congress and the president find some mu-

tually acceptable level of cooperation. The incentives for cooperation are great.

A president has many reasons for wanting to get along with Congress. His image as a masterful leader is enhanced if no senator or
representative creates conditions that make him look inept. He can
give more attention to his public and press relations, or even his
influence within the executive branch of the government, if strong
opposition emanating from the Capitol does not constantly threaten
him. He can comfortably leave the country for diplomatic ventures if
he knows that a group of "barons" a mile or so southeast of the White
House will not seize the occasion to aggrandize themselves at the
expense of the sojourning "chief."

None of these reasons for wanting amicable relations with Congress is ignoble, but one eminently practical motive is more important, if not necessarily more noble. As the Constitution makes explicit,
the laws of the land—including, critically, the essential functions of
raising and disbursing revenue—require the approval of Congress.
Thus, simply to keep the government functioning at a minimum level
a president must be concerned with at least some congressional legislative activity—taxation and appropriations. Since every president
also has grander programmatic ambitions, he must be concerned about
and involved in a large part of congressional activity.

Members of the House and Senate also have many reasons for
wanting to get along with a president, although their reasons are probably not as great as his. Nevertheless, members with broad programmatic aspirations stand a greater chance of realizing some of those
aspirations if the president can be induced to support or initiate
some of their ideas. Thus, for example, Congressional initiators of
anti-air pollution legislation in the late 1950s and early 1960s made a
major stride forward only when they finally induced President John
Kennedy to support their views. Even members with few legislative
ambitions will find White House support useful as they seek new post
offices, dams, and defense contracts for their districts.

There are also conditions that promote conflict between president
and Congress, however. These include: genuine disagreement over
policy goals (disagreement that may be magnified for partisan reasons); the almost inevitable jealousies of individuals each responsible
to their own constituencies; and the natural desire of potential
competitors to maintain some information not available to the other
party (this helps explain the continuing debate over "executive privilege" with regard to the sharing of information). Disagreement over
policy goals is the most important source of conflict. Examples include

the basically hostile reaction by Congress to President Nixon's initiatives in welfare and housing in the early 1970s and to much of President Kennedy's New Frontier program in the early 1960s.

The relationship between Congress and the bureaucracy is less visible to the public because of the relative lack of media coverage when compared to the attention given the relationship between Congress and the president, but it too is vital in determining the shape of national policy. The policies that emerge from this relationship are not as dramatically new as some emerging from the presidential-congressional relationship, but they are collectively important. And, equally important although less glamorous, the nexus between bureaus and committees determines many of the details of how ongoing programs will be implemented. These seemingly routine and dull decisions can shape programs in ways very different from what the proponents in the White House and in Congress originally envision. These decisions also impact most directly on the citizens of the nation.

In much of the writing on the relations between Congress and the bureaucracy (and, surprisingly, the literature on this subject is scarce) the element of conflict is stressed. Not only is conflict depicted as a central and normal condition, but the discussions of these relations are usually cast in polemical terms. Typically, bureaucrats are portrayed as either trying to administer programs in the public interest despite the limitations imposed by parochial-minded congressmen, or else as trying to avoid the attentive eyes of public-spirited congressional watchdogs who insist on economy and efficiency instead of the normal "bureaucratic" (that is, wasteful) methods of administration. Discussions of congressional oversight of administration usually focus on congressional aggressiveness in oversight and bureaucratic resistance to it. Depending on the point of view, congressional aggressiveness is either praised or condemned, and the bureaucratic resistance is described as dastardly or heroic.

By contrast, it is here argued that the bureaucratic-congressional relationship is at the center of public policy development in the United States and that cooperation characterizes this relationship far more than conflict. Basically, members of Congress and members of the bureaucracy have valuable items to trade and, unless the terms of trade strike one party or the other as outrageous, there are strong incentives to keep the relations smooth, cooperative, and devoid of disruptive conflict. Conflict can be costly to both sides and so both sides are reluctant to initiate it. Conflict does arise and should be noted, but the more usual situation is one of relative peace and harmony.

It has been suggested that even some of what seems to be conflict is symbolic only and, in fact, is indicative of a continuing arrangement between Congress and the bureaucracy that give both of them what they want: the bureaucracy receives increased authority, staff, and budget, and members of Congress are able to provide additional important services to their constituents. This argument is elaborated in a provocative short book by Morris Fiorina, whose central point is best summarized in his own words:

> Congressmen (typically the majority Democrats) earn electoral credits by establishing various federal programs (the minority Republicans typically earn credits by fighting the good fight). The legislation is drafted in very general terms, so some agency, existing or newly established, must translate a vague policy mandate into a functioning program, a process that necessitates the promulgation of numerous rules and regulations and, incidentally, the trampling of numerous toes. At the next stage, aggrieved and/or hopeful constituents petition their congressmen to intervene in the complex (or at least obscure) decision processes of the bureaucracy. The cycle closes when the congressman lends a sympathetic ear, piously denounces the evils of bureaucracy, intervenes in the latter's decisions, and rides a grateful electorate to ever more impressive electoral showings. Congressmen take credit coming and going. They are the alpha and the omega.
>
> The popular frustration with the permanent government in Washington is partly justified, but to a considerable degree it is misplaced resentment. *Congress is the linchpin of the Washington establishment.* The bureaucracy serves as a convenient lightning rod for public frustration and a convenient whipping boy for congressmen. But so long as the bureaucracy accommodates congressmen, the latter will oblige with ever larger budgets and grants of authority. Congress does not just react to big government—it creates it. All of Washington prospers. More and more bureaucrats promulgate more and more regulations and dispense more and more money. Fewer and fewer congressmen suffer electoral defeat. Elements of the electorate benefit from government programs, and all of the electorate is eligible for ombudsman services. But the general, long-term welfare of the United States is no more than an incidental by-product of the system.[11]

As members of a congressional committee and officials of a bureau interact, mutual support can be offered in several forms. The com-

---

11. Morris P. Fiorina, *Congress: Keystone of the Washington Establishment* (New Haven: Yale University Press, 1977): 48–49.

mittee can provide the bureau with favorable decisions on budget, authority, jurisdiction, procedure, organization, and reorganization. Committee members also provide bureaucrats with rewards in the form of public praise for jobs well done. Bureaus can provide committee members with "good" policy (that is, policy in accord with the preferences of the committee members) and with special treatment for the states, districts, and constituents of committee members on matters involving the application of regulations, the location of facilities, or the priority given a specific matter. Bureaucrats can also provide public support for senators and representatives by deferring to them as experts in given areas. A classic case of committee-bureau interaction in which virtually all of the above supports were traded occurred during the 1950s and 1960s between the National Institutes of Health and appropriations subcommittees chaired by Senator Lister Hill (D-Ala.) and Representative John Fogarty (D-R.I.).

The instances of conflict that do occur usually stem from genuine differences of opinion over what is good policy, disputes motivated by partisan considerations, or personal dislikes. The running dispute for several decades between the foreign aid agency and a House appropriations subcommittee chaired by Otto Passman (D-La.) provides an example of continuously hostile relations based on policy differences and personal considerations. Similar continuing disputes include those between Senator Warren Magnuson (D-Wash.) and the National Institute of Education and between Senator William Proxmire (D-Wisc.) and the National Science Foundation.

From the congressional point of view the danger of close cooperation is that it may, in fact, amount to cooptation by a bureau with a more numerous staff and more complete information about the subject matter of its own programs. The danger of generating programmatic conflict is that the benefits that the bureau can offer to committee members may be withheld or withdrawn.

In general, then, influence over the development of public policy is shared (unevenly, in most instances) by the president and individuals in the institutional presidency, members of the House and Senate, civil servants in the bureaucracy, and lobbyists representing various interests. In any given policy area various coalitions may emerge involving three basic participants. One particularly strong link is that between Congress and the bureaucracy—specifically, between a subcommittee or two and the top officials in a specific bureau. When this nexus adds a few supportive interest group representatives it becomes exceptionally powerful and can often withstand even pressure from the White House.

Congressional Involvement in Policy-Making:
Patterns of Interaction with The Executive Branch

Congress, because of both its constitutional position and the activity of its members, is involved in one way or another in every area of policy in which the federal government is active. But the nature of congressional activity varies from issue to issue and from time to time. Generalizations that Congress is losing power to the president and has been since the beginning of the twentieth century may make exciting rhetoric but reveal almost nothing about the nature of congressional involvement in policy-making. The reality of congressional involvement is much more complicated and cannot be caught in a facile general statement.[12]

There are four analytical models that are useful in understanding congressional involvement in policy-making. Congress never follows a single model at any given time. Rather it usually is involved in all four models simultaneously in different issue areas. It may be that trends develop in specific areas—that is, with Congress consistently moving from one model to another one—but any comprehensive generalization about the trend of congressional involvement is bound to be so general that most important variations will be obscured.

The first model can be labeled *executive dominance*. In this model the principal source of initiation for legislative ideas comes from the executive branch. The executive, usually the president on major matters, sets the agenda for Congress to consider. Congressional participation in shaping the details of specific programs is generally low. Not only does the executive serve as the principal source of initiation but it also produces the details of proposals, which are, for the most part, ratified by Congress. Congress simply legitimizes what the executive proposes. Thus there is a final legislative product that is broadly acceptable to both the executive branch (which gets what it wants without much change) and Congress (which seems quite content to approve the details of what the executive wants).

There are a number of easy generalizations in the literature that the whole of foreign policy and defense policy are typified by the executive dominance model. More careful examination, however, suggests that this generalization is only selectively true, as will be seen in chapter 12. The original proposal for a "war on poverty" in 1963–64 through programs such as community action, the job corps, the neigh-

---

12. See Huitt, "Congress: Retrospect and Prospect"; and John R. Johannes, "The President Proposes and Congress Disposes—But Not Always: Legislative Initiative on Capitol Hill," *The Review of Politics* 36 (1974): 356–370, for two recent balanced essays on presidential-congressional relations.

borhood youth corps, and operation headstart, provides a closer fit to the executive dominance model.

The second model is *joint program development*. In this model the principal source of legislative initiative can be either the executive branch or Congress or it can be a joint initiative either coordinated and planned or fortuitous and unplanned. Both the executive and Congress are heavily involved in decisions about details. There may be some conflict over these details but there is also a high degree of willingness both within Congress and the executive to compromise so a final product broadly acceptable to both can emerge.

A great variety of matters in the economic field—taxes, for example —seem to fit this model reasonably well. Additional examples include the "depressed areas" programs (Area Redevelopment and Economic Development) of the 1960s and the Model Cities program of the late 1960s. These programs were both aimed at promoting economic development—the first in primarily rural areas and the second primarily in inner city ghettos.

The third model is *congressional dominance*. In this model the principal source of initiation comes from within Congress; congressional involvement in shaping details is high. The executive branch in this case is willing to participate in the shaping of details in only a marginal way. The executive is also willing at least to acquiesce to the congressional initiative and decisions on details and may even be eager to embrace the congressional solution. Whatever the motivation and whatever the degree of eagerness, a final legislative product emerges because the important individuals in the two branches reach some form of agreement.

In recent years policies and programs relating to atomic energy, strip mining control, consumer protection, air pollution, and water pollution all seem to fit this model. In large part these programs fit this model because of aggressive members of Congress with decided policy views and institutional positions from which to push those views successfully.

The fourth model is *stalemate*. In this model there may be initiative in either branch, or there may be competing initiatives undertaken simultaneously in both branches. Both branches also get heavily involved in the attempt to shape details, but again their simultaneous efforts run counter to each other. Finally, all of this activity bears no immediate fruit because neither side is willing to yield to the views of the other or even compromise to reach some mutually agreeable solution.

The controversy over the supersonic transport in the early 1970s seems to fit this model. The executive branch was pushing federal funding for the development of the SST and Congress was balking. As a result some initial funds were spent but the entire project was finally cancelled. Welfare reform in the Nixon-Ford years also provides an example.

Oftentimes debate in an area will fit the stalemate model for several years and then a different model will finally apply as some form of compromise is reached. For example, in the late 1950s a large number of areas fit this model: aid to education, area redevelopment, medicare, and manpower development and training. But in the 1960s agreement was reached and measures passed. As this example suggests, the fourth model is often the product of partisan differences between Congress and the White House; it is most likely to appear in those periods when the major elective parts of the government are not in the hands of a single party. In general, it can be said that the same policy area can move between any combination of models over time. It is far too simple to think of a single dimension of presidential "strength" or "weakness" as explaining patterns of relative influence over all policy.

Table 1–3 summarizes the models of congressional involvement in policymaking.

Congressional Functions and Societal Impact

Congress performs a variety of functions, but one can be viewed as broadest and most important: it helps, or at least tries to help, resolve differences of opinion about public policy between different individuals and groups in society. These differences of opinion can be

Table 1–3

Models of Congressional Involvement in Policy-Making

Model	Principal Source of Initiation	Degree of Congressional Participation in Shaping Details	Degree of Executive Participation in Shaping Details	Final Legislative Product
Executive Dominance	Executive	Low	High	Yes
Joint Program Development	Executive or Congress or Both	High	High	Yes
Congressional Dominance	Congress	High	Low	Yes
Stalemate	Executive or Congress or Both	High	High	No

narrowly divided or they can be poles apart. They can be pursued peacefully through argument or they can be pursued in a more physical manner through such measures as strikes, lockouts, demonstrations, and violence—both planned and unplanned.

If Congress is largely successful in the performance of this function and if the other institutions of society are also largely successful in performing the same function, then society is likely to be relatively stable. If Congress and the other institutions of government are unsuccessful in resolving conflict, then societal instability may develop. Failure is, of course, possible; the Civil War is a classic example of what happens when the most fundamental societal conflict cannot be resolved through normal institutional channels.

Despite the ultimate importance of this broad function, it does not have much analytical utility. Four more specific categories of the policy-relevant functions of Congress include lawmaking, oversight of administration, education of the public, and representation. These categories do not include every function of Congress, but they do include those central to congressional impact on public policy.

Congressional performance of these functions is not fixed—it varies as the environment varies and as the membership of Congress varies. Although environmental factors can have an important influence on the way Congress performs its functions, Congress nonetheless has a great deal of latitude in choosing its direction. The wishes and preferences of the collection of individuals happening to serve in it at any particular time are a principal internal variable that influences the performance of basic congressional functions.

Congress and Lawmaking

Prior to the Civil War, congressional lawmaking activity in the domestic sphere was basically limited to promoting the development of the nation by subsidizing a large number of private activities (for example, turnpikes and canals). This sort of interest has persisted to the present day and Congress is still heavily involved in the subsidy of a wide range of state, local, and private development activities, in such fields as agriculture, education, health, airport construction, and the merchant marine.

Once the Civil War had demonstrated that the federal government was also a national government, new problems, largely associated with the rapid industrialization of the nation, began to arise that involved public discussion of what the government should do. Corporate wealth, which rapidly made the Republican party its political handmaiden, began to alter the dimensions of American opportunity. The end of the homesteading era and the massive waves of immigration from Eastern and Southern Europe compounded the new problems.

The political system took about twenty years to frame even the beginnings of a coherent response. The response came in the form of involving the government—including Congress—in regulation. In the late nineteenth century Congress began the long development of regulation of railroads and corporations with the passage of the Interstate Commerce Act in 1887 and the Sherman Antitrust Act in 1890. In the first fifteen years of the twentieth century other regulatory laws, such as the Hepburn Act of 1906, the Clayton Act of 1914, and the Federal Trade Commission Act of 1914, were enacted. Since then, congressional concern with regulation has expanded greatly to include such matters as unfair business practices, all modes of transportation, power, radio and television, food and drugs, labor relations, and the securities market.

It took the catastrophe of an economic depression seemingly irreversible by normal means to legitimize the activity of conscious and planned redistribution of economic and social benefits in society on the part of Congress and the government as a whole. The economic disaster of the 1930s revealed the corresponding social disaster that had been developing for a number of decades. Congress made some attempts to redraw more equitably the social and economic lines that the mythical "free market" had produced. In the last four and a half decades the congressional agenda has included a great number of topics involving debates over equality or inequality and degree and direction of redistribution; wages and hours, social security, medical care for the aged, national health insurance, aid to depressed geographic areas, public housing, aid to inner city public education, and job training serve as examples.

In the period after the Second World War—and in large part as a result of social forces unleashed by the domestic impact of the War— the congressional agenda of redistributive questions was expanded to include questions about racial discrimination.

Congress occasionally surrenders willingly some of its lawmaking activities in the domestic realm. For example, the adoption of the Reciprocal Trade Agreements Act in 1934 diminished the congressional role in the making of tariffs and increased the role of the executive branch, especially the president. Congress can also be aggressive in seeking out new areas of endeavor—congressional initiatives were responsible for the development of water and air pollution policy in the 1950s and 1960s, for example. Congress can also deliberately seek simply to maintain the existing situation in terms of the range of activities in which it is engaged.

Congressional performance of the lawmaking function in the realm of foreign affairs has varied from relatively passive to relatively aggressive. Congress can never absolutely control foreign policy—it is constitutionally prevented from doing so, given the powers specifically allocated to the president. It can put itself in a genuinely subservient role, however, as it did at the time of the passage of the 1964 Gulf of Tonkin Resolution, which gave the president a virtual carte blanche to proceed in Vietnam as he saw fit. In that resolution Congress responded to President Johnson's report on North Vietnamese attacks on two U.S. ships and the retaliatory air strike he ordered against North Vietnamese Naval bases by declaring their support for the President's "determination . . . to take all necessary measures to repel any armed attack against the forces of the United States and to prevent further aggression." [13] Only two senators and no representatives voted against this broad grant of authority that President Johnson used to justify rapid and massive escalation of the Vietnam War. Congress repealed the resolution in 1970, although the repeal was more important symbolically than in terms of any real impact on American involvement in Vietnam.

If Congress is relatively aggressive it can work jointly with the president and bureaucracy in a number of foreign policy areas to develop policy. This has been true in recent years in the consideration of some treaties and in the treatment accorded some aspects of foreign aid and immigration. In the making of war Congress has in the last few years become concerned about reasserting its constitutionally-granted powers. In November 1973 Congress passed a war powers bill over a veto. This provided that the president must report commitments of American troops to foreign combat within forty-eight hours. He must order the cessation of such combat after sixty days unless Congress has given its approval (although he can extend that period by thirty more days if he determines that American troops are endangered). There is no evidence yet, however, that presidential influence has been effectively curtailed in this area.

In short, when aggressive, Congress can be quite important in what might be called secondary areas of foreign policy-making and can have at least some importance in the primary areas. When passive, Congress

---

13. For the full text of this resolution see *Congressional Quarterly's Guide to the Congress of the United States* (Washington, D.C.: Congressional Quarterly, 1971, 1st ed.): 221.

gives up almost all influence in the primary areas and relegates itself to a small supporting role even in the secondary areas. It can never dominate foreign policy but its influence can never disappear altogether either.

Congress and Oversight of Administration

Congress has the responsibility of determining if its programs are being executed as it has intended and if the money it has appropriated is being spent on the purposes for which it was authorized. Oversight is the method of supervising both the programs Congress has created and the bureaucrats who administer them.

The General Accounting Office (GAO), the official watchdog arm of Congress, is vital in the oversight function, but its activities are necessarily limited by a sheer size problem—it has a limited number of personnel and cannot possibly oversee all of the programs run by the bureaucracy. Congress supplements the reports and information coming from the GAO with the oversight activities of its committees. In effect, almost all appropriations and authorization hearings become forums for Congress to oversee the activities of the bureaucracy as they administer programs.

An important feature of oversight, which is also tied to the lawmaking function, is the inclusion of standards for administration of programs and for program performance in original authorizing legislation. When standards are specified, Congress has a tool to use later in oversight hearings to assess how well a program is being administered.

Some programs have very specific standards included—the Social Security Act of 1935 contained remarkably clear standards to guide subsequent administration of the law. Other programs have poorly defined standards—the phrase "maximum feasible participation" (of the poor) contained in the Economic Opportunity Act of 1964 (an act designed to combat poverty in a variety of ways) proved to be confusing to most persons who came in contact with the law—federal administrators, city officials, and actual or potential beneficiaries. Some thought it meant only token formal participation of the poor. Others thought it meant genuine program control by a majority of the poor. Many took a middle position somewhere between the extremes. Congress never provided an authoritative interpretation.

The inherent nature of a program affects the kind of evaluation criteria, if any, that can be specified in authorizing legislation. In general, it is more difficult to devise measures of success for programs in human resource fields such as education, health, and rehabilitation, which attempt to improve the quality of individual lives. Evaluation criteria in other areas, for example, defense, seem to be more easily devised because the area deals with quantifiable items rather than with qualitative changes in education, health care, career opportunities, racial equality and similar aspects of human lives.

Congress can pursue its oversight activities in a variety of moods. It can be intent on very narrow questions, for example, "What did you do with the $10,000 for new downspouts at Fort Sill?"; or pursue very broad questions, for example, "What should the role of the federal government be in relation to the development of the nation's urban areas?" Much oversight approaches the "Fort Sill" end of the spectrum —in fact, some members of Congress seem intent on becoming day-to-day managers of specific programs. But a good deal of the other kind of oversight also takes place. In the 1960's, for example, hearings on the federal government and the cities chaired by Senator Abraham Ribicoff (D-Conn.), hearings on manpower chaired by Senator Joseph Clark (D-Pa.), hearings on national security organization chaired by Senator Henry Jackson (D-Wash.), and hearings on hunger chaired by Senator George McGovern (D-S.Dak.) all exemplified oversight of administration of the broadest kind—concerned not just with administrative details but with the scope and direction of policy in large and important areas. The Ribicoff hearings, for example, were conducted for thirty-three days scattered between August 1966 and June 1967. They dealt with all aspects of the federal government's relation to urban problems including, centrally, the problems of black citizens, the economic consequences of suburban development, and the enormous costs of education. These hearings helped focus governmental attention on a range of problems and helped stimulate discussion of possible solutions.

Congress and Education of the Public

Perhaps inevitably, Congress as an institution has never devised an appropriate mode of communicating its views about public policy to the public. As a multi-headed institution of members with differing party affiliations and policy views it is hard to imagine "the Congress" ever appearing as a single entity to the public. There is no one spokesman for Congress, even on relatively noncontroversial issues, and especially not on controversial ones. When members of Congress have locked horns with the president over some issue, the natural advantage lies with the president. He can state his position clearly in public with immediate and thorough coverage by the mass media. The leaders of the congressional majority on an issue can try to counteract it, but the congressional posture is almost always muddied because there will always be a vocal minority in Congress supporting the presidential position.

Individual members of Congress, however, can and do engage in educating the public. Indeed, most of the time that they spend in contact with the public, particularly constituents, is an attempt to educate (and usually to influence votes, but the two are not incompatible). Speeches, appearances, and newsletters to home states and districts are all opportunities for congressmen to convey informed views on issues important to the nation or some part of it.

Members take different stances with respect to education, and their stance is usually tied to their individual conception of representation. Some can play it safe by trying to take only positions they gauge to be popular. By following "the voice of the people" they try to maximize their chances for continued electoral success. In large part, of course, the "voice" they hear may be an echo of what they themselves have said and want to believe that "the people" support. Others, perhaps more courageous, may try to lead the public, taking positions they know may be unpopular.

Congress and Representation

The nature of representation is both a practical and philosophical question of great importance to those who write about government and to those practitioners who contemplate the deeper meaning of what they do. Numerous conceptions of representation have been advanced for the last several thousand years.[14] At root Congress can be called representative because it is an elected body and because a system of periodic free elections can remove from office any member judged by his constituents to be totally unrepresentative. It cannot be labelled representative in a variety of precise senses, however. For example, the characteristics of the members are different from the characteristics of the population as a whole. Members of Congress are better educated, wealthier, and more likely to be lawyers, white, and males than the general population. So in the traits by which we classify the

---

14. For recent useful discussions of representation see Hanna Pitkin, *The Concept of Representation* (Berkeley: University of California Press, 1967); and Charles E. Gilbert, "Operative Doctrines of Representation," *American Political Science Review* 57 (1963): 604–618.

population Congress is decidedly unrepresentative—or, to put it a different way, overrepresentative of certain characteristics. Nor can Congress be said to be representative in terms of exactly reproducing "public opinion" on a variety of issues. Senators and representatives clearly have and use freedom of judgment in acting on issues without, in most instances, specific instructions from the people they represent. Nor can Congress be said to represent all interests in society simultaneously. On some issues some individuals and classes of individuals are "losers" and, in a sense, their losses provide the benefits that are redistributed to other individuals and classes of individuals (the "winners").

But the fact of free elections coupled with the fact that most citizens acquiesce or consent to the legitimacy of Congress by accepting the results of those elections seem sufficient to establish a case for Congress as a valid representative institution. Even more important, it is evident that members of the House and the Senate think of themselves as representatives and worry about their behavior in that light. They are very conscious of being representatives of their districts or states. They are aware that conflict may exist between the presumed demands of the district and the demands of party. They almost uniformly cite constituency (and conscience) as legitimate reasons for deserting party stands.[15] They use this language in explaining defection to the party leaders who usually accept the explanation. Conversely, they occasionally cite the demands of party or the unaminity of their fellow party members from their state or region in explaining votes to questioning constituents.

Members of Congress are genuinely concerned with their constituencies' attitudes. But their perceptions may be incorrect, in part because they may take their cues from a very small and biased sample.[16] Some may conduct polls to determine sentiment (a few of these polls are professionally constructed and thus produce accurate results); most probably rely on a combination of intuition and discussion with individual constituents whose views they trust and respect or at least those with enough political influence to make consultation prudent. Members who come from highly competitive districts or states are probably more likely to worry about representing with some

---

15. Randall B. Ripley, *Party Leaders in the House of Representatives* (Washington, D.C.: Brookings, 1967): 140–141.
16. Warren E. Miller and Donald E. Stokes, "Constituency Influence in Congress," *American Political Science Review* 57 (1963): 45–56; and George R. Boynton, Samuel C. Patterson, and Ronald D. Hedlund, "The Missing Links in Legislative Politics: Attentive Constituents," *Journal of Politics* 31 (1969): 700–721.

precision the views of their district.[17] They may, however, badly misinterpret real feelings in their district.

A well-established fact—recognized by some members much more clearly than others—is that most constituents have no clear opinions on most issues with which senators and representatives must deal.[18] This means that an aggressive and self-confident member has a wide latitude within which to operate. It also means that when a member claims to be representing the opinion of his district he is, on most issues, representing the opinion of only a minority of his constituents, because most don't know or care about the issue at hand, and at any rate don't communicate any attitude to him at all.

Individual members of the House and Senate undertake a number of different kinds of activities that can be considered representative. First, they support the interests of individuals in a variety of "casework" activities. These cases typically involve deportation and immigration, selective service, social security, and tax matters. Casework activities may involve so-called "private legislation"—for example a bill to exempt named individuals from immigration quotas. They may also involve non-legislative congressional inquiries into various bureaucratic proceedings—for example, pursuing the question of the eligibility of a specific individual for social security or medicare benefits.

Members of the House and Senate also pursue casework for corporate entities. Typically, these cases involve enforcement and interpretation of the tax code or exemptions from various regulatory provisions. For example, when strict enforcement of federal safety standards threatened the last steamboat on the Ohio River with extinction, interested members of Congress from the region were successful in getting different standards applied to this particular boat. Defense contractors involved in cost overrun disputes with the government can regularly count on some congressional intervention on their behalf.

Members are also concerned with intervening in the division of federal largesse. Here they pursue not only such tangible and visible items as new post offices and dams for given localities and contracts for certain companies but also assist local units of government in seeking

---

17. See John C. Wahlke, Heinz Eulau, William Buchanan, and Leroy Ferguson, *The Legislative System* (New York: Wiley, 1962); and Heinz Eulau, John C. Wahlke, William Buchanan, and Leroy C. Ferguson, "The Role of the Representative," *American Political Science Review* 53 (1959): 742–756, for evidence at the level of the state legislature.

18. John C. Wahlke, "Policy Demands and System Support: The Role of the Represented," *British Journal of Political Science* 1 (1971): 271–290.

federal funds for such things as education, health, pollution control, job training, and housing.

Senators and representatives can also seek to represent broad classes or races. For example, some black members consider themselves representatives of the interests of all blacks; some conservative white southerners consider themselves representatives of the interests of all southern whites and perhaps all whites. Some members consider themselves spokesmen for all the poor or for some segment of the poor—perhaps urban, Appalachian, Indian, or Mexican-American.

Finally, senators and representatives can seek to represent "the national good." This applies to most members at least some of the time. In this vein some members are even led to take stands that are unpopular and endanger their seats. The early opposition of Senators Wayne Morse (D-Oreg.) and Ernest Gruening (D-Alaska) to the war in Vietnam provides a case in point. Their position on this issue—and their visibility in pushing it—contributed to subsequent defeats at the polls.

Most members of Congress pursue a mixture of these representative activities, although different members weight the activities differently. Thus it was not at all unusual to see the same Senator Morse who opposed Vietnam on grounds of national interest extremely vigorous in support of high tariffs to protect Oregon cherries. Nor was it unusual to see Senator J. William Fulbright (D-Ark.) simultaneously pursuing "national interest" concerns as chairman of the Foreign Relations Committee and promoting the welfare of Arkansas chicken and rice farmers.

Fulbright himself commented on the balancing act he felt most legislators, including himself, had to undertake between constituency interests and broader national interests: [19]

> The average legislator early in his career discovers that there are certain interests, or prejudices, of his constituents which are dangerous to trifle with. Some of these prejudices may not be of fundamental importance to the welfare of the nation, in which case he is justified in humoring them, even though he may disapprove. The difficult case is where the prejudice concerns fundamental policy affecting the national welfare. . . .
>
> As an example of what I mean, let us take the poll-tax issue and isolationism. Regardless of how persuasive my colleagues or the national press may be about the evils of the poll-tax, I do not see its fundamental importance, and I shall follow the views of the people of my state. . . . On the other hand, regardless of how strongly op-

---

19. Quoted in Vogler, *The Politics of Congress*: 81.

posed my constituents may prove to be to the creation of, and participation in, an ever stronger United Nations Organization, I could not
follow such a policy in that field unless it becomes clearly hopeless.

SUMMARY

Several broad generalizations emerge from this chapter that should
be kept in mind as the subsequent, more detailed chapters are read:

First, Congress is important in terms of its policy impact. It is not
merely of historical interest, but in fact affects the daily life of all
American citizens. It performs four principal functions that can and
do have major impacts on society.

Second, Congress is a dynamic institution that changes both in
response to outside events *and* in response to the deliberate plans
and choices of its members. It is not a museum featuring relics of the
past. Rather it is a complex institution in a constant state of change—
sometimes slow and occasionally rapid.

Third, the key relationship in determining the congressional policy
impact at any given time is that between Congress and the executive
branch—both the president and the bureaucracy, which themselves
are often pushing in different directions.

Fourth, it is useful to think about Congress as at any given time
lying somewhere along a spectrum between fragmentation and integration in terms of both its internal organization and its impact on
the policies of the federal government. Congress' position on the spectrum changes over time, although there are more "natural" forces
leading it to gravitate toward the fragmentation pole than toward the
integration pole. Achieving integration takes more deliberate will and
effort than achieving fragmentation. It is also well to remember that
any given mix of fragmentation and integration will serve somewhat
different values more effectively.

CHAPTER 2

CONGRESSIONAL DEVELOPMENT

SIMPLY PUT, CONGRESS WAS DELIBERATELY CREATED TO BE A fragmented institution. In its development, however, forces have emerged that have occasionally allowed it to be more integrated. Thus the history of Congress is, and continues to be, in a broad sense, a history of the debate between fragmentation and integration played out in a complex institution.

Although Congress has changed—especially in response to a developing presidency, the growth of the bureaucracy, and the vast expansion of the tasks undertaken by the federal government—it has always been an important force in the governing apparatus of the nation. In this it was following a tradition well-rooted in the colonial period of the seventeenth and eighteenth centuries as well as in British antecedents.

The development of a representative and powerful legislature in Great Britain (Parliament) evolved through at least four stages.[1] First, beginning late in the thirteenth century and for a few centuries thereafter the king called Parliaments to meet for his own purposes, primarily to levy taxes that would provide revenue. Second, this body called by the king to vote taxes also gradually acquired other legislative power. Third, by the late seventeenth century Parliament had evolved to the stage where it could put definite limits on what the king could do, both in lawmaking and in raising revenues. These gains were cemented by the Puritan Revolution of the mid-seventeenth century and especially by the Glorious Revolution of 1688. From that point until the late nineteenth century in Great Britain the representative and electoral base for Parliament was very limited, however. Only

---

1. See Charles A. Beard and John D. Lewis, "Representative Government in Evolution," *American Political Science Review* 26 (1932): 223–240.

the relatively well-to-do in society were effectively heard in Parliament. The fourth stage of development came in the late nineteenth century when the representative and electoral base was broadened.

American legislative development, stemming from the state of Parliament in the early seventeenth century, began immediately and took a different course than did that in Great Britain. The colonial legislatures, beginning with the Virginia House of Burgesses in 1619, became important very quickly. Whereas in Great Britain the contention between Parliament and the Crown for power was not resolved until 1688 (and even after 1688 there were some shaky moments for parliamentary supremacy for at least a hundred years), legislative power in the colonies immediately grew. Furthermore, although a broad electorate did not develop in Great Britain until the late 19th century, in some of the colonies such an electorate was present even before independence was achieved.

Thus American legislative development went much more quickly than the longer and slower process in Great Britain. The American Congress created at the constitutional convention in Philadelphia in 1787 was virtually automatically a powerful body and a body that was assumed to be broadly representative, certainly by the standards of the eighteenth century. Any other basic decisions would have run counter to the dominant traditions of specifically American legislatures (as contrasted to the British Parliament) that had begun to develop in 1619.

These twin characteristics of a national American legislature—powerfulness and representativeness—were a foregone conclusion in Philadelphia. The dominant political thinking in the country and at the convention accepted them as necessary and as proper. The strength of these views was reinforced by the fact that one of the most successful claims the rebellious colonists had made before and during the War of Independence was that they were not receiving adequate representation in the government of Great Britain. Therefore, they argued, they could not be expected to support that government through taxes and in other ways. In this claim, which made a question of legislative representation central, they had been supported by some leading British political figures, including Edmund Burke.

THE CONSTITUTIONAL MANDATE

Much lively debate and many detailed compromises characterized the decisions made by the members of the constitutional convention in 1787 that stated the powers Congress would possess.[2] But the principle

---

2. On the Constitutional Convention's decisions about Congress and for "founding fathers" interpretations of those decisions see Max Farrand, *The Framing of the*

that there would be a powerful national legislature was never jeopardized. The numerous provisions and clauses throughout the Constitution that refer to Congress, especially those in Article I, section 8, make evident the intent of the framers to have such a legislature. In that section Congress is given a variety of specific powers, including the power to tax, borrow and coin money, regulate foreign and interstate commerce, establish a post office, establish federal courts in addition to the Supreme Court, declare war, and provide for the creation and maintenance of armed forces. And, in the event that these grants did not prove sufficient, the framers of the Constitution also granted Congress the power "To make all Laws which shall be necessary and proper for carrying into Execution the foregoing Powers, and all other Powers vested by this Constitution in the Government of the United States, or in any Department or Officer thereof."

The members of the constitutional convention made several assumptions that most closely affected the place of Congress in the American scheme of government. First, as already indicated, they assumed that the legislature should and would be powerful and important. No other course was ever seriously considered. Second, they assumed that the government in general needed substantial restraints as well as substantial power. Third, they assumed that the legislature in particular needed to be restrained.

The decisions made on the basis of these assumptions produced the mix of powers and restraints that characterize the entire government. Specifically, they produced the mix of powers and restraints characterizing Congress—powers and restraints that primarily militate in favor of the fragmentation described in Chapter 1 rather than integration.

The thoughts of those who took the lead in creating the new government, including Congress, are revealed best in the *Federalist* papers. Two of those papers, numbers 10 and 51, are especially worth notice as a prelude to understanding the convention's vision of Congress.

In number 10 Madison outlined the dangers of what he called "faction" and sought a cure. That cure is alleged to be present in the proposed new governing scheme. Madison's analysis can best be summarized by a few quotations from the paper:

> Among the numerous advantages promised by a well-constructed Union, none deserves to be more accurately developed than its tendency to break and control the violence of faction. . . .

Constitution of the United States (New Haven: Yale University Press, 1913); and Alexander Hamilton, John Jay, and James Madison, *The Federalist* (New York: Random House).

By a faction, I understand a number of citizens, whether amounting to a majority or minority of the whole, who are united and actuated by some common impulse of passion, or of interest, adverse to the rights of other citizens, or to the permanent and aggregate interests of the community.

There are two methods of curing the mischiefs of faction: the one, by removing its causes; the other, by controlling its effects. . . .

The inference to which we are brought is, that the *causes* of faction cannot be removed, and that relief is only to be sought in the means of controlling its *effects*.

If a faction consists of less than a majority, relief is supplied by the republican principle, which enables the majority to defeat its sinister views by regular vote. It may clog the administration, it may convulse the society; but it will be unable to execute and mask its violence under the forms of the Constitution. When a majority is included in a faction, the form of popular government, on the other hand, enables it to sacrifice to its ruling passion or interest both the public good and the rights of other citizens. To secure the public good and private rights against the danger of such a faction, and at the same time to preserve the spirit and the form of popular government, is then the great object to which our inquiries are directed. Let me add that it is the great desideratum by which this form of government can be rescued from the opprobrium under which it has so long labored, and be recommended to the esteem and adoption of mankind.

By what means is this object attainable? Evidently by one of two only. Either the existence of the same passion or interest in a majority at the same time must be prevented, or the majority, having such coexistent passion or interest, must be rendered, by their number and local situation, unable to concert and carry into effect schemes of oppression.

Madison then concludes number 10 by showing that the proposed government will allow control over the evil effects of faction and will prevent the tyranny of the majority.

In number 51, also written by Madison, the guarantees against tyranny of the majority (recall that a majority was defined as but a special kind of faction in number 10) are made more explicit. These guarantees are embodied in an elaborate scheme of separated powers enhanced by checks and balances. The place of Congress in this scheme of limited power is clearly shown, again most succinctly in the words of the author:

To what expedient, then, shall we finally resort, for maintaining in practice the necessary partition of power among the several departments, as laid down in the Constitution? The only answer that can be given is, that as all these exterior provisions are found to be inadequate, the defect must be supplied, by so contriving the interior structure of the government as that its several constituent parts may, by their mutual relations, be the means of keeping each other in their proper places. . . .

In framing a government which is to be administered by men over men, the great difficulty lies in this: you must first enable the government to control the governed; and in the next place oblige it to control itself. A dependence on the people is, no doubt, the primary control on the government; but experience has taught mankind the necessity of auxiliary precautions. . . .

But it is not possible to give to each department an equal power of self-defence. In republican government, the legislative authority necessarily predominates. The remedy for this inconveniency is to divide the legislature into different branches; and to render them, by different modes of election and different principles of action, as little connected with each other as the nature of their common functions and their common dependence on the society will admit. It may even be necessary to guard against dangerous encroachments by still further precautions. As the weight of the legislative authority requires that it should be thus divided, the weakness of the executive may require, on the other hand, that it should be fortified. . . .

There are, moreover, two considerations particularly applicable to the federal system of America, which place that system in a very interesting point of view.

First. In a single republic, all the power surrendered by the people is submitted to the administration of a single government; and the usurpations are guarded against by a division of the government into distinct and separate departments. In the compound republic of America, the power surrendered by the people is first divided between two distinct governments, and then the portion allotted to each subdivided among distinct and separate departments. Hence a double security arises to the rights of the people. The different governments will control each other, at the same time that each will be controlled by itself.

Second. It is of great importance in a republic not only to guard the society against the oppression of its rulers, but to guard one part of the society against the injustice of the other part. Different interests necessarily exist in different classes of citizens. If a majority be united by a common interest, the rights of the minority will be insecure. There are but two methods of providing against this evil: the one by creating a will in the community independent of the majority —that is, of the society itself; the other, by comprehending in the society so many separate descriptions of citizens as will render an unjust combination of a majority of the whole very improbable, if not impracticable. The first method prevails in all governments possessing an hereditary or self-appointed authority. This, at best, is but a precarious security; because a power independent of the society may as well espouse the unjust views of the major, as the rightful interests of the minor party, and may possibly be turned against both parties. The second method will be exemplified in the federal republic of the United States. Whilst all authority in it will be derived from and dependent on the society, the society itself will be broken into so many parts, interests and classes of citizens, that the rights of individuals, or of the minority, will be in little danger from interested combinations of the majority.

In short, when Federalist numbers 10 and 51 are read together, a formula for a fragmented Congress is quite clear. It is to be a powerful Congress but one that will be limited by (1) being composed of two houses with different constituencies, (2) the powers of other branches of the federal government, (3) the powers of state governments, and (4) the necessities imposed by representing a large and diverse set of interests ("factions" or potential "factions") that will have trouble agreeing on any scheme that might be oppressive to a minority.

Within this general institutional and philosophical framework—to which all of the specific decisions of 1787 were faithful—several concrete decisions stand out as most important in the subsequent development of Congress: (1) the decision to create a separate and independent judiciary that could serve to check both the president and Congress; (2) the decision to make the legislature bicameral, with equal houses representing different constituencies; and (3) the decision to interweave the powers of the president and Congress thoroughly while maintaining their very distinct identities. The latter two decisions have been much more consistently important than the first. Judicial power has been an important potential check, even though not often used with major impact. Each of the three decisions will be considered in turn.

Judicial Power

The policy interaction between the federal courts and Congress has been sporadic and has mainly involved congressional statutes struck down by the Supreme Court as unconstitutional (beyond the power of Congress according to the constitution) in whole or in part. Between 1789 and 1976 a total of 125 such declarations of unconstitutionality were made.[3] These decisions often involved minor statutes or only parts

---

3. Henry J. Abraham, *The Judicial Process,* 3rd ed. (New York: Oxford University Press, 1975): 286; and P. Allan Dionisopoulos, "Judicial Review in the Textbooks," *DEA News* 1 (1976): 19–21.

of statutes. Court activity in this sphere has been cyclical. Between 1789 and 1864 the Court was very timid, declaring only two congressional acts unconstitutional. Then between 1864 and 1936 the Court became much more aggressive, declaring 72 statutes unconstitutional, at least in part. From 1936 until 1953 another phase of passivity seemed to grip the Court, and it found only three congressional acts to have gone beyond constitutional power. Then beginning in 1954 the Court again became more aggressive. From 1954 through 1976 it found 48 statutes unconstitutional, at least in part.

The courts have also had a major impact on Congress through their role in redistricting since 1962 (treated in Chapter 3).

Bicameralism

The decision to have two houses of the national legislature followed the precedent set by the British Parliament and ten of the thirteen colonies. The Convention opted for a two-house national legislature with little debate.

There was debate, however, over the basis on which the two houses should be organized and elected. There was only minimal sentiment against having at least one house popularly elected (a "popular" electorate by the standards of the eighteenth century included a large proportion of all adult white males, although some white males might be denied the vote on the grounds of not having sufficient property). The delegates also assumed that the House of Representatives (as the popularly elected branch was called) would represent "democratic" interests—that is, measures favored by the majority of the voters that were widely expected to be "radical." The institution of slavery was protected even in the House, however, because representatives were apportioned to the states on the basis of their white population plus three-fifths of their slave population, even though slaves could not vote. Thus southern states received extra seats in the House because of their large populations of black slaves. This compromise marked the first attempt to deal with a subject that would eventually tear the Union apart.

The Senate (as the second house of the legislature was called) was expected to serve as a check on the impetuosity of the House. But how the Senate should be organized and elected was a subject of some debate, although there was virtually no sentiment for having it popularly elected. It was expected to be representative of more privileged interests in society that presumably would be badly treated in the House. But the delegates could not find a way of defining interests other than in terms of states. Thus every state was given two senators and the power of their election was lodged in the state legislatures.

The overly simple assumption that individuals elected by what passed for a mass electorate in 1787 to represent "the people" would be radical and that individuals elected indirectly to represent states would be more conservative and solicitous of economic interests was not borne out in practice. Certainly there have been numerous important policy disagreements between the two houses. But relative degrees of "conservatism" and "liberalism" have fluctuated. In the last several decades, for example, the Senate has tended to be more consistently concerned about federal aid for urban problems than the House, in part because most senators have at least one large urban area in their states with problems of which they are personally aware. In contrast, many members of the House come from totally rural or suburban districts, where these problems are far less visible.

In 1913 the seventeenth amendment to the Constitution changed the mode of election of senators so that they too would be elected by a mass electorate. The electoral system had been moving toward popular election for some time. Even during the period of election by state legislatures, senatorial candidates had often involved themselves in the campaigns of candidates for the state legislatures so that citizens were informed who their senator might be when they made their choice among state legislative candidates.[4]

In theory, the Constitution made the two chambers equal partners in the making of laws, although some special functions were reserved for each house: the Senate was given sole power to try impeachments, ratify treaties, and approve presidential nominations; the House was given the sole power to bring impeachments and to initiate tax bills (by custom this has also included the sole power to initiate appropriations bills). In practice, the two houses have remained generally equal, although at various points in American history one house has seemed to overshadow the other one. Throughout most of congressional history it has also been true that as individuals senators have had more prestige than representatives; many representatives have willingly left the House to run for the Senate while virtually no one has gone the reverse route. Nevertheless, prestige is not "power" or "influence." Equality may vary between substantive fields and over time, but the fact of equality is real: both bodies are jealous of their independence and their impact on public policy. This means that both houses will

---

4. On the interweaving of senatorial campaigns and state legislative campaigns see William H. Riker, "The Senate and American Federalism," *American Political Science Review* 49 (1955): 452–469.

usually seek to have an impact in virtually all important areas of legislation. No substantive fields become the exclusive property of one house or the other. Relative importance of the two houses varies from area to area, but rarely is either house devoid of influence.[5]

Congress and the President

The second crucial decision made by Constitutional Convention involved the nature of the relationship envisioned between the Congress and the executive. The two were formally separated, each with particular "checks and balances" on the other, yet there are also some shared functions, and policy-making on a large scale is impossible without sustained close cooperation between Congress and the president. In Article II, section 3, the Constitution formally charges the president to give "to the Congress Information of the State of the Union, and recommend to their Consideration such Measures as he shall judge necessary and expedient." The president is also given the power to call special sessions of either or both houses. Finally, he can veto a measure passed by both houses if he feels it is unsound or otherwise improper.

Congress, however, is responsible for either passing or rejecting various proposals for laws—proposals coming from the president or from any other source. Although the president is commander-in-chief of the armed forces, only Congress can formally declare war. All operations of the executive branch are dependent on money that can be provided only by Congress. And the resources from which that money comes are derived from taxes that are imposed only after proper congressional action. Two-thirds of the voting members of both houses can override a presidential veto. Treaties and nominations made by presidents are subject to congressional veto.

A president can be removed from office by Congress. This is extremely difficult to achieve because most members fear the negative consequences for the stability of the political system and a majority of the House and two-thirds of the Senate must agree in separate actions in order to effect the removal of the president. Only two serious attempts have been made to impeach presidents in the whole course of American history. In 1868 President Andrew Johnson was impeached by the House but the Senate fell one vote short of conviction.

In 1974 Congress was well on the way to impeaching and convicting President Richard Nixon when he resigned. The House Judiciary

---

5. For evidence of vacillations in relative impact of the two chambers on legislation, see David J. Vogler, *The Third House* (Evanston: Northwestern University Press, 1971): 110–111.

Committee spent a number of months sifting the evidence against Nixon, and committee members from both parties recommended impeachment of the President on three different counts (articles) to the full House. These articles involved obstruction of justice, abuse of presidential powers, and contempt of Congress—all in connection with the attempt by Nixon to cover up the White House role in the break-in at the Watergate headquarters of the Democratic National Committee in June 1972, and, in the case of the second article, with the attempt by the president to use federal agencies to harass political "enemies." It seemed very likely that the House would support at least the first two articles and that the Senate would vote to convict on at least those two articles. The case became moot when Nixon, in effect, admitted to ordering a cover-up of Watergate activities six days after the break-in by releasing information not previously available to the Judiciary Committee. The reaction to this admission was so overwhelmingly negative that it took only three days (from the admission on 5 August 1974, until 8 August 1974) for Nixon to decide that resigning would be preferable to certain impeachment and conviction.

Article II, section 4 of the Constitution provides that "The President, Vice President and all Civil Officers of the United States, shall be removed from Office on Impeachment for, and Conviction of, Treason, Bribery, or other high Crimes and Misdemeanors." There is no specific definition either in law or precedent of what constitutes "other high crimes and misdemeanors." In the case of a president it certainly seems likely that offenses against the Constitution and oath of office to support it as interpreted by a majority of the House and two-thirds of the Senate could bring impeachment and conviction even though those offenses might not literally involve acts for which the president could be tried and convicted in a court of law. Before Nixon's final disastrous admission his defenders on the House Judiciary Committee had argued that impeachable offenses should be narrowly defined to those for which criminal conviction could be obtained in a court but their position was in a minority of about two-to-one in the Committee.

Presidents are chosen by the House if the electoral college does not provide a majority. This happened after inconclusive elections in 1800 and 1824. In the first instance the House chose Thomas Jefferson over Aaron Burr and in the second John Quincy Adams over several rivals including Andrew Jackson. On another occasion, following the election of 1876, Congress created an Electoral Commission that, in effect, determined the results of the election, probably contrary to the will of the majority of the electorate. Thus Rutherford B. Hayes became president instead of Samuel Tilden. The Senate is responsible for choosing the vice-president following an inconclusive election. This has happened only once, in 1837. When the vice-presidency is vacant, a majority of both the House and Senate must confirm the president's nominee. If a president declares himself able to resume his duties after a period of disability and the vice-president and a majority of the cabinet disagree, Congress must settle the issue.

In effect, no matter what vision the president has about the shape of public policy, the implementation of that vision is dependent on Congress. Congress can also take considerable initiative in shaping public policy according to some collective vision possessed by a large number of its members. Congress is also deeply involved when those policies are implemented through the bureaucracy. Thus both Congress and the president legislate, and both Congress and the president administer. Yet they are part of a governmental system in which their entities and their roles—that is, what is expected of them—are kept separate and distinct. They are mutually interdependent in producing results; but they are separate and independent in defending institutional prerogatives.

The Emergence of the Modern Congress

In the early part of the nineteenth century Congress bore only a partial resemblance to the institution with which we are familiar today. The electorate for representatives had not yet stabilized (in some states restrictions on voting on the basis of property continued through the first few decades) and state legislatures elected senators. Not all representatives were elected from specific districts; until 1842 states were free to elect all representatives on a statewide basis and many did. Congress dealt with only a few aggressive presidents (chiefly Washington, Jefferson, and Jackson) before the Civil War. Even more important, the workload of the government was not very demanding The main business of Congress consisted of debates on tariff policy every decade or so and two major efforts to preserve the federal union without civil war in 1820 and 1850.

By mid-century and particularly following the Civil War new conditions emerged. The remaining restrictions on voting based on property disappeared and black male citizens were added to the electorate by the fourteenth and fifteenth amendments to the Constitution. Virtually all representatives now came from districts that were only part of a state. Lincoln revived the tradition of a consistently aggressive president that had been dormant since the days of Jackson. And his successful prosecution of the War left little doubt that the government could be mobilized to pursue national policy. His immediate successors did not appear aggressive—in part because Congress had adopted an aggressive stance particularly with regard to Reconstruction. By late in the century Cleveland and McKinley began to revive the presidency and, in a sense, prepare it for the burst of activity that would come in the twentieth century. Following the Civil War the government—both executive and legislature—had a great deal more to do as the nation industrialized rapidly and the government sought to cope with the consequences of that development.

It is here argued, then, that roughly before the immediate post-Civil War period of the 1870s and 1880s Congress was in a "pre-modern" phase. After the 1870s and 1880s the "modern" Congress emerged. Naturally, change existed before the 1880s and has continued since then. But the process of emergence was rapidly accelerated for a few decades in the late nineteenth century.

The difference between the pre-modern Congress and the modern Congress can be illustrated in six important areas: (1) turnover of membership; (2) finality of electoral decisions; (3) workload and length of sessions; (4) orderliness of floor proceedings; (5) stability of committee memberships and criteria for assignments to committees; and (6) the level of party development within the House and Senate. Table 2–1 summarizes the differences, and discussions appear in the following sections.

These features were chosen because, collectively, their impact in the modern Congress has been to promote professionalism and stability in contrast with the relative amateurism and instability in the pre-modern era. As indicated in chapter 1, institutional stability has both costs and benefits in terms of maximizing substantive congressional policy impact. Congress can still consciously promote internal, institu-

Table 2–1
Primary Differences between Pre-Modern Congress and Modern Congress

Pre-Modern Congress	Modern Congress
High turnover of membership	Low turnover of membership
Many contested elections	Few contested elections
Short sessions, relatively light workload	Long sessions, heavy workload
Chaotic floor proceedings	Orderly floor proceedings
High turnover of committee personnel; shifting criteria for assignment	Low turnover of committee personnel; stable criteria for assignment
Undeveloped political party structures	Well developed political party structures

tional change, but it cannot recreate the radical instability of the pre-modern period.

Turnover of Membership

In the pre-modern Congress, members came and went rapidly. There were few senior members. Life in Washington was not pleasant, Congress did not seem very important, and the unstable party situation often made re-election difficult to achieve. In the modern Congress, members began serving for much longer periods of time. They became wedded to the notion of a career in Congress. This new desire stemmed from several factors: the strengthening of the parties and the emergence of one-party states and districts after the Civil War making re-election easier; the emergence of national problems raised a legislative career to a new level of importance; and the demonstration by Congress after Lincoln's death that it intended to be an aggressive part of the government.

Figure 2–1 summarizes this change in terms of average years of service for all senators and representatives since 1789. Until the 1880s the experience of the average senator and representative remained at a low and fairly constant level—representatives averaged two years (after a higher level of around three years during a peak of House influence on national policy in the 1810s and 1820s) and senators around four years. Members of both chambers, especially the House, routinely left Congress for other opportunities, both governmental and private. Mid-term resignations were common.

Beginning about 1880 the average years of service rose dramatically in both houses, doubling in the Senate in less than two decades and almost tripling in the House in three decades. This trend has continued. It is produced by two factors: the desire on the part of members to seek re-election and the decreasing competitiveness of many districts (and some states) so that re-election is relatively easy to achieve for the incumbent. Both the desire for long service and the requisite condition for fulfilling the desire emerged in the late nineteenth century.[6]

---

6. See H. Douglas Price, "The Congressional Career—Then and Now," in Nelson W. Polsby (ed.), *Congressional Behavior* (New York: Random House, 1971). On the general point of the development of a "career" in Congress see Nelson W. Polsby, "Institutionalization in the U.S. House of Representatives," *American Political Science Review* 62 (1968): 144–168; Samuel P. Huntington, "Congressional Responses to the Twentieth Century," in David B. Truman (ed.), *The Congress and America's Future*, 2nd ed. (Englewood Cliffs, N.J.: Prentice-Hall, 1973); T. Richard Witmer, "The Aging of the House," *Political Science Quarterly*, 79 (December 1964): 526–541; and H. Douglas Price, "Congress and the Evolution of Legislative 'Professionalism'," in Norman J. Ornstein (ed.), *Congress in Change* (New York: Praeger, 1975): 2–23.

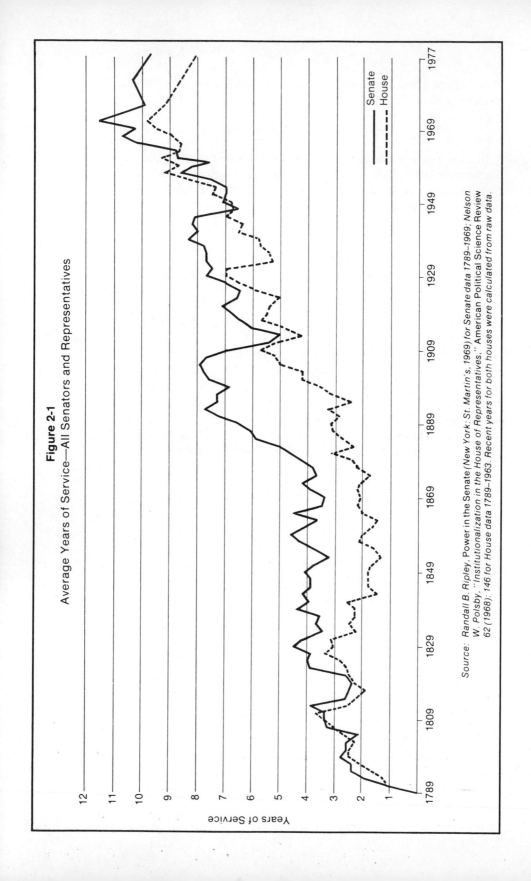

Figure 2-1

Average Years of Service—All Senators and Representatives

Source: Randall B. Ripley, Power in the Senate (New York: St. Martin's, 1969) for Senate data 1789–1969; Nelson W. Polsby, "Institutionalization in the House of Representatives," American Political Science Review 62 (1968): 146 for House data 1789–1963. Recent years for both houses were calculated from raw data.

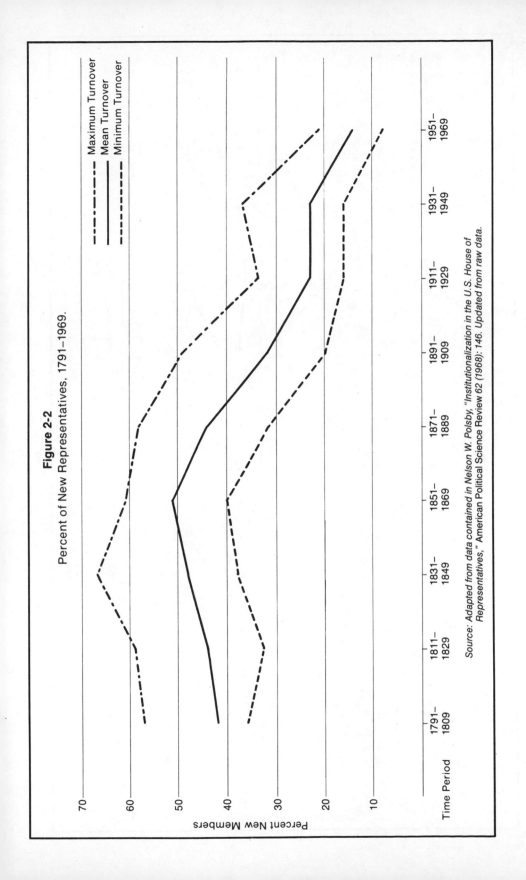

Figure 2-2

Percent of New Representatives, 1791–1969.

Source: Adapted from data contained in Nelson W. Polsby, "Institutionalization in the U.S. House of Representatives," American Political Science Review 62 (1968): 146. Updated from raw data.

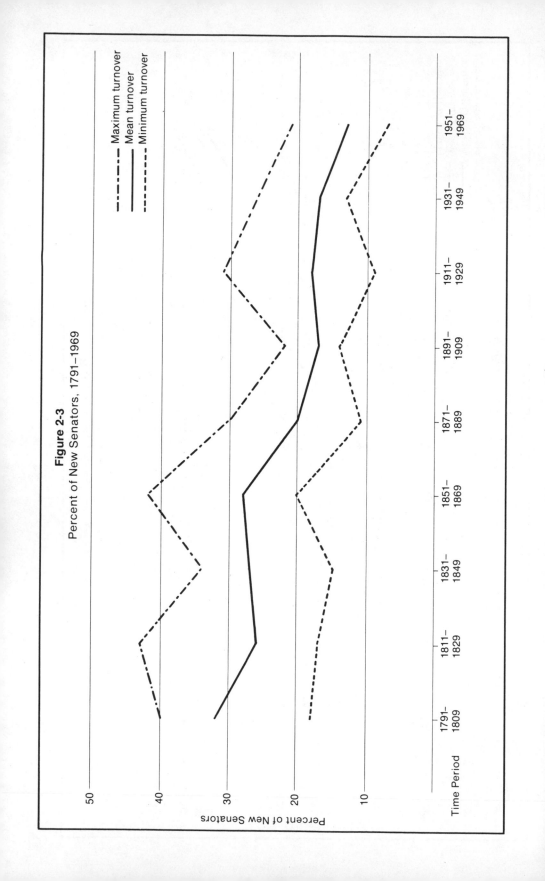

Figure 2-3
Percent of New Senators, 1791–1969

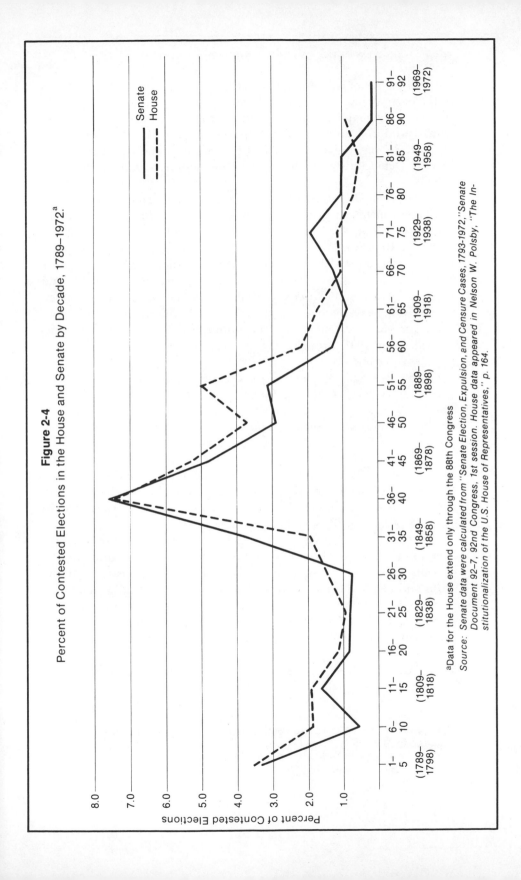

Figure 2-4

Percent of Contested Elections in the House and Senate by Decade, 1789–1972.[a]

[a]Data for the House extend only through the 88th Congress

Source: Senate data were calculated from "Senate Election, Expulsion, and Censure Cases, 1793-1972," Senate Document 92-7, 92nd Congress, 1st session. House data appeared in Nelson W. Polsby, "The Institutionalization of the U.S. House of Representatives," p. 164.

The critical factor in helping to produce safe seats was a strengthening of the party system in that period and a geographical division of party strength. The major reason for these developments was the Civil War, which produced an aggressive Republican party in the north that retained its aggressiveness after the War and was countered by a revived Democratic party, with a strong southern and border state base.[7]

In the pre-modern Congress there were always large numbers of new (freshmen) members in both houses. In fifteen of the first forty-eight Congresses (from 1789 until 1883) over half of all members of the House of Representatives were freshmen. During the same period of time (in fact, until 1901) the percentage of freshmen was never below 30 percent and was usually well above 40 percent.[8] Between 1789 and 1899 an average of 45.3 percent of all House members were freshmen in each Congress. Because length of service has been increasing there are fewer vacancies and hence the number of new members has decreased. From 1901 through 1977 the average number of freshmen has been 20.1 percent.

Figures 2–2 and 2–3 summarize the percentage of representatives and senators coming for the first time to their respective chambers since 1791 (the Second Congress) through the Ninety-first Congress (1969) in twenty-year periods. The First Congress is not included because, of course, all members were freshmen.

In the last four Congresses, beginning in 1971, 1973, 1975, and 1977, the percentage of new members has hovered around the average for the preceding twenty years, with one case of higher than average turnover in each house (19.8 percent of House members were new in 1975; 18 percent of the senators were new in 1977).

Figures 2–2 and 2–3 show a dramatic and continuing drop in turnover in the House beginning in the 1870s and continuing to the present. In the Senate the major drop in turnover occurred in the 1870s and 1880s and has continued somewhat sporadically since, particularly in the last two decades. Before the Civil War the turnover in both houses was very high: between one-quarter and one-third of every Senate was composed of freshmen senators and close to half of every House was composed of freshmen representatives. In the last several decades those figures have generally shrunk to between one in every seven or eight in both houses. The emergence of relatively

---

7. See Eric L. McKitrick, "Party Politics and the Union and Confederate War Efforts," in William N. Chambers and Walter D. Burnham (eds.), *The American Party Systems* (New York: Oxford University Press, 1967).

8. Polsby, "Institutionalization," 146.

strong parties with different geographical bases in the late nineteenth century is a powerful factor helping to explain the initial change.

Finality of Electoral Decisions

In the pre-modern Congress members were subject to challenges to their election. These challenges, on the grounds of electoral irregularities, were especially frequent from the end of the Civil War to the turn of the century. Virtually all contests were decided by the House and Senate on strictly partisan grounds.[9] Each seat was particularly valuable in the late nineteenth century because it was a period of close competition between the parties both in the electorate in terms of close elections and in Congress in terms of shifting control and small majorities. Partisan election contests in both houses dropped dramatically around the turn of the century, and have continued to decline since. Members who wanted to make careers in Congress—now a majority instead of a small minority—could no longer afford to tolerate arbitrary threats to their goal. Figure 2–4 summarizes the percentage of seats challenged in the House and Senate by decade.

Workload and Length of Sessions

The pre-modern Congress did not meet much of the time because it did not have a great deal to do. In fact, until early in the twentieth century Congress met less than twelve months out of every two years. Except for the First Congress, which met seventeen months for the purpose of creating a governing apparatus, and the Civil War and Reconstruction Congresses, which met between ten and twenty-two months, the length of sessions remained consistently short until roughly 1911. Since that time Congress has met over twelve months out of every twenty-four. In the last three decades Congress has been in session most of the time. This feature of the modern Congress has required that a large proportion of the members become full-time legislators. The reason for this change is primarily that the workload of the entire national government has increased steadily since the Civil War. Since Congress is a central unit in the governing apparatus its workload has also increased steadily. Gradually, Congress became involved in the whole range of foreign and domestic policies outlined in chapter 1.

Figure 2–5 summarizes the growth in the length of the Congressional session by decade through 1971. The three Congresses that met between 1971 and 1977 were in session an average of 630 days each.

---

9. Price, "Congressional Career," reports that only 3 of 382 contested seats in the House were given to the minority party candidate from 1789 to 1908.

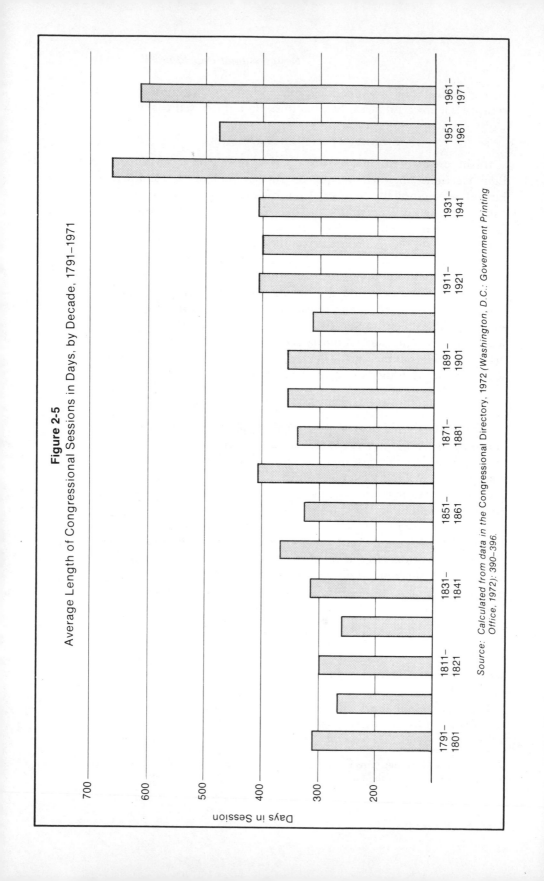

Figure 2-5

Average Length of Congressional Sessions in Days, by Decade, 1791–1971

Source: Calculated from data in the Congressional Directory, 1972 (Washington, D.C.: Government Printing Office, 1972): 390–396.

Orderliness of Floor Proceedings

In the pre-modern Congress, particularly in the House, floor proceedings were chaotic. H. Douglas Price described the House of the nineteenth century: "Members often used bitter and outrageous language, scathing ridicule, and sarcasm. Outbreaks of physical violence were not infrequent, and guns and knives were on occasion carried into the chamber." Neil MacNeil reports a number of instances of violence on the House floor and duels outside the House between members. In one famous encounter before the Civil War, Preston Brooks, a South Carolina representative, beat Charles Sumner, a Massachusetts senator, senseless on the Senate floor. Even more important, the rules of the House and Senate did not allow the orderly conduct of business.[10]

In the modern Congress decorum replaced raucousness and rules evolved that allowed Congress to dispatch large amounts of business on the floor rapidly. The development of such rules in the House was particularly important. The major developments came between 1876 and 1899 and were largely the result of the work of four Speakers: Samuel J. Randall (1876–1881), John G. Carlisle (1883–1889), Thomas B. Reed (1889–1891; 1895–1899), and Charles F. Crisp (1891–1895). Randall made the power of recognition absolute and not subject to appeal, obtained a general revision of the rules, and strengthened the Rules Committee, of which he was chairman. Carlisle was particularly astute in using the power of recognition and he further developed the Rules Committee as an instrument of party government. Reed had the House pass rules effectively outlawing dilatory motions and filibustering in the House. He also continued to use the power of recognition for party ends. Crisp extended the jurisdiction of the Rules Committee to bills still pending in standing committees. The Rules Committee also began to grant special orders or "rules" that would allow legislation to be brought to the floor more systematically.

The Speaker himself was shorn of some of his power acquired during this period in a House revolt against Speaker Joseph Cannon (1903–1911) that took place in 1909–1911 and reached a dramatic peak on the House floor on 19 March 1910. In 1909 the House established a consent calendar (which provided for the orderly consideration of bills to which there was no important opposition) and agreed to call the standing committees every Wednesday for consideration of business

---

10. Price, "Congressional Career," 18; Neil MacNeil, *Forge of Democracy* (New York: McKay, 1963): 306–309. See also Malcolm E. Jewell and Samuel C. Patterson, *The Legislative Process in the United States,* 3rd ed. (New York: Random House, 1977): 44–46.

on the Union or House calendars (calendars are simply lists of bills ready for floor action; different calendars include different types of bills). These changes limited the Speaker's arbitrary power to control the flow of business. In the March 1910 revolt the Speaker was removed from the Rules Committee, which was enlarged and made elective rather than appointive. Later that year, a method of discharging bills from standing committees was approved that gave the majority of the House the right to bring a bill to the floor even if it was opposed by a committee chairman and the Speaker. In 1911 the rules were changed to provide for the election by the full House of all standing committees and their chairmen. In practice, this led to the establishment of committees on committees (see chapter 5).

The Senate, which established decorum earlier than the House, has continued to take a more leisurely pace on the floor. But even in the Senate the wasting of time on the floor has declined. In the pre-modern period Congress could afford to waste time because the workload was so light. Once the workload grew and was attended to by professional legislators, time became valuable and procedures were invented to prevent gross waste of it.

Committee Membership: Stability and Assignment Criteria

In the pre-modern Congress there were shifting processes for assigning members to standing committees, and no consistent criteria were applied when such assignments were made. High turnover occurred in the membership of specific committees every two years, in part simply because turnover in Congress itself was so high. In the House the appointment power early gravitated to the Speaker, but it was not used with any consistency to promote policies he favored. Henry Clay, for example, the Speaker for eight years between 1811 and 1824, seems to have used this power merely to make friends and continue his tenure in the Speaker's chair.[11]

In the Senate even the location of appointment authority kept changing. The Senate had no standing committees until 1816 when eleven were authorized. Until 1823 the members of these committees were chosen by ballot by the whole Senate. From 1823 to 1833 the method of choice alternated between ballot, appointment by the president pro tempore of the Senate, and, for one short period, appointment by the vice-president. During much of the period before 1833 seniority for initial assignments and for rank on committees was so unimportant that chairmanships were rotated.

---

11. James S. Young, *The Washington Community, 1800–1828* (New York: Columbia University Press, 1966): 132–133.

After 1833 the Senate again resorted to balloting for all members. Chairmanships ceased to rotate, and party control of assignments began to appear. Committees began to divide on predictable ideological lines, and minority reports were written, whereas previously only majority reports were written. Party control was firm enough by 1846 that, although the formal requirement of balloting remained, the committee assignment lists supplied by the parties were routinely approved.

As the old parties split under the strain of dealing with the slavery question, the Senate found committee assignments more difficult to make. From 1849 to 1857 the president pro tempore again became the appointing agent, although the parties did not relinquish their influence. The southern Democrats dominated the committee chairmanships because of their number in the party. They supported the hardening of seniority to protect their position so that they could defend slavery. Democrats defended a version of the principle of seniority (not removing sitting committee members because of their experience) in an 1857 debate over proposed committee assignments. The Republicans had challenged the assignments as unfair; they had not been consulted by the Democrats when the assignments were made. When the Republicans became the majority in the Senate in 1861 they consulted the Democrats in that year but then ceased consulting them, instead filling all committee places themselves. This situation prevailed until the Democrats became numerous enough after the Civil War to force, in effect, the adoption of a seniority criterion.[12] Since then memberships on committees have been relatively stable—the same members tend to serve on the same committees term after term and develop both their own legislative career and the capacity of Congress to cope with the professionalism of the bureaucracy. Long service on specific committees has accompanied long service in the House and Senate as a whole.

Committee Chairmanships: Appointment Criteria

In the pre-modern Congress chairmen were selected by the same variety of methods by which other members were selected. And a variety of criteria for choice were used—including personal loyalty to the appointing authority. Turnover of chairmen was frequent.

In the modern Congress seniority developed as a virtually automatic

---

12. The preceding three paragraphs are taken from Randall B. Ripley, *Power in the Senate* (New York: St. Martin's, 1969): 22–23. The brief review is based on George Lee Robinson, "The Development of the Senate Committee System" (Ph.D. dissertation, New York University, 1954).

rule for apportioning committee chairmanships.[13] In the Senate, seniority became well-established very quickly in 1877, when the Senate again had a minority party large enough to pose a threat to the policy preferences of the majority party. Between 1865 and 1877, when vacancies occurred in the chairmanships of ten of the most important standing committees in the Senate the Republican party filled those vacancies only about one-quarter of the time on the basis of seniority. Since 1877 the seniority rule for chairmanships has been basically sacred, with only scattered violations.[14] The evidence suggests that the Democrats had begun to use seniority in the four Congresses preceding the Civil War (at which time most of them left the Senate). In the period after the War, until 1875, there were only a few Democrats in the Senate. When they reappeared in sizeable number seniority was rarely violated.[15]

In the House the development of seniority occurred more gradually. Speakers were struggling to get control of the House in the 1880s and 1890s and they frequently ignored seniority in the appointment of committee chairmen and ranking minority members in order to assure that individuals personally loyal to them and in general agreement with their policy views would hold key committee positions. (It should also be noted that, at least in formal terms, the Speaker made minority appointments as well as those from his own party until 1903, when he formally delegated the power to the minority leader.) The members who were removed or passed over in these non-seniority appointments were sometimes compensated by receiving better assignments, equal or better chairmanships, or positions of party leadership. However, a number of seniority violations went uncompensated —that is, a member eligible to become chairman or ranking minority member on the basis of seniority was effectively demoted and someone else with less seniority got the desired position; the senior member received no compensating assignment.

Figures 2–6 and 2–7 summarize all violations of seniority and uncompensated violations of seniority in the appointment of House chairmen between 1881 and 1977. It is clear from the figures that the

---

13. On this subject see Barbara Hinckley, *The Seniority System in Congress* (Bloomington: Indiana University Press, 1971); Michael Abram and Joseph Cooper, "The Rise of the Seniority System in the House of Representatives," *Polity* 1 (1968): 53–85; Nelson W. Polsby, Miriam Gallaher, and Barry Spencer Rundquist, "The Growth of the Seniority System in the U.S. House of Representatives," *American Political Science Review*, 63 (1969): 787–807; and George Goodwin, Jr., "The Seniority System in Congress," *American Political Science Review* 53 (1959): 412–436.

14. Ripley, *Power in the Senate*: 43–44.

15. Ibid., 45.

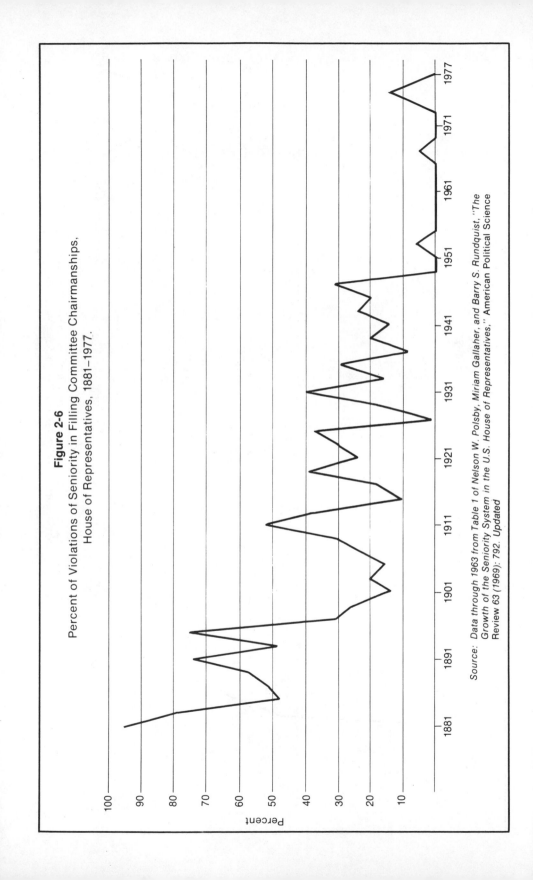

Figure 2-6

Percent of Violations of Seniority in Filling Committee Chairmanships,
House of Representatives, 1881–1977.

*Source: Data through 1963 from Table 1 of Nelson W. Polsby, Miriam Gallaher, and Barry S. Rundquist, "The
Growth of the Seniority System in the U.S. House of Representatives," American Political Science
Review 63 (1969): 792. Updated*

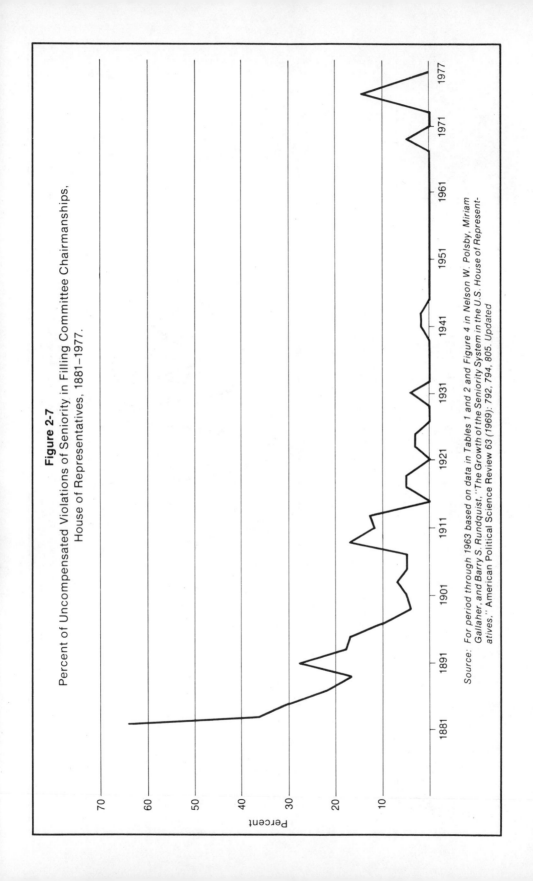

Figure 2-7

Percent of Uncompensated Violations of Seniority in Filling Committee Chairmanships, House of Representatives, 1881–1977.

Source: For period through 1963 based on data in Tables 1 and 2 and Figure 4 in Nelson W. Polsby, Miriam Gallaher, and Barry S. Rundquist, "The Growth of the Seniority System in the U.S. House of Representatives," American Political Science Review 63 (1969): 792, 794, 805. Updated

trend has been steadily away from violations of seniority. This is particularly evident in Figure 2–7, which shows a high level of uncompensated violations in the 1880s and 1890s declining in the first decade of the twentieth century. There is a spurt of uncompensated violations in the turmoil just before and after the drastic reduction of the power of the Speaker (including the removal of his power over committee appointments in 1910) and by 1921 uncompensated violations virtually disappear—with a total of eleven occurring between 1921 and 1977.

1975 obviously stands out on Figure 2–7 as an exceptional year. In that year three chairmen were removed and replaced by less senior members by new procedures that had been established in the Democratic caucus. A fourth was almost toppled. These men lost their seats because of a combination of age, unresponsiveness to the members of their committees, and ideological disagreements with the majority of their party. It would certainly be claiming far too much to say that seniority is dead in the House. In 1977, for example, all appointments to chairmanships were made in accord with seniority. It would be accurate, however, to say that the performance of chairmen can and will be monitored by the members and, if that performance is found sadly lacking, change not in accord with seniority may well be the result.

During the period of the highest number of violations of seniority the Speaker and minority leader (to the extent that the latter was consulted before 1903 and used his more formally delegated power after 1903) were selective in the non-seniority criteria for appointment that were used. Personal and programmatic loyalty, regional balance, and promotion of party unity were used most heavily in the most important committees—those deeply involved in politics as well as major policy decisions (Rules, Ways and Means, and Appropriations) and those involved with major policy (for example, Agriculture, Commerce, Foreign Affairs, Judiciary, and Naval Affairs). Committees involved in less important or relatively minor policy areas (for example, District of Columbia, Indian Affairs, and Territories) and those involved with only routine matters (for example, Claims, Invalid Pensions, and War Claims) were much more likely even before 1911 to have chairmen and ranking minority members appointed on the basis of seniority.

Table 2–2 summarizes the violation of seniority in the choosing of chairmen and ranking minority members in the House between 1881 and 1919. The data are presented separately for 1881 and 1911 and 1911 to 1919 to illustrate that an important change did in fact take place in 1911 (after the Speaker lost the appointment power) but that the change was gradual rather than immediate. This is in line with the data presented earlier in Figures 2–6 and 2–7. Note that in both

Table 2–2

The Violation of Seniority in Chairmanship and Ranking Minority Member Appointments for Selected House Committees, 1881–1919.

	Percent of Appointments that Violated Seniority							
	Chairmen				Ranking Minority Members			
Type of	1881–1911		1911–1919		1881–1911		1911–1919	
Committee	%	(N)	%	(N)	%	(N)	%	(N)
Political	65	(17)	0	(4)	73	(15)	40	(5)
Major Policy	49	(37)	17	(6)	28	(37)	0	(14)
Minor Policy	25	(24)	40	(5)	10	(31)	14	(7)
Routine	37	(19)	33	(3)	18	(22)	0	(7)
All Committees	43	(97)	22	(18)	20	(105)	9	(33)

Source: Based on raw data contained in Michael Abram and Joseph Cooper, "The Rise of Seniority in the House of Representatives," Polity 1 (1968): 52–85.

periods violations of seniority were much more frequent when a chairmanship was involved than when only the ranking minority position was involved.

Table 2–3 shows that before 1911 the violation of seniority was very similar in both parties. In the 1911–1919 period the differences between the parties may be attributed almost wholly to the fact that the Democrats were the majority party and the Republicans the minority. Thus the Democrats made all of the chairmanship appointments and, in a period of transition after the decision to limit the powers of the

Table 2–3

The Violation of Seniority in Selected Committee Leadership Appointments by Democratic and Republican Parties in the House of Representatives, 1881–1919.

	Percent of Appointments That Violated Seniority							
	Republicans				Democrats			
Type of	1881–1911		1911–1919		1881–1911		1911–1919	
Committee	%	(N)	%	(N)	%	(N)	%	(N)
Political	75	(20)	40	(5)	58	(12)	0	(4)
Major Policy	30	(50)	0	(14)	25	(24)	17	(6)
Minor Policy	12	(34)	14	(7)	24	(21)	40	(5)
Routine	27	(26)	0	(7)	27	(15)	33	(3)
All Committees	32	(130)	9	(33)	31	(72)	22	(18)

Source: See Table 2–2.

Speaker, had more at stake in filling chairmanships. But by 1921 both parties virtually rejected any criteria other than seniority for appointing committee chairmen and ranking members (and all other seats too). Bypassing seniority after 1921 usually came only in the most extraordinary circumstances—for instance, when the person under consideration supported a presidential candidate of the opposition party. The deviations in 1975 again stand out as particularly interesting and important.

The rise of seniority as virtually the single criterion for advancement toward committee chairmanships is explained principally by the emergence of a large number of career legislators. Because committee work is an important factor in the creation of a congressional reputation, career legislators could not tolerate arbitrariness in this area. Therefore, they supported—or perhaps demanded—an automatic role of advancement that would protect an orderly career development.

Development of Party and Leadership Structures

Pre-Modern Congress. In the pre-modern Congress there were few identifiable party leaders or institutions in either House. Members would occasionally rise to prominence in one House or the other, but this was usually a result of personal accomplishments, not of holding any position. The one institutional position that did have a number of influential incumbents was the speakership of the House (the only congressional office specified in the Constitution), but a large number of Speakers were figureheads[16]—either serving as pawns for others or purposely apolitical. There were no majority leaders or minority leaders or whips—positions that evolved well after the Civil War, either late in the nineteenth or early in the twentieth centuries. The few individuals who were widely recognized in their time as leaders came and went quickly, were often very junior at the time of their rise to eminence, and often voluntarily left Congress for other pursuits. Pre-Civil War Speakers such as Henry Clay and a host of individuals long since forgotten serve as examples. The speakership itself offers a good index in support of the point. Table 2–4 summarizes differences in years of service before becoming Speaker and in years of life after leaving the House for Speakers before and after 1875.

It is clear from the table that the average Speaker before 1875 had relatively few years of previous experience and tended to leave the speakership early in life (most lived about seventeen years after leaving

---

16. See Mary P. Follett, *The Speaker of the House of Representatives* (New York: Longmans, Green & Co., 1896).

Table 2–4
The Aging of the Speakership.

	Years of service prior to assuming the speakership	Years of life after leaving the House
Pre-1875 Speaker (N = 27)	6.5	16.7
Post-1875 Speaker (N = 17 or 20) [a]	19.7	5.6

[a] The two living ex-Speakers and the incumbent are included for column 1 but excluded from column 2.

Source: Adapted from data in Nelson W. Polsby, "Institutionalization in the U.S. House of Representatives," American Political Science Review 62 (1968): 148, 150–151. Updated for post-1875 period.

the House). Since 1875, however, Speakers have had a great deal of legislative experience and have remained in the speakership until late in life, living an average of less than six years after leaving the House.

"Careerism" in the speakership has grown. Table 2–5 presents information on the occupations of Speakers immediately following their speakerships. Before 1875 only two (Nathaniel P. Banks and William Pennington) out of twenty-seven Speakers finished their working lives either in the speakership, in the House (losing the speakership only

Table 2–5
Occupations of Speakers of the House of Representatives Immediately after Leaving the Speakership.

	Career Speakers [a]	"Higher" [b] Office	"Lesser" [c] Office	Private Business
1789–1875	2	8	16	1
1875–1977	14	4	0	1
Total	16	12	16	2

[a] These were individuals who died as Speaker, remained in the House but not as Speaker because their party lost control of the House, or simply retired because of old age or election defeat.

[b] This category includes the presidency (1), the vice-presidency (2), and the Senate (9).

[c] This category includes all other elective and appointive offices.

Source: Adapted from Nelson W. Polsby, "The Institutionalization of the U.S. House of Representatives," pp. 150–51. Updated for post-1875 period.

because of a party turnover), or in retirement. And neither of them really made a career in the House. After 1875 74 percent of the Speakers have been "career" Speakers. Before 1875 sixteen of the twenty-seven Speakers (almost 60 percent) left the speakership for some office that today would be regarded as distinctly inferior: for example, a receiver-general of the Pennsylvania Land Office, a state treasurer of Virginia, and a minister to Russia were all men fresh from the speakership. After 1875 no Speaker left office to take a lesser office, three left for the Senate, one (John N. Garner) left to become vice-president, and the only other, Thomas B. Reed of Maine, was in most ways a career Speaker but left the speakership to practice law when he became disgusted with the policies (and personality) of President McKinley.

Partisan patterns of voting on roll calls on the floor appeared from time to time in the pre-modern House and Senate. But at other times there appeared to be little partisan voting.[17]

More important, party was not a well-developed entity in the premodern House and Senate. Formal organization and consistent party leadership were missing until late in the nineteenth century. One important student of the early Congress, James Young, offers an accurate description of congressional parties in the era just before Jackson became president:

> If the party did not meet, neither did it attain, but momentarily, the status of an organized group in the congressional community. What degree of formal organization the party did achieve was only for the brief duration of its convocation as a nominating caucus [for President]. . . . In the periods intervening between caucuses the party had no officers, even of figurehead importance, for the guidance or man-

17. There is disagreement in the scanty historical literature on the pre-modern Congress on how much party unity there was in contrast to unity "caused" by other factors, such as region or rooming together in Washington. There is agreement, however, that little is known about how unity that does appear to be related to party was generated. It seems to have been at least partially spontaneous, not the result of any presidential leadership or party leadership or party organization, all of which were missing all or most of the time.

For empirically based discussions of these questions in different periods of the pre-modern Congress see Thomas B. Alexander, *Sectional Stress and Party Strength* (Nashville: Vanderbilt University Press, 1967); Rudolph M. Bell, *Party and Faction in American Politics: The House of Representatives, 1789–1801* (Westport, Conn.: Greenwood Press, 1973); Allan G. Bogue and Mark Paul Marlaire, "Of Mess and Men: The Boardinghouse and Congressional Voting, 1821–1842," *American Journal of Political Science* 19 (1975): 207–230; David J. Russo, The Major Political Issues of the Jacksonian Period and the Development of Party Loyalty in Congress, 1830–1840," *Transactions of the American Philosophical Society* 62 (1972): part 5; Joel H. Silbey, *The Shrine of Party* (Pittsburgh: University of Pittsburgh Press, 1967); and Young, *Washington Community.*

agement of legislative processes. Party members elected no leaders, designated no functionaries to speak on their behalf or to carry out any legislative task assignments. The party had no whips, no seniority leaders. There were no Committees on Committees, no Steering Committees, no Policy Committees: none of the organizational apparatus that marks the twentieth-century congressional parties as going enterprises.[18]

The same description, with minor alterations, could serve for any period in the pre-modern Congress.

Party membership was loose and unbinding even on the supposed members. There was little party cohesion even in voting for Speaker.[19] Party labels changed; before the Civil War the Whigs, National Republicans, Democratic Republicans, and Federalists came and went as major parties. In some Congresses there were no readily identifiable parties at all but merely pro-administration and anti-administration groups of members. In the period between 1830 and 1870, there were often sizable numbers of minority (third-party) party members in Congress. But after the Cvil War the two-party system crystallized nationally and congressionally.

Modern Congress. In the modern Congress, parties emerged as much more structured parts of the congressional apparatus, although their policy importance has fluctuated.[20] In the period between the Civil War and the present, both parties in both houses have identified formal leaders and established a variety of party committees. The sequence varied in the two houses, however. Since 1789 the Speaker of the House had been at least a nominal leader of the majority party; he became consistently important after 1869 (with the single major exception of 1919–1925, when internal politics in the House Republican party produced a Speaker explicitly elected because he agreed to be a figurehead). A formal minority leader emerged in the early 1880s and has been a consistently important figure in his party. In terms of status and function he has been parallel to the speaker for his own party.

---

18. Young, *Washington Community*: 126–127.

19. See Appendix C of Follett, *The Speaker of the House of Representatives*.

20. For studies, based on roll call votes, that show a powerful party leadership in the House achieving a high degree of unity, and therefore a high degree of party impact on policy, see David W. Brady, *Congressional Voting in a Partisan Era* (Lawrence, Kans.: The University Press of Kansas, 1973); and David W. Brady and Phillip Althoff, "Party Voting in the U.S. House of Representatives, 1890–1910: Elements of a Responsible Party System," *Journal of Politics* 36 (1974): 753–775.

In the period between 1897 and 1911 both parties in the House added additional central leadership positions as partisan conflict became more intense and the maintenance of party unity more difficult. Both the Speaker and the minority leader needed assistance. The majority leader became a formal and important leader in 1899 and has been generally influential in both parties since then. Both parties appointed their first whips in the last few years of the nineteenth century. Men in these positions were sporadically active until the 1930s. In the early 1930s both parties developed large whip organizations that have helped to make most chief whips more important figures. These organizations are heavily involved in the distribution and collection of information for the central leaders and in securing the most favorable attendance on the floor from a partisan standpoint. Their emergence in the 1930s was related to the vast increase in the congressional agenda as the New Deal responded to the Depression.

Both parties created important party committees after 1910–1911, when the speakership was substantially reduced in terms of potential influence. Chairmen of some of these committees have occasionally been prominent figures in the party.

In the Senate the development was reversed and the timing changed. The party committees and organizations emerged in both parties after the Civil War and became important in the decade between 1885 and 1895; no easily identifiable formal central leadership positions were created until the period between 1911 and 1915, although powerful leaders began to emerge after 1885.

The difference in the timing of Senate and House developments is largely explained by the development of the "career senator" several decades before the development of the "career representative." The professionalization of the Senate career occurred simultaneously with the centralization of power, whereas in the House the centralization of power preceded the professionalization of the representative career. Thus in the Senate there was a reluctance on the part of senators to trust single powerful leaders because their decisions could be so important (and so potentially harmful) to individual senators who wanted to stay in the Senate for the rest of their political lives. Seniority hardened at the time in the Senate in order to offer some protection to career senators. Party committees and organizations were thought to be less threatening than single leaders and they were first entrusted with leadership functions. Only after the Senate went through a period of leaderlessness in the early years of the twentieth century were senators willing to admit the need for strong single leaders.

In the House, power was centralized in the hands of the Speaker and minority leader before the career began to develop. When the career developed, the members of the House demanded restrictions on the central leaders (symbolized by the revolt against Speaker Cannon in 1910), and seniority and party committees were established as protections for the career-oriented House members.

Table 2–6 summarizes the chronology of the two separate developmental histories.

Table 2–6
Party Development and Related Events in House and Senate

Event	House	Senate
Centralization of Power	1875–95	1885–95
Professionalization of Career	1890–1910	1875–95
Hardening of seniority as criterion for advancement on committees	1911–25	1885–95
Creation of central leadership positions	1897–1900	1911–15
Creation of party committees and organizations	1919–present	1885–95

The majority leader in the Senate emerged as a formal and readily identifiable party leader in both parties in the period between 1911 and 1915. The minority leader emerged at the same time. After some dominant personalities left the Senate in the first few years of the twentieth century, the Senate experienced a period during which arriving at decisions had become very difficult. It also had experienced an aggressive president in the person of Theodore Roosevelt. Both party leaders have remained influential in the affairs of their respective parties since then. The majority and minority whips were created in the same period to aid the floor leaders, but these individuals have not been major figures in their parties until the last several decades. From 1935 to 1944, in fact, the Republicans did not bother to fill the position because they were such a small minority in the Senate.

Important party committees—the equivalents of policy committees and committees on committees—developed in both parties during the 1870s and were the vehicles used to centralize power in both parties in the Senate in the 1880s and 1890s by men who did not bear formal leadership titles but who were highly influential and effective leaders.

Table 2–7 summarizes the establishment of various formal leadership positions and party committees on a continuing basis in both houses. The activities of these leaders and committees in the modern House and Senate will be discussed in chapter 6.

By the beginning of the twentieth century, parties were an obvious, influential, and permanent feature of life in Congress. The development of strong parties in the electorate following the Civil War was reflected in Congress. When the national parties weakened again in the twentieth century the congressional parties also weakened although, given the vital procedural role of the leaders in providing order for a busy legislature, the pre-modern situation was not recreated.

Since the late nineteenth century members have been very clear about which party they belonged to and the identity of their formal party leaders. Third parties have almost vanished. Speakers have been elected by a straight party vote. There were still some major centrifugal forces in both houses—particularly the orientation of members to serving constituency interests before party interests when the two were perceived to clash—but well-organized parties became firmly enough entrenched to counteract such forces at least some of the time.

Much of the debate over "reform" in Congress centers around the role of parties and party leadership. Parties clearly have the apparatus to centralize much of the policy-making in the Senate and particularly in the House; whether their leaders have the will or the opportunity to develop such centralization as a prelude to policy integration is always an open and important question.

Summary

The above description and analysis points to one conclusion: on all of the criteria discussed the modern Congress has become both pro-

Table 2–7
The Establishment of Formal Party Leadership Positions and
Committees in Congress.

House [a]	Year of Creation on a Continuing Basis	
	Republicans	Democrats
Majority Leader	1899	1911
Minority Leader	1883	1889
Whip	1897	1900
Policy Committee	1919	1933
Committee on Committees	1917	1911
Senate		
Floor Leader (Majority Leader and Minority Leader)	1913	1911
Whip	1915	1913
Policy Committee	1874	1879
Committee on Committees	1865	1877

[a] Positions in addition to the Speakership.

[b] The House Republican Policy Committee has been only sporadically important; the House Democratic Policy Committee (called Steering Committee) has never been important.

fessional and stable. The professionalism has allowed Congress to cope with its increasing workload and also to face the fact of a powerful executive branch in such a way as to keep a considerable amount of legislative influence. The stability has permitted the processing of the workload in reasonably good and timely order.

On the other hand, stability also has its costs. It may be deemed necessary by a group of career-oriented professionals—such as most senators and representatives—but it may also lead to seemingly permanent alliances on major questions of public policy between the professionals in Congress and the professionals in the executive branch and in the interest groups. These alliances may result in good policy or bad policy, in programs that work or in programs that fail. But, in any event, such alliances are not likely to view dramatic changes in policy as necessary or useful. Such changes might threaten the existence of the alliances themselves and thus threaten the security of the members of those alliances, including the congressional members. Some would argue this is a wise way to make public policy—with any changes widely agreed on and only relatively minor in scope. Others would argue that such excessive stability and concern with preserving the status quo inhibits the government's ability to meet pressing national problems.

CHAPTER 3

CONGRESSIONAL
ELECTIONS

CONGRESSIONAL ELECTIONS USUALLY CONTRIBUTE IN A MAJOR WAY TO the fragmentation that typifies Congress. First, they serve to keep Congress permeable *and* concerned with representation. Permeability and attention to representation come both in the form of challengers ousting incumbents in elections (although this does not happen with much frequency at present) and in the responsiveness of members to communications from at least some of their constituents.

Second, the character of the American party system, when coupled with elections for all seats in both houses, pushes in the direction of fragmentation through providing little stress on agreement on national issues among members professing the same party identification. The stress instead tends to be on local issues. One of the leading students of American political parties, the late V.O. Key, makes several observations underscoring this point:

> Observation of the nomination of candidates for the House and Senate brings forcibly to attention at least two peculiar characteristics of the American party system. First is the odd mixture of centralization and decentralization in the organization of American parties. . . .
>
> In the national conventions a consensus is sought among the divergent interests within the party; in the nominations for House and Senate those same interests are free to impose their special policy coloration on the party's local candidates. The differences compromised in the national convention are perpetuated, even accentuated, in the party's congressional slate.
>
> A focus on nominations also brings to the fore another feature of the American system, namely, the fact that much of our politics is intraparty, not interparty, politics. . . .

Despite the capacity of the party system to confront the nation's electorate with great alternatives, the independence of the choice of executive and legislature assures that elections will produce a mixed mandate. To some extent the affairs of senatorial politics in each state and of congressional politics in each district are governed, not by the great considerations of national politics, but by questions peculiar to the locality. . . .

This mixture of nationalism and parochialism in elections contains the roots of the conflicting tendencies of amalgamation and cleavage in executive-congressional relations. . . .

The fundamental characteristics of the American parties—their diversity of composition, their dominant policy orientations, their inner contradictions—manifest themselves in bold relief in the membership of the party groups in the House and Senate.[1]

In many ways members of Congress are always running for re-election. As one House member put it: "You should say 'perennial' election rather than 'biennial.' It is with us every day." [2] Members perceive virtually everything they do as affecting re-election, and much of their behavior is shaped by that perception. "The electoral connection" is central in explaining what goes on inside Congress.[3] That fact is perhaps ironic when one considers that many potential or actual voters do not share the overriding interest in elections exhibited by members. Many individuals will not vote. Of those who do vote a large proportion will have little precise knowledge about the behavior of their senators or representatives. Many will not even recognize their names. Fewer still will know anything about the challengers.

There are, however, some voters in every district and state who do pay attention to the behavior of their representatives and senators. Much of the time members try to be particularly responsive to these individuals and to groups in which they are active.

Elections provide the main occasion of authoritative contact between constituents and members. Constituents control the ultimate sanction or reward for a member or an aspiring member through the electoral process. This fact motivates much of the contact that occurs between members and constituents between elections.

Elections are also the mechanism linking almost nonexistent national political parties, constituency parties that are usually weak

---

1. V. O. Key, Jr., *Politics, Parties, and Pressure Groups,* 5th ed. (New York: Crowell, 1964): 434–435, 545–546, 665.

2. Quoted in Charles L. Clapp, *The Congressman: His Work as He Sees It* (Washington, D.C.: Brookings, 1963): 330.

3. See David R. Mayhew, *Congress: The Electoral Connection* (New Haven: Yale University Press, 1974).

organizationally, and congressional parties that, although often weak forces, are sometimes relatively strong influences over the agenda and policy results emanating from Congress.

Congressional elections can best be understood by first considering the voters and electoral districts, then candidates and campaigns, election results, and, ultimately, the implications of elections for congressional behavior.

The Voters

From its beginning, the House of Representatives was conceived to be a popular body—representing "the people" and chosen by them. The Senate did not formally become a popular body until the ratification of the seventeenth amendment to the Constitution in 1913. In practice, however, the Senate was well on its way to becoming a popular body before 1913.[4]

The opportunity for direct popular impact on both the House and Senate is thus present, but it is an opportunity that is never fully exercised by the electorate. Turnout for elections of representatives is always less than 60 percent and sometimes much less. For senatorial elections turnout is rarely more than 60 percent (see Figures 3–1 and 3–2) and is usually much lower.

Low turnout has been interpreted in several different ways. Some suggest that it indicates satisfaction with the governmental system. Others argue that it is a sign of alienation from the system, that people are cynical and do not believe that their vote will make any difference. Still others argue that it is merely a sign of apathy, that a large number of people just do not much care about the political system and are neither supportive nor hostile.[5]

---

4. This was true for two basic reasons: (1) state legislatures had only infrequently tried to bind their senators' voting and policy positions in the Senate, a practice that virtually disappeared after the Civil War, and (2) several events occurred that introduced popular control, albeit indirectly, prior to adoption of the seventeenth amendment. These included the active involvement of senatorial candidates in the campaigns for state legislatures (so that voting by the populace for state legislators was in effect a referendum on U.S. senatorial candidates). The development of the primary election system after 1888 also offered popular control. Finally, shortly before the seventeenth amendment was adopted, a system was invented and used in Oregon that provided for direct popular vote on senatorial candidates in connection with the regular election, even though formal electoral power remained in the state legislature.

On all of these developments and their impact see William H. Riker, "The Senate and American Federalism," *American Political Science Review* 49 (1955): 452–469.

5. On some of these issues see E. E. Schattschneider, *The Semi-Sovereign People* (New York: Holt, Rinehart, and Winston, 1960).

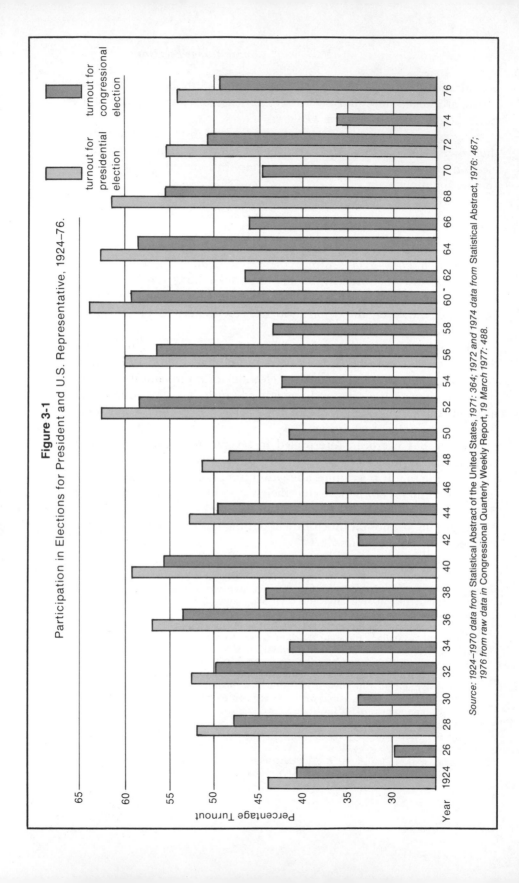

Figure 3-1

Participation in Elections for President and U.S. Representative, 1924–76.

turnout for presidential election

turnout for congressional election

Source: 1924–1970 data from Statistical Abstract of the United States, 1971: 364; 1972 and 1974 data from Statistical Abstract, 1976: 467; 1976 from raw data in Congressional Quarterly Weekly Report, 19 March 1977: 488.

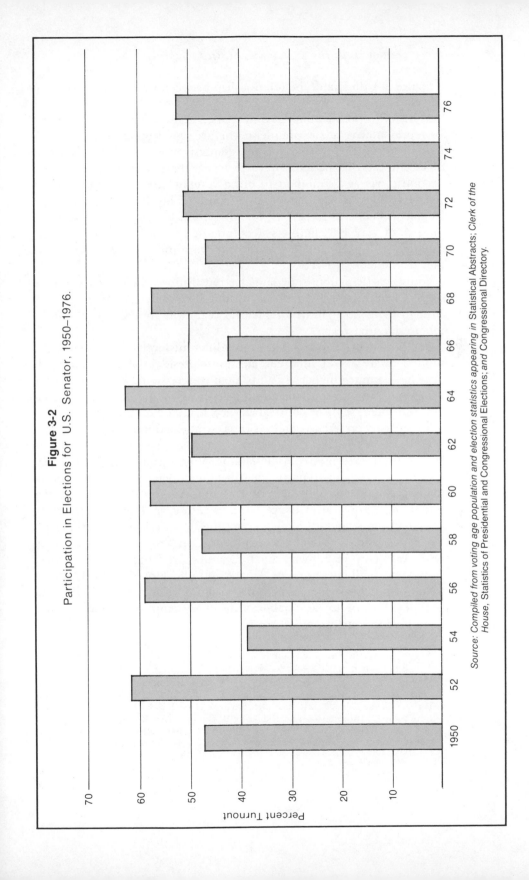

Figure 3-2

Participation in Elections for U.S. Senator, 1950–1976.

Percent Turnout

70　60　50　40　30　20　10

1950　52　54　56　58　60　62　64　66　68　70　72　74　76

Source: Compiled from voting age population and election statistics appearing in Statistical Abstracts; Clerk of the House, Statistics of Presidential and Congressional Elections; *and* Congressional Directory.

Figure 3–1 illustrates the relationship between turnout for presidential elections and turnout for congressional elections for the years 1924–1976. In presidential election years, almost as many people voted for representative as for president; the average dropoff between presidential voting and voting for representatives was slightly less than 4 percent for this period. In years when there was no presidential election to act as a stimulant to bring voters to the polls, the turnout rate for congressional elections was considerably lower. The average dropoff was close to 13 percent for the period between 1924 and 1976. That is, of very 100 eligible voters, almost 13 who voted for a representative in a presidential year did not vote for that office two years later in the off-year election.

Voting participation in Senate elections follows the same pattern as House races. Figure 3–2 reports turnout in those elections from 1950 through 1976. Turnout in presidential years was always higher than in non-presidential years.

One persistent factor related to the different levels of turnout is the public's awareness of different elections—presidential elections obviously have a much higher visibility than congressional elections. Other factors affecting turnout include the level of competition in the contests, the voter's sense of political efficacy, his sense of duty, the strength of his partisan preference, and his interest in the campaign.[6]

Those voters who turn out have mixed motives in making their choices for representative and senator. Voters can consider (not always consciously) their party identification, their opinion of the individual candidates, and their view of the issues as they relate to the candidates. Empirical evidence suggests, however, that the electorate collectively does not know much about the relationship between parties and issues, about which party controls Congress, and about policy stands taken by incumbent senators and representatives. Thus most voting for candidates for the Senate and the House is likely to be devoid of much specific policy content and is related instead either to party loyalties or to personal loyalties. One empirical study reaches the following conclusions: [7]

---

6. Angus Campbell, Philip E. Converse, Warren E. Miller, and Donald E. Stokes, *The American Voter* (New York: Wiley, 1964).

7. Donald E. Stokes, and Warren E. Miller, "Party Government and the Saliency of Congress," in Angus Campbell and others, *Elections and the Political Order* (New York: Wiley, 1966): 209–210. See also Barbara Hinckley, Richard Hofstetter, and John Kessel, "Information and the Vote: A Comparative Election Study," *American Politics Quarterly* 2 (1974): 131–158; and Barbara Hinckley, "Issues, Information Costs, and Congressional Elections," *American Politics Quarterly* 4 (1976): 131–152.

In the congressional election . . . the country votes overwhelmingly for party symbols, but the symbols have limited meaning in terms of legislative policy. . . . The electorate sees very little altogether of what goes on in the national legislature. Few judgments of legislative performance are associated with the parties, and much of the public is unaware even of which party has control of Congress.

What the public's response to the parties lacks in programmatic support is not made up by its response to local congressional candidates. Although perceptions of individual candidates account for most of the votes cast by partisans against their parties, these perceptions are almost untouched by information about the policy stands of the men contesting the House seat. The increment of strength that some candidates, especially incumbents, acquire by being known to their constituents is almost entirely free of policy content.

This absence of policy content in congressional elections in the mass sense enables members to exercise relatively independent judgment in weighing personal feelings about policy issues against the perceived needs or claims of constituencies. Congressmen do not need to feel terribly constrained to vote exactly as they think their districts would prefer, although some feel more independent than others.

The absence of policy content in mass voting also contributes to the incumbent members' chances for re-election. Basically, members are not judged at election time on the basis of their policy stands or performance. They are well aware that a very large part of the electorate in their districts does not know their policy stands and, even if it did, it would not vote solely on that basis.[8]

THE ELECTORAL DISTRICTS [9]

The apportionment of Senate seats and the provision of constituencies for senators present no problem: each state gets exactly two senators and all senators represent entire states. House seats, however, are more difficult to create. First, the number of seats must be *apportioned* among the fifty states on the basis of population. Then, within each

---

8. See Clapp, *The Congressman*: 377 for a discussion of representatives' attitudes in 1959. See also Charles O. Jones, "The Role of the Campaign in Congressional Politics," in M. Kent Jennings and L. Harmon Zeigler (eds.), *The Electoral Process* (Englewood Cliffs, N.J.: Prentice-Hall, 1966).

9. See Lewis A. Froman, Jr., *Congressmen and their Constituencies* (Chicago: Rand McNally, 1963): Chapter 6, on the policy differences generated by the fact that senators come from whole states and representatives from districts. See also Chapter 1 of this volume.

state that has more than one representative, geographic areas must be delineated. This distribution of seats within a state, formally called *districting,* is also done on the basis of population. Apportionment is done by Congress itself (now using a virtually automatic formula based on the census figures that are collected every ten years). Districting is done by state governments. In recent years, federal courts have also become heavily involved in the redistricting process.

Apportionment can have some impact on the content of congressional decisions as regional strength changes. Districting within states is even more important, however, as skillful manipulation of district lines can alter the party and ideological complexion of both individual seats and entire state delegations. For example, in the 1972 elections for the House only 13 out of 378 incumbents who ran were defeated. Eight of these individuals were defeated primarily because of redistricting. Democratic strength was particularly hurt because seven of the eight were Democrats who lost districts whose electoral base had shifted to rapidly growing suburbs, dominated by Republican voters.

Reapportionment

Reapportionment has taken place every tenth year immediately after the census. This practice began following the 1790 census, and has occurred regularly with the exception of 1920. Different methods have been used, but all of them have been based on population. The size of the House grew rapidly from 1790 until 1830 (inceasing from 65 to 242 members). For the next several decades the size was stable, but growth resumed following the 1870 census, until the number of seats reached the present 435 in 1913.

The size of the House was not fixed permanently at 435 by Congress until 1929, because no agreement on an alternative number could be reached before that time. Then, as now, reapportionment touched fundamental political nerves. Prior to the 1920 census, all states had benefited from reapportionments by receiving an increased number of seats in the House. But following that census (and the impressive population shifts following World War I) many states were faced with a loss of seats for the first time. The result was a stalemating of reapportionment efforts until 1929 when President Hoover convened a special session of Congress and insisted on apportionment legislation. By that time it was evident that population distributions were not going to return to prewar patterns, and new urban areas were clamoring for greater representation; Congress relented, fixing permanently the number of seats at 435, and requiring that these seats be distributed among the states on the basis of population after each census. With the single exception of a temporary increase to 437 from 1959 to 1963 to accommodate the inclusion of Alaska and Hawaii in the Union, there have been no changes in the size of the House since 1913. Attempts to increase its size, usually initiated by states faced with the loss of seats because of reapportionment, have met with failure.

Redistricting

The districting of states has even more explosive potential than reapportionment, since the way in which district lines are drawn define constituencies and hence affect the chances of election success or failure for representatives of those constituencies. It is not uncommon to see districts redrawn after the censuses to the explicit benefit of the party in the majority in the state legislatures. Gerrymandering (named after Elbridge Gerry, a governor of Massachusetts in the early nineteenth century) is the name given to the manipulation of the shape of a district to benefit a specific party or candidate. It would be too idealistic to expect state legislators to strive for impartiality and resist the political influences that bear on them as they grapple with redistricting. These forces are strong and elemental: parties want to maximize the number of their seats in Congress, incumbent representatives want to be assured of re-election through the creation of "safe" districts, and potential candidates want to create districts for themselves in which they can win.

Until the 1960s state legislatures were free to manipulate district lines without regard to the distribution of population within a state, with the result that a single district could have as many as four times the number of people as another district in the same state. This practice was challenged in a 1946 court suit in Illinois.[10] When the case reached the Supreme Court, however, the majority declined to intervene, claiming that it was inappropriate for the Court to enter the "political thicket."

In a 1962 apportionment case [11] the Court reached an opposite conclusion: the majority ruled that legislative apportionment *was* a justiciable issue, and that if a violation of rights was involved then a judicial remedy was appropriate. Applying the equal protection of the laws clause of the fourteenth amendment, the Court ruled that district for state legislatures must be equal in population. This decision led to a broader decision in a 1964 case,[12] the *Wesberry* case,

---

10. *Colegrove* v. *Green* (328 U.S. 549).
11. *Baker* v. *Carr* (369 U.S. 186).
12. *Wesberry* v. *Sanders* (376 U.S. 1).

when a six to three majority ruled that the Constitution (Article I, section 2—not the fourteenth amendment) required that House districts created by state legislatures must be equal in population. As Justice Black, writing for the majority, put it: "We hold that, construed in its historical context, the command of Article I, Section 2, that Representatives be chosen 'by the People of the several States' means that as nearly as is practicable one man's vote in a Congressional election is to be worth as much as another's." [13] In short, the Court was endorsing the much used phrase "one man, one vote."

The unsuccessful dissenters in this case continued to claim that the courts had no business in a political area. Justice Harlan stated the minority position succinctly: "The claim for judicial relief in this case strikes at one of the fundamental doctrines of our system of government, the separation of powers. In upholding that claim, the Court attempts to effect reforms in a field which the Constitution, as plainly as can be, has committed exclusively to the political process." [14]

The *Wesberry* case did not address the question of precisely how equal districts had to be in order to satisfy the requirements of the majority opinion. Federal courts involved in various redistricting suits following the *Wesberry* decision applied a variety of standards in determining what equality of size meant in practice. In 1969 the Supreme Court gave its own meaning to equality in the case of *Kirkpatrick* vs. *Preisler*.[15] Again by a six to three majority the Court held that equality meant absolute equality. Justice Brennan, writing for the majority, said "Equal representation for equal numbers of people is a principle designed to prevent debasement of voting power and diminution of access to elected Representatives. Toleration of even small deviations detracts from these purposes." [16]

Virtually every state has had to redistrict, sometimes more than once, as a result of these court decisions in the 1960s. Although requiring equality between districts, the courts have not, at least to date, involved themselves in prescribing the shape of districts. State legislatures still gerrymander in order to include or exclude blocs of voters, according to the prevailing dictates of political expediency. The latitude for manipulating the complexion of a state's representation in Congress has been decreased since the *Wesberry* decision, but it has by no means been eliminated.

---

13. *Wesberry* v. *Sanders* (376 U.S. 7–8).
14. *Wesberry* v. *Sanders* (376 U.S. 48).
15. *Kirkpatrick* v. *Preisler* (394 U.S. 526).
16. *Kirkpatrick* v. *Preisler* (394 U.S. 531).

Both before and after the Supreme Court's *Wesberry* decision the issue of reapportionment engendered much public debate, especially concerning the effects of having or not having reapportioned districts. Liberals in particular argued that the pre-*Wesberry* conditions favored rural areas over urban areas, and that as a result, congressional policy was conservatively biased. A study by *Congressional Quarterly* in 1962, however, showed that it was not urban but suburban areas that were underrepresented.[17] Andrew Hacker, in an empirical study of what an equally districted House might look like (undertaken before *Wesberry*), came to the conclusion that liberals were almost certainly not underrepresented in the House and might be even slightly overrepresented.[18] In fact, the redistricting that has occurred in accord with the *Wesberry* decision has produced a greater suburban representation in Congress, but neither political party nor any particular political ideology has benefited. In short, court action on redistricting may make good theoretical sense in a representative system but it has not basically affected the nature of Congress or its decisions. The central fact that members of the House come from fairly small districts, many of them relatively homogeneous, remains unchanged.

CANDIDATES AND CAMPAIGNS

The question of why individuals choose to run for Congress has no single answer. Empirical research suggests that there are various motives. Some individuals value a political career and see the opportunity of election to Congress as furthering that career. Others think of politics more broadly than just elected office and may run for Congress simply as one more way of being politically active. Still others may not be interested in a political career and may not be consistently interested in politics per se but may run out of a rather vague sense of civic duty or because they are persuaded that it is an appropriate thing to do. If elected, many members who may not have thought seriously about the satisfaction that might come from a political career are increasingly attracted to seek re-election and remain in the House or Senate or at least in electoral politics for a long time. A few, even if they win, never really become very interested in the House or Senate or politics and voluntarily retire rather quickly. In short, members come to Congress (or lose races for Congress) for many different reasons and

---

17. *Congressional Quarterly Weekly Report,* 1962: 153–169.
18. Andrew Hacker, *Congressional Districting* (Washington, D.C.: Brookings, 1964, revised ed.): 95–96.

with many different self-images. Once in Congress, socializing pressures may impose more uniformity on what was at the outset a reasonably diverse lot of people.[19]

Nominations

Virtually all nominations for the House and Senate are made in primary elections held within the parties in the various states and districts. In a few districts and states the primaries merely serve to ratify the choice of the dominant political organization, but most primaries have at least the potential for being genuinely competitive. Likewise, in most districts and states the "party organization" is relatively unimportant in selecting nominees. As one commentator has put it, "Nominations are . . . generally on a do-it-yourself basis." [20] The primaries that actually attract competition are, understandably, in states and districts where the nominee of the party has a reasonably good chance of winning.

Incumbents have very important advantages in nominating primaries. These advantages are not ironclad guarantees of success, however—some incumbents are defeated in their party's primary. In the elections of 1972, 1974, and 1976, for example, eighteen House members met defeat in a primary and four senators ended their Senate careers involuntarily in the same fashion. Five of the House seats and one of the Senate seats were then lost to the other party in the general election. To put these figures in perspective, however, during these same three elections 1160 incumbent House members successfully sought renomination and seventy-five senators did likewise. Thus the eighteen who lost represent about 1.5 percent of all who tried for renomination to the House; the four losing senators represent about 5 percent of all who tried for renomination. There is some evidence that an incumbent senator who survives a competitive primary is more likely to lose the following general election than a senator who does not have such a primary.[21]

In some districts and states the primary is, in effect, the most important election because the general election is virtually always won

19. See Jeff Fishel, *Party and Opposition* (New York: McKay, 1973): Chapter 3; and Clapp, *The Congressman:* 31–34.
20. H. Douglas Price, "The Electoral Arena," in David B. Truman (ed.), *The Congress and America's Future* (Englewood Cliffs, N.J.: Prentice-Hall, 1965): 41. For a good viguette of one primary campaign see Daniel J. Balz, "One Primary Day in Iowa—Traveling the Long Road to Congress," *National Journal* (11 September 1976): 1280–1283.
21. Robert A. Bernstein, "Divisive Primaries Do Hurt: U.S. Senate Races, 1956–1972," *American Political Science Review* 71 (1977): 540–545.

by the candidate of the same party. This is still true of a number of southern seats, which are reliably Democratic, although two-party competition has increased steadily in this region over the last several decades.

The primary system of nominating candidates for Congress underscores the decentralized nature of American politics. National party leaders very rarely play any part whatsoever in seeking or supporting candidates for House and Senate seats. The men and women who run emerge in a variety of ways, but not because of the labors of national figures of virtually non-existent national parties.[22]

General Election Campaigns [23]

A candidate for Congress faces one central problem: how to make himself known to enough people and preferred over his opponent. Solving this problem is predicated on solving another vast problem: the acquisition of sufficient finances to achieve the goal. Incumbents have a natural advantage in solving the first problem and this helps, to some extent, reduce the magnitude of the second problem. Challengers of incumbents have a much more difficult time in the areas of both recognition and money.

The high rate of success among incumbents (which will be examined later in the chapter) can be explained in both personal terms and in terms of the electorate. At the personal level the incumbent is known to a much larger proportion of his constituents than his opponent because of the media coverage he receives while in office. He receives a salary while campaigning. He can use his congressional staff to help in the campaign. He can use his franking privileges to mail materials to his constituents that will help establish both his name and a favorable image of himself. He can use that same privilege to conduct polls of his constituents' opinions. He has established links to contributors and campaign workers who have helped him in the past and for whom, presumably, he has provided favors, both tangible and intangible, while in office.[24]

---

22. For a good discussion contrasting the situation in the United States with the centralized nature of nominations for seats in the House of Commons in the United Kingdom see Mayhew, *Congress: The Electoral Connection:* 19–27.

23. For interesting stories of seven campaigns for House seats in 1974 see Alan L. Clem et al., *The Making of Congressmen: Seven Campaigns of 1974* (North Scituate, Mass.: Duxbury, 1976).

24. For some details on specific campaigns between incumbents and non-incumbents for the House in 1962 in the San Francisco Bay area see David A. Leuthold, *Electioneering in a Democracy* (New York: Wiley, 1968).

The high rate of incumbents' electoral success can also be explained by the relatively stable party identification of the voters. Since voting for Congress tends to be largely on the basis of party labels, most districts elect members to Congress who share the most popular label. Thus party identification and voting stability are closely linked in the case of congressional elections. (They are much less closely tied in the case of presidential elections, in which there is room for the large-scale intervention of other factors such as personality.)

Like nominations, election campaigns are run largely on a do-it-yourself basis. Most members of the House and Senate do not receive extensive aid (financial or otherwise) from their political parties, even though those political parties have various state organizations, national committees, and congressional campaign committees that are presumably in business partially to provide such aid.[25]

Campaign Finance

The cost of campaigns for House and Senate seats is, in the aggregate, enormous. In 1974, for example, candidates in primary general elections spent about $74 million.[26] Two years earlier the comparable amount was over $66 million. Of the total in 1974 about $45 million was spent on House races and almost $29 million was spent on 34 Senate races. In 1976 there were 31 contested Senate races. Total spending for these campaigns was over $38 million.[27]

Spending in individual races varies greatly. In contested Senate races in 1976, for example, the range was from $697 (for the winner in Wisconsin) to over $3 million (for the winner in Pennsylvania). The average spending by all candidates in an average Senate campaign was over $1.2 million. In one House race in a portion of Chicago in 1974 the winner and loser combined to spend over half a million dollars.[28] In some other races, costs were very low. In a few races where there are only nominal contests the winner and loser combined may spend only a few thousand dollars.

What impact does spending have? Empirical research has provided

---

25. Clapp, *The Congressman:* 29, 352–53, 363.
26. Herbert E. Alexander, *Financing Politics* (Washington: Congressional Quarterly Press, 1976).
27. Rhodes Cook, "Money, Incumbency Failed to Guarantee Success in 1976 Senate Races," *Congressional Quarterly Weekly Report* (25 June 1977): 1291–1294.
28. "$74-Million Spent in Congressional Races," *Congressional Quarterly Weekly Report* (19 April 1975): 789–794.

at least some partial answers. One summary of such research noted the following items: [29]

1. Spending seems to be more productive of votes in primary elections compared to general elections.

2. Spending increases turnout.

3. Spending by challengers is more important than spending by incumbents. As the challenger's spending increases, his or her chances of victory increase, although they are far from guaranteed.

4. At some point there appears to be "threshold effect"—that is, a challenger to an incumbent needs to spend a sizable amount to be in the race at all, but beyond that threshold amount extra spending seems to have little impact on his or her chances for winning. In 1974 in congressional contests the threshold amount was estimated to be $125,000.

Where does all of this money come from? For the 1976 Senate races, as reported by the Federal Election Commission, about 68 percent of the money came from individual contributions (which, of course, varied greatly in size). Another 15 percent came from interest group committees, 13 percent came from the candidates themselves, and less than 4 percent came from party committees.[30]

Despite new reporting requirements in recent laws, the figures for interest group contributions seem low. In 1976, for races for both Senate and House, Common Cause calculated interest group spending at about 30 percent of total campaign spending ($22.5 million of a total of about $74 million).[31] In any event, wherever actual spending by interest groups falls between 15 percent and 30 percent, it is important. It is especially important because it tends to be targeted on a few races of most concern to specific groups.

The $22.5 million given by interest groups in 1976 compares with $12.5 million given in 1974. Common Cause calculates that about one-third of the 1976 total came from organized labor groups and close to another one-third came from business groups. Other large contributors included health professional groups (doctors and dentists) and agricultural groups (principally milk producers).

29. Gary W. Copeland and Samuel C. Patterson, "Reform of Congressional Campaign Spending," *Policy Studies Journal* 5 (1977): 424–431. For evidence on point 3 see also Stanton A. Glantz, Alan I. Abramowitz, and Michael P. Burkart, "Election Outcomes: Whose Money Matters?," *Journal of Politics* 38 (1976): 1033–1038.

30. Cook, "Money, Incumbency Failed to Guarantee Success in 1976 Senate Races."

31. "Interest Group Donations to Congressional Campaigns almost Doubled in 1976," *Congressional Quarterly Weekly Report* (19 February 1977): 321; and "Interest Group Gifts to 1976 Congressional Campaigns," *Congressional Quarterly Weekly Report* (16 April 1977): 710.

The targeting of the interest group donations in 1976 was evident. Labor groups gave more than $100,000 to each of 11 senatorial candidates (all Democrats) and more than $40,000 to each of eight House candidates (all Democrats). On the other side ideologically, business-professional-agriculture groups gave more than $100,000 to eight Senate candidates (six Republicans and two Democrats) and more than $40,000 each to at least ten House candidates (eight Republicans and two southern Democrats).

Candidate contributions and loans (which, of course, may never be repaid) to their own campaigns can also be very important in the case of wealthy candidates. In 1976 fifteen Senate candidates contributed or loaned more than $50,000 each to their own campaigns. Nine of these individuals gave more than $100,000. At the upper end a losing Republican in Maine contributed more than $500,000 to his own campaign, a losing Democrat in Rhode Island gave almost $700,000, and a winning Republican in Pennsylvania contributed and loaned close to $2.5 million to his own campaign.

Personal wealth and contributions do not guarantee victory, however. Of the nine candidates giving more than $100,000 four won and five lost.

The high cost of gaining a House or Senate seat raises important questions. Can only rich men and women seek these offices? Are interested groups and individuals in a position to contribute so much of the needed money that they in fact "buy" public policy when they support a winning candidate heavily? The dangers implied by even qualified affirmative answers to such questions are certainly real.

Even if one assumes totally honorable winners and undemanding campaign contributors members of Congress will at the minimum unconsciously give extra weight to the interests and opinions of the largest contributors to their campaigns in reaching some of their decisions. And, of course, not all large contributors are undemanding, and the definition of honor by members of the House and Senate varies from individual to individual.

Before the 1970s there were only weak statutory efforts that tried to deal with limiting campaign contributions and spending and requiring open reporting. Many states have laws that supposedly limit the amount of spending in congressional campaigns, but they have had virtually no impact. In 1925 Congress passed a Corrupt Practices Act that basically had no impact on the financing of congressional campaigns.

In the 1970s, however, Congress began to deal seriously with questions of reporting, limits on contributions, limits on spending, and public financing of campaigns. Much of the attention has been focused on presidential campaigns. But congressional elections have also received substantial attention and continue to be the subject of debate.

Congress passed laws in 1971, 1974, and 1976 dealing with campaign finance. They are complicated laws and will not receive full treatment here.[32] Essentially, as of mid-1977 the laws affecting congressional campaigns contained fairly effective reporting requirements, generous limits on contributions, no limits on spending, and no provision for public financing.

The 1974 Act did contain limits, which were used only in the 1974 campaign. In a Senate primary the limit was eight cents per voter or $100,000 (whichever was greater). In a general election for a Senate seat the limit was twelve cents per voter or $150,000 (whichever was greater). House limits were $70,000 for both primaries and general elections. In 1976 the Supreme Court declared these limits to be an unconstitutional limitation on free speech as guaranteed by the First Amendment to the Constitution.[33] At the same time the Court approved limits on presidential campaign spending because there was also public financing. Therefore, Congress could reinstitute limits on congressional campaign spending by providing public financing. As of mid-1977 Congress was debating proposals in this area. The timing and content of new legislation was far from certain, but it seems very likely that there will be additional legislation in the area of campaign finance in the near future. Real solutions, however, remain hard to achieve.

ELECTION RESULTS

Congressional election results can be analyzed in many different ways. This section focuses on five important aspects of congressional elections. First, because elections determine which individuals get to Congress, a profile of the characteristics of the members is presented. Second, because elections determine which party will control the House and the Senate in organizational terms, patterns of party control are summarized. Third, the question of turnover of members (or lack thereof) is examined, which leads to a fourth consideration, the relationship of turnover to policy and institutional change. Finally, some general influences on the results of congressional elections are discussed.

---

32. For an excellent summary see *Congressional Quarterly's Guide to Congress,* 2nd ed. (Washington: Congressional Quarterly, 1976): 544–557. On limits on contributors see also the summary in Michael J. Malbin, "Labor, Business and Money—a Post-Election Analysis," *National Journal* (19 March 1977): 414.

33. *Buckley* v. *Valeo* (424 U.S. 1).

A Profile of the Members

The winners of seats in the House and Senate are by no means a cross section of the American population. By almost any measure they come from a social and economic elite. The same is true of the men and women they defeat.[34] The system of nominations and elections used in this country produces a certain kind of member, defined in socioeconomic terms. Thus, in a narrow sense, Congress is never fully representative of the American people. This does not mean that only upper class interests prevail in the decisions of Congress but it does suggest that some of the less well-off classes in society may have little reason to identify with the decisions reached by Congress because they do not identify with the decision-makers.

Education. One striking characteristic of members of Congress is that they are highly educated. Table 3–1 summarizes the formal education of members of the House and Senate and the general population in 1966. It is clear that representatives and senators are equally well educated in formal terms and, in addition, they are vastly more educated than the general public.

Occupation. The majority of the members of the House and Senate are lawyers. Most of the non-lawyers come from a business or banking

Table 3–1

Educational Attainments of House and Senate Members and General Population, 1966.

Level of Education	House	Senate	General Population
No College	7%	4%	82%
Some college	14%	13%	10%
BA degree (or equivalent)	19%	14%	
Law degree	53%	59%	} 9%
Advanced degrees	7%	10%	
Total	100	100	101 [a]

[a] Does not sum to 100 because of rounding.

Source: The figures on House and Senate members came from Charles O. Jones, Every Second Year *(Brookings, 1967). Those on the general population came from De-partment of Commerce, Bureau of the Census,* Current Population Reports, *Series P-20, no. 158, 19 December 1966.*

34. Fishel, *Party and Opposition.*

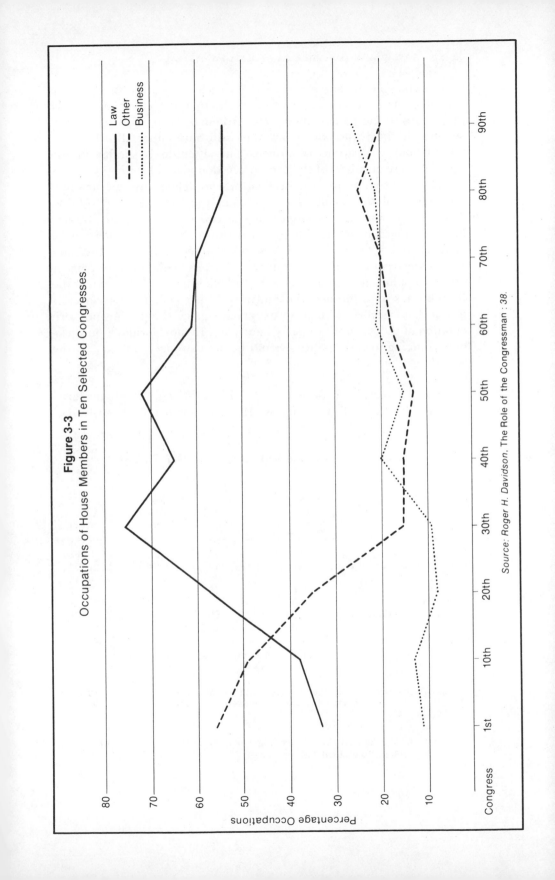

Figure 3-3

Occupations of House Members in Ten Selected Congresses.

Law

Other

Business

Percentage Occupations

Congress

1st 10th 20th 30th 40th 50th 60th 70th 80th 90th

10 20 30 40 50 60 70 80

Source: Roger H. Davidson, The Role of the Congressman : 38.

background. There are scatterings of teachers, journalists, farmers, and other occupations. Figure 3–3 summarizes the changing mix of professions in the House since 1789. Although the proportion of lawyers has declined since the 1850s, they still outnumber all other professions and occupations combined. The situation is similar in the Senate, where members of the legal profession abound.

Table 3–2 summarizes the occupations (as defined by the members themselves) of the members of the Ninety-fifth Congress (1977–78). The distribution of occupations in the two houses is quite similar; however, there are some differences between the parties in terms of occupation. For example, of all senators who served between 1947 and 1957, 63 percent of the Democrats were lawyers, while only 45 percent of the Republicans were lawyers. On the other hand, 40 percent of the Republicans were businessmen but only 17 percent of the Democrats fell in that category. This is not surprising, given the pro-business orientation of the Republican party in general. In most locales a businessman choosing to enter politics would be most strongly attracted to the Republican party.[35]

Age. The mean age of senators and representatives, about forty-eight in the Ninety-fifth Congress (1977–78) has dropped in the last

Table 3–2

Occupations of Members of the 95th Congress, 1977–78.

Occupation	House Percent of Total Membership[a]	Number	Senate Percent of Total Membership[a]	Number
Law	51%	223	68%	68
Business or banking	27	118	24	24
Education	17	72	12	12
Agriculture	4	16	9	9
Journalism	3	14	4	4
Public Service/Politics	14	60	26	26
Other	6	25	3	3

[a] The percentages sum to more than 100 because many members listed several occupations.

Source: Adapted from Congressional Quarterly Weekly Report, 1 January 1977: 20. "Other" includes engineering, labor leader, law enforcement, medicine, clergyman, and scientist.

35. Donald R. Matthews, *U.S. Senators and Their World* (Chapel Hill: University of North Carolina Press, 1960): 36.

few years after remaining constant in the low fifties for several decades before that. The average senator in 1977 was older (between fifty-four and fifty-five) than the average representative (almost forty-seven). Ages of individual members range from the twenties into the eighties. The average age of all members was about forty-three until roughly the Civil War and then climbed to the early fifties by the 1930s.[36] Increased life expectancy for all persons in the country explain this nineteenth-century change. Better pensions and a hectic pace help explain the recent drop in the House as older members have exhibited increased willingness to retire.

Race and Sex.[37] Before Reconstruction no blacks served in Congress. During Reconstruction there were two black senators and twenty black representatives. All of these individuals were Republicans from former Confederate states. The first black member after Reconstruction was not elected until 1929. Since that time there have been twenty-one representatives and one senator who have been black. All except the senator and one representative have been Democrats. Only three have come from southern states.

As of 1977 a total of ninety-six women had served in Congress as members of the House or Senate. Eleven had been in the Senate (only three won election; the rest were appointed to fill unexpired terms). Eighty-five had been elected to the House (including one who later won election to the Senate). The first woman was elected to the House in 1917. The first woman senator was appointed in 1922.

In the Ninety-fifth Congress (1977–78) there were sixteen black members of the House and one black senator. Seventeen women were members of the House.

In short, Congress is overwhelmingly white and male, although women and blacks have increased their numbers substantially in recent years. Most of the black members came from predominantly black districts.

Political Experience. The average member of the House and Senate is a politically experienced individual who has previously held public office. For example, of the 179 senators who served between 1947 and 1957 only 10 percent of them had never held public office. Almost 80 percent of them had held public office for more than five years

---

36. Roger H. Davidson, *The Role of the Congressman* (New York: Pegasus, 1969): 38.
37. Information on black and women members through 1975 is contained in *Congressional Quarterly's Guide to Congress:* 525–528.

before coming to the Senate and 55 percent of them had held public office for more than ten years. Twenty-eight percent of them had been governors immediately before coming to the Senate and 28 percent came to the Senate directly from the House.[38]

Representatives are also politically experienced when they come to the House. For example, a sample of members of the House in the Eighty-eighth Congress showed that three-quarters of them had held a state or local party position, almost half of them had served in a state legislature, and only 6 percent had no discernible political experience.[39]

Elections and Party Control

Virtually every congressional election in American history has provided a clear single majority party in the House and in the Senate. Before 1855 several different parties took their turn at organizing the House and Senate. Since 1855 only Republicans or Democrats have had majorities in either House.

Which party controls the House and Senate is important because of their differences on at least some major policy issues. Thus party control has implications for eventual policy decisions, even allowing for a great deal of slippage between party promises and performance and for a considerable amount of diversity within a party.

Figure 3–4 shows the relative strength of the majority party and largest minority party in the House between 1789 and 1853 in terms of the percentage of the total seats held (lesser minority parties are omitted). Figure 3–5 presents the same information on the Senate between 1789 and 1853. Figure 3–6 shows the relative strength of the Democrats and Republicans, again omitting small minority parties, from 1855 through 1977 in the House. Figure 3–7 presents information on the post-1855 period for the Senate. It is clear from these four graphs that there has been considerable competition overall for control of Congress.

The pre-1855 House was not a particularly competitive body. For 61 percent of the time between 1789 and 1855, there was a very large majority party that held 60 percent or more of the seats. This meant that the difference in the size of the majority and the minority parties was so large that the minority had little chance of defeating the wishes of the majority. For only 39 percent of the time between

---

38. Matthews, *U.S. Senators and Their World:* chapter 3.

39. Davidson, *The Role of the Congressman:* 50.

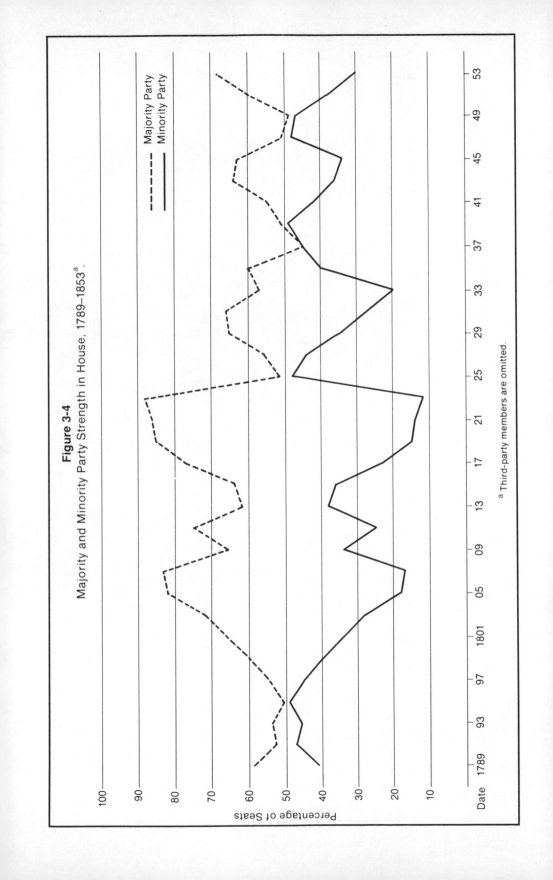

Figure 3-4

Majority and Minority Party Strength in House, 1789–1853[a].

Majority Party
Minority Party

Percentage of Seats

Date   1789   93   97   1801   05   09   13   17   21   25   29   33   37   41   45   49   53

[a] Third-party members are omitted.

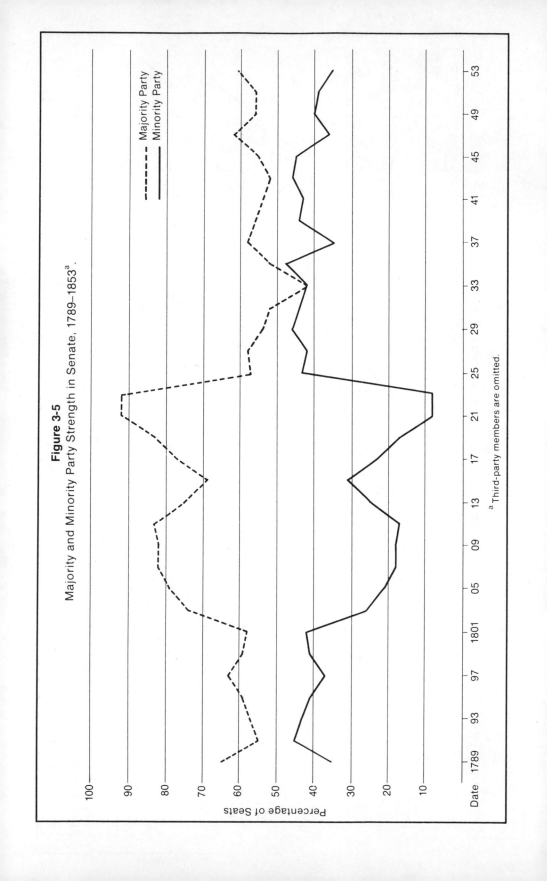

Figure 3-5

Majority and Minority Party Strength in Senate, 1789–1853[a].

Percentage of Seats

Majority Party

Minority Party

Date 1789 93 97 1801 05 09 13 17 21 25 29 33 37 41 45 49 53

[a] Third-party members are omitted.

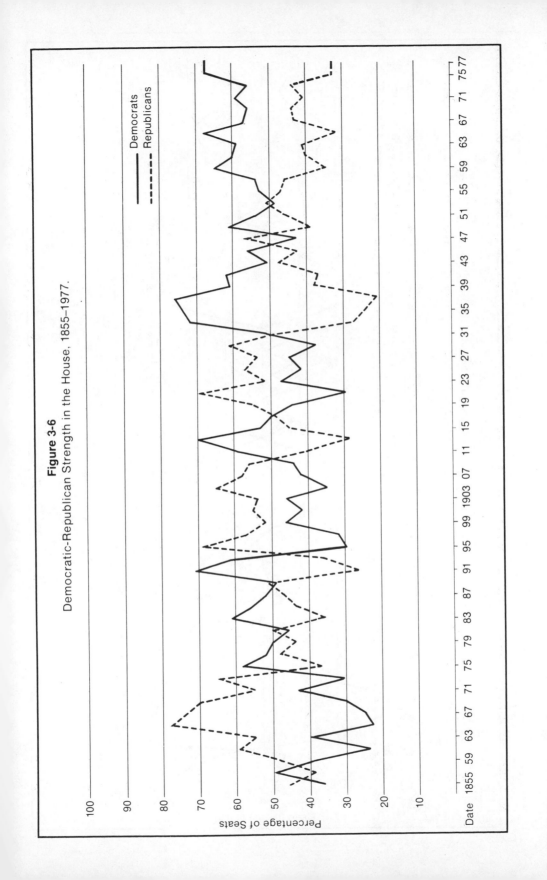

Figure 3-6

Democratic-Republican Strength in the House, 1855–1977.

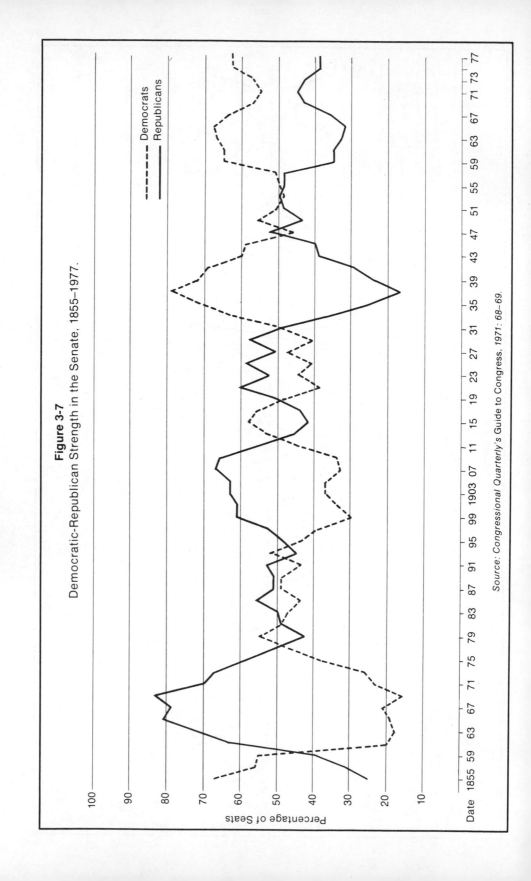

Figure 3-7

Democratic-Republican Strength in the Senate, 1855–1977.

- - - - - Democrats
———— Republicans

Percentage of Seats

100 90 80 70 60 50 40 30 20 10

Date 1855 59 63 67 71 75 79 83 87 91 95 99 1903 07 11 15 19 23 27 31 35 39 43 47 51 55 59 63 67 71 73 77

Source: Congressional Quarterly's Guide to Congress, 1971: 68–69.

1789 and 1855 was the size of the majority and minority parties less uneven, giving the minority a better chance to defeat majority party wishes.

In the House of the post-1855 period there has been a majority party holding 60 percent or more of the seats only 37 percent of the time. Because large (60 percent or more) majorities were less frequent than in the pre-1855 period, there was more opportunity for competition between the majority and minority parties. For over three-fifths of the time from 1855 to 1977 the minority party had a realistic chance of defeating the legislative wishes of the majority party because only a few defections from the majority party to the minority party were necessary to make the majority party lose.

Table 3–3
Percentage Democratic House Members, by Region, Elected in Selected Years between 1924 and 1976.

Region	Democratic Percentage of Seats Held by Republicans and Democrats Combined following Election of:					
	1924	1936	1948	1960	1972	1976
South	98	98	98	93	69	75
Border States	60	95	88	84	77	77
New England	13	48	39	50	60	68
Mid-Atlantic	26	68	49	49	54	70
Midwest	16	78	44	41	38	56
Plains States	13	45	16	19	36	48
Rocky Mountain	21	100	75	73	42	53
Pacific Coast	11	82	36	51	58	72
Difference between highest and lowest Democratic percentages	87	55	82	74	41	29

The states contained in the various regions are as follows: South (Alabama, Arkansas, Florida, Georgia, Louisiana, Mississippi, North Carolina, South Carolina, Tennessee, Texas, and Virginia), Border States (Kentucky, Maryland, Missouri, Oklahoma, and West Virginia), New England (Connecticut, Maine, Massachusetts, New Hampshire, Rhode Island, and Vermont), Mid-Atlantic (Delaware, New Jersey, New York, and Pennsylvania), Midwest (Illinois, Indiana, Michigan, Ohio, and Wisconsin), Plains States (Iowa, Kansas, Minnesota, Nebraska, North Dakota, and South Dakota), Rocky Mountain (Arizona, Colorado, Idaho, Montana, Nevada, New Mexico, Utah, and Wyoming), and Pacific Coast (Alaska, California, Hawaii, Oregon, and Washington).

Third party members are omitted; the percentages are calculated on the combined Democratic and Republican seats.

Source: *Adapted from Milton C. Cummings, Jr.,* Congressmen and the Electorate *(New York: Free Press, 1966): 221. Updated from raw data.*

In the Senate the level of party competition as measured by the percent of seats held by each party has been higher than in the House. In the pre-1855 Senate, the majority party held 60 percent or more of the seats 45 percent of the time. That figure was also 45 percent in the post-1855 Senate. This indicates that competition was more nearly equal in both time periods. The minority party had a realistic chance of legislative success (that is, defeating the wishes of the majority party) more than half of the time.

Not only are the modern House and Senate often competitive in terms of a majority party with less than 60 percent of the seats, but the sectional ties of the parties have become more diffused. No longer is the south reliably Democratic in terms of its representation in Congress and in terms of the dominant place of southerners in the congressional Democratic party. Likewise, the midwest, plains, and New England have all become competitive instead of being reliably Republican. Members of the House and Senate from those areas no longer necessarily dominate the Republican Party. Table 3–3 summarizes the changing regional mix of seats in the House of Representatives for selected years between 1924 and 1976.

Table 3–4
Success of Incumbents Seeking Re-election to House Seats, 1954–1976.

Year	Number Seeking Re election[a]	Number Who Won	% Who Won
1954	401	379	95
1956	403	389	97
1958	390	355	91
1960	400	375	94
1962	385	370	96
1964	386	344	89
1966	405	362	89
1968	401	396	99
1970	389	378	97
1972	378	365	97
1974	383	343	90
1976	381	368	97
1954–1976 Totals	4702	4424	94

[a] This includes only general elections, not primaries or special elections.

Source: The data on 1954 through 1960 came from Charles O. Jones, "The Role of the Campaign in Congressional Politics," in M. Kent Jennings and L. Harmon Zeigler (eds.) The Electoral Process (Englewood Cliffs, N.J.: Prentice-Hall, 1966): 24. Data from 1960 through 1976 were compiled from Congressional Quarterly materials.

Similarly, contests for individual Senate seats have been getting closer as larger numbers of states have become competitive rather than being dominated by one party.[40]

Competition, Turnover, and Incumbency

Despite a reasonable degree of competitiveness between the parties inside Congress and despite the decline of one-party regions and states, competition for individual seats in Congress has declined in several senses in the last several decades.[41] First, in any given election most incumbents seeking re-election win. Second, the margin of victory has risen for most seats. Third, competition between the parties for individual seats has stabilized at a relatively low level.

Table 3–4 shows the high degree of success for incumbent members of the House in general elections since 1954. About 90 percent of all general election contests for House seats in the twelve elections from 1954 through 1976 involved incumbents. In those elections the incumbent won 94 percent of the time on the average. In one year (1968) an incredible 99 percent of the incumbents running won. In the years that were the most difficult for incumbents (1964 and 1966) 89 percent still won. As was seen in chapter 2, this means that at present about 85 percent of each "new" House that convenes in January of odd-numbered years is made up of individuals that were in the previous Congress. This figure ranged from 91 percent return-

---

40. Price, "The Electoral Arena," 42–45.
41. There has been an outpouring of political science literature in recent years on various aspects of the decline of competition. Of particular interest are the following: Charles S. Bullock III, "Redistricting and Congressional Stability, 1962–72," *Journal of Politics* 37 (1975): 569–575; Albert D. Cover and David R. Mayhew, "Congressional Dynamics and the Decline of Competitive Congressional Elections," in Lawrence C. Dodd and Bruce I. Oppenheimer (eds.), *Congress Reconsidered* (New York: Praeger, 1977): 54–72; Robert S. Erikson, "The Advantage of Incumbency in Congressional Elections," *Polity* 3 (1971): 395–405; Erikson, "Is there Such a Thing as a Safe Seat?," *Polity* 8 (1976): 623–632; Erikson, "A Reply to Tidmarch," *Polity* 4 (1972): 527–529; John A. Ferejohn, "On the Decline of Competition in Congressional Elections," *American Political Science Review* 71 (1977): 166–176; Morris P. Fiorina, "The Case of the Vanishing Marginals: The Bureaucracy Did It," *American Political Science Review* 71 (1977): 177–181; Fiorina, *Congress: Keystone of the Washington Establishment* (New Haven: Yale University Press, 1977); Fiorina, David W. Rohde, and Peter Wissel, "Historical Change in House Turnover," in Norman J. Ornstein (ed.), *Congress in Change* (New York: Praeger, 1975): 24–57; Warren Lee Kostroski, "Party and Incumbency in Postwar Senate Elections: Trends, Patterns, and Models," *American Political Science Review* 67 (1973): 1213–1234; and David R. Mayhew, "Congressional Elections: The Case of the Vanishing Marginals," *Polity* 6 (1974): 295–317.

ing members after the 1968 election to 79 percent returning members after the 1974 election.

Table 3–5 shows the situation for incumbent victories in the Senate in the same twelve elections. Only elected (not appointed) incumbents are included in the table. About 80 percent of all contests involved incumbents. An average of 85 percent of those incumbents seeking re-election were successful. In the best years for incumbents in this period (1960 and 1966) 96 percent won. In the worst year, 1976, 64 percent still won.

A comparison of Tables 3–4 and 3–5 makes it clear that incumbent senators are more vulnerable to defeat than incumbent House members. However, given that only one-third of the Senate is elected at any single election, this still means that about 85 percent of all senators in a given Senate will have been there in the previous Senate.

In short, members of the House and Senate who already hold seats and seek to retain them usually do so. Charles Clapp reported, on the basis of his roundtable discussions and interviews in 1959, that members of the House "agree that as incumbents they possess extraordi-

Table 3–5
Success of Incumbents Seeking Re-election to Senate Seats, 1954–1976.

Year	Number Seeking Re-election [a]	Number Who Won	% Who Won
1954	26	22	85
1956	29	25	86
1958	26	17	65
1960	28	27	96
1962	30	27	90
1964	30	28	93
1966	26	25	96
1968	24	20	83
1970	26	23	88
1972	25	20	80
1974	25	23	92
1976	25	16	64
1954–1976 Totals	320	273	85

[a] This includes only general elections, not primaries or special elections.

Source: *1954–1970 data come from Kostroski, "Party and Incumbency in Postwar Senate Elections," 1217. 1972–1976 data are compiled from information in* Congressional Quarterly *materials.*

nary advantages over their opponents. There is a tendency to believe that, aside from isolated instances where an overriding issue is present, there is little excuse for defeat. At the beginning of a new Congress legislators often discuss the defeat of former colleagues in terms of failure to make full use of the many perquisites of incumbency." [42] One estimate of the impact of incumbency for House members is that simply holding the seat adds somewhere between 2 percent and 5 percent to the incumbents' vote—an amount usually sufficient to in-sure victory.[43] The margin of the advantage, according to the same analysis, has increased in recent congressional elections. Another study confirmed the value of incumbency for House seats and also found the same advantage for incumbent senators.[44]

The proportion of elections that are won by large margins (defined as 60 percent or more of the two-party vote) has increased in the last several decades.[45] For the House, for example, in the five elections between 1956 and 1964 the percentage of incumbents winning by 60 percent or more of the vote ranged between 59 and 64 percent and averaged 61 percent. In the five elections between 1966 and 1974 that percentage ranged between 66 and 78 and averaged 72. Figures on northern Senate seats (southern seats were not competitive until recent years and so are excluded) show the same pattern. Between 1946 and 1962 about 22 percent of incumbents won at least 60 percent of the two-party vote. From 1964 through 1974 this figure jumped to about 40 percent.

Competition between the parties for individual House seats has been quite low since the 1940s. Table 3–6 shows the level of competi-tion from 1914 through 1970. It has stabilized at a low level for the last three decades.

All of the above information suggests a great deal of stability in the membership of the House and Senate. Such is the case. On the other hand, it is easy to overlook the fact that incumbents—including some very senior incumbents—are defeated and that, over a series of elec-tions, there is substantial change in the membership of Congress specifically because of electoral defeat. Thus if Congress is looked at over a series of years rather than election-by-election, a somewhat different picture emerges. One study that took this perspective reached the following conclusion:

---

42. Clapp, *The Congressman:* 331.
43. Erikson, "The Advantage of Incumbency in Congressional Elections"; and Erikson, "A Reply to Tidmarch."
44. Cover and Mayhew, "Congressional Dynamics and the Decline of Competitive Congressional Elections."
45. Ibid., 55–56.

Table 3–6
Inter-Party Competition for Congressional Seats, 1914–1970.

Years	Percentage of Fluidity [a]	Percentage of No-Change Districts [b]
1914–26	12.0	62.1
1932–40	10.6	69.9
1942–50	11.9	74.0
1952–60	7.8	78.2
1962–70	8.2	76.5

[a] Fluidity measures the proportion of elections within the time periods indicated that resulted in a change of party control of the seat. Thus, if 1000 elections were held in a time period, and 100 resulted in a party change, the fluidity percentage would be 10.

[b] A no-change district is simply one in which the same party won every election within the time period (the first time period contains 7 elections, the others all contain 5).

Source: Data for first four periods come from Charles O. Jones, "Inter-Party Competition for Congressional Seats," Western Political Quarterly 17 (1964): 465. Data for last period comes from Bullock, "Redistricting and Congressional Stability, 1962–72," 575.

Many a congressional district will send one congressman to Washington for a number of terms and be stereotyped as "safe" for his party. Then, its veteran representative is defeated in an "upset" win by a new challenger, who goes on to win a series of elections, perhaps only to be unseated himself in another "upset." . . . A sizable proportion of congressmen get to Washington by defeating the previous incumbent. Many are themselves forced out of office by a defeat at the polls.[46]

To support his point the author examined the circumstances of victory for 322 members of the House elected or re-elected in 1972 (he excluded members first elected prior to 1954 and those elected from "new" [that is, drastically altered by redistricting] districts). Of these 322 individuals, 28 percent first came to Congress by defeating an incumbent in a general election. Another 8 percent defeated an incumbent in a primary election. Thus, 36 percent had entered Congress by defeating an incumbent.

When the circumstances surrounding leaving the House are examined, the same kind of picture emerges. After the 1972 election 378 of the 435 members of the House who had won election or re-election in 1952 had left. Of those individuals, 25 percent had left because of defeat in a general election. Another 10 percent had left

---

46. Erikson, "Is There Such a Thing as a Safe Seat?," 632.

because of defeat in a primary. Thus, 35 percent had left Congress by being defeated.

Even tempered by the longer-range view, turnover and competition are both relatively low for seats in Congress and incumbency is a great advantage. Why has this situation developed? Redistricting prompted by the Supreme Court decisions in the early 1960s has been investigated as a cause but has been found neither to hurt incumbents nor to offer them extra support.[47] Two reasons that interact with each other help explain the situation of lessened competition outlined above.

First, voters have become much less likely in recent years to vote a "party ticket" in balloting for a number of offices, including the House and Senate. Since the level of information on the part of voters on issues in congressional campaigns is very low, the factor of familiarity with an incumbent—at least by name—when compared to unfamiliarity with a challenger works to the electoral advantage of the former. Voters seem to be using the fact of incumbency increasingly as a cue for prompting their choice in congressional campaigns. When voters deviate from their normal party identification in voting for members of the House, they have been increasingly deviating in the direction of the incumbent, regardless of party.[48]

Second, members of Congress have become more adroit at creating and exploiting the advantages of incumbency that allow numerous opportunities for self-promotion at home. These advantages include such items as free mail privileges, a large staff to work on constituency problems, and considerable subsidized travel. Members also focus much of their total activity and energy on constituency-oriented matters such as bringing federal largesse into their district or state and concerning themselves with constituents' problems through casework activities.[49]

What are the consequences of low competition and turnover? As with most important questions about American politics, there are no

---

47. Bullock, "Redistricting and Congressional Stability, 1962–72"; and Cover and Mayhew, "Congressional Dynamics and the Decline of Competitive Congressional Elections."

48. For specific evidence on deviation from party identification related to incumbency see Cover and Mayhew, "Congressional Dynamics and the Decline of Competitive Congressional Elections," 65. See also Ferejohn, "On the Decline of Competition in Congressional Elections."

49. See Fiorina, *Congress: Keystone of the Washington Establishment;* Fiorina, "The Case of the Vanishing Marginals: The Bureaucracy Did It"; and Cover and Mayhew, "Congressional Dynamics and the Decline of Competitive Congressional Elections."

easy answers. Several consequences seem possible, some of which push in opposite directions from others:

(1) The Democratic dominance of Congress, which has been almost unbroken since 1933 and absolute since 1955, is likely to be perpetuated, given that most incumbents are Democrats. (An even more important perpetuating factor is, of course, the predominantly Democratic identification of the electorate.)

(2) Fragmentation of policy will be promoted because members will continue to pay most of their attention to constituency-oriented matters or casework rather than broad national policy questions.

(3) Alternatively, incumbents may feel secure enough to reduce somewhat their attention to narrow policy questions and casework and pay more attention to broad national policy.

(4) Incumbents will feel increasingly independent of their party leaders in the House and Senate, thereby reducing the chances of party cohesion in support of integrated policy.

(5) Incumbents will also feel increasingly independent of the President, thus increasing congressional impact on policy.

Turnover of Members Related to Policy and Institutional Change

Although turnover is relatively low in Congress and new members typically enter in small groups rather than masses, Congress is still a dynamic and changing institution, capable of changing its collective mind both about the substance of policy and about the procedures by which it arrives at decisions. This dynamism is enhanced because the electoral system in the United States allows such turnover, because elections are automatically held every two years, because even slow turnover aggregates fairly quickly, and because there are occasional elections in which there are unusually large numbers of newcomers who win (such as happened in the House in the 1974 election and in the Senate in the 1976 election).

The fact of turnover and the constant replacement of old members by new members help keep Congress dynamic in at least three specific ways.

First, new cohorts of members stemming from a single election or several elections in a row help alter the general liberal-conservative balance in Congress.[50]

---

50. Alan L. Clem, "Do Representatives Increase in Conservatism as They Increase in Seniority?," *Journal of Politics* 39 (1977): 193–200.

Second, changed policy outcomes can be generated by Congress specifically because of new members who bring altered perspectives, values, and commitments to Congress. For example, the large group of new members who won in the 1964 election helped produce the mass of domestic legislation collectively labeled as "The Great Society" by President Johnson.[51]

Third, new members are often important in efforts to revise the procedures by which Congress conducts business.[52] It seems very unlikely, for example, that the House Democratic party would have instituted such major changes in its way of proceeding in 1975 (changes to be discussed in subsequent chapters) without the presence of seventy-five new Democrats generated by the 1974 election.

There is also evidence that "marginal" congressmen—that is, those who win by small margins or think that their next election will be decided by a small margin—are particularly important as policy innovators in Congress. They use policy innovation as a way of distinguishing themselves to their constituents and as a way (they hope) of creating or reviving a winning electoral coalition at home.[53] The number of "marginal" members has shrunk in recent years and is now quite small.

Influences on Congressional Elections

Congressional elections in presidential years and in "off" (that is, nonpresidential) years can best be explained separately because, in part, different forces seem to be at work.

Presidential Year Congressional Elections. Until the election of 1960 there was a reasonably high correlation between voting for members of Congress and voting for President on a district-by-district basis. But since that time the correlation has gone dramatically down, indicating that voters are engaging in more and more ticket-splitting. Therefore, the close articulation between presidential and congres-

---

51. David W. Brady and Naomi B. Lynn, "Switched-Seat Congressional Districts: Their Effect on Party Voting and Public Policy," *American Journal of Political Science* 17 (1973): 528–543. See also Thomas P. Murphy, *The New Politics Congress* (Lexington, Mass.: Lexington Books, 1974); and Michael J. Malbin, "Times Change, but Congressmen Still Vote the Way They Used to," *National Journal* (20 March 1976): 370–374.
52. See Murphy, *The New Politics Congress.*
53. David J. Vogler, *The Politics of Congress,* 2nd ed. (Boston: Allyn and Bacon, 1977): 89–91. See also Morris P. Fiorina, *Representatives, Roll Calls, and Constituencies* (Lexington, Mass.: Lexington Books, 1974).

sional voting discussed in most of the older standard treatments of elections no longer exists.[54]

There are "coattail" effects in presidential year voting, but they can run in both directions. That is, a heavy vote for a popular presidential candidate in a state or district can help candidates of his party for the Senate and House win. But popular candidates for Congress can also help pull a weaker presidential candidate to victory in a state or district. Even before the period of reduced articulation of party voting (specifically, in the period between 1924 and 1964) the coattails ran from presidential candidate to House candidate about 60 percent of the time and in the other direction about 40 percent of the time.[55] It seems reasonable to assert that the basic strength of the Democratic party in congressional elections helped carry President Truman, Kennedy, and Carter to their victories in 1948, 1960, and 1976, respectively. In 1964 Lyndon Johnson's strong showing pulled some Democrats to victory. But Richard Nixon in 1968 and 1972 and Jimmy Carter in 1976 did not exhibit electoral appeal that helped congressional candidates of their party win.

One factor that seems to have a predictable impact on voting for House and Senate candidates in both presidential and nonpresidential years is the state of the economy. In general, the candidates of the party of the incumbent President suffer if there is an economic downturn in the year prior to the election, although an upturn does not reliably produce extra votes for the same candidates.[56]

Midterm Congressional Elections. Until very recently it was thought that midterm congressional elections represented the "decline" phase of a "surge and decline" phenomenon characterizing the relationship

54. For older treatments see Key, *Politics, Parties, and Pressure Groups:* Chapter 20; and Milton C. Cummings, Jr., *Congressmen and the Electorate* (New York: Free Press, 1966). On the decay of the correlation between presidential voting and voting for congressional candidates see Walter Dean Burnham, "Insulation and Responsiveness in Congressional Elections," *Political Science Quarterly* 90 (1975): 411–435.

55. Cummings, *Congressmen and the Electorate.*

56. See Howard S. Bloom and H. Douglas Price, "Voter Response to Short-Run Economic Conditions: the Asymmetric Effect of Prosperity and Recession," *American Political Science Review* 69 (1975): 1240–1254; Saul Goodman and Gerald H. Kramer, "Comment on Arcelus and Meltzer, The Effect of Aggregate Economic Conditions on Congressional Elections," *American Political Science Review* 69 (1975): 1255–1265; and Gerald H. Kramer, "Short-Term Fluctuations in U.S. Voting Behavior, 1896–1964," *American Political Science Review* 65 (1971): 131–143. For a contrary view see Francisco Arcelus and Allan H. Meltzer, "The Effect of Aggregate Economic Variables on Congressional Elections," *American Political Science Review* 69 (1975): 1232–1239; and Arcelus and Meltzer, "Aggregate Economic Variables and Votes for Congress: A Rejoinder," *American Political Science Review* 69 (1975): 1266–1269.

between presidential year and nonpresidential year congressional elections.[57] Presidential year congressional elections were thought to produce an abnormally large congressional majority, and the almost inevitable loss of seats two years later by the President's party was thought to reflect primarily a return to the "normal" party balance rather than a negative judgment about the President's performance. This view had considerable plausibility when there was high correlation between presidential and congressional vote in presidential years. But given the collapse of that correlation and the increased value of incumbency, some alternative explanations seem necessary.

Two factors have emerged as particularly important in explaining midterm results as other than a return to a "normal" party balance: presidential popularity and the state of the economy.[58] There is substantial support for the view that midterm results can be interpreted at least in part as a referendum on presidential performance for the preceding two years, especially performance in terms of how the economy is thought to be doing. It is still "natural" for the in-party to lose seats, but those losses are cut substantially if the President is popular and/or if the economy is doing well.

THE IMPLICATIONS OF ELECTIONS
FOR CONGRESSIONAL BEHAVIOR

The continuous presence of frequent elections has a profound influence on the ways in which Congress works. In general, the virtually universal desire for re-election on the part of incumbents has led Congress to structure itself internally to maximize re-election chances and also leads Congress to handle policy questions in ways supportive of the same end.[59] The frequency of elections and the desire for

57. For presentations of variations of this general view see Key, *Politics, Parties, and Pressure Groups:* chapter 20; Angus Campbell, "Surge and Decline: A Study of Electoral Change," in Campbell and others, *Elections and the Political Order:* chapter 3; and Barbara Hinckley, "Interpreting House Midterm Elections: Toward a Measurement of the In-Party's 'Expected' Loss of Seats," *American Political Science Review* 61 (1967): 694–700.

58. On these factors see Samuel Kernell, "Presidential Popularity and Negative Voting: An Alternative Explanation of the Midterm Congressional Decline of the President's Party," *American Political Science Review* 71 (1977): 44–66; James E. Piereson, "Presidential Popularity and Midterm Voting at Different Electoral Levels," *American Journal of Political Science* 19 (1975): 683–694; Edward R. Tufte, "Determinants of the Outcomes of Midterm Congressional Elections," *American Political Science Review* 69 (1975): 812–826; and the articles cited in footnote 56, above.

59. See Mayhew, *Congress: The Electoral Connection,* for a particularly intriguing elaboration of this generalization.

re-election lead to both institutional and policy fragmentation most of the time.

The next four chapters will focus on congressional institutions, and the general bias of those institutions toward fragmentation will be analyzed in detail. To conclude the present chapter, a summary of the policy consequences of the electoral system for seats in the House and Senate will be offered.

In many ways the electoral system pushes in the direction of policy conservatism, in the sense that members normally have a stake in avoiding highly controversial issues, keeping the substantive agenda static, and not exploring fresh solutions to problems, many of which may have been present for years. Six different aspects of congressional elections push in the direction of policy conservatism, thus defined.

First, only certain kinds of individuals tend to be electable to Congress—generally white, upper-middle-class males. This tendency toward socioeconomic homogeneity in Congress probably helps limit the perspective and imagination of members, although it is certainly not absolutely deterministic of what Congress can achieve if it wants to.

Second, the low turnout for congressional elections helps result in at least a partially stagnant congressional agenda. Rarely are new voices in the electorate loud enough or numerous enough to add items to the congressional agenda.

Third, the high rate of electoral success on the part of incumbents also promotes stability of agenda and solutions. Few freshmen members are sent to Congress every two years. And even when they arrive, they usually have limited opportunities to make major policy inputs in their early years, particularly in the House.

Fourth, the low degree of competition for most seats—especially in the House—also tends to reduce the innovative potential within Congress. Knowledge is limited on the question of the link between election margins and policy behavior by members, but the most persuasive evidence suggests that those elected by relatively narrow margins tend to be the most "innovative" or "extreme" in their policy positions rather than instinctively always seeking a presumably safe middle of the road.[60] Their "innovation" may stem from a need to gain higher visibility in their constituencies.

---

60. Morris P. Fiorina, "Electoral Margins, Constituency Influence, and Policy Moderation: A Critical Assessment," *American Politics Quarterly* 1 (1973): 479–498; Fiorina, *Representatives, Roll Calls, and Constituencies;* Barbara Sinclair Deckard, "Electoral Marginality and Party Loyalty in House Roll Call Voting," *American Journal of Political Science* 20 (1976): 469–481; and Vogler, *The Politics of Congress:* 89–91.

Fifth, the high cost of campaigns helps reinforce the attractiveness of "playing it safe" in Congress. If members do not offend important constituents with unusual stands or new ideas, serious threats in either the primary or general election may be avoided. Thus they may run relatively inexpensive campaigns. Since incumbents of both parties share this interest it seems reasonable to assert that they may seek to protect each other from controversial issues. They may not share either party labels or beliefs but all have a common stake in returning to Washington as cheaply as possible. This fact also helps freeze the agenda so that only highly familiar items are on it.

Sixth, for much significant policy change to occur, a change in the partisan control of Congress is often necessary. Yet the great advantage of incumbents, coupled with the predominantly Democratic sympathies of the electorate, have made such party turnover extremely rare for the last four and a half decades. Even when voters do alter the percentage of the vote they give the Democrats on a national basis, that drop is not reflected in a corresponding drop in the percentage of the seats controlled by the Democrats. Increased competitiveness in the vote in all districts aggregated is usually not reflected very well in increased competitiveness inside Congress.[61]

The electoral system, however, also has some features that can promote responsiveness to changing views in the electorate, a broadened policy agenda, and innovativeness in seeking solutions.

Two features that promote an activist and innovative stance are the existence of a strong two-party system and single-member districts. This means that every Congress meets with a single majority party in at least nominal control of the House and Senate (only very rarely have different parties controlled the two chambers). Thus a real majority is potentially present in every Congress. When the nominal majority is also a new majority—that is, when the electorate has put a different party in control—a situation is created in which the likelihood of aggressiveness on the part of that majority is relatively high *because* it is likely to have come into majority status after a number of frustrating years in minority status.

Apathy and ignorance on the part of the electorate are features of the electoral scene that can cut two ways. They may allow members to be lethargic, uninnovative, and responsive to only a few selected interests. But they also allow members the freedom to be creative, in-

---

61. For a discussion of this phenomenon see Edward R. Tufte, "The Relationship between Seats and Votes in Two-Party Systems," *American Political Science Review* 67 (1973): 540–554.

novative, and responsive to some larger vision of the pressing needs of public policy. Given adequate leadership and possessing adequate skills in manipulating the internal machinery of Congress, a majority, usually partisan, can emerge and can help create new directions in the solution of national problems.

Finally, it needs to be repeated that the electoral system does allow turnover of members, even if it does not encourage it. These new members are critical in terms of helping produce policy change over time in Congress.[62] New perspectives and commitments, based on new electoral coalitions, are not guaranteed by new members, but electing new members is the most reliable way of infusing substantive change into the congressional agenda and the congressional policy product.

---

62. See the items cited in footnotes 50–53, above, and Warren L. Kostroski, "Elections and Legislative Reform: External and Internal Influences and Legislative Behavior," *Policy Studies Journal* 5 (1977): 414–418.

PART II

THE INTERNAL
ENVIRONMENT
FOR
CONGRESSIONAL
POLICY-MAKING

CHAPTER 4

___

CONGRESSIONAL
DECISION-MAKING

As THE MODERN CONGRESS MAKES DECISIONS IN THE MANY SUBSTANTIVE fields for which it is responsible, its members have to face three central facts that have shaped the character of the institution: (1) the fact that they are elected representatives, (2) the fact of a powerful presidency, and (3) the fact of a vast professional bureaucracy. In the following sections the congressional response to this environment is outlined. Detailed attention is paid to the central processes—both formal and informal—by which Congress makes specific decisions. These processes include the inculcation of general norms, the giving and receiving of behavioral cues, and the formal rules and procedures of the House and Senate.

THE BROAD CONGRESSIONAL RESPONSE
TO INSTITUTIONAL ENVIRONMENT

All members of the House and Senate are elected from individual constituencies (with the relatively insignificant exception of a few senators who may hold short-term appointments from governors to fill vacant seats). Virtually all of them are genuinely concerned with the way they "represent" their constituents. Virtually all of them bear one of two party labels both in the electoral process and in Congress. These labels, however, are associated with a national party system that is weak and somewhat mythical, with district parties that are often unimportant, and with congressional parties that are only sporadically cohesive and demanding. This combination of circumstances allows individual members a maximum of freedom as they make up their minds on substantive questions. They can easily rationalize whatever behavior they decide on in terms of representation of constituents despite the competing demands of the president, party leaders, committees, interest groups, or bureaucrats.

Given that most members prize the independence they derive from this situation, there is a strong norm in Congress that legitimizes a member's policy stances and behavior as long as that member justifies them in the name of representation. At the same time, the norm does not demand rigorous attention to ferreting out "real" constituency opinion, so that members are free to provide their own definition of the interests and opinions that deserve attention. Members can maximize their freedom of action in Congress by playing off presumed constituency pressure against pressures brought by party leaders in Congress, the executive branch, or committees. If, for example, the president and party leaders actively advocate a gun control bill, a member opposed to the bill can claim in talking with a leader urging him to vote for it that he would like to but that constituency opinion prohibits a "yes" vote. The leader will neither check (because he has no way) nor rarely even challenge the member's assertion about the views of his constituents. This freedom is not granted members simply for its own sake; the main point of allowing members such latitude is to maximize their chances of re-election—a goal virtually all members have in common.

Congress must also confront a president endowed by the Constitution with great powers that have been expanded in practice through the aggressiveness of a number of specific presidents and the attentions of the media and the public. On selected issues the president can appeal directly to the electorate for support, thus pressuring Congress for a favorable response. John Kennedy made such an appeal on tax reform, Lyndon Johnson did the same on civil rights, Richard Nixon took a similar route in promoting revenue sharing, and Jimmy Carter followed suit on energy policy. The institutionalization of the presidency has also enhanced its potential for influence.

The existence of a powerful chief executive has stimulated the development of elaborate Congressional leadership structures and apparatus, the function of which is not only to centralize congressional response to presidential proposals but also, importantly, to mediate between the rank-and-file members (and sometimes the chairmen and senior members) and the president. The leaders are channels for information and presumed influence flowing both ways. If the members have a grievance or a strongly felt position the leaders are expected to so inform the president. If the president has a strongly held position, the leaders of his party are expected to communicate that position to the members. There is a natural tension surrounding the positions of leadership: the president tends to view the leaders of his party as his lieutenants; members often prefer to think of the leaders as being responsible for defending congressional autonomy against the encroachments of the president and executive branch.

The professional bureaucracy that Congress must face is nominally under the control of the president but is, in practice, a set of independent forces. The presence of such a bureaucracy, which administers the programs Congress legislates, has contributed to the growth and entrenchment of a well-developed structure of relatively autonomous committees and subcommittees with fixed jurisdictions and fairly stable memberships. In addition, the presence of the bureaucracy helps determine the functions that the committees will perform: oversight (review of bureaucratic activities), authorization of new programs or renewals of existing programs, and appropriation of funds are all carried on with specific reference to parts of the bureaucracy. To facilitate oversight of existing programs and consideration of new legislation, the subject matter division of labor among the committees roughly parallels that in the bureaucracy. Within the committees the workload is further divided among subcommittees whose jurisdictions often parallel the responsibilities of specific units in the bureaucracy.

The advantage of this method of division of labor is that it encourages members to become knowledgeable and expert in particular issue areas and enables them to compete with the experience and expertise of the bureaucrats with whom they interact. The disadvantage of this same division of work, particularly when coupled with the fact that committee memberships are stable, is that it encourages the formation of cozy relationships between a small number of bureaucrats and legislators who come to see eye-to-eye on matters in their particular policy sphere. This results in policy that does not change much.

An additional effect of the large bureaucracy has been that Congress has turned to the use of professional staff in an effort to compete with the bureaucrats' generally superior command of information about programs. Individual members simply have too many responsibilities to delve deeply into all of them, and they need assistance to match the advantage that size alone gives the bureaucracy. Thus they have created a sizeable group of knowledgeable staff members who possess considerable technical competence in a variety of legislative fields. Many of these individuals become permanently tied to a committee regardless of personnel or even party turnover.

NORMS AND SOCIALIZATION

Norms are simply standards that prescribe acceptable and unacceptable behavior in an organization. They are "informal rules, frequently unspoken because they need not be spoken, which may govern conduct more effectively than any written rule. They prescribe 'how things are done around here.' " [1]

Norms do not appear in Congress by magic. Rather, they stem from institutional process and interaction. By the same token, they are not immutable. They change when personnel, times, and the issues confronting Congress change. The single most important source of change in norms is turnover in personnel.

New people are rarely socialized perfectly into an institution in the sense that they both understand and accept its norms totally. The greater the number of newcomers to an institution the more likely that the norms will change. Newcomers bring their own views to an institution. These views are the result of differing ideologies, ages, and societal norms acquired during childhood and young adulthood. New members may affect the views of more senior members toward congressional norms, particularly if the senior members sense a widespread feeling in support of some changed views.

A classic example of changing norms and the differences those changes make is provided by the Senate between the 1950s and 1970s. Observers of the Senate during the late 1940s and 1950s concluded that that body was in the grip of norms that produced an ideologically conservative bias in the decisions it made.[2] It was implied that these specific norms—that junior members should act as apprentices, work hard mainly on legislative details, defer to the widom of senior members (who also happened to be the most conservative senators), and that all senators should approach the task of legislating in a sober spirit that would produce only minor changes from a status quo—were permanent features of Senate life.

Subsequent studies of the Senate, however, have pointed out that the norms of the Senate differed both before and after the particular period of the 1950s. The norms of that era were not fixed nor was the stance of the Senate. In the 1960s and 1970s it became clear that

---

1. Barbara Hinckley, *Stability and Change in Congress* (New York: Harper and Row, 1971): 59.
2. See William S. White, *Citadel* (New York: Harper and Brothers, 1956); and Donald R. Matthews, *U.S. Senators and Their World* (Chapel Hill: University of North Carolina Press, 1964).
3. See Ralph K. Huitt, "The Outsider in the Senate: An Alternative Role," *American Political Science Review* 55 (1961): 566–575; Norman J. Ornstein, Robert L. Peabody, and David W. Rohde, "The Changing Senate: From the 1950's to the 1970's," in Lawrence C. Dodd and Bruce I. Oppenheimer (eds.), *Congress Reconsidered* (New York: Praeger, 1977): 6–9; Nelson W. Polsby, "Goodbye to the Inner Club," *Washington Monthly* (August 1969): 30–34; and Randall B. Ripley, *Power in the Senate* (New York: St. Martin's, 1969).

junior members, often of an aggressively liberal persuasion, could also wield substantial legislative influence and produce important changes from the status quo that were not to the liking of the senior, conservative members. The norms changed to become less restrictive.

A summary of the status of Senate norms in the mid-1970s compared to the mid-1950s [4] concluded that only three of the six norms observed two decades earlier still continued in force without much change: courtesy, reciprocity, and institutional patriotism. Two more —legislative work and specialization—had diminished considerably. And one—apprenticeship—had been altered so substantially as to be almost unrecognizable. It should also be noted that during the same period of time the norm of apprenticeship in the House had also been altered significantly.[5]

Predominant Norms in the House and Senate[6]

Four norms or clusters of norms are most significant in the contemporary House and Senate. Two of them—institutional loyalty, reciprocity and accommodation—are strong, relatively stable, and very similar in both houses. Two others—specialization, seniority and apprenticeship—are changing in both houses and are also different in form and meaning in the two houses.

Institutional Loyalty. Both houses have strong norms demanding the loyalty of the members to their respective institution. This means that members should not, by and large, make public criticisms of their fellow members or of the functioning of their institution, although considerable deviation from this norm is tolerated during election campaigns. Members should take the place of the House or Senate in the governmental scheme seriously and make this seriousness evident. For the most part members are expected to anticipate a career in the

---

4. Ornstein, Peabody, and Rohde, "The Changing Senate: From the 1950's to the 1970's," 6–9.

5. Lawrence C. Dodd and Bruce I. Oppenheimer, "The House in Transition," in Dodd and Oppenheimer, *Congress Reconsidered:* 21–53.

6. For the fullest discussion of Senate norms, see Matthews, *U.S. Senators and Their World*, chapter 5; Matthews, "The Folkways of the United States Senate: Conformity to Group Norms and Legislative Effectiveness," *American Political Science Review* 53 (1959): 1064–1089; and David W. Rohde, Norman J. Ornstein, and Robert L. Peabody, "Political Change and Legislative Norms in the United States Senate," (paper prepared for delivery at the 1974 annual meeting of the American Political Science Association). On the House see Richard F. Fenno, Jr., "The Internal Distribution of Influence: The House," in David B. Truman (ed.), *The Congress and America's Future* (Englewood Cliffs, N.J.: Prentice-Hall, 1973, 2nd ed.): 83–90. For another useful discussion of norms, see Hinckley, *Stability and Change in Congress:* 59–69.

House or Senate, although many House members are eager to obtain Senate seats. Members are expected to defend the institution against the encroachment of the president or the bureaucracy and are expected to defend the prerogatives of their own chamber against perceived imperialistic behavior of the other chamber.

Most of the few senators and representatives who have been disciplined by the House and Senate by removal or by loss of seniority or committee assignments were guilty mainly of bringing discredit to their chamber. In two of the most celebrated recent cases—the censure of Senator Joseph McCarthy in 1954 and the refusal to seat Representative Adam Clayton Powell in 1967—it seems clear that one of the prime offenses of both was that they brought the "good name" of the Senate and House, respectively, into public question. McCarthy was censured because of excesses connected with his chairmanship of the Permanent Investigations Subcommittee and his refusal to testify before the Senate Rules Committee in connection with accusations he and another Senator, William Benton of Connecticut, had made against each other. Powell was excluded from his House seat because of misuse of funds of the committee he chaired, refusal to pay a New York libel judgment, and noncooperation with House committees investigating his behavior.

In the last few years a number of senators and representatives have felt free to criticize the decline of congressional power. Included in this general criticism are specific allegations that outmoded procedures may help relegate Congress to a subordinate position. This criticism is tolerated because the motivation behind it is the desire to restore Congress to its "rightful" place in the governmental scheme—a place in which it cannot be dominated by the president and bureaucracy.

Reciprocity and Accommodation. The House and Senate process a vast number of bills each year. Each bill must go through a large number of stages. It is imperative that senators and representatives help each other or very little would be accomplished. It is expected of all members that they will learn to be mutually helpful, to accommodate themselves to each other's needs, and to bargain in a way that always leaves room for compromise. This norm necessarily requires an extensive amount of mutual courtesy and deference, particularly on matters in which one individual is reputed to be expert. This norm also tends to reduce extreme partisanship, which makes bargaining and accommodation more difficult.

In impact, it underscores the virtues for members of bargaining, compromise, and logrolling (that is, trading support for a variety of matters each important to only a few members). The tie between reciprocity (which sounds fancy) and logrolling (which sounds earthy) is well illustrated by a comment by former Senator Sam Ervin, a Democrat from North Carolina, on his relations with Senator Milton Young, a Republican from North Dakota (to a North Dakota audience): "I got to know Milt Young very well. And I told Milt, 'Milt, I would just like you to tell me how to vote about wheat and sugar beets and things like that, if you just help me out on tobacco and things like that.' " [7]

Specialization. In the House, members are expected to specialize in one or, at most, a very few legislative areas. Each member has only a few subcommittee assignments, and the specialization is supposed to coincide with these assignments. Concomitant with this norm is an additional norm that legislative work should be taken seriously. Many House members choose their specialties to coincide with important interests in their districts. This is not made mandatory by the norms, but it is certainly approved behavior.

In the Senate the norms of specialization and legislative work are not nearly as specific or constraining. Because the Senate has fewer members than the House, each senator has a large number of committee and subcommittee assignments. Furthermore, there is no expectation that senators will speak and develop their ideas primarily in committee or only on topics under the jurisdiction of their committees and subcommittees. In part, they are expected to help develop a national policy agenda rather than proceeding primarily as craftsmen in relatively small and technical areas. Also, given the relatively large numbers of senators who explore the possibility of running for president, their tendency to make statements on a wide range of topics is reinforced.[8]

Seniority and Apprenticeship. Until recent years the grip of the seniority and apprenticeship norms and practices was very strong in both the House and Senate. And the two fitted together: senior members had most of the good positions and made most of the important

---

7. Quoted in *Minot (N.D.) Daily News,* June 17, 1976.
8. On the Senate as "a hot-house for significant policy innovation" see Nelson W. Polsby, "Strengthening Congress in National Policymaking," in Polsby (ed.), *Congressional Behavior* (New York: Random House, 1971): 3–13. On the Senate as "a presidential incubator" see Robert L. Peabody, Norman J. Ornstein, and David W. Rohde, "The United States Senate as a Presidential Incubator: Many Are Called but Few Are Chosen," *Political Science Quarterly* 91 (1976): 237–258.

decisions while junior members mainly kept quiet and worked hard on less important matters while waiting to become senior.

This situation has changed in both houses. It began changing slowly in the Senate in the 1950s and slowly in the House in the 1960s. The 1970s saw a great acceleration of change in both houses so that, at present, the hold of seniority in both a formal and informal sense has been weakened and only a few vestiges of apprenticeship remain.

By far the most important use of seniority was in making committee assignments and in the advancement of committee members toward chairmanships (these topics will be considered in more detail in Chapter 5). Changes began in the Senate when Minority Leader Lyndon Johnson instituted the "Johnson rule" in 1953 that all Democratic senators would have a seat on one major committee before senior Democrats would be able to go on a second major committee. The Republicans adopted a similar practice informally in 1959 and made it formal in 1965, along with the provision that no Republican could serve on more than one of the four most important Senate committees (Appropriations, Armed Services, Finance, and Foreign Relations).

Then in the 1970s changes were adopted by both parties in both houses that involved the choosing of committee leaders—chairpersons in the case of the majority Democrats and ranking minority members in the case of the Republicans.

In 1973 the *Senate Republicans* agreed to an arrangement whereby the Republican members of each standing committee elect the ranking minority member and that choice is then subject to approval by all Republican senators through a vote in the Republican Conference (the meeting of all Republicans).

In 1975 the *Senate Democrats* agreed to hold a secret ballot on any chairman when such a ballot was requested by one-fifth of the membership of the Democratic caucus (all Democrats). Nominations for chairmanships come from the Steering Committee.

In 1971 the *House Republicans* agreed to vote in Conference on the nominations for ranking minority members coming from the Republican Committee on Committees.

The *House Democrats* made changes in their procedures in 1971, 1973, and 1975, each with more potential for limiting strict seniority appointments than the previous change. In 1971 the House Democrats agreed that the caucus should vote on any nomination for a chairmanship coming from the Committee on Committees (at that time the Democratic members of the Ways and Means Committee) if as many as ten members requested such a vote. In 1973 the procedure was changed virtually to guarantee secret ballot votes on each chairmanship nomination in the Democratic caucus. Three party leaders were also added to the Committee on Committees. In 1975 the power of making assignments was transferred to the Steering and Policy Committee and all chairpersons plus the chairpersons of the Appropriations Committee subcommittees were made subject to secret ballot votes in the caucus, with additional provisions for nominations from the floor.

Except for the House Democrats, the procedures have not resulted in non-seniority appointments to the top spots on committees. In the case of the House Democrats one chairman almost lost his position in a hard 1971 fight and in 1975 three senior southerners did lose their chairmanships and a fourth chairman almost lost. In 1977 one Appropriations Subcommittee chairman was replaced. Thus the specific change in personnel resulting from these procedures has been relatively small. But the spirit of the changes has certainly made senior members more aware of and responsive to both procedural equity for less senior members and, in some cases, differing substantive commitments on the part of large numbers of members of their committees or parties.

With these formal supports for awarding the most powerful institutional positions to the most senior members weakened, attitudes toward the relative place of junior and senior members have also changed in the last few years. It is no doubt true—and is probably usually true in any human group—that those individuals with more experience are likely to have more influence. But those with less experience can also have considerable influence.

The norm of apprenticeship—the belief that junior members should serve for a period of time as apprentices before beginning to speak out and take an active role in legislative matters—has almost vanished in the Senate and has been substantially weakened in the House. This norm had two applications—on the floor and in committees. On the floor it meant that junior members should be restrained in speaking, offering bills, and offering amendments. In committee it meant little participation in the questioning of witnesses in hearings and deference to the judgment of more senior members on substantive matters.

More senior members may continue to be the most potent in floor actions simply because they can, in many instances, generate respect and support by their mastery of certain subject matters. But junior members have become much more active. By the mid-1960s apprenticeship for senators on the floor was very rarely evident. Likewise, good committee assignments were so widespread that having less seniority was not terribly limiting even within the committee structure. Thus, a study of the Senate as it was in the mid- and late-1960's concluded:

Virtually all senators can acquire substantial legislative influence. Those who do not have it usually have disqualified themselves by violating the Senate's code of acceptable conduct that is understood by most members. The code is not highly restrictive, and only repeated violations bring sanctions.

The Senate is not composed of a few omnipotent and happy senior senators and a great many impotent and unhappy junior senators. Most senators are content with their lot. Most of them feel that they have a considerable amount of legislative potency, at least in selected fields.[9]

Several recent studies of the House have also shown the norm of apprenticeship to be weakening its hold on freshmen members. Herbert Asher has written that

The need for a lengthy inactive apprenticeship no longer seems to be accepted; freshmen appear to be participating more frequently and earlier in their careers than the traditional description of the newcomer would lead one to expect. . . . The objective measures did suggest an improvement in the committee assignments given to freshmen.[10]

In both houses it remains true that, despite improvements in the committee assignments of junior members, some seniority is generally still very helpful in obtaining the best assignments. One recent study of committee assignments in the House concluded, "The apprenticeship model is useful in understanding committee assignments despite the changing values of some of the variables in the assignment process."

Within Senate committees there seems to be little concern for maintaining apprenticeship. The status of junior members varies more from committee to committee in the House. Given the general "legislative craftsman" self-image of most House members and committees and subcommittees, seniority continues to play a large role in some committees in terms of allocating influence over substantive outcomes.

In short, the picture of Congress slavishly devoted to elevating senior members to positions of power and suppressing junior members is no longer accurate, although that picture is based on the practices and performance of Congress for most of the twentieth century until

9. Ripley, *Power in the Senate*, 185.
10. Herbert B. Asher, "The Changing Status of the Freshman Representative," in Norman J. Ornstein (ed.), *Congress in Change* (New York: Praeger, 1975): 233. See also Asher, "The Learning of Legislative Norms," *American Political Science Review* 67 (1973): 499–513.

the 1960s in the Senate and the 1970s in the House. Senior members are still important, but junior members can also be important too, even though they are operating from less imposing formal positions than their senior colleagues.

Summary of Operative Norms in the Late 1970s. The omnipresent norm in both the House and Senate is to take representation of constituents seriously. These additional major normative mandates are also present:

1. Speak well of Congress and particularly of your own chamber. If you criticize, do it constructively and in a way designed to make clear that your goal is to strengthen the institution.

2. Respect your fellow members—both as individuals and as experts in specific substantive areas. Deal with them openly and courteously in ways that will lead to the maximum achievement of their goals and your own. Do not let party or ideological stances get in the way of making mutually agreeable and profitable bargains.

3. If you are a House member, specialize in a few substantive areas and work hard in those areas. If you are a senator, be active in the legislative arena but do not necessarily restrict your activity to any particular subject matter areas.

4. If you are a House member, be sure you have something to say before saying it, but do not let the fact of relatively junior status inhibit you from contributing to the legislative process.

The Process of Transmitting Norms: The Socialization of Freshmen

Freshmen members of Congress seem to know the general norms of the House or Senate before they even arrive in Washington. One study observed that freshman representatives are conversant with congressional norms simply because these norms parallel the codes of behavior common to many institutions.[12]

This is not to argue, however, that freshmen have nothing to learn. They certainly need to learn how the system actually operates: what committees do what, which individuals have what kinds of influence, what specialization means in practice, and so on. This kind of information often fleshes out the bare bones of norms, and to acquire it, new freshmen observe and talk to such knowledgeable people as senior

11. Charles S. Bullock III, "Apprenticeships and Committee Assignments in the House of Representatives," *Journal of Politics* 32 (1970): 720.
12. Asher, "The Learning of Legislative Norms," 512.

colleagues, staff members, and the press when they come to Washington.[13] Freshmen also spend a considerable amount of time with each other, sharing experiences, observations, and the information they have picked up. Likewise, they tend to hire at least some experienced staff members who are able to pass on relevant information to them.[14]

Freshmen members also begin to learn where to look for cues on how to vote on the floor. It has been found that in the House, they initially look to their state delegations; as the session wears on they broaden their search for cues to members of relevant committees.[15]

The best evidence is that freshmen in both the House and Senate are now incorporated into the life of those two bodies very quickly. The new members come to Washington already aware of the norms of the chamber in which they will sit; they learn additional details quickly and soon are assimilated into the institution. Their voting does not distinguish them from others, nor do their committee assignments, except for scarce representation on the most prestigious committees.[16]

After the seventy-five freshmen Democrats in the Ninety-fourth Congress played such a visible and major role in the procedural reforms emanating from the House Democratic party in late 1974 and early 1975, it was widely speculated that a new "force"—freshman power—would become a permanent feature of life in the House. However, other pressures and interests, which lead all freshman "classes" to diverse stances (much like their elders) soon helped break apart the new "force." [17] A large number of new members is an important factor

13. See Richard F. Fenno, Jr., "The Freshman Congressman: His View of the House," in Nelson W. Polsby (ed.), *Congressional Behavior* (New York: Random House, 1971): 125–135.

14. On these two sources of information see Irwin N. Gertzog, "The Socialization of Freshmen Congressmen: Some Agents of Organizational Continuity" (paper prepared for delivery at the meeting of the American Political Science Association, September 1970).

15. Herbert B. Asher, *Freshmen Representatives and the Learning of Voting Cues,* Sage Professional Paper in American Politics 04–003 (Beverly Hills: Sage, 1973).

16. On voting see Theodore Urich, "The Voting Behavior of Freshmen Congressmen," *The Southwestern Social Science Quarterly* 39 (1959): 337–341; William Mishler, James Lee, and Alan Tharpe, "Determinants of Institutional Continuity: Freshmen Cue-taking in the U.S. House of Representatives" (unpublished paper); and J. Richard Emmert, "Freshmen Congressmen and the Apprenticeship Norms," *Capitol Studies* 2 (1973): 49–64. On assignments of freshmen to committees see Charles S. Bullock III, "Freshmen Committee Assignments and Re-Election in the United States House of Representatives," *American Political Science Review* 66 (1972): 996–1007.

17. On the "disintegration" of the Democratic class of freshmen first elected in 1974 see Matt Pinkus and Bruce F. Freed, "Freshmen in the House: A Sobering Six Months," *Congressional Quarterly Weekly Report* (2 August 1975): 1674–1677; and Michael J. Malbin, "Congress Report/A Year Older and Wiser, Freshmen Reassess Their Role," *National Journal* (14 February 1976): 189–195.

in change in Congress, as has already been noted, but there is no reason to expect continuing "class unity" and every reason to expect the other factors will be much more explanatory of coalitions on policy matters. Perhaps the most fitting comment came from a new Democrat in mid-1975, in reflecting on the experience of his own class: "Anyone who thought the freshmen would be doing anything together beyond the first month was mistaken." [18]

The Impact of Norms on Congressional Behavior

The most effective members of Congress are those who observe the norms of institutional loyalty and reciprocity and accommodation. In the House the most effective members also observe the norm of specialization. But in both houses there is great tolerance of deviant behavior. Short of actions so outrageous as to call into question the good name of the House or Senate, there is little or no "punishment" for any kind of behavior. The psychological pressure to conform to the norms is probably stronger in the House than in the Senate.[19] The Senate is now a very tolerant body, and certainly the "Club" dominated by conservative southerners that seemed to rule the Senate in the 1940s and 1950s has long since been laid to rest.[20]

In both houses the norms of specialization and reciprocity and accommodation give added support to the dominance of substantive decisions by the standing committees and particularly by subcommittees. This, in turn, underscores the fragmented nature of policy emerging from Congress. This effect of these two norms may not have a conservative effect in terms of substance in all cases but it has a conservative effect in the sense that it helps make centralized leadership very difficult except for short periods of time. Thus coordinated programs of legislation are less likely to emerge from a number of committees simultaneously in response to leadership requests. Scattered bills are

---

18. The quotation is from David W. Evans, an Indiana Democrat, in Pinkus and Freed, "Freshmen in the House: A Sobering Six Months," 1674.

19. On the use of psychological pressure on House members who consistently oppose their party see Randall B. Ripley, *Party Leaders in the House of Representatives* (Washington: Brookings, 1967): 158–159.

20. For highlights of the debate over whether there was or was not a club in the Senate and its alleged impact see White, *Citadel;* Matthews, *U.S. Senators and Their World;* Joseph S. Clark and other senators, *The Senate Establishment* (New York: Hill and Wang, 1963); Wayne R. Swanson, "Committee Assignments and the Non-Conformist Legislator: Democrats in the U.S. Senate," *Midwest Journal of Political Science* 13 (1969): 84–94; Huitt, "The Outsider in the Senate"; Ralph K. Huitt, "The Morse Committee Assignment Controversy: A Study in Senate Norms," *American Political Science Review* 51 (1957): 313–329; Polsby, "Goodbye to the Inner Club"; and Ripley, *Power in the Senate.*

reported on a sporadic basis but central direction of a range of measures is rare.

Many of the operating norms of the House and Senate acknowledge the members' concern with representation and re-election, and allow them considerable freedom in balancing perceived constituency pressure against pressure from party leaders. The consequence of these norms is that the power of the party system in Congress to command and receive cooperation from party members in policy matters is limited. There are other factors contributing to a relatively weak and decentralized party system; none, however, is more critical than the recognition of each member's need to vote in accord with the presumed interests of his constituency.

Because many of the governing norms are oriented toward promoting a stable membership, this means that the norms operate against handling controversial (that is, potentially politically damaging to at least some incumbents) matters openly. If they are handled at all an effort is made to arrive at compromises that either defuse explosive issues or at least minimize the political costs of the detonation.

CUES FOR INDIVIDUAL BEHAVIOR

Members of the House and Senate are called on to make a very large number of decisions each year. They must vote publicly hundreds of times on the floor. They must vote many more times on the floor by voice vote or in other less visible ways. They must vote in committee and subcommittee. They must make a raft of other decisions in committee and subcommittee on which no formal vote is taken. They are basically asked to be familiar enough with everything the government does to make intelligent choices.

Obviously, no single individual can become even semi-expert in everything on the governmental agenda. Therefore, members seek shortcuts as they try to make up their minds. They seek cues for how to behave and how to vote on a great variety of policy matters. They want sources for those cues whose judgment they trust and who will lead them to "proper" decisions—that is, decisions that will help the senator or representative reach his own goals: whether they be re-election, ideological consistency, the "public good," personal status, or a combination of these goals.

Some observers have argued that if only Congress had more "information" on the substance of policy available to it, it could make "better" decisions. In fact, however, there are at least three limits to this view. First, good information is very difficult to come by in many areas. Second, even if it were available, it would be so vast in quantity that no member could absorb it, even for part of the policy areas with which each member must deal. Third, the norms of Congress that support fragmentation also support a limited search for information and a limited responsiveness to what has come to be called "policy analysis." [21] Thus the shortcuts that members seek include a deliberate decision to limit the amount of information they want and to which they will pay any attention.[22]

Figure 4–1 portrays, in highly simplified fashion, the pressures (or cues) involved in the decision process by which an individual senator or representative makes up his mind on what position to take on any specific policy.

In this figure, pressures from outside Congress include those stemming from the public (mass opinion, the opinion of various specialized publics, and the opinion of voters as registered in their electoral decisions), interest groups, the various parts of the executive branch (the presidency and bureaucracy), and state and local officials. These pressures have an impact on the institutional clusters within Congress (relationship A in the figure) and also have an impact on the individual member directly (relationship B).

Pressures from inside Congress include those generated by party leaders, committee delegations, state delegations, informal clubs and groups, and staff members. These pressures impinge on the individual

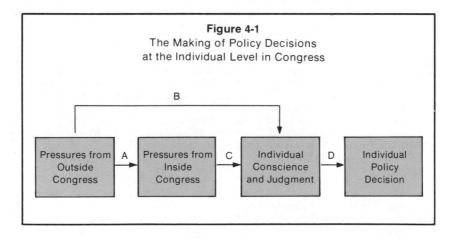

Figure 4-1
The Making of Policy Decisions
at the Individual Level in Congress

21. On some of the issues on the relations between Congress, information, and policy analysis see Charles O. Jones, "Why Congress Can't Do Policy Analysis (or words to that effect)," *Policy Analysis* 2 (1976): 251–264; and Allen Schick, "The Supply and Demand for Analysis on Capitol Hill," *Policy Analysis* 2 (1976): 215–234.
22. See John W. Kingdon, *Congressmen's Voting Decisions* (New York: Harper and Row, 1973): Chapter 9. See also the discussion of Kingdon's findings, below.

senator and representative (relationship C). It should also be noted that these sources of outside and inside pressure have a vast array of interrelations among themselves.

Once the individual legislator has received the various outside and inside pressures he views them through the filters of his conscience and judgment and reaches his decision on his position (relationship D).

A number of studies have attempted to determine the cues to which members respond. Many of these studies examine the relationship between potential cues and roll call voting on the floor. They do not prove causality in the sense that a member consciously searches for a cue, receives it, and behaves accordingly; instead they infer that patterns of behavior reflect patterns of cue-giving and cue-taking.[23] Such studies of the House have outnumbered those of the Senate, but it is reasonable to assume that senators and representatives share similar thought processes.[24] They are also confronted with approximately the

23. For discussions relying specifically on an analysis of decision-making, cue-giving, and cue-taking see Kingdon, *Congressmen's Voting Decisions;* Donald R. Matthews and James A. Stimson, *Yeas and Nays: Normal Decision-Making in the U.S. House of Representatives* (New York: Wiley, 1975); Matthews and Stimson, "Decision-Making by U.S. Representatives: A Preliminary Model," in S. Sidney Ulmer (ed.), *Political Decision-Making* (Cincinnati: Van Nostrand Reinhold, 1970); and Aage R. Clausen, *How Congressmen Decide* (New York: St. Martin's, 1973).

Other relevant studies include Herbert B. Asher and Herbert F. Weisberg, "Voting Change in Congress: Some Dynamic Perspectives on an Evolutionary Process," *American Journal of Political Science* (1978), forthcoming; Cleo H. Cherryholmes and Michael J. Shapiro, *Representatives and Roll Calls* (Indianapolis: Bobbs-Merrill, 1969); Aage R. Clausen and Richard B. Cheney, "A Comparative Analysis of Senate-House Voting on Economic and Welfare Policy: 1953–1964," *American Political Science Review* 64 (1970): 138–152; James W. Dyson and John W. Soule, "Congressional Committee Behavior on Roll Call Votes: The U.S. House of Representatives, 1955–64," *Midwest Journal of Political Science* 14 (1970): 626–647; Thomas A. Flinn and Harold L. Wolman, "Constituency and Roll Call Voting: The Case of Southern Democratic Congressmen," *Midwest Journal of Political Science* 10 (1966): 192–199; Lewis A. Froman, Jr., *Congressmen and Their Constituencies* (Chicago: Rand McNally, 1963); John E. Jackson, *Constituencies and Leaders in Congress: Their Effects on Senate Voting Behavior* (Cambridge, Mass.: Harvard University Press, 1974); David Kovenock, "Influence in the U.S. House of Representatives: A Statistical Analysis of Communications," *American Politics Quarterly* 1 (1973): 407–464; Gregory B. Markus, "Electoral Coalitions and Senate Roll Call Behavior: An Ecological Analysis," *American Journal of Political Science* 18 (1974): 595–607; David R. Mayhew, *Party Loyalty Among Congressmen* (Cambridge: Harvard University Press, 1966); Leroy N. Rieselbach, "The Congressional Vote on Foreign Aid, 1939–1958," *American Political Science Review* 58 (1964): 372–388; W. Wayne Shannon, *Party, Constituency and Congressional Voting* (Baton Rouge: Louisiana State University Press, 1968); David B. Truman, *The Congressional Party* (New York: Wiley, 1959); and Julius Turner and Edward V. Schneier, Jr., *Party and Constituency: Pressures on Congress* (Baltimore: The Johns Hopkins University Press, 1970).

24. Clausen, *How Congressmen Decide.*

same workload. There is evidence that "Senators are less subject to constituency pressures and more independent of partisan constraints," [25] because most states have more diverse constituencies than most House districts and because Senate party leaders are usually less demanding than House party leaders. But these differences are not so great as to suggest that completely different decision-making processes exist in the two houses.

A number of studies have tried to assess the impact of constituency on individual decision-making. The patterns that emerge from these studies are less than crystal clear. The safest conclusion seems to be that in terms of socio-economic characteristics, certain kinds of districts (for example, poorer urban districts) are more likely to elect Democrats, other kinds of districts (for example, relatively well-off suburban districts) are apt to elect Republicans, and that some ideological and programmatic differences are built into the basic difference between "Democratic districts" and "Republican districts." [26] The effect of typical constituency characteristics on the voting habits of congressmen is not at all clear.[27]

Occasionally constituency interests (as opposed to constituency characteristics) will clearly be a factor accounting for changed voting patterns. Southern Democratic attitudes about foreign trade, for example, changed markedly from free trade to protectionism as the southern states industrialized and brought in industries concerned with protection—particularly the textile industry. At a more general level, of course, it can be argued that constituency characteristics (for example, percent blue collar workers, percent Catholic) reflect constituency interests (higher minimum wages, urban renewal, aid to parochial schools).[28]

A number of cue-givers inside the House have also been identified. Usually they have been studied in isolation—that is, the impact of state delegations as a separate topic, the impact of committee delegations as a separate topic, the impact of party leaders as a separate topic, and so on. But recently several studies have looked at these influences simultaneously in order to compare them. One of the most interesting studies was done by Matthews and Stimson on the period between 1957 and 1964.[29] They investigated the relative potency of state party delegations, the president, party leaders, party majority, majority of

25. Clausen and Cheney, "A Comparative Analysis of Senate-House Voting," 151.
26. See Froman, *Congressmen and Their Constituencies:* 95; and Shannon, *Party, Constituency, and Congressional Voting:* Chapter 9.
27. See Shannon, *Party, Constituency, and Congressional Voting:* 178.
28. Flinn and Wolman, in "Constituency and Roll Call Voting," make this argument.
29. Matthews and Stimson, "Decision-Making by U.S. Representatives."

the House, committee chairmen and ranking committee members, and the Democratic Study Group as cue-givers.

Matthews and Stimson summarize their principal findings succinctly:

> The consistently most important single cue-giver in both parties is the member's state party delegation. . . . Two additional collective cues—the party majority and the House majority—are also potent, especially among the Democrats (who were in the majority all eight years). The President as a *direct* cue-giver is seemingly less significant, although Kennedy and Johnson did considerably better among Democrats than Eisenhower did among Republicans as a direct source of cues.[30]

Table 4–1 summarizes the Matthews-Stimson findings. It should be noted that the possible variation in the figures reported ranges from .50 (perfect agreement between the average Democratic or Republican congressman and a cue-giver) to −.50 (perfect disagreement). Thus figures greater than .30 are quite high. The table reports two periods: 1957–1960, when a Republican was president, and 1961–1964, when a Democrat was president.

State party delegations were the most important cue-givers in both parties, although they were more important for the Democrats than for the Republicans. The president was an important positive cue-giver for the Democrats when he was a Democrat and a relatively important

Table 4–1

Cue Sources for Congressmen, 1957–1964.

| | Average Cue Scores | | | |
| | Democrats | | Republicans | |
Cue Source	1957–60	1961–64	1957–60	1961–64
State Party Delegation	.42	.43	.37	.38
President	.04	.32	.13	−.16
Party Leaders	.27	.34	.26	.28
Party Majority	.34	.37	.35	.37
House Majority	.31	.39	.20	.23
Committee Chairmen	.19	.31	−.05	−.09
Ranking Members	−.05	−.01	.08	.19
Democratic Study Group	.29	.35	−.09	−.09

Source: Adapted from Donald R. Matthews and James A. Stimson, "Decision-Making by U.S. Representatives: A Preliminary Model," in S. Sidney Ulmer (ed.) Political Decision-Making (Cincinnati: Van Nostrand Reinhold, 1970): 31.

30. Ibid., 31–32.

negative cue-giver for the Republicans. The Republican president was only moderately important as a cue-giver for the Republicans and was about neutral as far as the Democrats were concerned.

Party leaders, particularly for the Democrats under a Democratic president, were important cue-givers. The party majority was consistently and about evenly important for members of both parties. The House majority was, predictably, a more important cue-giver for the members of the majority party throughout the period.

Committee chairmen were important as cue-givers for the members of their party and provided some negative cues for the members of the other party. Like the party leaders, they were most important when a member of their party was also president. This underscores the point that the party becomes most important when the president and congressional majority are of the same party.

Ranking minority members are not quite the mirror image of committee chairmen. They provided mildly negative cues for the members of the majority party, but were only moderately important in providing positive cues for the members of their own party. They were also more important in this regard when a Democrat was president, lending support to the image that the Kennedy-Johnson term was much more partisan in Congress than the second Eisenhower term.

The Democratic Study Group did about as well providing cues to the Democrats as the party leaders and party majority, largely because the views of the DSG were similar to the views of most Democrats except the southern conservatives. The DSG also provided mildly negative cues for the Republicans.

There is valid evidence that members of the House and Senate take stable positions over time on general classes of policy issues. Voting change on the floor is evolutionary, not rapid.[31] Clausen has identified five predominant policy dimensions: government management, social welfare, international involvement, civil liberties, and agricultural assistance.[32] He found that in the 1950s and 1960s members' positions on these issues exhibited great stability. He also found that the influential factors on the five dimensions remained quite stable: party influence dominated the government management dimension, a combination of party and constituency influence dominated the social welfare and agricultural assistance dimensions, constituency influence dominated the civil liberties dimension, and a combination of constituency and presidential influence dominated the international involvement dimension. These findings suggest that the

---

31. See Asher and Weisberg, "Voting Change in Congress."
32. See Clausen, *How Congressmen Decide.*

Matthews-Stimson analysis would be even more potent if it were done separately for the different policy dimensions. In any event, the work of Matthews-Stimson and Clausen suggest that cue-giving and cue-taking is not a random matter in Congress but that patterns of regularity and predictability do exist. The varying sources of influence will be examined in detail in subsequent chapters.

One of the most convincing summaries of how individual members of Congress make up their minds is provided by Kingdon, based on his close first-hand observation and interviewing in the House of Representatives in 1969.[33] Kingdon's basic argument can be summarized as follows:

1. Members search for information about a decision they must make only if they define that decision as having some kind of "problem" associated with it.

2. There are no problems with, or difficulty in making, many decisions. This is true when: (a) all of the forces that normally affect the member's decisions (interest groups, constituency, staff, administration, party leadership, fellow congressmen, and own attitude) agree that a given decision is proper; or (b) he or she feels very strongly about the matter at hand in a personal sense; or (c) the member has a well-established voting record on the same or similar issues.

3. Members make up their minds in a "consensus mode of decision" most of the time. This means that they first determine if a vote is controversial. If the answer to that is no, then any decision is relatively cost-free. When controversy is perceived then the member will check his or her "field of forces" to see how much conflict is present. If the actors in the field of forces all agree on the proper decision, the member will go along with them. If only one actor is out of line, most of the time the member will vote against that actor (93 percent of the time in Kingdon's data). If two actors are out of line, then the chances of going with the minority of forces rise (17 percent of the time in Kingdon's data). It is worth noting that the force called "own attitude" is by far the most potent in explaining defections by the member from the majority of a field of forces in agreement against his or her own attitude.

THE SUBSTANTIVE IMPACT OF RULES AND PROCEDURES

The general impact of the rules in both the House and the Senate is the same: the rules protect the power and prerogatives of the standing committees of the House and the Senate by making it very

---

33. Kingdon, *Congressmen's Voting Decisions:* Chapters 9 and 10.

difficult for a bill that does not have committee approval to come to either floor and by making it very difficult to amend bills reported from committee (this is particularly true in the House).[34] Thus the fragmenting impact of stable standing committees and particularly subcommittees is enhanced and perpetuated.

The rules create a situation in which there are multiple "veto points" through which every piece of legislation must pass. Every item that finally becomes a statute must usually be acted on affirmatively by two subcommittees (one in each house), two committees (one in each house), the House Rules Committee, the entire House, the entire Senate, a conference committee, and the president. At each step in the congressional process there are opportunities for delay or defeat. There are also opportunities for amendment that may render the final product unrecognizable to the orginal sponsors. Ultimately, a statute may also face review by federal courts on constitutional questions. Some statutes and portions of statutes are declared unconstitutional and, therefore, void.

The rules of the House and Senate underscore the necessity of bargaining if anything is to be accomplished in Congress. The rules are structured to prevent domination of the process by any one person or small group. An unavoidable result of the rules is that coalitions must be built for positive action to be taken.

The Sanctity of Committee Decisions

The House. Ordinarily no legislation can come to the floor of the House unless it has been considered and reported on by a standing committee. There are ways around the committee system, but they are cumbersome and rarely successful. For example, a discharge petition to remove a bill from a committee and bring it to the floor requires the signatures of an absolute majority of the House (218 individuals). Between 1923 and 1975 only twenty-five petitions of 396 filed received the necessary signatures. Of those twenty-five bills that were discharged, twenty passed the House but only two ultimately became law.

A procedure called suspension of the rules can also be used to circumvent House committees, but this procedure requires a two-thirds vote and thus controversial bills have a difficult time passing under it.

---

34. For excellent discussion of the impact of the rules see Lewis A. Froman, Jr., *The Congressional Process* (Boston: Little, Brown, 1967); and Leroy N. Reiselbach, *Congressional Politics* (New York: McGraw-Hill, 1973); Chapter 5. The following discussion incorporates some of the insights of these works, but for information on details, these books should be consulted. See also *Congressional Quarterly's Guide to Congress* (Washington: *Congressional Quarterly*, 1976, 2nd ed.): 335–364.

The Rules Committee can also bring any bill to the floor regardless of committee action. It rarely does so, because its members properly perceive that they too have a stake in preserving the sanctity of the committee process.

When bills come to the House floor through the regular committee process they may have special safeguards to insure their prompt consideration and perhaps their passage. Appropriations and tax bills, for example, may come to the floor as privileged business at any time, although the Appropriations Committee and Ways and Means Committee may prefer to go through the Rules Committee in order to obtain conditions they deem favorable placed on the debate.

The rules of the House plus the actions of the Rules Committee make it difficult for committee bills to be amended. Debate on amendments is strictly limited. Amendments rejected in the Committee of the Whole (a procedure used to facilitate floor debate by the whole House) cannot be made subject to a formal roll call after the Committee has risen; but amendments that are passed in the Committee of the Whole can be retested on a roll call. On most bills the minority party is, in effect, limited to one major effort to amend or kill the bill —the recommittal motion that immediately precedes the vote on final passage. Thus if the majority party members of the committee are in agreement with a large part of the majority party in the House the committee version of a bill is likely to pass unchanged.

The Senate. The Senate rules have a discharge provision that is very difficult to use. But there are other provisions, easier to use, that can bypass a committee stage and produce floor action. The Senate suspension of the rules procedure is easier to use than the House procedure and requires only a majority vote; it is used mainly for appropriations bills. Non-germane amendments (also called "riders") can also be added to Senate bills through the normal amending procedure in committee or on the floor, again unlike the House, which has a strict rule of germaneness. With some frequency, important measures reach the Senate floor as riders to trivial bills. Finally, bills passed in the House can be brought directly to the Senate floor without consideration by a Senate committee. Civil rights bills have sometimes been kept out of the hostile Judiciary Committee in this way.

All of these measures are unusual; but their greater availability suggests that the Senate is less dedicated to protecting the sanctity of the committee stage than is the House. Similarly, on the floor even those bills coming through the normal committee procedure (the vast majority of bills) are less protected against amendment than in the House. Senators have a number of committee assignments; in some ways this helps lead them to attach less negative symbolism to the amendment of committee products.

Multiple Vetoes

In both houses there are a number of points at which a few determined members (or perhaps even a single determined member) can stop or at least significantly delay the passage of a piece of legislation. Committee procedure and floor procedure are both very complex. As a bill travels between houses and from the committee to the floor in either house (particularly the House) there are other dangers. Table 4–2 summarizes the points at which delay or defeat may occur in the House alone. The same table would apply to the Senate with the deletion of the references to the Rules Committee, some minor changes in the details of stalling action on the floor, and the significant addition of the filibuster as a weapon for either delay or defeat.

The Special Case of the Senate Filibuster

The right of senators to engage in "unlimited debate" unless a special majority of their fellows vote to deny them that right is regarded as the oldest of the rules of Congress by the public and in many

Table 4–2

Points at which Delay or Defeat May Occur in the House.

Delay	*Defeat*
Committee inaction in referring to a subcommittee	Committee inaction
Subcommittee inaction (prolonged hearings; refusal to report)	Negative vote in committee
	Subcommittee inaction
Committee inaction (prolonged hearings; refusal to report)	Negative vote in subcommittee
Rules Committee inaction (refusal to schedule hearings; prolonged hearings; refusal to report)	Rules Committee inaction
	Negative vote in Rules Committee
Slowness in scheduling the bill	Defeat of rule on the floor
Floor action (demanding full requirements of the rules)	Motion to strike enacting clause
reading of the journal	Motion to recommit
repeated quorum calls	Final passage
refusing unanimous consent to dispense with further proceedings under the call of the roll	
prolonging debate	
various points of order	

Source: Lewis A. Froman, Jr., The Congressional Process *(Little, Brown, 1967): 18.*

ways was so regarded by most senators themselves until very recently. The filibuster has been used by minorities that, knowing they were in the minority position, were nonetheless so intense in their opposition to some issue that they were willing to disrupt the normal proceedings of the Senate in an effort to prevent the action they found abhorrent.

Filibusters will sometimes go unchallenged and thus succeed. This is most true at the end of a session, particularly at the end of a Congress, when time simply has run out. Since 1917 the Senate has provided a cloture mechanism by which filibusters can be ended. From 1917 to 1949 and again from 1959 to early 1975 this rule provided for cloture by two-thirds of those senators present and voting. Between 1949 and 1959 the rule was interpreted to mean that two-thirds of the entire Senate had to vote for cloture before it could be imposed. Since March 7, 1975, the rule is that three-fifths of the entire membership (sixty senators out of the hundred members) must agree to cloture.

From 1917 through 1977, 132 cloture votes were taken, of which thirty-nine were successful. But the pattern of usage has varied enormously. In the early years in which the rule was in effect (1917–1929) the procedure was used ten times and was successful four times. None of these votes involved civil rights questions. However, in the next three decades (1930–1959) the procedure was used only twelve times; eight of those occasions involved civil rights questions, and none of the cloture motions were successful. It was during this period that the reputation of the filibuster as the absolutely unbeatable southern weapon against civil rights legislation was established.

However, the 1960s and 1970s have seen a very different attitude toward cloture emerge, in terms of frequency, subject matter, and success. During the 1960s cloture was attempted twenty-three times, only eleven of which involved civil rights matters. (Four of the twenty-three motions were successful, and three of the four successes were on civil rights bills.) From 1970 through 1977 cloture motions were voted on eighty-seven times. Thirty-one of the votes imposed cloture. No filibuster successfully prevented civil rights legislation from being enacted.

Thus the filibuster and cloture play a very different role in the Senate in the late 1970s than they did earlier. Cloture is voted on so frequently as to be almost routine (twenty-one times in 1974 and twenty-three times in 1975 alone). And, especially since the change in the rule in 1975, success is relatively easy to achieve. After the change in March, 1975, cloture was imposed in fourteen of the twenty-four cases in which a vote was taken in 1975 and 1976.

Given the rule change in 1975 and the attitude of present senators, the filibuster is no longer a reliable weapon in the hands of a minority. One study of the filibuster even dismissed its potency in its supposed period of invulnerability in the 1940s and 1950s:

> (1) Filibusters have been so unthreatening to various presidents' legislative programs that the actual postwar occupants of the White House either have remained aloof from attempts to curb this presumed impediment to their power or have even covertly helped defeat and distract such efforts. (2) With one possible exception, in no case between the war and 1966 was the filibuster responsible for the death of a civil rights bill supported by majorities in Congress.[35]

The threat of a filibuster is, however, also used to gain concessions even if the filibuster itself is not invoked. Often, the proponents of a bill will agree to amendments that weaken the bill in order to build the special majority needed for cloture. Thus, filibusters may well achieve part of their aims even if cloture is voted. Sometimes just the threat of a filibuster may bring forth the desired concessions.[36]

Despite the lack of reliability on the part of the filibuster as a weapon to prevent action, it can still work. In the summer of 1977, for example, a plan to finance congressional elections with public funds was defeated by a filibuster. A cloture vote was taken three times, but the majority failed each time: 49–45, 47–46, and 52–47. There was always a majority opposed to the filibuster, but it fell short of the sixty votes needed for cloture. The bill was passed only after the public financing section had been removed.

Rules, Bargaining, and Coalition-Building

The rules and procedures in both houses are constructed so that they enhance the influence of the members skilled in parliamentary maneuver. More important, they underscore the necessity of bargaining, compromise, and coalition-building in order to achieve anything in terms of legislative products.

Three recent cases follow that illustrate a number of points about the relationship between the rules of the House and Senate and the processes of bargaining and coalition-building.

---

35. Raymond E. Wolfinger, "Filibusters: Majority Rule, Presidential Leadership, and Senate Norms," in Wolfinger (ed.), *Readings on Congress* (Englewood Cliffs, N.J.: Prentice-Hall, 1971): 305.
36. See, for example, Howard E. Shuman, "Senate Rules and the Civil Rights Bill: A Case Study," *American Political Science Review* 51 (1957): 955–975.

Food Stamps, Tobacco, Wheat, and Cotton: House Action in 1964.[37] In 1964 Congress passed a food stamp act making permanent a program that had begun under executive order a few years earlier. The passage of that bill in the House illustrates how the rules and procedures of the House are used to affect substantive outcomes.

In early February 1964 the House Agriculture Committee voted to table the administration's food stamp bill by a vote of nineteen to fourteen. The fourteen Republicans had been joined by five Democrats (four southerners and a Missourian) in favor of the tabling motion. All fourteen opposed to it were Democrats. The chairman of the Committee had favored the bill (and opposed the tabling motion). He was not personally enthusiastic about the food stamp bill but was willing to support the administration, which had worked very hard in December 1963 to help him get a cotton bill through the House.

Liberal Democrats both on and off the Agriculture Committee sought a lever to persuade the committee to reconsider the tabling motion. They chose to use a bill the committee had reported that would authorize public funds for the support of a study of tobacco and health. The Agriculture Chairman, Harold Cooley, from a large tobacco-growing district in North Carolina, had a special interest in having the tobacco bill passed. A moderate California Democrat on the Rules Committee, B.F. Sisk, determined that he would work to prevent the Rules Committee from granting a rule to the tobacco bill until the Agriculture Committee had reported out the food stamp bill favorably. He was successful in this maneuver, although he reserved a motion to reconsider the tobacco bill, implying that it could be saved given favorable Agriculture Committee action on the food stamp bill.

The Agriculture Committee responded as Cooley and Sisk hoped it would: three of the dissident Democrats changed their votes and the Committee reported the bill. (Sisk kept his end of the implied bargain and the tobacco bill came out of the Rules Committee soon thereafter.)

The involvement of the food stamp bill in trades involving the House rules did not end there, however. In early March the Senate had added a wheat program to the cotton program passed by the House the preceding December. The administration feared that the wheat-cotton bill would lose in the House because of solid Republican opposition and the defection of some liberal northern Democrats. Agriculture Department officials, Cooley, and the House Democratic

37. The discussion of the food stamp program is based on Randall B. Ripley, "Legislative Bargaining and the Food Stamp Act, 1964," in Frederic N. Cleaveland and Associates, *Congress and Urban Problems* (Washington, D.C.: Brookings, 1969): 279–310.

leaders wanted to arrange a trade in which northern liberals would vote for wheat-cotton if southern conservatives (*very* interested in cotton) would vote for something important to the liberals. Until the House on 12 March defeated a pay raise bill for government employees (including members of Congress) there had been talk that the pay raise and wheat-cotton bills might be linked. However, votes by rural representatives had helped kill the pay raise, which increased the antagonism of the urban Democrats toward agriculture bills.

Gradually, during late March, it became clear that the hoped for trade would involve the food stamp bill and the wheat-cotton bill. No formal announcement was made of such a trade. Indeed, no formal meeting was held at which leaders of urban-liberal and rural-conservative blocs agreed on it. Instead, as is typical of the implicit bargaining that takes place in Congress, a favorable psychological climate developed. The more the individual members and the press talked about a specific trade of southern rural votes on food stamps for northern urban votes on wheat-cotton, the more firmly the exchange became implanted in the minds of the members. Individual lobbying efforts by the Agriculture Department and the House leaders reinforced this attitude.

The Rules Committee granted rules to both bills and the House leaders scheduled them back-to-back in early April. Liberals insisted that the food stamp bill go first, as they were mistrustful of their southern colleagues.

When debate ended on the food stamp bill the Republicans used a familiar delaying tactic: a Republican demanded an engrossed copy of the bill (that is, a bill printed with all amendments) before the final vote could be taken. The Democrats had anticipated this ploy and had alerted the printer ahead of time so that he could accomplish the task in a few hours. In the interim the Speaker of the House let debate on the rule for the wheat-cotton bill begin. Within a few minutes liberal Democrats realized that this might mean that the final vote on wheat-cotton would come before the final vote on food stamps. They protested to the Speaker and he, employing a power that had been temporarily granted to him earlier that day for an entirely different purpose (paying respects to the remains of General Douglas Mac-Arthur in the rotunda of the Capitol), declared a recess so that the "proper" ordering of the bills could be re-established. When the House resumed its deliberations both bills passed, adjournment coming near one o'clock the next morning.

In this case the liberal proponents of food stamp legislation used the rules to cement an ad hoc coalition that allowed their position to prevail. They skillfully used the existence of the Rules Committee and the procedures under which the House votes on the floor to give themselves every chance of success. If the leaders of this group had not been thoroughly familiar with House rules and procedures they might have let success slip away from them.

The Senate and Legislative Reapportionment, 1964–1966.[38] Shortly after the Supreme Court declared in 1964 that both houses of state legislatures had to be reapportioned on a one-man, one-vote basis, Senator Everett Dirksen, Illinois Republican and the Senate minority leader, introduced a constitutional amendment that would remove federal court jurisdiction over legislative reapportionment cases. Constitutional amendments are time-consuming and require two-thirds majority votes; therefore, Dirksen also introduced a bill that would provide a two-year stay of federal court decrees involving reapportionment. The subsequent debate illustrates how delays possible under Senate rules can be used to defeat seemingly popular initiatives. This case is particularly interesting because "liberals" used the delaying tactics and "conservatives" were eager for action.

Dirksen got approval for the bill from the Judiciary Committee but then offered it on the floor as a rider to the foreign aid bill. A liberal coalition announced its intention to filibuster, and the filibuster began. Dirksen sought cloture, but this move failed. Then another senior Republican moved to table the rider. He anticipated—correctly —that the Senate would defeat his motion. This would show that a majority of the senators favored the bill but were being frustrated by the filibusterers. It would also presumably force Majority Leader Mansfield to find a way out of the impasse. This Mansfield did by offering a sense of Congress resolution (not literally a law but simply a formal statement of opinion passed by a majority) that was not binding on federal courts and was inapplicable to the Supreme Court but that counseled moderation in application of the basic decision. Dirksen found this language unacceptable, but the liberals picked up enough moderate support to pass it (effectively, it had no impact on the courts) and win the battle in 1964.

In 1965 Dirksen resumed his drive for a constitutional amendment. The liberals' first tactic was to prolong discussion of the proposal (and several variants that appeared throughout 1965 and 1966) in the subcommittee of the Judiciary Committee handling the bill. Then in the

---

38. The following account is based on Edward Keynes, "The Senate Rules and the Dirksen Amendment: A Study in Legislative Strategy and Tactics," in Lawrence K. Pettit and Edward Keynes (eds.), *The Legislative Process in the U.S. Senate* (Chicago: Rand McNally, 1969): 107–145.

full committee the liberals were able to gain a tie, which prevented the bill from being reported out favorably. Dirksen succeeded in bringing the amendment to the floor by substituting it for a joint resolution proclaiming National American Legion Baseball Week on the floor. This is a rarely used procedure in the Senate, but it got the Dirksen amendment to the floor in 1965. Dirksen had a majority of the Senate in support of his proposal but did not have the necessary two-thirds. Thus the Senate defeated the amendment fifty-seven to thirty-nine.

Dirksen submitted a watered-down version of his amendment to the Judiciary Committee. In a trade with the president, Dirksen allowed an immigration bill important to the president to be reported out by the Judiciary Committee (of which Dirksen was a member); in exchange, one anti-Dirksen Democrat on the committee changed his vote so that the Dirksen amendment could be reported out by the committee. This new version also failed to get the needed two-thirds vote on the floor in 1966 (the vote was fifty-five to thirty-eight).

Keynes' conclusions about the whole process are instructive:

In the two-year struggle over state legislative reapportionment, the strategic needs of the two coalitions determined the selection of relevant and appropriate rules of procedure. While the members of the Dirksen coalition were confronted with the problem of promoting congressional action before too many state legislatures were reapportioned under court order, the liberals attempted to delay action and ultimately defeat any legislation designed to undermine the Reynolds decision.

Both sides employed the rules to affect the timing of decisions. The liberals delayed action in the 88th Congress by selectively filibustering H.R. 11380 (as amended) until the closing days of the session. In the 89th Congress they structured events in the Senate Judiciary Committee to delay floor action until the beginning of August 1965. Senator Dirksen also employed the rules in the 89th Congress to circumvent the Judiciary Committee, thereby expediting floor action on his constitutional amendment (S.J. Res. 66, as amended). The very timing of the decision, as both sides realized, was important in determining the final outcome of the struggle.

The rules were also employed as tools in the legislative process to bargain over substantive changes in the proposed legislation. Senator Dirksen offered a series of substantive concessions or 'sweeteners' to attract additional support for his measure. By bargaining down an initially untenable position Dirksen hoped to expand the base of his Senate coalition. The liberals, however, met each concession with still further demands for changes in the proposed resolutions. The liberals used the rules to slow down the momentum of the legislative process in the Senate and to bargain for substantive changes in the Dirksen legislation.[39]

The 1973 Farm Bill. In 1973 Congress passed a comprehensive farm bill that included sections on feed grains, wheat, cotton, dairy products, and food stamps. It was a very complex bill that engendered a great deal of controversy and debate. Various disputes erupted in various locations: in the Agriculture Committees of the House and Senate, on the Senate floor, in conference, between the administration and various members of Congress, between interest group representatives and members of Congress, and, above all, on the floor of the House. These disputes illustrate how the rules allow compromise to be worked out on the floor. They also illustrate that when final compromise cannot be reached at any one stage the matter under consideration can usually be shunted on to a succeeding stage (in this case, the conference committee) with the hope that the elusive winning bargain can be struck there.

When the bill first came to the House floor on 10 July 1973 it was already in tenuous shape. Its ultimate success depended on ratification by the House of an agreement reached by the senior members of the Agriculture Committee and the administration whereby the committee members agreed to remove a provision that would have increased price support payments as production costs increased (a provision opposed by the administration as too expensive and inflationary) in exchange for administration support of other key provisions including, critically, those on cotton supports. On July 10 and 11, however, the roof fell in on the committee, particularly the senior southern Democrats most solicitous of cotton interests. First, the House refused to remove the escalator clause for price support payments. Then the House itself turned on cotton interests and limited the amount of subsidy that could be paid to any individual farmer to $20,000 (many large cotton growers receive a great deal more); it also deleted a $10 million subsidy to a private organization engaged in research and promotional work for cotton. On July 12 the chairman of the Agriculture Committee, W.R. Poage of Texas, used the rules of the House to give himself some more time to put a winning combination together again. He moved to postpone consideration of the bill until further notice and the House agreed.

39. Keynes, "The Senate Rules and the Dirksen Amendment," 139.

Four days later, on July 16, Poage was ready to try again. In the interim a presumably winning bargain had been struck between cotton interests and organized labor. Labor spokesmen agreed to support an amendment eliminating all specific references to cotton in the bill (this would effectively eliminate the ceiling provision on subsidy amounts) if cotton interests would agree to oppose an amendment to the bill that would prevent the families of individuals on strike from using food stamps. Presumably, conservative members from cotton districts would support labor's position on the food stamp amendment in return for the support of liberal members from heavily unionized districts in the north for cotton's position on subsidy ceilings. But only some of the southerners voted with the labor bloc when three separate votes were taken on the question of stamps for strikers, even though a majority of the northern Democrats had gone along with an earlier successful motion to strike all references to cotton from the bill. The conservative position, with a majority of southerners supporting it, triumphed. Thus when the cotton questions again came up the northerners defected and the anti-cotton provisions were reinserted in the bill. Now the bill was satisfactory to neither the northern pro-labor Democrats nor to the pro-cotton southerners. The rules had permitted an incredible chain of amendments and amendments to amendments as the various interests sought to negotiate their varied interests on the House floor itself. But the bargain simply did not hold.

However, the rules, in effect, permitted one more appeal—to the conference committee. With neither of the major Democratic blocs happy but with a large number of members still having considerable interest in other provisions of the bill (food for peace, the other provisions for food stamps, and the other crops) the leadership on the bill frankly appealed to the House to pass the bill even in its unsatisfactory form so that more quiet and private negotiation could take place in the conference committee. The hope was that the combination of senior senators and representatives on that committee could quietly satisfy all of the major interests and thus insure the ultimate adoption of the conference report. And, in fact, the conference committee did succeed and deleted or modified the provisions offensive to organized labor and the cotton interests.

Thus, in a single case, the rules of the House were used first to stall when time was needed for working out an agreement between interests, second to allow elaborate extensive amendment designed to implement the agreement, and third to send the bill to conference for a second chance at satisfying all major interests when the agreement could not be successfully implemented on the House floor.

SUMMARY: AN OVERVIEW OF CONGRESSIONAL DECISION-MAKING

This chapter has outlined the setting in which both Congress as an institution and senators and representatives as individuals operate. In general, a number of regularities in congressional behavior, both individual and collective, are visible. These regularities have been explained primarily in terms of major environmental features—the electoral and representational system, the nature of the executive branch, and the nature of the workload. These features impinge on individual members directly and are also transmitted through the norms of behavior in the two houses, the cue-taking patterns used by the members, and the nature and impact of the rules and procedures of both houses.

The norm of specialization is a reaction to the existence of a specialized bureaucracy and a large and demanding workload. It also serves to promote narrow constituency interests. The norm of reciprocity and accommodation also facilitates the representation of those interests as well as making feasible the processing of an extensive agenda.

Among the cue-givers that have the most impact on patterns of congressional decisions, the constituency (including state delegations) and the president stand out, in addition to political parties and party leaders in the House and Senate. This fact highlights both the importance of the constituencies and president in the congressional environment and the complex role of the congressional parties as entities that in some ways serve the interests of the constituencies and president but in other ways are the main potential rallying points for a genuinely *congressional* point of view on policy.

The rules also afford members the opportunity to respond to perceived constituency interests (often by delaying or preventing action) if they so desire. At the same time, skillful parliamentarians can also maximize their responsiveness to the president or to some party position on policy. These activities are allowed by the rules, even though in general the rules also promote the relatively orderly disposition of the large workload. At times, however, orderliness takes second place to serving constituency, president, or party.

CHAPTER 5

COMMITTEES
AND SUBCOMMITTEES

IN LATE JULY, 1977, THE HOUSE AND SENATE QUICKLY AND ROUTINELY
passed S. 1474, a bill authorizing $3.7 billion for military construc-
tion projects for Fiscal 1978 (October 1, 1977–September 30, 1978).
The passage of this bill through the legislative process was unspectacu-
lar and noncontroversial; it went virtually unnoticed except by those
directly involved in the process. The brief and undramatic story of
this bill illustrates a number of general points about the congressional
impact on public policy: that even legislation involving a great deal
of money (and $3.7 billion is still a sizable sum) does not necessarily
attract wide attention; that Congress is generally responsive to executive branch requests but also makes some substantial alterations, even
in the area of national defense; that defense policy and domestic policy
are intertwined; that members of Congress are particularly sensitive to
constituency interests in any piece of legislation; and, above all, that
the standing committees and subcommittees of Congress effectively
make most of the substantive decisions for the entire body.

The Ford administration requested only $2.7 billion for military
construction before it left office. Once the Carter administration had
made its budget alterations in early 1977, it upped that request to
$3.58 billion.

The Military Construction and Stockpiles Subcommittee of the
Senate Armed Services Committee and then the full committee reviewed the bill first. They recommended changes in the bill from the
administration request that added about $150 million to it, making
the total in the bill $3.73 billion.

The full Senate quickly adopted the committee report by voice vote
with only one minor change. That change added an authorization of

$1.3 million for completion of a visitors' center at Pearl Harbor, Hawaii. The amendment was offered by a senator from Hawaii and presumably would please his constituents.

The Senate committee justified its additions to the administration's request principally by referring to the need for stimulation of the construction industry and asserting that the additions in the bill would create 50,000 construction jobs. The Senate Committee also added a provision to the bill that no base in the United States with a civilian payroll of 1,000 or more could be closed or have its civilian work force cut by 50 percent or by 1,000 workers until sixty days after the Secretary of Defense had notified Congress.

The House Subcommittee on Military Installations and Facilities and the full Armed Services Committee also reviewed the bill and held hearings on it in the spring. Floor action on the bill took a very short time, as there was virtually no debate and no amendments were added. Only one amendment was offered and was defeated easily.

The House committee was somewhat more frugal than the Senate Committee and reported a bill containing total authorizations of $3.51 billion. They added a program designed to achieve energy conservation in family housing on military bases. The largest project they deleted was a new plant scheduled to be built in Mississippi to produce artillery shells. Members of the Kansas congressional delegation had lobbied against the new plant on the grounds that it would cut jobs at two existing plants, including one in Kansas. The Senate had funded this project—no doubt in part because the Chairman of the Senate Armed Services Committee came from Mississippi.

The conference committee that was appointed to adjust the differences between the House and Senate bills did not take long to do its work. The final figure authorized in the bill was $3.72 billion, very close to the Senate figure and considerably more than the initial administration request. The Senate additional projects (aimed at adding construction jobs and at financing energy conservation and pollution control on military installations) was retained. About half of the House's addition of an energy conservation program was retained on a pilot basis. The Mississippi ammunition factory was funded—the chairman of the Senate committee was apparently more influential than the Kansas House delegation, which had no members on the Armed Services Committee.

The conferees also agreed on a permanent procedure to facilitate and guarantee congressional review of any proposed base closing or reduction in civilian payroll (always a touchy subject because of the economic ramifications at the local level). Before any base could be closed or a civilian payroll of more than 500 cut by 50 percent or

1,000 people (whichever was smaller) the Secretary of Defense would have to: inform Congress that he was considering such a change; file an environmental impact statement; inform the Armed Services Committee in both houses of the final decision and justify it; and wait sixty days before taking final action (which would allow time for contrary congressional action).

President Carter signed the bill shortly after the House and Senate approved the conference report. As is customary, the Congress of the United States had made a major commitment of the nation's resources by passing virtually without question the recommendations of that tiny fraction of its membership sitting on two subcommittees with jurisdiction in the area.

Virtually since its beginning, Congress has conducted its business through committees. The modern Congress is characterized by a stable system of standing committees with fixed jurisdictions and relatively unchanging memberships. This committee structure is at the heart of all congressional activities; it embodies the principal congressional response to the subject specialists in the bureaucracy and to its own heavy workload. Without resorting to this labor-saving device, a body of 535 members would be incapable of processing the extensive amount of legislation necessary to govern this nation. And yet the very device that permits the legislature to legislate contains the potential for dilution of congressional impact: individual committees and subcommittees can become highly responsive principally to selected interests. When allowed to operate with virtual autonomy, the committee structure becomes a fragmenting force—the numerous specialized clusters of individuals each proceed on their separate courses never united by any common vision of national policy goals. However, the presence of party leaders, and the types of interaction that must occur between the leaders and the committees help curb the fragmenting tendency of committees. When working in accord with the party leaders, the committee system offers Congress its principal opportunity to shape national policy in detail.

The congressional committee system has been in flux in the last few years. But its centrality and importance in determining what emerges from Congress in terms of policy substance has remained unchanged. The changes have all been procedural (and, of course, such changes have substantive implications in many instances) and will be discussed throughout the rest of this chapter. They involve committee assignment processes, sizable dents in the "rule" of seniority for determining chairmanships, open meetings, restrictions on chairpersons, and the devolution of power to subcommittees to a point that many are nearly autonomous.

AN OVERVIEW OF THE PRESENT COMMITTEE SYSTEM

A Description of the Committee System

There are several different kinds of committees in Congress. By far the most important are the *standing committees* and their *subcommittees*. These are committees that exist from Congress to Congress, with stable memberships and jurisdictions. The entire range of legislation that Congress considers is parceled out to the standing committees. At present (1977) there are twenty-two standing committees in the House and fifteen in the Senate. The jurisdictions are relatively well denoted by the names of the committees. In general, the two houses have parallel committee structures, although they use different titles for some committees (for example, Ways and Means in the House and Finance in the Senate have roughly the same jurisdiction; Education and Labor in the House and Human Resources in the Senate have about the same jurisdiction).

The House has seven committees that the Senate does not have: District of Columbia, and Post Office and Civil Service (these matters are handled by the Governmental Affairs Committee in the Senate); Merchant Marine and Fisheries, and Science and Technology (these matters are handled by the Commerce, Science, and Transportation Committee in the Senate); Small Business, and Standards of Official Conduct (these matters are handled by two separate select committees in the Senate); and Rules (this is a committee unique to the House because of its rules of procedure). Table 5–1 lists the committees of the House and Senate along with the number of members on each and the number of subcommittees established by each.

There is a wide range in the size of committees. House committees are uniformly larger than Senate committees. There is also a wide range in the number of subcommittees established by any given committee. A few have no subcommittees and conduct all of their business in full committee. Most have a sizable number of subcommittees. Some conduct virtually all of their business through subcommittees and the full committee becomes like a holding company for the subcommittees. Subcommittees are discussed in more detail below.

Both houses make some use of *special* and *select* committees. Table 5–2 lists these committees for 1977 and indicates their size. The importance of the committees varies. The Select Committee on Small Business in the Senate, for example, has considerable importance. The House had a similar select committee for many years and it became so

Standing Committees of Congress, 1977

Committee in House of Representatives	No. of Members	No. of Subcommittees	Parallel Committee in Senate	No. of Members	No. of Subcommittees
Agriculture	46	10	Agriculture, Nutrition, and Forestry	18	7
Appropriations	55	13	Appropriations	25	13
Armed Services	40	7	Armed Services	18	8
Banking, Finance and Urban Affairs	46	10	Banking, Housing and Urban Affairs	15	8
Budget	25	0[a]	Budget	16	0
District of Columbia	19	3	—	—	—
Education and Labor	37	8	Human Resources	15	8
Government Operations	43	7	Governmental Affairs	17	7
House Administration	25	7	Rules and Administration	9	0
Interior and Insular Affairs	43	7	Energy and Natural Resources	18	5
International Relations	37	9	Foreign Relations	16	9
Interstate and Foreign Commerce	43	6	Commerce, Science, and Transportation	18	6
Judiciary	34	7	Judiciary	17	10
Merchant Marine and Fisheries	40	6	—	—	—
Post Office and Civil Service	25	7	—	—	—
Public Works and Transportation	43	6	Environment and Public Works	15	6
Rules	16	0	—	—	—
Science and Technology	40	7	—	—	—
Small Business	37	6	—	—	—
Standards of Official Conduct	12	0	—	—	—
Veterans' Affairs	28	5	Veterans' Affairs	9	3
Ways and Means	37	6	Finance	18	10

[a] Uses task forces instead of subcommittees.

Source: *Compiled from data in* Congressional Directory, 1977.

important that it was made a standing committee.[1] In 1977 the House Select Committee on Assassinations and the House Select Committee on Ethics both got considerable publicity, the former because of its seeming ineptness in handling its own staff and the latter because of its mandate to investigate the buying of influence in the House by an alleged agent of the Government of South Korea. A few select and special committees proceed very quietly on matters that attract little attention—the House Recording Studio and the Modernization of House Gallery Facilities are good examples.

In 1977 the House Ad Hoc Select Committee on Energy played a particularly important role in overseeing the passage of President Carter's energy program in the House.[2] This was a special device concocted by the Speaker of the House, Thomas P. O'Neill, to accomplish three purposes. First, he wanted to avoid jurisdictional fights over the legislation, which was complicated and was parceled out to sev-

Table 5–2
Select and Special Committees in Congress, 1977

Name of Committee	No. of Members
House of Representatives	
Ad Hoc Select Committee on Outer Continental Shelf	19
House Recording Studio	3
Select Committee on Aging	34
Select Committee on Assassinations	11
Select Committee on Ethics	19
Select Committee on Narcotics Abuse and Control	18
Special Commission on Modernization of House Gallery Facilities	5
Senate	
Select Committee on Ethics	6
Select Committee on Indian Affairs	5
Select Committee on Intelligence	17
Select Committee on Nutrition and Human Needs	9
Select Committee on Small Business	9
Special Committee on Aging	9

Source: Compiled from data in Congressional Directory, *1977.*

1. See Dale Vinyard, "Congressional Committees on Small Business," *Midwest Journal of Political Science* 10 (1966): 364–377.
2. Martin Tolchin, "The Energetic Role of the Energy Panel," *New York Times,* July 3, 1977.

eral standing committees. Second, he wanted to select a broad range of members who were not tied in to patterns of decision and interest representation well ensconced on the standing committees. Third, he wanted to maximize his own substantive role so that he could continue to coordinate between the White House and the House in substantive terms, not just on procedural matters. The Speaker named a close friend in the House as chairperson of the committee. The importance of the committee is attested to by the fact that 107 Democrats applied for the twenty-seven Democratic seats on the committee. The committee represented all of the major interests with a large stake in energy decisions: consumers, oil producers, automobile manufacturers, coal producers, and health and environmental interests. In a very real sense the speaker here put together a committee that helped the House achieve some degree of policy integration in a complex policy area rather than simply proceeding in the normal fragmented fashion.

Congress has also established some *joint* committees made up of equal numbers of senators and representatives. In 1977 only four such committees existed (five years earlier there had been nine joint committees). Table 5–3 lists the 1977 committees and the size of their memberships. Two of these have considerable importance: the Joint Committee on Taxation primarily because of the work of its staff in the tax field [3] and the Joint Economic Committee because it produces reports and holds hearings that receive considerable publicity and help shape thinking about economic policy.

One joint committee that went out of existence in 1977 after over thirty years of important life was the Joint Committee on Atomic Energy. In its heyday the committee virtually ran the atomic energy

Table 5–3
Joint Committees of Congress, 1977

Name of Committee	Number of Members
Joint Committee on the Library	10
Joint Committee on Printing	6
Joint Committee on Taxation	10
Joint Economic Committee	20

Source: Compiled from data in Congressional Directory, *1977. Three joint committees that went out of existence on July 1, 1977, are not included.*

---

3. See John F. Manley, "Congressional Staff and Public Policy-Making: The Joint Committee on Internal Revenue Taxation," *Journal of Politics* 30 (1968): 1046–1067.

program of the nation. It was unusual among joint committees in that it had authority to report legislation directly to the House and Senate floors.[4]

When standing committees, select and special committes, and joint committees are viewed together, two impressions emerge. First, the division of a vast jurisdiction into a finite number of units inevitably helps promote some fragmentation of matters that should logically be considered together rather than separately. On the other hand, the impression also emerges that Congress can and does change the committee units with which it conducts its primary substantive business. Committees are created and committees die. New developments in the realm of policy and in the organization of the executive branch are reflected in changes made by Congress itself in its own organizational structure. Some of these changes are slow. A good example is the death of the House Internal Security Committee (formerly the House Un-American Activities Committee), which did not come until 1975, despite the fact that it had never been important legislatively and had even ceased being important politically many years before. On the other hand, more speed is sometimes shown. For example, after a variety of investigations stemming from Watergate had revealed substantial abuses by American intelligence agencies in terms of violating rights of Americans, the Senate created a Select Committee in 1976 and the House followed suit in 1977.

Congress uses *conference* committees to resolve differences between the House and Senate versions of bills. These committees are appointed only for the duration of the discussion of a single bill; they disband once their report has been accepted by both houses and the bill is forwarded to the president for his signature. The same members may serve on a large number of conference committees in any given session. Typically, senior members are assigned to many more conference committees than junior members.

In general, the ratio of Democrats to Republicans on committees is determined by approximating the ratio of Democrats to Republicans in the whole House or Senate.

There are constant pressures to expand the size of the most sought after committees in order to increase the number of choice seats open. Table 5–4 summarizes the growth of committees in both houses between 1947 and 1977 for committees that existed during those years.

---

4. Harold P. Green, "The Joint Committee on Atomic Energy: A Model for Legislative Reform?" in Ronald C. Moe (ed.), *Congress and the President* (New York: Goodyear, 1971). See also J. Dicken Kirschten, "Is Doomsday at Hand for the Joint Atomic Energy Committee," *National Journal* (November 20, 1976): 1658–1665.

Table 5–4
Growth of Committee Size, 1947–1977 [a]

	Number of Members		Net Change
	1947	1977	
House Committees			
Agriculture	27	46	19
Appropriations	43	55	12
Armed Services	33	40	7
Banking, Finance, and Urban Affairs	27	46	19
District of Columbia	25	19	–6
Education and Labor	25	37	12
Government Operations	25	43	18
House Administration	25	25	0
Interior and Insular Affairs	25	43	18
International Relations	25	37	12
Interstate and Foreign Commerce	27	43	16
Judiciary	27	34	7
Merchant Marine and Fisheries	25	40	15
Post Office and Civil Service	25	25	0
Public Works and Transportation	27	43	16
Rules	12	16	4
Veterans' Affairs	27	28	1
Ways and Means	25	37	12
Senate Committees			
Agriculture, Nutrition, and Forestry	13	18	5
Appropriations	21	25	4
Armed Services	13	18	5
Banking, Housing and Urban Affairs	13	15	2
Commerce, Science, and Transportation	13	18	5
Energy and Natural Resources	13	18	5
Environment and Public Works	13	15	2
Finance	13	18	5
Foreign Relations	13	16	3
Governmental Affairs	13	17	4
Human Resources	13	15	2
Judiciary	13	17	4
Rules and Administration	13	9	–4

Source: Congressional Directory, *1947 and 1977.*

[a] Some committees had different names in 1947. Committees created after 1947 are not included.

As the table shows, only one minor committee in each house shrank in size. Two minor House committees remained stable in size. All other committees—fifteen in the House and twelve in the Senate—grew. The growth was very large in a number of cases and generally reflected those areas in which the requests for membership were the greatest. Between 1947 and 1977 the total number of seats on standing committees grew from 203 to 244 in the Senate and from 484 to 771 in the House.

The Politics of Major Change in the Committee System

Any change in the committee structure of either house inevitably involves a variety of political and substantive considerations. These considerations are more numerous when the House or Senate is looking at its total committee structure and pondering changes. Each house has undertaken such a major investigation and decision process in recent years. In general, the same pattern was followed in the two instances—fairly substantial changes were proposed by the panel that had studied the situation most closely and the full chamber finally made some changes, but only after those most threatening to the entrenched interests of incumbent members had been removed.

In 1973 the House created a Select Committee on Committees to study the House committee structure and to make recommendations. The Committee made extensive studies and held extensive hearings. Members of the House, lobbyists, academics, and a capable staff were all involved. The report of the Committee proposed some substantial changes. But then members whose own personal position or, in some instances, whose policy position seemed threatened mobilized to oppose a number of specifics in the plan. Lobbyists for various organizations and interests that felt that change would jeopardize their close and productive relationships with existing committees also began to push against specific parts of the bill. Consequently, a much milder version of change was adopted by the House in October, 1974.[5]

The House experience was repeated in the Senate in 1976–77. A Select Committee to Study the Senate Committee System was created in 1976. It reported an ambitious plan of reorganization, although not as ambitious as the one proposed in the House. But both in the Rules Committee and on the Senate floor the changes were moderated, largely because of the opposition of senators who would lose

---

5. For a summary of House action see "Hansen Reorganization Plan Adopted," *Congressional Quarterly Weekly Report* (October 12, 1974): 2896–2898. For a thorough description and analysis of the whole process see Roger H. Davidson and Walter J. Oleszek, *Congress Against Itself* (Bloomington: Indiana University Press, 1977).

important positions and jurisdiction (including chairpersons) and because of the opposition of lobbyists who felt threatened. Some shifts of jurisdictions and organizations were made. Limits were also placed on the number of assignments any individual could receive—memberships on three committees and eight subcommittees and chairmanships of no more than three committees and subcommittees beginning in 1979.[6]

The general lesson from these experiences is that reorganization is difficult to accomplish because, by definition, members of the House and Senate as well as important outside interest groups have a stake in maintaining existing arrangements. They are comfortable with them and are afraid of the unknown. It should also be observed, however, that the outside interests are likely to reassert and reestablish themselves in alliance with key members of Congress almost no matter what jurisdictional and organizational structure is adopted.

COMMITTEE ASSIGNMENTS

Each of the four parties in Congress (House Democrats, House Republicans, Senate Democrats, and Senate Republicans) uses slightly different methods for assigning members to vacancies in standing committees.[7]

The House Democrats used the Democratic members of the Ways and Means Committee to recommend assignments to the Democratic caucus from 1911 through 1974. Beginning in 1975, this recommending power was transferred to the Steering and Policy Committee. The caucus possesses the final authority to accept or reject the recommendations. Acceptance of the full slate of assignments is usually virtually automatic, with the possible exception of a few nominations to chairmanships. The Speaker appoints all Democratic members of the Rules Committee.

The House Republicans have a special committee on committees comprised of a member from every state having at least one Republican. The actual work of making assignments, however, is done by

---

6. For a good summary of the Senate experience see Thomas P. Southwick, "Senate Approves Committee Changes," *Congressional Quarterly Weekly Report* (February 12, 1977): 279–284.

7. Still the best treatment of committee assignments in the House is Nicholas A. Masters, "Committee Assignments in the House of Representatives," *American Political Science Review* 55 (1961): 345–357. See also "Politics of House Committees: The Path to Power," in *Congressional Quarterly Weekly Report* (February 10, 1973): 279–283; and David W. Rohde and Kenneth A. Shepsle, "Democratic Committee Assignments in the House of Representatives: Strategic Aspects of a Social Choice Process," *American Political Science Review* 67 (1973): 889–905.

an executive committee that always includes representatives of the states with the largest Republican delegations (New York, California, Ohio, Pennsylvania, Michigan, and Illinois). Since voting is on the basis of the number of Republicans from a state, those states with the most Republicans dominate the process. The House Republican Policy Committee approves the nominations. The Republican Conference approves only the ranking minority members.

The Senate Democrats have a steering committee appointed by the floor leader that makes the Democratic appointments. The steering committee is comprised of the senior members of the party (many of them committee chairmen); once on the committee they are automatically reappointed. The decisions of this committee are limited by the unwritten rule that all Democrats should have one choice assignment before any Democrat is given two (this is called the "Johnson rule" because it was first implemented in the early 1950s when Lyndon Johnson was the Democratic floor leader). The Democratic Conference must approve the Steering Committee nominations.

The Senate Republicans have a committee on committees that makes initial assignments on the basis of seniority. They are limited, however, by a rule adopted by the Republicans in 1965 that no Republican can hold seats on more than one of the four most desired committees (Appropriations, Armed Services, Finance, and Foreign Relations) before every Republican senator at least has a chance to refuse such a seat. The Republican Conference does not approve nominations.

Many criteria are used in making initial assignments to committees. These include seniority, region, ideology, preferences of the indivdual members, and—at least in some cases—religion and race. In general, all of the parties use the same mix of criteria. Additional factors that affect committee assignments include the expressed preferences of individuals such as party leaders, senior committee members, and, occasionally, representatives of interest groups. In general, the assigning authorities are amenable to the argument that a particular assignment will help a member retain his seat in forthcoming elections. This is the most commonly used criterion and the most persuasive argument a member can make.

But the criteria change from year to year, from committee to committee, and from member to member. A veteran member of the House who became Majority Leader in 1977, Jim Wright (D-Tex.), provides a nice summary:

> Being appointed to the committee of one's choice is a matter of application and luck. The freshman member should certainly make

his wishes known to the Speaker (if he is of the same political faith) and the leaders of his party in the House in either event. He also should try to line up as much support as he can muster among the colleagues of his own state delegation.

Sometimes, however, even the most careful plans will not avail an aspirant. Naturally, if a freshman is to be successful in his quest there must be a vacancy on the desired committee, and generally there must be no one with seniority from his cwn geographic zone and in his own political party who wants this particular assignment. . . .

But other considerations might prevail. During President Eisenhower's Administration, for instance, the conservative bloc of the Republican Party in the House controlled the party leadership. They would not permit any Republican member to be appointed to the powerful Ways and Means Committee unless he *opposed* Eisenhower's liberal position on reciprocal trade. On the other hand, while Sam Rayburn held sway as Speaker, no Democrat was chosen to this committee unless he agreed to *support* the reciprocal trade program.[8]

Members seek to achieve one or more of three general goals as they seek committee assignments: to increase their influence on some policy area that interests them, to increase their chances of re-election, or to increase their influence in the House or Senate. Interviews with freshmen in the Ninety-second Congress (1971–72) showed most of them interested either in policy or in re-election (or in both) as they sought their first assignments.[10]

At different periods in congressional history, policy preferences and ideological biases get built into assignment patterns, although the biases are likely to change over time. For example, for many years both parties in the Senate assigned their more conservative members to the Finance Committee. Until recently Senate Democrats also tended to put an unusually large proportion of conservatives on the Appropriations, Armed Services, and Judiciary Committees.[11] A systematic study of the progress of senators through shifting committee assignments supports the claim that for the period from 1947 through 1963, Senate Democrats regularly discriminated against liberal sena-

8. Jim Wright, *You and Your Congressman* (New York: Coward-McCann, 1965): 131.

9. Richard F. Fenno, Jr., *Congressmen in Committees* (Boston: Little, Brown, 1973).

10. Charles S. Bullock, III, "Motivations for U.S. Congressional Committee Preferences: Freshmen of the 92nd Congress," *Legislative Studies Quarterly* 1 (1976): 201–212.

11. See Randall B. Ripley, *Power in the Senate* (New York: St. Martin's, 1969): Chapter 3.

tors who were eager to change the rules of the Senate.[12] In the House, by contrast, a study of assignments in the early 1960s suggested that the more liberal Democrats were more likely to get their preferences.[13] In the House Republican party the more conservative members generally do better.

Since both the House and Senate have equally elaborate committee and subcommittee structures it is inevitable that senators will have more assignments than representatives (unless the size of Senate committees were kept very small). In the Ninety-third Congress (1973–1974) each member of the House had an average of 1.6 assignments to standing committees and 3.5 subcommittee assignments. Every senator, however, had an average of 2.6 standing committee assignments and 9.7 subcommittee assignments.[14]

The Impact of Seniority

No assignment system is likely to be neutral or unbiased. Seniority as a primary consideration in committee assignments in the United States Congress is no exception. For many years it was argued that seniority promoted the interests of conservatives, especially southern Democrats. Even that claim was exaggerated, although there was some truth to it.[15]

Even during the period in which southerners, mostly conservatives, did seem to be unusually important in Congress—especially the Senate —seniority was only one factor that promoted and sustained their importance. By 1977 southern power, even in the Senate, had declined substantially. And, of course, not all southern Democrats are conservatives. Table 5–5 summarizes the shifting fortunes of southern power in the Senate by comparing the percentage of all Democratic senators who are southerners to the percentage of all chairmanships of both full committees and subcommittees held by southerners. Southern overrepresentation reached its peak in the late 1950s and early 1960s and has been declining ever since.

A recent study shows that in the late 1970s and on into the 1980s

12. Wayne R. Swanson, "Committee Assignments and the Nonconformist Legislator: Democrats in the U.S. Senate," *Midwest Journal of Politics* 13 (1969): 84–94.

13. See Randall B. Ripley, *Party Leaders in the House of Representatives* (Washington, D.C.: Brookings, 1967): 60.

14. The figures come from Herbert B. Asher, "Committees and the Norm of Specialization," *Annals of the American Academy of Political and Social Science* (January, 1974): 68.

15. See Barbara Hinckley, *The Seniority System in Congress* (Bloomington: Indiana University Press, 1971).

the use of seniority as a criterion for advancement on committees toward chairmanships will actually favor northern Democrats and liberals.[16] Several studies also show that freshmen members of the House have been getting progressively better assignments in recent years.[17] There are legitimate questions about placing reliance on seniority as a criterion for assignment and especially for advancement to committee chairmanships, but there is certainly nothing automatic in its use that favors either liberals or conservatives. Electoral results and career patterns in the House and Senate also play independent roles in determining the nature of the bias that appears in committee assignments and is often mistakenly attributed to seniority alone. Perhaps the main impact of using seniority as a primary criterion for choosing chairpersons is that they are notably older than the rest of the members, on the average. But there is no empirical support for the proposition that the older members are necessarily more conservative.

Table 5–5
Southern Democratic Strength in the Senate, 1941–1977

Congress (Year)	Percentage of Southerners [a] among:		
	All Democratic Senators	Committee Chairpersons	Subcommittee Chairpersons [b]
77th (1941)	33	62	—
81st (1949)	41	40	—
85th (1957)	45	53	45
89th (1965)	29	62	35
93rd (1973)	26	47	26
95th (1977)	27	40	27

[a] Southerners are defined as senators coming from the eleven states of the Confederacy.

[b] Accurate data on subcommittee chairmanships are difficult to obtain before 1955.

Source: Compiled from raw data in Congressional Directory *for each year for the first two columns and from raw data in* Congressional Quarterly *for the third column.*

16. Norman J. Ornstein and David W. Rohde, "Seniority and Future Power in Congress," in Norman J. Ornstein (ed.), *Congress in Change* (New York: Praeger, 1975).

17. Irwin N. Gertzog, "The Routinization of Committee Assignments in the U.S. House of Representatives," *American Journal of Political Science* 20 (1976): 693–712; and David N. Farnsworth and John E. Stanga, Jr., "Seniority, Reform and Democratic Committee Assignments in the House of Representatives," *Policy Studies Journal* 5 (1977): 431–436.

The Attractiveness of Committees

Committees vary in their attractiveness to the members of the House and Senate. Some committees—such as Appropriations, Ways and Means, or Finance—offer their members increased visibility as legislators. Some committees—such as Public Works and Transportation or Agriculture—enable the members to do things for their constituents that they might not otherwise be in a position to do; this enhances the standing of the member at home and may well increase the safety of his or her seat at election time. Some committees—such as Foreign Relations, International Relations, Education and Labor, or Human Resources—allow the members to maximize their ability to influence national policy in an area of special interest to them.

Compilations are done from time to time of patterns of transfers between committees. These patterns give a good guide to the attractiveness of the various committees because members are not likely to seek a transfer except when they value a different committee more highly. The patterns of "prestige" or attractiveness are quite stable. In the House the most attractive committees are Rules, Ways and Means, Appropriations, and Armed Services. In the Senate the most attractive committees are Foreign Relations, Finance, Appropriations, Judiciary, and Armed Services.[18]

In large part the most attractive committees are the most important committees in terms of policy. This suggests that individual members take seriously their desire to influence policy. Finance, Ways and Means, Armed Services, and Appropriations also offer a number of opportunities to perform major services for constituents and for fellow members in terms of such items as special tax provisions, protection of defense installations against closing, and appropriation of funds for pet projects.

THE INTERNAL OPERATIONS OF COMMITTEES

The standing committees of the House and Senate vary in the way they work. Both houses have increasingly delegated substantive decision-making power to subcommittees, although there are variations among individual committees. Both houses now have limits on the

---

18. For rankings in both houses from 1949 through 1968 see George Goodwin, Jr., *The Little Legislatures* (Amherst: University of Massachusetts Press, 1970). For additional material on the House see Charles S. Bullock, III, "Committee Transfers in the United States House of Representatives," *Journal of Politics* 35 (1973): 85–120; and Malcolm E. Jewell and Chu Chi-hung, "Membership Movement and Committee Attractiveness in the U.S. House of Representatives, 1963–1971," *American Journal of Political Science* 18 (1974): 433–441.

power of chairpersons, although again those limits are different on different committees and some chairpersons are still extremely powerful. Some committees seek internal integration that presumably enhances their autonomy and the chances that their policy decisions will go unchanged in the full House and Senate and in conference committees. Others are much more oblivious to any necessity for a high degree of integration. Some virtually eschew partisanship as they pursue agreement on policy statements and actions. Others not only carry general party disagreements into committee deliberations but also magnify and intensify them. Some, in effect, prescribe a period of apprenticeship for junior members. Others admit junior members to full participation immediately. No committee is immune to changes in the way it works.

Subcommittees [19]

Most congressional committees use subcommittees to process their work. The natural tendency is for the subcommittees to move toward autonomy and for the full committees to ratify the work of the subcommittees almost automatically.

In general, the substantive work of Congress gets done largely in subcommittees. This fact maximizes the impact of individual members (particularly the senior members of the subcommittees) on policy but it also opens the committee system to the special representations of the bureaucracy and interest groups. Every bureau and every interest group can seek out "its subcommittee," and if they can befriend the chairman and perhaps the ranking minority member they can help control federal policy in areas that interest them. In such a situation it is hard to say which persons in a triangular arrangement have the most influence: the senator or representative or the bureau chief or the lobbyist (or even, particularly in the Senate, a staff person for the subcommittee).

Power devolved to subcommittees in the 1960s in the Senate in most cases. This created a situation in which virtually all Senators were either the chairperson or ranking minority member of at least one

19. On various aspects of subcommittee functioning see Lawrence C. Dodd and Bruce I. Oppenheimer, "The House in Transition," in Dodd and Oppenheimer (eds.), *Congress Reconsidered* (New York: Praeger, 1977): 21–53; Goodwin, *The Little Legislatures:* 45–63; Charles O. Jones, "The Role of the Congressional Subcommittee," *Midwest Journal of Political Science* 6 (1962): 327–344; Norman J. Ornstein, "Causes and Consequences of Congressional Change: Subcommittee Reforms in the House of Representatives, 1970–73," in Ornstein (ed.), *Congress in Change* (New York: Praeger, 1975): 88–114; and Ripley, *Power in the Senate:* Chapters 3, 6, and 7.

subcommittee—and many served in those capacities on several sub-committees. Although the committee reorganization in the Senate in 1977 reduced the number of subcommittees to 100, that still left more than enough for every senator to be a critical person in one or more substantive areas. Given the relatively small number of senators, this situation also left staff members as critical persons in the decision-making on many subcommittees. Thus even the most junior senators are able to develop legislative influence and this, in turn, is likely to make them relatively content with the way in which the Senate conducts its substantive business.

Subcommittees have become much more important in the House in the 1970s. Before the last decade they were consistently dominant only on the Appropriations Committee. Now they have become the central fact of legislative life in the House on virtually all committees. Between 1955 and 1977 the number of subcommittees has grown from 83 to 137. Because of the new rules requiring the key positions (chairmanships and ranking minority member positions) to be spread among different members, in 1977 close to half of the Democrats and most of the Republicans held such a position. Influence over subcommittee business is still not as widespread as in the Senate and, given the relative size of the two bodies, probably will never become so. But power is much more widespread in the House than even five or ten years ago.

A number of developments in the 1970s have produced the present situation.[20] First, in 1971 the House Democrats adopted the rule that no member can be chairperson of more than one subcommittee. Prior to that time a number of senior members had dominated the sub-committee chairmanships.

Second, the Democratic caucus adopted a subcommittee "bill of rights" in 1973. This bill of rights protected subcommittees from domination by the chairperson of the full committee. Specifically, the Democratic membership on each full committee (a mini-caucus) was given power to select the chairpersons of subcommittees by vote. In the last few years several sitting subcommittee chairmen have been replaced by these mini-caucus votes, although seniority on the full committee continues to be the most important criterion for selection as a chairperson.[21] The bill of rights also provided that subcommit-

---

20. What follows is based on Bruce F. Freed, "House Reforms Enhance Subcommittees' Power," *Congressional Quarterly Weekly Report* (November 8, 1975): 2407–2412, especially 2408.

21. See Thomas R. Wolanin, "Committee Seniority and the Choice of House Sub-committee Chairmen: 80th–91st Congresses," *Journal of Politics* 36 (1974): 687–702; and Jack A. Goldstone, "Subcommittee Chairmanships in the House of Representatives," *American Political Science Review* 69 (1975): 970–971.

tees had to have fixed jurisdictions; that they were authorized to meet without approval of the chairperson of the full committee; that they would have adequate budgets under their own control; that they would have staff directly responsible to the subcommittee chairperson and ranking minority member; and that all members of the full committee would have a right to at least one "choice" subcommittee assignment. By these moves chairpersons of the full committees were deprived of a number of powers some of them had been able to use in past years to keep subcommittees tightly under their own control.

Third, all full committees with more than twenty members except the Budget Committee must establish at least four subcommittees. Only three committees had fewer than twenty members in 1977. This reform was initially aimed at the Ways and Means Committee, in which Chairman Wilbur Mills had maintained a high degree of control by having no subcommittees, but it also prevents the emergence of any similar situation in the future.

Fourth, all House committees are now required to have written rules of procedure. These offer additional guarantees for individual members and for subcommittees that decisions will not be made in such a way as to thwart the will of the majority, particularly the majority of subcommittees.

Fifth, in December, 1974, the Democratic caucus specified that no member of a committee could hold more than two subcommittee memberships. This was aimed particularly at dispersing power on the Appropriations Committee.

Sixth, beginning in 1975 all chairpersons on the Appropriations Committee had to win approval of the full Democratic caucus. This resulted in the deposing of one chairperson in 1977, when the caucus removed Robert Sikes of Florida from an appropriations subcommittee chairmanship for what the majority considered to be ethical violations.

In short, Woodrow Wilson's aphorism that "our form of government" is "a government by the chairmen of the Standing Committees of Congress" might best be changed to "a government by subcommittees of Congress." [22]

Committee Chairpersons

The powers of committee chairpersons have been reduced in recent years, and they are certainly not the unfettered autocrats sometimes portrayed in the popular press. They remain, however, critical in-

---

22. Woodrow Wilson, *Congressional Government* (New York: Meridian, 1956): 82.

dividuals in shaping the substantive impact of Congress on legislation. In general, the chairperson of a committee still has more influence than anyone else on the committee in terms of shaping its policy decisions. They command this kind of influence either because they successfully exert independent judgment supported by the use of the resources they possess or because they are faithfully reflecting the policy preferences of a number of committee members.

For well over a century in the Senate, committee chairpersons have almost all been chosen on the basis of their seniority in a given committee, as distinguished from their seniority in the Senate as a whole. The person in the majority party who has longest service on a committee at the beginning of any given Congress is designated as chairperson; everyone below him in committee seniority is ranked accordingly for purposes of succession and, in some committees, for purposes of receiving subcommittee chairmanships. The minority party adopted the same pattern for choosing ranking minority members. The Civil War created some delay in the final consolidation of the seniority system but by the mid-1870s it was well established. Violations have occurred since but they have been rare.

In 1973 the Senate Republicans decided to make their ranking minority positions elective within the Republican delegation on each committee. This policy has not yet resulted in any violations of seniority. The most senior members are likely to continue to hold the ranking positions, even if formal "elections" are held. But at least the change gives the Republican senators on individual committees a weapon to use if they are actually confronted with an incompetent, senile, gravely ill, or tyrannical ranking member.

In 1975 the Senate Democrats adopted a rule that makes committee chairpersons subject to secret ballot vote in the Conference if one-fifth of the membership requests it. This has not yet resulted in any violations of seniority but is certainly a check on arbitrary behavior by chairpersons.

The principle of seniority was used in the House by both parties for selection of committee chairpersons with only a few exceptions from about the time of World War I until the mid-1970s. Then in the mid-1970s the Democrats made chairmanships elective within the Democratic caucus. This procedure resulted in no violations of seniority in 1973 and 1977 but in 1975 it resulted in three sitting chairmen being deposed. Seniority is still the single most important criterion used in the House in selecting chairpersons, but as the bloodletting in 1975 demonstrates, it is no longer the only criterion.

Despite limits on the power of chairpersons—limits that have been particularly well developed in the House in recent years in connection with the promotion of subcommittee influence—a skillful chairperson can parlay both his remaining powers and his knowledge of procedures and substantive matters into considerable influence. There is still considerable respect for the powers of chairpersons in both houses, in part because other members hope to rise to chairmanships themselves and do not want to inherit empty shells. Deference to a chairperson is often based on his genuine expert knowledge in the areas within the jurisdiction of a committee. A knowledgeable chairperson can usually make a strong case for the position he favors on legislation and can persuade a large proportion of the members to follow his lead.

Even before the formal rules changes adopted in the House in the last few years, committees faced with a chairperson they felt was unfair had ways of limiting his powers and influence. Chairpersons who consistently antagonized committee members with tyrannical or erratic behavior sometimes found themselves severely hemmed in by unwelcome new rules—an event that has occurred in recent years in the House Committees on Education and Labor, Post Office and Civil Service, and Government Operations.

In 1966 the House Education and Labor Committee reported a major antipoverty bill (a series of amendments to the 1964 Economic Opportunity Act) on June 1. The Chairman of the Committee, Adam Clayton Powell, did not schedule the bill for floor action until September 26 and even suggested that it might not come to the floor until after the November elections. The great majority of the committee members—particularly his fellow Democrats—viewed this as the last straw in what they considered a history of irresponsible behavior on Powell's part since assuming the chairmanship of the committee. They were particularly critical of his high rate of absenteeism, and made allegations about arbitrary hiring and firing of committee staff, misusing committee funds, and simply refusing to report legislation favored by the committee. As a result the committee—by a vote of twenty-seven to one with three abstentions—adopted new rules for the committee that no longer left Powell in a position to thwart the majority of the committee. Among other things these rules set a regular weekly meetings that could be held even without the chairman, created six standing subcommittees not under the chairman's control, divided control of staff between the majority members as a unit, the minority members as a unit, and the subcommittees, guaranteed that bills approved by the committee would be reported to the floor, guaranteed that bills coming into the committee would be referred to a subcommittee, required reports on the use of committee funds, and specified that subcommittee members should sit on conference committees considering bills that had come from their particular sub-committee.

In 1973 and 1974 the Ways and Means Committee underwent major changes. Even before the departure of Wilbur Mills from the chairmanship he had held for seventeen years, these changes had begun. Mills' dominance of the committee in favor of moderate policy positions was threatened. The House rejected a major Ways and Means compromise engineered by Mills involving cost-of-living increases in social security payments. A reform adopted by the Democratic caucus left room for opening committee bills to floor amendment, whereas previously most Ways and Means bills had been granted a "closed rule" (one that allowed no amendments on the floor of the House). The Republicans became less willing to cooperate with Mills, and liberal Democrats seemed more demanding on issues such as tax reform and health insurance.

Then in October, 1974, the House required Ways and Means to establish subcommittees in the next Congress after defeating an effort to remove considerable jurisdiction from the Committee. And in December, 1974, the Democratic caucus removed committee assignment powers from the Democratic members of Ways and Means and increased the size of the committee from twenty-five to thirty-seven as a prelude to adding a number of new liberal Democrats in early 1975 when the Ninety-fourth Congress convened.

In the House, subcommittee power has become the rule of the day. The situation is more variable in the Senate. Some committees are still dominated by very powerful chairmen and the members have not insisted on subcommittee government.

The powers of Senate committee chairpersons and ranking minority members were succinctly summarized by Walter Oleszek, a Congressional Research Service staff member:

> Committee chairmen are important figures because they can call meetings and establish agendas, appoint staff members, refer bills to one rather than another subcommittee, retain bills or oversight hearings in full committee rather than refer them to a subcommittee, designate conferees, act as floor managers, control committee funds, control committee rooms, chair hearings and executive sessions, and, depending on committee rules, create subcommittees and establish their party ratios.
>
> Ranking minority members are also important and influential figures on committees. Among their powers are nominating conferees; hiring and discharging minority staff; fixing minority staff salary rates; assisting in scheduling hearings both in Washington, D.C. and

outside; authorizing the interrogation of witnesses by professional staff; sitting ex officio on all subcommittees; appointing minority members to subcommittees; and influencing the appointment of special or ad hoc subcommittees.[23]

House chairpersons have lost many of the powers still residing in the hands of Senate chairpersons. They still have some formal powers, however, including control over the staff of the full committee and considerable control over agendas and the scheduling of meetings. Above all, if they have knowledge of their subject matter, they can still be very important figures in committee deliberations.[24]

The symbolism of either ousting or severely restricting the power of a chairperson is important. And, no doubt, there are values to be served by "democratizing" committee procedure. But simply changing or restricting chairpersons is not likely to change the substantive output of a committee by itself. Other changes are necessary. For example, one study of the three House committees whose chairmen were deposed in 1975—Armed Services, Agriculture, and Banking and Currency—shows that the committees proceeded about the same in the following year.[25] But when other factors with which a committee must deal are also changing, then the change of chairpersons can be an additional, important factor producing change in its policy performance.

Perhaps the best example of a powerful chairman in the late 1970s is Senator Russell B. Long (D-La.) of the Senate Finance Committee.[26] Long dominates his committee, which also happens to be a committee with a vast and important jurisdiction, including taxes, welfare, social security, medicare, health insurance, and foreign trade.

Long retains all important business for the full committee; there is no subcommittee autonomy on Senate Finance. And the members of the Committee support him in his desire to keep a centralized committee, apparently feeling that such a procedure enhances their own influence too.

In the years of his chairmanship (since 1966) he has used his powers to consolidate his influence. He has been particularly adept at expanding the staff of the committee in such a way as to buttress

23. Walter Oleszek, "Overview of the Senate Committee System," in Commission on the Operation of the Senate, *Committees and Senate Procedures* (Washington: U.S. Government Printing Office, 1977): 15.

24. On the changed position of House chairpersons see Dodd and Oppenheimer, "The House in Transition," 37–40.

25. John Berg, "Reforming Seniority in the House of Representatives: Did It Make Any Difference?," *Policy Studies Journal* 5 (1977): 437–443.

26. Alan Ehrenhalt, "Senate Finance: The Fiefdom of Russell Long," *Congressional Quarterly Weekly Report* (September 10, 1977): 1905–1915.

positions he favors. He knows the substantive business of the committee very well and is a tireless exponent of his positions in debate and conversation, but he also knows when to compromise and is not given to pushing hopeless crusades. Perhaps above all, he also knows how to trade important favors, particularly amendments to the tax code, for support for his positions.

In the trading process Long is usually quite open about what he is doing. The committee now holds all of its meetings in the open and keeps transcripts of the proceedings, but that has not affected the bargains that are struck. An exchange in a 1975 committee meeting typifies the kind of openness about bargaining that characterizes Long's style. Another member of the Committee, Gaylord Nelson (D-Wis.) said during a session at which a bill was undergoing final specific changes in language, "I understand that in my absence, we passed the tax breaks for railroads, but omitted railroad-over-water ferries—such as the one in Wisconsin." Long replied, "I'll be happy to give you that one without need of further discussion, but I expect you in exchange to vote for this next tax credit we're about to discuss."

Integration

Integration refers to how well the parts of a committee (that is, the individuals and, to a lesser extent, the subcommittees) mesh as the committee operates from day to day. The classic example of a highly integrated committee is the House Appropriations Committee.[27] Individuals who are recruited for this committee are not passionate partisans and must maintain an aura of "responsibility" about them. These qualities are sought to perpetuate the dominant norms about the job of the committee: to cut the federal budget and guard the treasury. In general, committee members believe—regardless of party—that the proposals coming from the executive branch almost always contain some fat. Their job is to trim that fat while providing enough money to maintain federal programs, particularly those vital to constituents, at adequate levels. Agencies that receive the largest percentage of their requests from the committee are likely to be those with non-controversial tasks, stable workloads, and leaders held in high esteem by the committee. Agencies involved in controversy, with shifting workloads, and leaders held in low esteem by committee members are unlikely to fare very well. Agencies with strong support from external

---

27. Richard F. Fenno, Jr., "The House Appropriations Committee as a Political System: The Problem of Integration," *American Political Science Review* 56 1962): 310–324; and Fenno, *The Power of the Purse* (Boston: Little, Brown, 1966).

clientele groups are likely to grow more rapidly from year to year than agencies without clientele groups or with weak, apathetic, or hostile groups. Bureaus such as the Forest Service, Office of Education, and Soil Conservation Service are in a particularly strong situation because they have strong support from within and without the committee simultaneously. At the other extreme, agencies such as the Bureau of Mines, the Bureau of Reclamation, and the Census Bureau, have had neither external nor committee support.

Virtually all of the work of the committee is conducted in the appropriations subcommittees, and the full committee routinely accepts nearly all of their budget decisions. This means that individual members specialize in one or two specific areas and are expected to become experts on whom the rest of the committee (and the House) can rely for sound judgments. The prime integrating factors in this committee seem to be the mutual deference paid to one another by the various subcommittees and the widely shared vision of the central purpose of the committee.

Another example of a highly integrated committee was the House Committee on Ways and Means until 1975.[28] The integrating mechanisms of this committee were different from those of the Appropriations Committee. The committee is not united substantively: the tax matters (the tax code, social security and medicare, welfare, the tariff) that the committee handles have long had major partisan aspects that divide members both of the committee and of the House. On the other hand, the committee members do seem to be agreed that their task is to legislate so well and so thoroughly that their work will be accepted virtually without question by the House and, hopefully, by the Senate Finance Committee and the whole Senate, too. The chairman of the committee from 1958 through 1974, Wilbur Mills of Arkansas, was adept at managing the substantive policy tensions that are part of his committee's province. He showed great skill in emphasizing points of agreement and minimizing points of disagreement while treating all participants fairly.[29]

A classic example of Mills at work occurred in 1965 on the question of establishing a federal program supporting medical care for the aged (medicare). The administration was supporting a bill that was funded through a payroll tax but that provided mainly hospitalization costs

28. John F. Manley, "The House Committee on Ways and Means: Conflict Management in a Congressional Committee," *American Political Science Review* 59 (1965): 927–939. See also, Manley, *The Politics of Finance* (Boston, Little, Brown, 1970).

29. See Manley, "Wilbur D. Mills: A Study in Congressional Influence," *American Political Science Review* 63 (1969): 442–464.

and left other medical expenses largely uncovered. The ranking Republican on the committee had introduced a bill with a more generous benefits package but funded on the basis of voluntary enrollment supplemented by money from general federal revenues. After listening and helping guide the debate between the contending forces, Mills cleverly proposed a compromise that adopted the more generous benefits package of the Republican bill but retained the compulsory membership-payroll tax feature of the Democratic bill. Thus he left virtually all members of the committee with some reason for satisfaction and yet was instrumental in creating a program that was more far-reaching than anyone thought could come out of the Ways and Means Committee.

Yet another pattern of integration is evident in the House Committee on Agriculture.[30] The main work of the committee is conducted by subcommittees dealing with specific crops; the principal integrating factor is the mutual deference of these subcommittees to one another. The growers of all crops—particularly those important to the southern Democrats who have dominated the committee's majority party contingent for a number of years (for example, cotton and tobacco)—receive good treatment in the subcommittees; the full committee ratifies subcommittee decisions. When there are partisan issues before the committee that are not tied to specific crops, however, integration is likely to be diminished as the demands of partisanship take over. The basic question of level of parity (the percent of a "fair market price" supported by governmental subsidy) has often been such a partisan issue.

The House Committee on Education and Labor provides an example of a committee not preoccupied with integration, probably because it would be virtually impossible to achieve.[31] The committee handles issues that not only provoke partisan differences (labor-management relations and federal aid to education, for example) but that also raise thorny racial and religious questions (federal aid to parochial schools, federal programs to force unions to open their ranks to black members). There is no agreement on the substance of what the committee should do (as in the case of Appropriations). There is the use of subcommittees but no mutual deference among them (as in the case of Appropriations and Agriculture). There have been no chairmen particularly skillful in muting conflict on partisan issues (as in

---

30. Charles O. Jones, "Representation in Congress: The Case of the House Agriculture Committee," *American Political Science Review* 55 (1961): 358–367.
31. Frank J. Munger and Richard F. Fenno, Jr., *National Politics and Federal Aid to Education* (Syracuse: Syracuse University Press, 1962).

the case of Ways and Means). And there has not even been agreement that the committee should aim for a product that will be accepted almost automatically by the House. Rather the expectation seems to be that the debate over the divisive aspects of the committee's work will continue on the floor and in the Senate and in conference committees.

Committee integration in the Senate presents a different picture from the House. The average size of Senate committees is smaller and the average senator has many more committee assignments. Whereas a House member becomes expert in a particular field and develops a personal stake in the most minute of outcomes, the individual senator develops a personal stake in only a few scattered items. He is much more reliant on staff than is the House member. Mutual deference to subcommittee decisions is widely accepted in the Senate as a norm, and is not a question that each individual committee must decide.

One study of Senate committee integration found that integration (measured by agreement of committee members in roll call voting on the floor) was related to similarity of members' constituencies (measured by income inequality) and to members' seniority in the Senate.[32] Committees whose members were relatively junior and who represented rather similar states were more highly integrated than committees whose members were more senior and represented states that differed. When integration was related to the members' success in getting their own bills reported from their committees, it was found that members on more integrated committees had greater success than members on less integrated committees. Pork barrel committees (those dealing primarily with tangible physical benefits—"pork"—for constituencies) were an exception to this finding.

What are the results of committee integration? Well-integrated committees are more likely to be able to offer inducements to members of the House and Senate that will lead them to seek membership on such committees (for example, members may receive important psychological gratification from seeing their efforts in committee result in successful legislation). Well integrated committees (Ways and Means, Appropriations) are more desired than a partially integrated committee (Agriculture,) which is, in turn, more desired than a relatively

32. Lawrence C. Dodd, "Committee Integration in the Senate: A Comparative Analysis," *Journal of Politics* 34 (1972): 1135–1171. It should also be noted that there is no universal agreement on how to measure integration. And different measures may produce different results in terms of the presumed consequences of integration. See Lawrence C. Dodd and John C. Pierce, "Roll Call Measurement of Committee Integration: The Impact of Alternative Methods," *Polity* 7 (1975): 386–401.

unintegrated committee (Education and Labor). There seems to be no convincing evidence, however, that better integrated committees "succeed" more on the floor.

Partisanship

It has already been suggested that committees vary in terms of their partisanship.[33] Some, like House Education and Labor and Public Works, are unabashedly partisan. Others, like Ways and Means, exhibit a restrained form of partisanship. Others, like Appropriations, are virtually nonpartisan. In general, in the House, reduced partisanship makes integration more likely. In the Senate there is less evidence about the extent and impact of partisanship within committees. There is, however, clearly a range of behavior. The Senate Appropriations Committee, for example, generally operates on a nonpartisan basis.[34] In general, most Senate committees have a tradition of minimizing partisan considerations whenever possible. No committees always split along party lines but there are occasions—predictable on the basis of the issues at stake and personalities of the most important committee members—in which committees will proceed on a highly partisan basis. The attitude of the chairman toward partisan questions is an important factor explaining the relative presence or absence of partisanship. Only a few Senate chairmen act as aggressive partisans. Most seek accommodation with at least a sizable part of the contingent from the minority party.

Apprenticeship

Virtually all of the committees in both houses rely on division of labor and specialization on the part of members. Only a few committees do not use subcommittees and even on those committees individual members develop reputations for expertise on specific matters that come under committee purview. Specialization is necessary for committees to process their generally heavy workloads and to compete with the level of information that bureaucrats possess.

In some committees specialization involves a differentiation between senior and junior members of the committee or subcommittees. The senior members are viewed as the genuine specialists and are

---

33. On Education and Labor, Ways and Means, and Appropriations see the material cited in footnotes 27, 28, and 31, above. On Public Works see James T. Murphy, "Political Parties and the Porkbarrel: Party Conflict and Cooperation in House Public Works Committee Decision Making," *American Political Science Review* 68 (1974): 169–185.

34. See Stephen Horn, *Unused Power* (Washington, D.C.: Brookings, 1970).

given both formal and informal recognition (for example, more time for questioning during hearings) within the committee and on the floor of the chamber of which the committee is a part. On other committees junior members are accorded full rights virtually from the day they join the committee and they may, in fact, develop subject matter expertise that leads to deference very quickly. The apprenticeship norm is more prevalent in the House than in the Senate, although it has waned in many House Committees in recent years.

The Special Case of the House Rules Committee [35]

The House of Representatives operates under a much tighter set of rules on the floor than does the Senate. In large part this difference is dictated by the differing sizes of the two bodies. The much larger House must have a more orderly and restricted floor procedure in order to work effectively. To help govern the conditions under which specific measures are discussed on the House floor, the House has long used a committee on rules.

The Rules Committee plays a role both before and after House passage of legislation and also has some general powers. Before House passage its central role is to decide whether a bill can come to the House floor and, if so, the conditions under which it will be debated. In deciding whether it is ready for floor action at all, the Committee has the option of reviewing the work of the standing committee reporting the bill, sometimes in a fair amount of detail. If it decides to grant a "rule" (the provisions for floor debate) then it decides whether to leave the bill open to amendments, whether to restrict the number of amendments, or whether to eliminate the possibility of floor amendments altogether. It also sets the time limit for the debate, always splitting the time evenly between those in favor of the bill and those opposed to it.

After House passage of legislation the most important power of the Rules Committee is either to grant or to avoid a conference with the Senate over two differing versions of the bill. The Committee can also help revive House-passed bills that were defeated in the Senate. And

---

35. On the Rules Committee see James A. Robinson, *The House Rules Committee* (Indianapolis: Bobbs-Merrill, 1963); Douglas M. Fox, "The House Rules Committee's Agenda-Setting Function, 1961–1968," *Journal of Politics* 32 (1970): 440–443; Douglas M. Fox and Charles Clapp, "The House Rules Committee and the Programs of the Kennedy and Johnson Administration," *Midwest Journal of Political Science* 14 (1970): 667–672; Spark M. Matsunaga and Ping Chen, *Rulemakers of the House* (Urbana: University of Illinois Press, 1976); and Bruce I. Oppenheimer, "The Rules Committee: New Arm of Leadership in a Decentralized House," in Dodd and Oppenheimer, *Congress Reconsidered*: 96–116.

it can promote final passage of legislation by waiving points of order against conference reports that contain extraneous (non-germane) provisions.

There are provisions by which the full House can overrule the decisions of the Rules Committee either before or after floor action on a bill. But these procedures are difficult and complex and are rarely used successfully.

In addition to its legislative power, the Rules Committee also helps settle jurisdictional disputes between standing committees, it helps kill bills that in fact few members of the House want to be forced to vote on publicly, it approves the creation of select committees, it helps regulate travel by committee members, and it proposes general rules governing the House.

From its creation in the nineteenth century until 1910, the Rules Committee was virtually the personal vehicle of the Speaker. He appointed its members and served as its chairman. From 1910 until the late 1930s, although the Speaker could no longer sit on the committee and had lost the power of making committee appointments, the committee continued to be an instrument loyal to the wishes of the Speaker and other majority party leaders. The committee members from the majority party believed their main function was to assist the leaders of their party in the achievement of their legislative objectives.

From the late 1930s until the early 1960s, however, a group of conservative southern Democrats on the committee allied with the Republicans (who were all conservatives) to kill a number of liberal Democratic initiatives on domestic legislation. This legislative deadlock resulted in the committee becoming the focus of hot political division between liberals and conservatives. In 1961 the House agreed to increase the size of the committee temporarily in order to give the Democratic leaders a better chance of control of the committee; this increased size was made permanent in 1963.

Since 1963 the Rules Committee has basically ceased stifling major liberal Democratic initiatives in the House and has become a generally reliable arm of the leadership of the House Democratic party. Occasionally the committee will hold up House consideration of a major bill, as it did with a land-use bill and a mass transit conference report in 1974, but it would be surprising to find the committee opposing the wishes of the Speaker. To help solidify the formal hold of the Speaker on the committee, although he still cannot be a member, the House Democrats gave the Speaker the power to appoint all Democratic members of the committee (a safe majority of the committee) beginning in 1975. The Speaker thus has an important committee at his disposal to help him make complicated rulings and decisions so as to maximize both his control of the House in procedural terms and the success rate in terms of substantive legislation he favors.

CONFERENCE COMMITTEES [36]

When the House and Senate pass two different versions of the same bill, a conference committee is appointed to reconcile the differences and present a final product that both houses must ratify before sending the bill to the president for his signature. About 15 percent of all bills —including most of the important ones—go to conference. This committee is typically made up of a few senior members from the relevant standing committees and subcommittees in each house. Both parties are represented on the conference committee. The decision-making is not by majority vote of the whole committee but is by agreement of the majority of each of the two delegations. In the last few years many conferences have been open to the press and public.

Some committees routinely appoint the same members to all conferences. Other appoint the senior members of the relevant subcommittee (plus, usually, the chairman of the full committee and the ranking minority member). Some appoint all of the members of the relevant subcommittee. The senior members of the House and Senate clearly dominate the conference process, although in recent years there has been increasing participation by junior members.

It is expected that the delegations from each house will "fight to win" in any disagreements between the two contingents. However, it is also assumed that disagreements will have to be compromised so that a final bill can be produced that will be acceptable to both houses. Thus the conferees know that they will have to bargain and cannot expect to win all points in dispute. Sometimes, particularly in the Senate, committee leaders will accept amendments on the floor that they really do not favor so that later on, in conference, they will have trading chips that they can give away in order to save some provision they really care about.

---

36. On conference committees see David J. Vogler, *The Third House* (Evanston: Northwestern University Press, 1971); Gilbert Y. Steiner, *The Congressional Conference Committee* (Urbana: University of Illinois, 1951); Ada C. McCown, *The Congressional Conference Committee* (New York: Columbia University Press, 1927); Fenno, *The Power of the Purse:* chapter 12; Gerald S. Strom and Barry S. Rundquist, "A Revised Theory of Winning in House-Senate Conferences," *American Political Science Review* 71 (1977): 448–453; John Ferejohn, "Who Wins in Conference Committee?," *Journal of Politics* 37 (1975): 1033–1046; and "Reform Penetrates Conference Committees," *Congressional Quarterly Weekly Report* (February 8, 1975): 290–294.

Conference committees usually have considerable leeway in reaching final agreement. On some occasions they may even insert new legislative language in the bill, provisions contained in neither the House nor the Senate bill. On a few bills, however, they will receive specific instructions from their parent chamber on provisions on which they must insist.

Usually the conference reports are routinely accepted in both houses. Occasionally, one or both houses will reject a conference report; this necessitates a new conference committee (even though it may contain the same individuals). Conference committees almost always reach agreement; when they do not, the bill may die in conference; or the bill may be returned to the two houses in hopes that revisions will be adopted that allow the conference committee to agree. The few seemingly irreconcilable disagreements stem either from an issue on which basic House and Senate attitudes are poles apart (for example, the supersonic transport aircraft in 1970) or from personal rivalries between committees or individuals (for example, the 1962 dispute between the chairmen of the two appropriations committees that blocked a number of bills in conference for several months).

The evidence is solid that, since World War II, the Senate has dominated conference committees in terms of having more of its provisions adopted than those of the House. This represents a change from an earlier period between 1927 and 1949 when the House dominated conference committee results. But for the post-1949 period Richard Fenno found, for example, that when there were contested provisions in appropriations bills the Senate "won" almost two-thirds of the time in the sense of having the final figure closer to its own figure rather than being closer to the House figure. This pattern of dominance stretched across almost all issue areas. Fenno concluded that this pattern prevails because the Senate usually supports higher figures than the House and, late in the process, a presumption in favor of higher spending develops because all of the participants (interest groups, executive agencies, House and Senate members and the Senate Appropriations Committee and conferees) except the members of the House Appropriations Committee have reasons for wanting higher spending. All want to satisfy clients and constituents; only the House Committee members remain primarily concerned with the value of "economy in government" for its own sake.

In another study, based on five Congresses scattered between 1945 and 1966, David Vogler found that the pattern of Senate dominance extended to virtually all issue areas, although there were significant differences between the areas. Table 5–6 summarizes Vogler's findings.

That the Senate is more influential in conference committees does not signify that it dominates the congressional impact on public policy. On all appropriations bills and on many other bills the House acts first, which means that the Senate frequently is left in the position of amending the House bill and reacting to the agenda set by the House. One study of "who wins" in conference concluded that the chamber that acted second had an advantage in terms of agreement on specifics.[37] But, of course, this may be more than offset by the influence implied by acting first and thus setting much of the agenda for eventual compromise. Perhaps the most intriguing suggestion is that conferees find a way to accommodate the most strongly held preferences of both houses. This seems to be the case in such widely diverse fields as water resource development, foreign aid, and defense appropriations, for example.[38]

The vital role that can be played by conference committees is well illustrated by a conference in the summer of 1973. It worked for three months to produce a highway bill acceptable to a large number of competing interests and points of view—including those of mass transit proponents (primarily urban lobbyists and environmentalists) and pro-highway interests (road builders, concrete and asphalt makers, tire

Table 5–6

Percentage of Conferences Won by Senate by Policy Area, 1945–48, 1953–54, 1963–66.

Policy Area	Percentage of Senate Victories	Number of Conferences
Appropriations	78	119
National Security	67	21
Public Works and Resources	67	15
General Government	57	7
Agriculture	56	16
Education and Welfare	50	16
Foreign Policy	50	26
Taxes and Economic Policy	48	48

Source: David J. Vogler, The Third House (Northwestern University Press, 1971): 59.

38. See Ferejohn, "Who Wins in Conference Committee?"; Randall B. Ripley, "Congressional Government and Committee Management," *Public Policy* 14 (1965): 28–48; and Arnold Kanter, "Congress and the Defense Budget," *American Political Science Review* 66 (1972): 129–143.

37. Strom and Rundquist, "A Revised Theory of Winning in House-Senate Conferences."

makers, car makers, and oil companies). Congress had failed to enact a highway bill in 1972 because of some of the same disagreements. When the House and Senate passed new bills in the spring of 1973 the same potential for irreconcilable disagreement existed because of the major differences between the two bills. Also complicating the work of the conferees was the threat of a presidential veto if the total amount of money in the bill was too large or if the bill provided for the subsidization of operating expenses of mass transit systems.

The most critical point of disagreement between the two houses had to do with whether Highway Trust Fund money could be diverted for use in mass transit facilities. (The fund had been created in 1956 to finance the construction of the interstate highway system. By 1973 about $5 billion was spent each year from the fund, which is replenished by taxes on gasoline, trucks, and other highway "user" taxes.) The Senate position was that the fund could be used for mass transit and the House position was negative. The conferees, over a period of three months, worked out an ingenious compromise that gave everyone a partial victory. In 1974 the inviolability of the trust fund for non-highway uses would be formally preserved (by an elaborate paper shuffle proposed by Jim Wright (D-Tex.), the central figure among the House conferees), in 1975 some limited diversion of money would be allowed for buses only, and in 1976 the Senate position became operative: money could be diverted for rail rapid transit as well as for buses. But the language was also written in such a way as to encourage the formation of a separate mass transit trust fund by 1976 or at least the creation of a single trust fund covering a wide variety of transportation needs.

The conferees also placated the administration by removing anti-impoundment language (but endorsing a court decision forbidding this practice by which the administration can refuse to spend money appropriated by Congress for specific purposes), by keeping spending levels within acceptable limits (in some cases below both the House and Senate versions), and by removing the operating subsidies section from the act. Mass transit proponents and pro-highway interests were at least partially satisfied because both got large subsidies.

In short, the conferees took a situation that looked very bleak and —by writing legislative language that appeared in neither the House nor the Senate bill—produced a winning compromise in three months.[39]

---

39. For a much more detailed description of the highway conference committee see Michael J. Malbin, "Transportation Report/Long Deadlock Ends in Compromise Opening Highway Trust Fund for Mass Transit," *National Journal* (August 11, 1973): 1163–1171.

A conference in the summer of 1977 illustrates a case in which energetic and committed persons in both houses got part of what they wanted added to a new program, even though in many cases these parts appeared in only the House version of the bill *or* the Senate version of the bill before Conference. This conference was on a new set of programs aimed at providing training and employment for youth, particularly unemployed and disadvantaged youth. The various parts of the package were formally amendments to the Comprehensive Employment and Training Act of 1973. Most of the ideas represented in the final legislation were generated in Congress rather than receiving any central direction from the White House.

The details of the legislation are very complex and need not concern us here. What is evident from an analysis of the final bill, however, is that almost everyone with an idea got a good part of what he wanted. Table 5–7 summarizes the money authorized in the bill for five major programs and for four specific programs within those major categories. The most interesting cases are those four instances in which one chamber had provided no money and the idea (and money) originated in the other chamber. In each of those instances the "compromise" reached in conference was to include the program and to grant well more than half the money contained in the version of the

Table 5–7
Authorization of Programs under Youth Employment and
Demonstration Projects Act of 1977
(dollars in millions)

Major Program Segment	House Bill	Senate Bill	Conference
National Youth Conservation Corps	350.0	350.0	350.0
Youth Incentive Entitlement	287.5	0	172.5
Community Improvement Projects	0	250.0	172.5
Secretary's Discretionary Grants	215.6	225.0	143.7
State and Local Programs	646.9	675.0	661.2
Selected Specific Programs within Major Segments			
Native American and Farmworker set-aside	0	57.5	43.7
Governors' statewide program	32.4	90.0	57.5
Direct allocations to local governments	614.5	585.0	603.7
In-school youth program	0	135.0	132.8

Source: Adapted from Employment and Training Reporter 8 *(June 22, 1977): 538.*

bill passed in the initiating chamber. Thus 60 percent of the House-initiated youth incentive entitlement program remained, and 69 percent, 76 percent, and 98 percent of the three Senate-initiated programs (community improvement projects, native American and farmworker set-aside, and in-school youth program) remained.

THE IMPORTANCE OF COMMITTEES

Explaining the Content of Committee Decisions

There are at least three major factors that help to explain the policy statements and actions that emerge from different committees.[40] First, the goals of the members in seeking membership on a committee are important. Second, the specific environment within which the committee works has a decided impact. Third, the basic decision rules adopted (perhaps unknowingly) by the committee help predetermine the kinds of policy statements and actions emerging from a committee. Table 5–8 summarizes the influence of these factors for six committees in the House. By discussing the general shape of the policy decisions emerging from each of the committees in the 1960s and early 1970s, one can see these factors at work.

The Appropriations Committee (in practice, its subcommittees) generally cuts budgets for all programs proposed by the executive branch by almost a fixed percentage (rarely greater than 10 percent and usually considerably lower), but the basic reliance is still on the executive request—the executive branch sets the agenda. Thus the committee responds to the executive-led coalitions and follows its basic decision rules of reducing executive budget requests while still providing adequate funding for the programs administered by the executive branch. At the same time the power of the committee to cut at least some things selectively (and also the power to add some things selectively) helps the members realize their private goal of increasing their influence in the House.

The Ways and Means Committee passes carefully worked out versions of essentially majority party positions on the range of subjects within the committee's jurisdiction (principally trade, social security, and taxation). The craftsmanship that goes into the final versions is de-

---

40. The following discussion is based on Richard F. Fenno, Jr., *Congressmen in Committees* (Boston: Little, Brown, 1973). See also Barbara Hinckley, "Policy Content, Committee Membership, and Behavior," *American Journal of Political Science* 19 (1975): 543–557.

Table 5–8

Factors Related to Policy Decisions for Six House Committees

	Appropriations	Ways and Means	Foreign Affairs	Education and Labor	Post Office and Civil Service	Interior and Insular Affairs
Members' Goals	Maximize influence in the House	Maximize influence in the House	Maximize influence in a given policy area	Maximize influence in a given policy area	Maximize chances of re-election to the House	Maximize chances of re-election to the House
Environmental Constraints	Parent chamber coalitions led by executive agencies	Parent chamber coalitions led by partisan clusters in the House and by executive agencies	Coalitions led by executive agencies (mainly State Department and AID)	Coalitions led by partisan groups in and out of the House	Coalitions led by clients (civil service unions; and 2nd and 3rd class mailers)	Coalitions led by clients (many and diverse)
Basic Decision Rules	1. Reduce executive budget requests 2. Provide adequate funding for executive programs	1. Write bills that will pass the House 2. Allocate credit to majority party for policies adopted	1. To approve and help pass the foreign aid bill	1. Allocate credit to parties for policies adopted 2. To pursue individual policy preferences regardless of partisan implications	1. To support maximum pay increases and benefits for civil servants; and to oppose all postal rate increases 2. To accede to executive branch wishes if necessary to assure some pay and benefits increases	1. To secure House passage of all constituency-supported, member-sponsored bills 2. To balance the competing demands of conservationists and private users of land and water resources so as to give special benefits to users

Source: Adapted from Richard F. Fenno, Jr., Congressmen in Committees (Boston: Little, Brown, 1973).

signed to insure that the final product will pass the House. The majority party stamp is also clearly on that product so that, when it passes, the majority party can take most of the public credit for it, even though the minority party may have made a considerable contribution. The products coming from the committee show responsiveness to partisan coalitions, especially that within the majority party, and responsiveness to the views of the Social Security Administration, the president, the Treasury, and other parts of the executive branch coalitions. But the Ways and Means Committee rarely simply passes an executive request without putting its own stamp on it as it did in the case of welfare and trade in 1962, medicare in 1965, and major tax revisions in 1964, 1969, and 1971.

The highly visible nature of the issues with which the Ways and Means Committee deals and the important ramifications of these issues for constituents means that subject matter alone will make the members visible and sought after by their colleagues. This enhances their influence. In addition, until 1975 the Democratic members served as members of the Democratic Committee on Committees and were, therefore, accorded additional influence. Thus the committee members realize their goal of enhancing their influence in the House.

The Foreign Affairs Committee's major policy activities involve the annual foreign aid authorization bill. The committee always approves the bill in a form generally acceptable to the executive branch. Minor cuts and alterations may be made but the committee does not make major changes. This product obviously shows that the committee is responsive to the executive-led coalition and follows its basic decision rule of approving and helping to pass the foreign aid bill. To the extent that individual members go on the committee to help support foreign aid they perhaps can feel that they are maximizing their impact on this policy area, although that impact does not appear to be independent but rather dependent on the executive branch.

The Education and Labor Committee is in almost a constant state of partisan turmoil. Much of its policy activity consists of heated debates and arguments inside the committee over a whole range of controversial measures involving labor relations; and a variety of poverty, welfare, and educational aid measures. When agreement is possible among a majority of the committee members (usually composed almost entirely of members of the majority party), controversial measures are brought to the floor, although without the guarantee that they will be passed by the House. If the measures reported by the committee pass, then certainly the majority party will receive the bulk of the credit.

At the same time all members of the committee can pursue matters that interest them personally because there is no norm within the committee that winning on the House floor is very important. Therefore, if "teams" and majorities emerge that is fine, but if they do not, members can still pursue their own interests and have the feeling that they are maximizing their influence on policy areas that intrigue them. When a majority of the committee is able to agree on a major issue then it is responsive to partisan groups within the committee and within the House.

The Post Office and Civil Service Committee increases the pay of federal civil servants rather steadily. First class postage rates also increase fairly frequently. Commercial users of the mails (magazines and "junk" mailers) are protected by the committee and increases in their rates are more gradual. These policy activities by the committee reflect their basic decision rule of supporting pay raises. That postal rates also go up indicates that the executive branch basically demands such increases as part of the price for increasing pay rates; the committee accedes to at least some of these demands rather than jeopardizing the increased pay. Certainly the policy decisions made by the committee reflect their responsiveness to the civil servant and postal employee unions, which are constantly pressing for higher wages, and to the second and third class mailers, who are constantly pressing for continued government subsidy of their mailing privileges with rates below cost. The favors that committee members do for federal workers (and every district has lots of postmen and many have other major federal installations) helps them maximize their chances for re-election by earning votes and also campaign contributions. The conversion of the Postal Service to corporation status has altered the jurisdiction of the committee and is likely to result in different patterns of behavior in the future.

The Interior and Insular Affairs Committee produces a mixture of legislation, some of it applauded by conservationists and sportsmen and offensive to the users of public resources (grazers, timbering interests, mining interests) and some of it favorable to the users and anathema to the conservationists and sportsmen. This mixed pattern of legislation reflects the conflicting pressures on the members of the committee, virtually all of whom come from western districts in which there are large numbers of users and increasing numbers of vocal conservationists. These cross-pressured members seeking to maximize re-election chances naturally seek to turn out a balanced product that will placate all of the interests partially and offend none of them totally. The committee also gets involved in disputes between different geographical areas, particularly in the West when diversion of water is involved. In such instances the committee often tries to do something for all of the competing areas.[41]

Committee Success on the Floor

Committee bills usually pass on the floor of the House and Senate. In the ten years between 1955 and 1964, for example, 90 percent of all bills in the House that went through the normal committee process and came to a roll call vote passed. There were numerous other bills that were not the subject of roll calls that also passed.

Committees vary, however, in the ease with which their handiwork is accepted on the floor. One study of roll call voting on committee bills in the House between 1955 and 1964 [42] showed that over the ten year period the most successful committees never had a bill that went to a roll call defeated (there were two such committees); the least successful committee had a little over 18 percent of its bills that went to a roll call defeated on the House floor.

The number of committee bills passed without amendment on the floor is another measure of committee success. The assumption is that amendments reflect a "second-guessing" of the judgment reported by the committee majority. Table 5–9 reports data on the passage of House and Senate committee bills for the period from 1963 through 1971. The table supports the proposition that the House is somewhat more likely to pass the handiwork of its committees unamended than is the Senate (70 percent of the time as compared to 65 percent). The range of unamended bills is similar in both houses. In the Senate the three committees whose bills got amended most often are all pork barrel committees. This suggests that senators will tack on amendments to spread the benefits of governmental activity—whether public works, military installations, or appropriations in general—more widely. The parallel pork barrel committees in the House also ranked low—although not among the lowest three. (Armed Services was ninth, Pub-

---

41. It should be noted in general that although there is "conventional wisdom" that members who serve on committees responsible for passing out federal largesse do better for their districts than other members there is no consistent evidence to support the conventional wisdom. See, for example, Leonard G. Ritt, "Committee Position, Seniority, and the Dstribution of Government Expenditures," *Public Policy* 24 (1976): 463–489. For a case in which states represented on a committee (House Public Works) benefitted more than those not represented see Gerald S. Strom, "Congressional Policy Making: A Test of a Theory," *Journal of Politics* 37 (1975): 711–735.

42. James W. Dyson and John W. Soule, "Congressional Committee Behavior on Roll Call Votes: The U.S. House of Representatives, 1955–1964," *Midwest Journal of Political Science* 14 (1970): 626–647.

Table 5–9

Percentage of Committee Bills Passing Unamended, 1963–1971.

	Percent of Bills Passing Unamended	Number of Bills
Senate		
All Senate Committees	65	1174
Top Three Committees		
Rules and Administration	92	25
Interior and Insular Affairs	88	80
District of Columbia	80	25
Bottom Three Committees		
Public Works	57	61
Armed Services	51	61
Appropriations	40	165
House		
All House Committees	70	1139
Top Three Committees		
Ways and Means	96	99
House Administration	93	29
Veterans' Affairs	93	27
Bottom Three Committees		
Banking and Currency	54	74
District of Columbia	47	17
Science and Astronautics	41	17

Source: Data compiled from Congressional Quarterly Almanacs, *1963–1971.*

lic Works was fourteenth, and Appropriations was seventeenth.) In both houses the top three committees were in five cases out of the six either relatively minor committees or specifically concerned with housekeeping in the House and Senate themselves. The only important substantive committee in the top three was the House Ways and Means Committee; this can be explained largely because most bills from that committee were considered under a closed rule—that is, a rule that simply does not allow amendments.

Change in Committees

Committees of Congress change. They change in procedures (both formal and informal), members, and policy positions. As with Congress as a whole, there is nothing static about the life and performance of committees. Some of the changes are generated from within individual committees. Some changes are imposed by the whole House or Senate. Some are in reaction to changes in the presidency, the bureaucracy, the agenda of government, or societal developments. Many changes are responding to all of these forces at once.

One recent change that has affected all committees in both houses is the opening of sessions, including decision-making meetings, to the public. Both houses adopted "sunshine" rules in 1973. Throughout the 1950s and 1960s until 1973 roughly two out of every five meetings were closed to the public. By 1975 this figure had declined to less than one in every twelve meetings.

One study of four House Committees—Agriculture; Interstate and Foreign Commerce; Government Operations; and International Relations—in 1975–76 concluded that the personnel and procedural changes of the 1970–1975 period had had definite effects on them, despite the different histories, "styles," and jurisdictions of the four.[43] All four of the committees became ideologically less distinctive from one another and from the two parties in the House. The membership of each of the four came to represent the ideological complexion of the House as a whole. Power had become less centralized in the four committees; subcommittee autonomy or at least increased importance was in evidence. At the same time the leaders of the committee, particularly the chairpersons of the full committees and the subcommittees, were more responsible and responsive to the memberships of the committees.

On the floor of the House the decisions of the committees were being accepted less automatically than before. The whole House appeared to feel more of a stake in the decisions they were ratifying than in previous years. Thus at the same time that subcommittees were winning considerable independent influence from the full committees, their decisions were more likely to be questioned and amended on the floor than previously.

A study of the House Ways and Means Committee at the end of the same reform era also found considerable change in a short period of time.[44] Central reforms included expansion of committee size, the creation of subcommittees for the first time in many years, and an

---

43. Norman J. Ornstein and David W. Rohde, "Shifting Forces, Changing Rules, and Political Outcomes: The Impact of Congressional Change on Four House Committees," in Robert L. Peabody and Nelson W. Polsby (eds.), *New Perspectives on the House of Representatives* (Chicago: Rand McNally, 1977, 3rd ed.): 186–269.

44. Catherine E. Rudder, "Committee Reform and the Revenue Process," in Dodd and Oppenheimer, *Congress Reconsidered:* 117–139.

opening of committee decisions to amendment in both the Democratic Caucus and on the floor of the House (this was accomplished by changing the "closed rule" practice that had virtually always allowed Ways and Means bills to be considered on the floor without the possibility of amendment). In addition, one critical personnel change occurred in 1975: a new chairperson replaced the powerful chairperson of the previous sixteen years, Wilbur Mills (D-Ark.). The replacement was caused by a personal scandal involving Mills and was not generated by the reformers in the House Democratic party, but the sudden absence of a central figure was important.

The principal results of all these changes were to open and democratize committee procedures, to expand the number of participants in decision-making both within the committee and outside the committee, and to allow some decisions that were not possible before, such as the removal of the oil depletion allowance. In a sense, the price the committee and the House paid for these changes was that in conference with the Finance Committee of the Senate, House influence waned.

The Overall Impact of Committees

The standing committees and subcommittees of Congress are critical in determining the substantive impact of Congress on policy and also in determining which interests will have the most access to the policy process at the national level. Representatives of bureaus and interest groups know this and cultivate their contacts with individual members and staff members on committees and subcommittees important to them. Presidents and party leaders alike can be frustrated by their own relative lack of access to the committee system.

In the late 1970s the autonomy of House committees in particular has been called into question in two ways. First, subcommittees have sought more autonomy from full committees with considerable success. Second, the Democratic caucus and to some extent the full House have sought to have more impact on committee deliberations, also with some success. However, the general proposition that substantive congressional decisions for the most part are made in committees and subcommittees still remains true even for the House. Change has been much less in evidence in the Senate in the late 1970s. If anything, the changes adopted in 1977 should strengthen the hand of Senate committees.

In general, then, the committee and subcommittee structure of Congress still promotes policy fragmentation much more than policy integration. In many ways this is virtually inevitable. However, some elements of integration can be inserted into the committee decision process by "outsiders." Potentially the most important outsiders are the President (and the institutional presidency) and especially the party leaders in Congress. The party leaders have the most potential because, although "outsiders" on specific committees, they are the epitome of "insiders" in the House and Senate. In the next chapter, which focuses on the party leaders, relations between leaders and committees will be examined in some detail.

CHAPTER 6

PARTY
LEADERSHIP

I N 1977 BOTH THE HOUSE AND THE SENATE CHOSE NEW LEADERS OF THE
majority party: Thomas P. O'Neill, Jr., to be Speaker of the
House and Robert C. Byrd to be Majority Leader of the Senate.
These choices illustrated two general points about leaders and leadership in the political parties in Congress. First, both houses showed
themselves capable of selecting more aggressive and activist leaders
after a period of relatively quiet (critics might say somnolent) leadership. Second, the careers of both men were typical for party leaders in
that both were devoted to a career in their respective chambers, both
had worked for their party in a variety of formal positions before
achieving the top position, and both had enormous skills in relating to
all different kinds of members holding a great variety of beliefs about
desirable public policy.

In the House in the Ninety-fourth Congress (1975–76) the Speakership of Carl Albert, an Oklahoma Democrat, had run into trouble. Albert was relatively old (late sixties) and in uncertain health. Most important, he was under constant pressure from the activist, liberal wing
of his party to be more assertive and to push legislative proposals and
positions they favored through the House. In the vanguard of this
activist group were most of the seventy-five freshmen Democrats who
had been elected in the Democratic triumph of 1974.

Albert's instincts were to proceed quietly. His view of his leadership
position was summed up a number of times in his own words at press
conferences. He was quoted as saying, for example, "I don't want to do
anything to offend anyone." "I want to be remembered as a congressman's speaker, well liked by his colleagues, from whom I am able to
get the most cooperation without too much arm-twisting." [1] Early in

---

1. Albert, quoted in Roulhac Hamilton, "Albert Reveals Cause of Weakness,"
Columbus Dispatch, June 29, 1975.

1975, when pushed by the freshmen particularly to exert more forceful leadership, Albert said, "They don't want a Speaker, they want a bouncer." [2]

Albert and his predecessor as Speaker, John McCormack of Massachusetts, held the speakership from 1962 through 1976. Both proceeded without consistent force or drive. Neither aspired to be a "strong" speaker in the sense of being the highly visible focus of legislative activity in the House who could in some major ways "speak for the House." The new Speaker in 1977, Thomas P. (Tip) O'Neill, had different aspirations and set out in 1977 to realize them.

O'Neill had come to the House in 1953. He had been a loyal member of the party and had come into a leadership position in 1971 when newly elected Speaker Albert and Hale Boggs, the majority leader, had chosen him to be Democratic whip. After Boggs' death in a plane crash in late 1972, O'Neill was elected majority leader by the Democratic Caucus. When Albert announced his retirement as Speaker at the end of 1976, there was no opposition to O'Neill as the next speaker. During his two years as whip and four years as majority leader he had shown himself to be both forceful and sympathetic and responsive to the membership simultaneously. In addition, he had used the powers of his offices to do a lot of favors for a lot of members who repaid him with their support of his rise up the leadership ladder.

It had been clear during the last years of the Albert speakership that O'Neill was the strongest person on the leadership team. Early in his speakership he gave every evidence of delivering on his pledge before being elected Speaker: "I intend to be a strong Speaker. I believe in strong leadership." [3]

O'Neill openly laid his prestige on the line on important issues such as the adoption of a code of ethics for the House and the House passage of the president's energy program in 1977, and he won. The secret behind his early successes was his ability to talk to all sides on an issue within his party, to help engineer winning compromises, and to assert his preferences in a personal manner that left even those opposed to his positions in agreement that he was a fine person and an effective

---

2. Albert, quoted in Richard L. Lyons, "Speaker, Activists Confer," *Washington Post,* June 19, 1975.

3. O'Neill, quoted in Michael J. Malbin, "House Democrats Are Playing with a Strong Leadership Lineup," *National Journal* (June 18, 1977): 940. For early assessments of O'Neill's performance in addition to the Malbin article see Richard L. Lyons, "A Powerful Speaker," *Washington Post,* April 3, 1977; Mary Russell, "Tip O'Neill: The Great Accommodator," *Washington Post,* June 19, 1977; Spencer Rich, "Tip O'Neill: A Legend Being Born," *Washington Post,* August 7, 1977; and Martin Tolchin, "An Old Pol Takes on the New President," *New York Times Magazine,* July 24, 1977.

leader. He was tireless in visiting with members of the House, lobby-ists, the president, and other executive branch officials. He even flew to Chicago to talk with the mayor and other officials in an attempt to sell the president's bill allowing same-day registration of voters. He had seemingly boundless capacities for hard work, compromise, and doing a series of personal favors for individuals. Thus, despite the de-centralization of power throughout the subcommittee system that had occurred in the previous years, O'Neill could operate as the un-doubted central figure of the House.

A long-time colleague and astute observer of the House, Richard Bolling of Missouri, offered a good capsule description of O'Neill: "He's an Irish politician. No table pounder. He puts an arm around your shoulders and says he needs you. . . . When he's going some-where he's like a tank, a kind tank." [4]

O'Neill himself was consistently candid in talking with the press about his own speakership. In an interview in the spring of 1977 he spoke insightfully about the kinds of things he could do to build per-sonal ties and loyalties that would pay off in policy decisions to his liking:

You know, you ask me what are my powers and my authority around here? The power to recognize on the floor; little odds and ends—like men get pride out of the prestige of handling the Com-mittee of the Whole, being named the Speaker for the day; those little trips that come along—like those trips to China, trips to Russia, things of that nature; or other ad hoc committees or special commit-tees, which I have assignments to; plus the fact that there is a certain aura and respect that goes with the Speaker's office. He does have the power to be able to pick up the telephone and call people. And Members often times like to bring their loyal political leaders or a couple of mayors. And often times they have problems from their area and they need aid and assistance, either legislativewise or ad-ministrativewise. We're happy to try to open the door for them, hav-ing been in the town for so many years and knowing so many people. We do know where a lot of bodies are and we do know how to advise people.

And I have an open door policy. Rare is the occasion when a man has a personal fund-raiser or being personally honored that I don't show up at it. I've made more public appearances and visited areas if they believe I can help them. I'm always accessible. These are part of the duties and the obligations of the Speaker, and it shows the warm hand of friendship. . . .

---

4. Bolling, quoted in Lyons, "A Powerful Speaker."

So that's what it's all about.[5]

In the Senate there was also a considerable change in the style of majority party leadership in 1977, although not as dramatic a change as in the House. The majority leader from 1961 through 1976 had been Mike Mansfield, a gentle, scholarly Montana Democrat, who had succeeded one of the most active and flamboyant of all Senate floor leaders, Lyndon Johnson of Texas. Mansfield's style and philosophy of leadership were the antithesis of that of Johnson (and also of Tip O'Neill): "I don't collect any IOUs. I don't do any special favors. I try to treat all Senators alike, and I think that's the best way to operate in the long run, because that way you maintain their respect and confidence. And that's what the ball game is all about." [6] Mansfield kept the flow of business moving through the Senate but—except on matters affecting Montana, when he became a bulldog—he did not often stamp his own imprint on the substance of what emerged.[7]

In 1977 Robert C. Byrd, West Virginia Democrat, was elected majority leader of the Senate by the Democratic Caucus. Just before the vote his only opponent, Hubert Humphrey, withdrew because, much like Tip O'Neill, Byrd appeared unbeatable. He had few enemies. And, also like O'Neill—although with a very different personal manner —he had patiently built up personal indebtedness and commitments through hard work in the Senate for many years. Beginning in 1967 he held two leadership posts: secretary of the Senate Democratic Conference (1967–71) and whip (1971–77). His first position—secretary of the Conference—did not amount to much when he acquired it, but he made it a position of service to his fellow Democrats. He treated the whip's position in the same way. So when the majority leadership became vacant through Mansfield's retirement, Byrd had ten years of favors to draw on in building support.

Byrd's style is to proceed relatively quietly (more like Mansfield than Johnson) but with considerable unrelenting purpose and efficiency in

5. O'Neill, quoted in Malbin, "House Democrats Are Playing with a Strong Leadership Lineup," 942.

6. Mansfield, quoted in Daniel Rapoport, "Congress Report/It's Not a Happy Time for House, Senate Leadership," *National Journal* (February 7, 1976): 171.

7. For good discussions of Mansfield's leadership see Richard E. Cohen, "Marking an End to the Senate's Mansfield Era," *National Journal* (December 25, 1976): 1802–1809; Andrew J. Glass, "Mike Mansfield, Majority Leader," in Norman J. Ornstein (ed.), *Congress in Change* (New York: Praeger, 1975): 142–154; and John G. Stewart, "Two Strategies of Leadership: Johnson and Mansfield," in Nelson W. Polsby (ed.), *Congressional Behavior* (New York: Random House, 1971): 61–92. For an excellent description of Johnson as leader in the Senate see Rowland Evans and Robert Novak, *Lyndon B. Johnson: The Exercise of Power* (New York: New American Library, 1966): chapters 3–10.

achieving that purpose (more like Johnson than Mansfield).[8] Like most party leaders in both houses, he focuses on providing procedural conditions that allow decisions to be made. He also intervenes in some substantive questions in order to suggest what he hopes will be winning compromises. He has complete mastery of the procedures of the Senate and understands well the personal views and political sensitivities of his colleagues. Although he does not like the term "facilitator," in fact his principal skill comes in facilitating the work of the Senate by manipulating procedures and substantive compromises in tandem.

An effective Senate leader must, of necessity, proceed differently than an effective House leader. A chief reason for this situation is the different rules used by the two chambers. The House is relatively highly structured and tightly controlled by formal rules. The Senate has a number of formal rules, but most of the time the proceedings are governed by the necessity of acquiring "unanimous consent" (that is, one objector can prevent a debate or decision from going forward or can at least stall the proceedings). Byrd himself has remarked of the Senate that "It would be impossible for Jesus Christ to do anything without unanimous consent." [9]

Byrd defined the essential tasks he saw in the job of majority leader: "He facilitates, he constructs, he programs, he schedules, he takes an active part in the development of legislation, he steps in at crucial moments on the floor, offers amendments, speaks on behalf of legislation and helps to shape the outcome of the legislation." [10]

The General Importance of Congressional Parties

Despite much commentary to the effect that American political parties are weak both in the electorate and in the national legislature, they are, inside Congress, one of the major potential integrating forces to counteract the numerous forces that push in the direction of fragmentation. This does not mean that parties always realize their integrating potential, but sometimes that potential can be stimulated by leadership either from within the House and Senate or from the White House or, most effectively, from both simultaneously.

---

8. On Byrd as leader see Richard E. Cohen, "Byrd of West Virginia—A New Job, A New Image," *National Journal* (August 20, 1977): 1292–1299; and Martin Tolchin, "Byrd Persuasive as Senate Chief," *New York Times,* March 27, 1977.

9. Byrd, quoted in Adam Clymer, "Leadership Gap in the Senate," *New York Times,* September 28, 1977.

10. Byrd, in Cohen, "Byrd of West Virginia . . .": 1294.

Political parties in the House and Senate played a central role in the emergence of the modern Congress in the late nineteenth century. In that period and in the first two decades of the twentieth century it appeared as if an American form of strong party government might become a permanent feature of Congress.

But, at about the time of World War I, support for consistently strong parties and party leaders in Congress waned among the members. Strong parties threatened the independence prized by the members. Consequently, the type of congressional parties that have dominated in Congress since World War I have been strong and effective shapers of the policy impact of Congress only sporadically. They are still important elements in the working of Congress but have usually played a more modest role than their predecessors between roughly 1890 and 1915.

The potential for change is always present in Congress, however. Thus parties could again emerge as even more potent and central features of the congressional landscape, if the members put programmatic considerations ahead of maximizing individual freedom from party constraints.

A candidate who has been elected to the House or Senate is confronted immediately with a congressional party. This party is likely to have a much greater impact on him than either the national party under whose banner he ran for office or the state and local parties, whose organization may have helped him as he campaigned. Party leaders, caucuses, committees, and other elements impinge on his daily life and are responsible for items crucial to his congressional career such as committee assignments. They control floor business, so he must come to terms with his party if he desires success in pushing those bills and policies he favors through Congress. In short, congressional parties provide absolutely essential procedural controls over congressional business. Centrally, they provide order and efficiency in the legislative process.

Congressional parties also possess substantive content. Until the twentieth century, congressional parties generated their own substantive positions, but their attention during the course of a Congress was narrowly focused, mainly on changing tariffs and a few other areas (for example, roads, canals, and other internal improvements).

In this century the leaders of the party of the president have typically (and without exception since 1933) accepted most of his policies and program preferences as their own. The leaders of the president's party in the House and Senate usually lend support to these proposals without seriously questioning them. The president's preferences aggregated in his legislative program are generally consistent with the national party platform, although rarely identical to it.

When the president's program comes to the committees and the floor in each house of Congress it generally receives support from most of the members of his party. There may be considerable dissent over portions of his program, but the party label they share with the president helps motivate most members to avoid dissent when possible. Party label is both a symbol and a reality that provides a focus for loyal behavior on substantive issues. Shared experiences, friendships, party machinery all help reinforce the natural feelings of loyalty to the president and his program.

These natural ties to the president on the part of his party's members are most dramatically visible when the House or Senate considers the question of overriding a presidential veto. Typically, many members of the president's party who voted for the bill the first time it went through the chamber will change their vote and support the president's veto.

Table 6–1 summarizes Republican voting in the House and Senate in 1973 and 1976 on seven different bills vetoed by Presidents Nixon and Ford. These vetoes represent all vetoes on which both initial roll calls and override votes were taken in one or both chambers in both the first six months of 1973 and the first six months of 1976. All seven vetoes were ultimately sustained, although in two cases one house voted to override. The Nixon vetoes in 1973 were of the Vocational Rehabilitation Act, the Consolidated Farm and Rural Development Act (with a provision directing the president to spend all funds authorized for water and sewer construction), a bill requiring Senate confirmation of the incumbent director and deputy director of the Office of Management and Budget as well as their successors, and a supplemental appropriations bill that contained a provision requiring the immediate cessation of bombing in Cambodia. The Ford vetoes in 1976 were of the Public Works employment bill (containing more money and jobs than the president desired), a bill providing federal aid to day care centers (containing standards the administration found objectionable), and revisions in the Hatch Act that would allow more political activity by federal civil servants.

When the initial voting by Republicans on each of these bills is compared to the vote on the veto override, it can be seen that Republican support for the president increased in every case, even though the president had, in effect, asked for Republican support at the time of initial passage too. Some of the changes in the direction of increased support for the president revealed in Table 6–1 are dramatic. In four of

Table 6-1

Republican Voting on Vetoed Bills, 1973 and 1976

Bill and Chamber (Year)	Vote on Original Passage		Vote on Veto	
	Republican Voting	% Supporting Nixon or Ford Position	Republican Voting	% Supporting Nixon or Ford Position
Vocational Rehabilitation Act— Senate (1973)	35–2	5	10–31	76
Water-Sewer Program—House (1973)	105–48	31	24–161	87
OMB Confirmation—Senate (1973)	16–17	52	14–22	61
OMB Confirmation—House (1973)	20–164	89	18–167	90
Cambodia Bombing Halt— House (1973)	63–120	66	53–133	72
Public Works Employment— House (1976)	62–71	53	56–82	59
Public Works Employment— Senate (1976)	20–16	44	12–25	68
Aid to Day Care Centers— Senate (1976)	18–16	47	11–26	70
Hatch Act Revisions—House (1976)	49–93	65	22–113	84

the seven cases a majority of voting Republicans had favored initial passage but moved to support the veto by a ratio of at least seven to three in every case.

The party that does not have a president in the White House has a difficult time in generating loyalty to a substantive program. This party can decide either to oppose the president and his party with or without proposing programmatic alternatives or to support partially the president's program or to try to participate in the development of some of it (an exceedingly difficult task). Typically, the party without the presidency has far less programmatic or substantive identity than the presidential party.

There are interactive factors that push party members in the House and the Senate to act in concert. In part there are genuine shared attitudes about public policy issues. These attitudes are reinforced by the requests and actions of the party leaders and of the president for members of his party. They are also reinforced because members of a party typically seek out other members of their party for most of their discussion of and advice about policy.[11]

Congressional parties serve to predict voting on the floor of the House and Senate better than any other factor. A recent study of voting in Congress from 1921 through 1964 concluded that "by any measure party remains the single most important factor in roll call voting." [12] The trend during this time period was toward weaker party unity on controversial issues, principally because of the growing ideological conservatism on the part of a number of southern Democrats. Nevertheless, party remained a relatively strong unifying force in Congress.

PARTY LEADERS

The functioning of congressional parties is shaped in large part by the individuals who hold critical institutional positions in those parties. This does not mean that other individuals are prevented from developing influence; it simply means that the most influential are those with formal titles.

The Positions of Leadership

In the House the principal leaders of the majority party in this century have been the Speaker and majority leader. In recent years the majority whip has also emerged as an important leader. The principal leader of the minority party has been the minority leader, sometimes joined by the minority whip.

In the Senate the principal leader of the majority party in this century has been the majority leader. The minority leader has generally been the chief leader of the minority party. Whips have become increasingly important in both parties.

Individuals selected for the five principal positions in the two houses (the majority leaders, the minority leaders, and the Speaker of the House) have been relatively senior members of their respective chambers, but they are not chosen on the basis of seniority. Table 6–2 summarizes the mean years of service in the House and Senate for the five principal leaders plus the whips in the four parties. This table makes it clear that the House Democrats consistently look to their more

---

11. See John W. Kingdon, *Congressmen's Voting Decisions* (New York: Harper and Row, 1973); and Helmut Norpoth, "Explaining Party Cohesion in Congress: The Case of Shared Policy Attitudes," *American Political Science Review* 70 (1976): 1156–1171.

12. Julius Turner, *Party and Constituency: Pressures on Congress* (Baltimore: Johns Hopkins Press, 1970, revised ed.), Edward Schneier (ed.).

Table 6–2
Average Seniority of Principal House and Senate Leaders at Time of Initial Selection, by Party, Twentieth Century.

	Speaker	(N)	Mean Seniority Floor Leader	(N)	Whip	(N)
House Democrats	25.2	(9)	18.8	(16)	11.1	(16)
House Republicans	22.4	(5)	16.1	(10)	7.2	(11)
Senate Democrats	—		9.2	(11)	6.6	(15)
Senate Republicans	—		13.5	(13)	6.0	(12)

senior members to fill their vacant leadership positions, as do the House Republicans. Neither Senate party produces leaders who are as senior. The Senate Republican floor leaders have been more senior than the Senate Democratic floor leaders.

Except for the House Democrats no geographical region has dominated any of the four parties in Congress. In the case of the House Democrats southerners have been most frequently chosen.[13] Four of the nine Democratic Speakers from 1911 to the present have been southerners and two more have been from border states. Eleven of the sixteen Democratic floor leaders from 1899 to the present have been southerners and two more have been from border states. Eight of the sixteen Democratic whips from 1900 to the present have been southerners and two more have been from border states. The Senate Democratic party has also chosen a number of southern and border state men as their leaders, but not as many: four of the eleven Democratic floor leaders from 1911 to the present were southerners and two more

Table 6–3
Average Length of Service in Principal Leadership Positions, by Party, Twentieth Century.

	Speaker	(N)	Mean Service Floor Leader	(N)	Whip	(N)
House Democrats	6.3	(8)	5.4	(15)	4.4	(15)
House Republicans	5.6	(5)	8.3	(9)	7.9	(10)
Senate Democrats	—		6.6	(10)	4.6	(14)
Senate Republicans	—		5.3	(12)	4.8	(11)

13. The South is defined as the eleven states of the Confederacy. Border states include Delaware, Maryland, West Virginia, Kentucky, Missouri, and Oklahoma.

were from border states; only four of the fifteen Democratic whips from 1913 to the present have been from the South and two more have been from border states.

Overall, 56 percent of the principal House Democratic leaders in this century have been southerners and 71 percent have been either southerners or from border states. But in the Senate only 31 percent have been southerners and only 46 percent have been either southerners or from border states.

Once selected, the leaders in all of the five principal positions tend to serve about the same length of time. Table 6–3 summarizes their service and shows the exceptions to be the floor leadership and whip's position in the House Republican party, which have more stability than the other offices.

Leadership Selection and Change[14]

The problem of succession from one leader to another is critical for any institution. Contests over succession can disrupt the institution. Smooth transition can facilitate the functioning of the institution, although perhaps at the price of continuing outmoded policies or procedures. In the House and Senate, experience over the last several decades leads to a number of generalizations about change in leadership.

The most striking pattern that emerges is that succession is handled quite differently in the majority party from the way it is handled in the minority party. In the majority party, particularly in the case of a long standing majority, succession is likely to be smooth and divisive internal contests rare. The longer a party is in the majority the more likely it is to develop established patterns of leadership succession. For example, during the long period of dominance of the House by the Democrats from 1931 to the present (with only two two-year breaks) a pattern has emerged whereby, first, a sitting majority leader virtually automatically succeeds to the speakership when it becomes vacant and, second, the majority whip regularly wins election as majority leader when that job opens, although he failed to do so in 1977. The 1977 failure of John McFall (D-Cal.) to advance can be attributed in large part to revelations he had received secret contributions from a Korean businessman accused of seeking to buy Congressional support

---

14. On leadership change see Robert L. Peabody, *Leadership in Congress* (Boston: Little, Brown, 1976); and Garrison Nelson, "Partisan Patterns of House Leadership Change, 1789–1977," *American Political Science Review* 71 (1977): 918–939. On the backgrounds of leaders see Garrison Nelson, "Change and Continuity in the Recruitment of U.S. House Leaders, 1789–1975," in Norman J. Ornstein (ed.), *Congress in Change* (New York: Praeger, 1975): 155–183.

for Korean interests. Any contests in the majority party are most likely to take place for lesser leadership positions, not the top positions.

In the minority party, however, particularly in the House, internal fights of an intense character are likely to occur over leadership positions. These contests are likely to occur at all levels of leadership and are most likely to occur at the times of highest frustration for the minority—for example, after a major electoral disaster.

In general, there are no good predictive characteristics about which individuals in the four congressional parties will be selected as leaders except for a few relatively obvious ones. Individuals chosen in the last century have all been making their career in Congress, although a few in the Senate aspired to the presidency. The art of compromise has been highly prized by those both electing and appointing leaders; ideologues have rarely won leadership positions. Individuals selected have had to be concerned with the welfare of their party, but this has not meant that a person could never have deviated from party positions, even on important issues. Thus far only white males have attained positions of party leadership in Congress.

The Party Loyalty of Leaders

If loyalty to party is defined in terms of the propensity to vote with the majority of the party on the House or Senate floor, then the principal party leaders are much more loyal than the average senator or representative or any other subset of senators or representatives. Table 6–4 summarizes party loyalty in voting on the floor of the House and Senate for all members of each party, for the chairmen or ranking minority members of each party, and for the floor leader of each party for the period between 1935 and 1970. As can be seen, party leaders are considerably more loyal in both parties in both houses compared either to all members or to the committee chairmen and ranking minority members as a group. It should also be noted that all categories

Table 6–4

Average Length of Service in Principal Leadership Positions, by Party, Twentieth Century.

	Speaker	(N)	Mean Service Floor Leader	(N)	Whip	(N)
House Democrats	6.3	(7)	5.3	(14)	4.6	(11)
House Republicans	5.6	(5)	8.3	(8)	5.2	(9)
Senate Democrats	—		5.6	(9)	4.5	(13)
Senate Republicans	—		5.2	(11)	4.6	(10)

in both parties in the House are slightly more loyal than the same categories in the Senate, suggesting that party is a more important phenomenon in the House than in the Senate. Likewise, it is worth noting that the gap between the loyalty of the leaders on the one hand and the loyalty of the general membership and committee leaders on the other is greater for the Democrats than for the Republicans. This is largely a product of differences in ideology between northern and southern Democrats during the period covered in the table.

The attitudes toward manifestations of loyalty vary somewhat between the two houses. In both houses general loyalty is expected. But in the Senate there is more tolerance of some overt behavior running contrary to generally understood party stands. For example, in 1973 the Senate Republican whip both voted and spoke against the president's position on the veto of the bill involving confirmation for the top officials in the Office of Management and Budget. Yet this occasioned no particular notice on the part of his party colleagues. In the same year, however, when the House Democratic whip voted against an anti-Cambodian bombing amendment and suggested on the floor to the manager of the bill that a point of order might be raised against the amendment there was considerable negative reaction on the part of his party colleagues, who had earlier been successful in getting the House Democratic caucus to endorse the amendment.

In 1977 the new House leadership—O'Neill as Speaker, Wright as majority leader, and Brademas as whip—supported all of President Carter's major legislative initiatives and skillfully worked to line up sufficient House support to pass them. In the Senate the new majority leader, Byrd, facilitated Senate consideration of all of the initiatives but did not take unequivocally supportive personal stands on all of them (for example, on the energy program) and opposed some of them (foreign aid, for example). Critically, from the president's point of view, he did support the Panama Canal treaties.

Contemporary Patterns of Leadership

Throughout history many patterns of leadership have been used by both parties in the House and the Senate. Since roughly the 1880s the formal leaders of both parties in both houses have been consistently important in helping to determine the timing and character of legislation emerging from the House and Senate.

Examination of leadership patterns in the House and Senate in the 1960s and 1970s reveals both stability and changes in terms of institutional arrangements. In those two decades the turnover in individuals holding leadership positions has been complete.

House Democrats [15]

The House Democrats in the 1960s and 1970s had a leadership pattern in which a three-man group (the Speaker, the majority leader, and the majority whip) formed the core. But, over time, the core leaders—especially the Speaker—have involved a growing number of individuals and party committees in performing leadership tasks. Thus by 1977 the three individuals at the center were meeting daily with the chief deputy whip and the caucus chairman. The Speaker was also attending a weekly meeting of the whip organization, an organization of twenty-eight individuals important in helping the leadership perform a number of tasks. The Speaker also convenes the Democratic Steering and Policy Committee two or three times a month. This committee, which he chairs, has the majority leader, chief whip, chief deputy whip, three deputy whips, caucus chairman, four additional members appointed by the Speaker, and twelve members elected by regional caucuses. The Committee performs two major functions: it serves as the Democratic Committee on Committees (it obtained this role in 1975) and it discusses and endorses party policy. The increased importance and activism of both the whip system and the Steering and Policy Committee involve a great many individuals in party leadership, without in any way diminishing the centrality of O'Neill. In fact, he is expert at using these other individuals and institutions to buttress his aims.

Over all of the party apparatus stands the party caucus, which became newly active in the House Democratic Party after many decades of slumber. The caucus discusses and adopts party positions, occasionally instructs Democratic contingents on standing committees on positions they must take, and elects leaders (including committee chairmen). With a relatively weak Speaker like Albert, the caucus seemed to be autonomous. With an activist speaker like O'Neill, the caucus seems much more an organ that interacts with the Speaker—both partially shaped by his wishes and partially shaping the positions he takes.

The core leadership group also coopts committee and subcommittee chairpersons when specific bills are ready for floor consideration. This

---

15. On the House Democrats see the material cited in footnote 3, above; Larry Dodd, "Emergence of Party Government in the House of Representatives," *DEA News Supplement*, No. 10 (Summer, 1976); Lawrence C. Dodd and Bruce I. Oppenheimer, "The House in Transition," in Dodd and Oppenheimer (eds.), *Congress Reconsidered* (New York: Praeger, 1977): 40–49; and Dodd, "The Expanding Roles of the House Democratic Whip System," (paper prepared for delivery at the 1977 Midwest Political Science Association meeting).

slightly expanded group then works on the tactical details of scheduling and passing the bill.

House Republicans [16]

The House Republicans had a more diffuse pattern of leadership during the 1960s and 1970s. Nine formal positions carried at least some leadership status in the Republican party during much of the period, even though it was in the minority and much smaller in size than the Democratic party. These positions were the minority leader; the chairman, vice chairman, and secretary of the conference (the Republican version of the Democratic caucus); the minority whip; the chairman of the Policy Committee; the chairman of the Research Committee; the chairman of the National Congressional Committee (a campaign committee); and the ranking minority member of the Rules Committee.

The Republican leaders were also aided by a whip organization and by the members of the Policy Committee and the Research Committee. The Republicans also had a large committee on committees to perform the function of assigning Republicans to standing committees. This committee tended to be relatively independent of the principal individual leaders. The full conference also helped organize the party.

In addition, the norms and traditions of the Republican party in the House also gave unusually heavy weight to the senior Republican members of various standing committee delegations. Senior Democrats on standing committees were also important in their party but not as independent within the party as the senior Republicans.

Senate Democrats [17]

The Senate Democrats operate with only a few leaders. By far the most important is the majority leader. He is aided by the majority whip and by the secretary of the party conference (the name for the whole Democratic membership). There are also four deputy whips, a steering committee, and a policy committee. But the majority whip, secretary, and deputy whips perform mainly housekeeping chores. The majority leader himself chairs the Steering Committee (which makes

---

16. On the House Republicans see Richard E. Cohen, "House Republicans Under Rhodes—Divided They Stand and Fret," *National Journal* (October 29, 1977): 1686–1690.

17. On the Senate Democrats see the material cited in footnote 8, above.

committee assignments) and the Policy Committee. He is constrained by the decisions reached in those committees but is certainly the most important figure in their deliberations. Mansfield chose to keep a low profile in most decision-making situations. This is in marked contrast to Lyndon Johnson's style in the 1950s. Where Mansfield was tolerant of dissent, Johnson would often charge disloyalty; where Mansfield refused to apply even mild pressure, Johnson would skillfully "arm-twist" using his full range of resources; where Mansfield was consistently calm and quiet, Johnson would run through a range of moods and appeals, including some dramatic and boisterous ones. Robert Byrd, who became majority leader in 1977, seems inclined to speak softly but to be much more assertive about his preferences than Mansfield.

Senate Republicans [18]

The Senate Republicans also have what amounts to corporate leadership. In the 1960s Everett Dirksen of Illinois was clearly the pre-eminent figure in the party, holding the position of minority leader. After his death in 1969 he was succeeded by Hugh Scott of Pennsylvania, who, although not as self-effacing as Mansfield, promoted the idea of corporate leadership. Thus in the 1970s the Republicans came to expect a number of leaders at the top. This expectation is reinforced because, unlike the Senate Democrats, the floor leader chairs no other party committees. Thus the minority leader, although the single most important leader, is aided by the whip, the chairman of the Conference, the chairman of the Policy Committee, and the secretary of the Conference. The Senate Republicans also have a committee on committees with a separate chairman, but this committee does not have much to do except for automatically ratifying what seniority dictates in most cases (the Senate Republicans are the one congressional party that uses seniority heavily in making initial assignments to committees).

Table 6–5 lists the principal leadership positions and the incumbents in those positions in 1977. Lesser positions and the memberships of committees and whip organizations are omitted. If they were included there would be a very large number of members of the House and Senate who would have some legitimate claim to functioning in the party leadership apparatus. But the realities were that both of the

---

18. On the Senate Republicans see Michael J. Malbin, "The Senate Republican Leaders—Life without a President," *National Journal* (May 21, 1977): 776–780.

Table 6–5
Principal Party Leadership Positions and Incumbents, 1977

House Democrats
 Speaker: Thomas P. O'Neill, Jr., Massachusetts
 Majority Leader: James C. Wright, Jr., Texas
 Majority Whip: John Brademas, Indiana
 Chairman of the Caucus: Thomas S. Foley, Washington

House Republicans
 Minority Leader: John J. Rhodes, Arizona
 Minority Whip: Robert H. Michel, Illinois
 Chairman of the Conference: John B. Anderson, Illinois
 Chairman of the Policy Committee: Del Clawson, California
 Chairman of the Research Committee: Bill Frenzel, Minnesota

Senate Democrats
 Majority Leader: Robert C. Byrd, West Virginia
 Majority Whip: Alan Cranston, California
 Secretary of the Conference: Daniel K. Inouye, Hawaii

Senate Republicans
 Minority Leader: Howard H. Baker, Jr., Tennessee
 Minority Whip: Ted Stevens, Alaska
 Chairman of the Conference: Carl T. Curtis, Nebraska
 Secretary of the Conference: Clifford P. Hansen, Wyoming
 Chairman of the Policy Committee: John G. Tower, Texas

Democratic parties were relatively centralized in terms of leadership
(with the House more so than the Senate), the Senate Republicans had
a corporate leadership, and the House Republicans had elements of
a corporate leadership but with an experienced floor leader who had
grown in influence with his fellow partisans.

LEADERSHIP FUNCTIONS

The leaders of all four congressional parties perform (or at least
have the potential of performing) five major functions.

First, the leaders help organize the party to conduct business. Essentially this means that they participate in the selection of new leaders
and the decisions concerning who will sit on which committees. This
choice determines which individuals will be sitting in the most critical
institutional positions when policy decisions are made.

In the House Democratic party the caucus elects the Speaker and the majority leader, and, until 1975, elected Ways and Means members. Usually, the Speaker can determine who the majority leader will be if he announces his preference publicly or lets it be widely known privately, although some Speakers have refrained from making their choice known. The Speaker could also usually endorse winning candidates for Ways and Means vacancies, although occasionally the caucus chose someone other than the Speaker's candidate. The Speaker and the majority leader appoint the whip, and the Democratic caucus has continued to resist moves to make the whip elective. The central leadership serves on the Steering and Policy Committee, which makes all committee assignments. Half of the committee is, in effect, appointed by the Speaker and he serves as chairman. Thus it is reasonable to assume that major committee assignments are pleasing to the Speaker and his lieutenants. (Prior to 1975 the influence of the leaders over committee assignments had to be much more selective, given the process for assignments that was then used.)

In the House Republican party the conference elects the minority leader, the minority whip, and the chairman of the conference. The Committee on Committees is constituted entirely through the state delegations—with one member of the committee coming from every state that has at least one Republican in the House. The minority leader (and the other central leaders too) have minimal influence on the decisions of the Committee on Committees and on the choice of other leaders.

In both Senate parties the leadership seems disposed not to play a very active role in helping with the leader and committee choices in the party. Every individual senator seems to fend for himself and little central direction is evident in organizational terms in either party.

The second of the five functions that the leaders of all four congressional parties perform is the scheduling of business to come to the House and the Senate floors. In the House the Speaker and majority leader make these decisions, although they occasionally consult the minority leader to make sure that his sense of fairness is not violated. In the Senate the majority leader routinely consults the minority leader; if they agree they have great flexibility because the Senate usually proceeds in an ad hoc fashion under so-called unanimous consent, which is based on agreements among everyone present to proceed in a specified way (time of debate, day of debate, control of time, allowable amendments) regardless of any formal Senate rules. Naturally, the scheduling decisions made in both houses are not neutral and can be used to influence the chances of success or failure of specific pieces of legislation. For example, if the majority party leaders fear a close vote they will postpone floor consideration if they know that some of their reliable supporters have to be absent. Or they may move floor action to a day on which some known opponents have to be absent.

Third, the leaders are responsible for promoting attendance on the floor of the House and the Senate. Both of the parties in the House do this primarily through their whip organizations, which are responsible for informing all party members that a critical vote is at hand and that their presence on the floor is required. This is done through an established telephone network between staff members in the regional whips' offices and staff members in the offices of individual congressmen who are responsible for knowing the whereabouts of the "boss." In the Senate, neither party routinely uses their whip apparatus that exists on paper. Consequently, a senator who is interested in a particular piece of legislation will frequently do his own "whipping" to increase attendance. Beginning in 1977 the Democratic Whip became more active.

Obviously, selectivity is exercised in this attempt to increase attendance. For example, the whip organization of one of the House parties may well not contact a known opponent of the leaders' position when a critical vote is imminent.

Fourth, the leaders are constantly engaged in the collection and distribution of information. Reliable information is a precious commodity in both houses. In the House the whip organizations in both parties serve as focal points for this function. They solicit members' attitudes on selected upcoming bills and disseminate the leaders' preferences and limited information on the content of proposed legislation to party members. In the Senate, however, individual senators particularly interested in a bill usually wind up doing their own "headcounts" and their own distribution of substantive information. In 1977 the official whips for both parties became more active in conducting headcounts.

Fifth, the party leaders in both houses maintain a liaison with the White House on policy matters. This involves the leaders of the president's party more frequently than the leaders of the other party. Between the late 1930s and the late 1960s the leaders of the president's party met with him weekly. President Nixon had less frequent meetings with the Republican leaders in Congress. Presidents Ford and Carter reinstated more frequent meetings. There may also be meetings on an emergency basis and the members of the opposition party may be invited from time to time for specific briefings and consultation. Presumably the leaders can serve as mediators between the president and the rank-and-file members, helping to facilitate the flow of policy-related information and preferences in both directions.

All five of these functions can be performed in such a way as to enhance the possibility of attaining specific desired policies and programs and reducing the possibility of producing undesired policies and programs. The leaders' central task is to persuade members to support their policy preferences on the floor of the House and the Senate. It should be noted, however, that the content of a leader's preferences is usually based on the stance of his party's delegation in the relevant standing committee for any given issue. That is, the leaders usually take their substantive cues from a committee delegation and then exercise their persuasive powers to gain ratification for that position, rather than attempting to push a personal position on their party in an authoritarian manner. They may also take major cues from the President or, in the case of the House Democrats, from the party caucus.

One relatively minor function the leaders perform that should logically be more important is to maintain contact with the leaders in the other house to facilitate both the flow of business and the adoption of common party positions in the two chambers. In recent years there has been increased interaction between the leaders, by party, across the houses on both a routine basis and on an ad hoc (usually signifying a crisis) basis. But these contacts have almost all been about procedural matters and have almost never dealt with the substance of policy.[19]

The leaders also are responsible for some administrative chores—simply making the House and Senate function as organizations that must meet payrolls, monitor expenses, buy supplies, and so on. In the mid-1970s both houses undertook studies of their ways of conducting business (some of which smacked of quill pens and 1789). The two commissions (the House Commission on Administrative Review and the Commission on the Operation of the Senate) both issued a number of specific recommendations for modernizing and streamlining the business arrangements. In late 1977, however, the House rejected the proposals of the Commission.[20]

---

19. See Walter Kravitz, "Relations between the Senate and the House of Representatives: The Party Leadership," in Commission on the Operation of the Senate, *Policymaking Role of Leadership in the Senate* (Washington: Government Printing Office, 1976): 121–138.

20. On this defeat see Ann Cooper, "House Refuses to Consider Obey Proposals," *Congressional Quarterly Weekly Report* (October 15, 1977): 2183.

The Principal Leadership Resources
for Affecting Legislative Results

The party leaders in both houses have four principal resources at their disposal as they labor to influence the policy statements and actions emerging from the Senate and the House.

The first is their ability to use the rules of the House and the Senate. Leaders, out of desire and necessity, develop considerable expertise in manipulating the intricacies of the rules.

In the House the majority party leaders, particularly the Speaker, are in a very strong position to use the rules to further their policy ends. The minority leaders in the House have some obstructive powers, but the House rules generally put the majority party in a consistently dominant position. For example, the Speaker can be selective in placing legislation on the "suspension calendar," a device for expediting relatively non-controversial bills (bills brought to the floor on this calendar are debated for only forty minutes and require a two-thirds vote for passage). Many bills of low visibility would die if they were not moved through the House quickly in this fashion. This means that the Speaker is in a good position to build credits for the future, to reward past loyalty, or to punish past disloyalty by either granting or withholding a member's request to place a low visibility bill that is important to him on the suspension calendar.

In the Senate the leaders of both parties have influence over the use of the rules. The legislative process in the Senate is highly flexible because of the use of unanimous consent agreements. The leaders play a central role in arranging these agreements, thereby enhancing their ability to collect IOU's for the future and to reward or punish past behavior.

The second resource possessed by the leaders of both houses is their control over a number of forms of tangible preferment. Tangible preferments include: appointments to special and select committees, commissions (such as those overseeing service academies), and delegations to foreign meetings (such as the NATO parliamentarians); appointments to standing committees; help in pushing specific bills; and help aimed at re-election. Again the granting or withholding of such preferments is used selectively to shorten the odds that the leaders will succeed when they ask for specific policy actions.

The leaders' control over assignments to standing committees is, with the partial exception of the House Democrats, less direct than their control over other appointments. But even indirect influence can be important.

In the House at present, as has been noted, the Speaker and his lieutenants are in a position to name the Democrats on the Rules Committee and to influence initial assignments to other committees heavily. Even before these formal powers were given to the leaders in the mid-1970s they expanded the number of seats on the most desirable committees to help add to their resource base.[21] And the leaders would intervene selectively in the assignment process even during the period when they had little formal role to play. In the 1950s, for example, Speaker Sam Rayburn saw to it that the Democratic membership on the Education and Labor Committee was reoriented from conservative to reliably liberal. Since at least the 1960s the Democratic Committee on Committees has paid some attention to party loyalty in making assignments—those members more loyal to the party are more likely to receive their preferred assignments when they request transfers.[22]

The House Republican leaders have less influence over standing committee assignments. The Committee on Committees is selected and operated so that, typically, a few senior conservatives from the states with the largest Republican delegations effectively make the assignment decisions. This means that the Republican delegations on the most important committees are heavily weighted in the conservative direction.

In the Senate the leaders have only minor influence on committee assignments. This is particularly true in the Republican Party where the Committee on Committees makes initial assignments on the basis of seniority (that is, with only minor exceptions, if two individuals apply for the same opening the more senior man automatically gets it). The influence of the Republican leaders can be seen only occasionally when they might ask a more senior man to apply for an opening in order to keep an undesirable senator off the committee. The Democratic Steering Committee, which is the committee on committees, is not bound by seniority and the majority leader chairs the committee. But his degree of influence is related to his degree of aggressiveness.

The leaders of all four parties can facilitate or impede committee and floor consideration of specific bills.

An additional tangible preferment is campaign help, which leaders can channel to particularly helpful members. Both of the congressional Republican parties have several million dollars at their disposal

---

21. Louis P. Westefield, "Majority Party Leadership and the Committee System in the House of Representatives," *American Political Science Review* 68 (1974): 1593–1604.

22. See Randall B. Ripley, *Party Leaders in the House of Representatives* (Washington: Brookings, 1967): 59–61.

to aid candidates, both incumbents and non-incumbents. This can be given on a selective basis, with maverick incumbents getting little or no aid. The Democratic congressional parties have much less money at their disposal and so the impact of the aid is considerably reduced. The leaders of all four parties can personally campaign for a few incumbents each year. Obviously it is very flattering for a rank-and-file congressman to have the Speaker or the majority leader speak personally in his or her district during a campaign. These appearances are rare and, like most scarce commodities, are highly valued by those who benefit.

The third resource the leaders can use to affect policy statements and actions is psychological preferment. This simply means that the leaders, particularly in the House, are in a position to give cues on how highly they value an individual member. These cues, once given, help establish a member's reputation. A member with a high reputation is likely to be more successful legislatively than a member who is not so highly regarded. House members know they need the respect and good will of their fellows to help make their careers successful in terms of achievement of legislative goals, and therefore are extremely sensitive to the leaders' cues. Skillful leaders can help sway member behavior by the content and timing of the cues and by selective publication of those cues to appropriate audiences. For example, if the Speaker stops a group of four congressmen and singles out one for praise on a floor speech, that is a signal to the others about the esteem in which that individual is held. Likewise, if he pointedly ignores one member of the group, that also conveys a message.

Senators also need respect and good will in the Senate if they are to be deemed successful legislators. On the other hand, senators can also command wider attention than that accorded to House members and many may not worry excessively about their perceived legislative effectiveness. They can also attain gratification by being public figures in their states or regions or even nationally. Almost any senator can command good newspaper space in his state and with a little extra effort can be quoted and pictured regionally or nationally. This opportunity is not open to most House members, which means that they are very sensitive to their standing in the House. Senators who want above all to be considered effective legislators are susceptible to psychological preferment manipulated by the leaders. Senator Mansfield did not use this tactic, although his predecessor, Lyndon Johnson, was masterful at it. The Republican leaders in the 1960s and 1970s were somewhere between Mansfield and Johnson in their level of activity.

The fourth resource that can be used by the leaders in seeking specific legislative action is their dominance over the communications processes internal to the House and Senate. The leaders are in a unique position to control what is learned by members about the schedule and rules affecting pending legislation and about the legislative intentions of the president, key members, and the leaders themselves. Particularly in the House, members of both parties routinely look to their party leaders for reliable information on such matters. They are not, however, heavily dependent on their party leaders for information on the substance of legislation; for that they rely on the standing committee members from their party. Even in the Senate a skillful leader like Lyndon Johnson can make the senators of his party (and even of the other party) come to him or his staff members for the most current and most reliable information.

The dominance over the communications process means that the leaders occupy a critical place. They learn as well as inform and can use their knowledge to enhance their chances for success by urging minor but critical amendments, for example, or by changing the schedule to accommodate a number of members who are in the leaders' camp on a given bill.

THE IMPACT OF THE LEADERS

The Leaders and Individual Members

The members of the House and Senate have definite expectations about the intrusion of the party leaders into their lives as legislators. House members are more likely to consider aggressive leadership legitimate than are senators. Senators acknowledge the legitimacy of their leaders stating party positions on at least some legislative matters, appealing for unity and loyalty on important bills, and distributing and collecting information on scheduling and substance. They do not, however, accept coercion as legitimate, nor do they think that the party leaders should interfere with the business of standing committees, aside from urging them to keep on schedule.[23] Most House members accept the same tasks as legitimate for the leaders to perform but they are more willing than senators to accept the coercive activities of leaders as legitimate.[24] This difference is rooted both in history and tradition (the simple fact that House leaders have usually been more aggressive than their Senate counterparts) and in the perceived necessities of managing a body of 435 people as opposed to a body of only 100 people.

---

23. See Randall B. Ripley, *Power in the Senate* (New York: St. Martin's, 1969): 104–106.
24. See Ripley, *Party Leaders in the House.*

The leaders understand that they must lead through a complicated process of interaction with the members. They can state preferences and apply a variety of pressures to get maximum support. But their job is persuasion—they do not have sanctions available that will always produce compliance. Leaders feel the need, however, to be restrained in the use of the sanctions they do possess because they realize the party membership can balk if it feels it is being subjected to unfair pressure. Members of Congress are keenly aware that they have been elected largely on the basis of their own resources and wits, and they inevitably feel a strong pull toward their constituencies. Likewise, members prize their own independence and resent what they consider to be unfair attempts at coercion to achieve unity for its own sake or even for a specific policy goal. When the pull of constituency or the dictates of conscience conflict with the demands of the party leaders, the member's decision can go either way. The most successful leaders acknowledge the existence of these cross-pressures and undertake a constant balancing act between demanding partisan unity and loyalty and deferring to constituency interests and the dictates of individual judgment.

The Techniques of the Leaders. The party leaders of both houses have a number of specific techniques they can employ to gain the support of their members for specific legislative ends, although they must constantly decide how aggressive to be in using them. Among these techniques are the following:

1. Using personal contact to ask for such actions as favorable roll call votes, votes in committees, certain kinds of speeches on the floor, absence or presence on the floor.
2. Promulgating permanent or temporary changes in the rules, procedures, and practices of the House or Senate that will make favorable legislative outcomes easier to achieve.
3. Using influence over committee assignments to achieve a certain ideological balance on a committee.
4. Encouraging the development of unanimous positions by standing committee contingents before floor debate begins.
5. Announcing official party positions on pending legislation by a letter to all members, by a statement from a policy or steering committee, or by the adoption of an official party position in one of the caucuses or conferences.
6. Coopting key members into the leadership circle for the duration of a given legislative struggle.

7. Stimulating key intra-party groups such as state delegations to unify behind specific positions.

8. Influencing the distribution of tangible rewards such as federal patronage, federal projects and electoral aid.

9. Distributing information selectively to the members on substance and procedure.

10. Giving special concessions to a few key members of the opposition party when a winning coalition cannot be formed from within a single party.

11. Manipulating floor proceedings by scheduling critical business at the most propitious time, arranging for influential speakers, managing the pattern of voting, and helping arrange the optimum time and amendment limits for a particular bill.

Conditions for Success.[25] Not all leaders are equally successful in achieving what they want as they seek to stimulate certain kinds of behavior from the members of their party. The leaders of the minority party are, by definition, dependent on some support from members of the majority party. Their hand is strengthened when the president is also of their party, but the problem of insufficient numbers remains. The leaders of the majority party, who presumably have the numbers on their side, must labor to maximize the unity of their members and prevent defections that could cause losses. In general, majority party leaders have greater chances of legislative success when their majority is large, when it is a relatively new majority, and when there is supportive activity coming from the president and the White House.

The leaders of both parties have increased chances for success on issues not terribly visible or salient to constituents. This leaves members freer to succumb to the blandishments of the leaders. Leaders are also more likely to prevail with specific requests at relatively invisible points in the legislative process. That is, if a member perceives that his position might cause some negative reaction in his constituency, he would feel insecure in honoring a leadership request on a final roll call on the floor. His action in a committee, however, is likely to go unnoticed at home by either the press or public whereas his action in the floor is likely to be reported. Leaders are also more likely to gain converts on issues that are defined in procedural terms than on

25. See Randall B. Ripley, *Majority Party Leadership in Congress* (Boston: Little, Brown, 1969): 184–187; and Lewis A. Froman, Jr. and Randall B. Ripley, "Conditions for Party Leadership: The Case of the House Democrats," *American Political Science Review* 59 (1965): 52–63. See also Barbara Deckard Sinclair, "Determinants of Aggregate Party Cohesion in the U.S. House of Representatives, 1901–1956," *Legislative Studies Quarterly* 2 (1977): 155–175.

issues that are defined in substantive terms. For example, a motion to adjourn may really be a motion that will kill a bill. A person who may mildly favor the bill can still claim that position and yet vote with his party leaders in favor of adjournment and rationalize his action—if it is ever questioned—as "only procedural." Again the relative visibility of actions on procedurally-defined issues is lower than on the substantively-defined issues and this allows members to adhere to the requests of the leaders without worrying in detail about constituency reaction.

The Leaders and Standing Committees

The party leaders are potentially the main centralizing forces in the legislative process, the standing committees the main decentralizing forces. Leaders and committees must necessarily interact in conducting the business of the two chambers. The exact nature of the interaction, however, can vary as can the relative importance of leaders and committees on critical items of substance.

In many ways leaders and committees are interdependent. As party leaders seek specific legislative ends they must rely on the standing committees for a number of things: the detailed substance of bills, the timetable within which bills are ready for floor consideration, the transmission of leaders' legislative preferences to the members of the committee during committee deliberations, and aid in the transmission of those preferences to all party members during floor consideration. Committee leaders must rely on the party leaders for scheduling business for the floor and working for its passage or defeat, for communicating important information about members' preferences to the committee, and for helping distribute committee opinions to non-committee members.

The Nature of Leader-Committee Interaction. There are three particularly important points of interaction between party leaders and committee leaders. The first involves assignments to committees. Who sits on a committee may, in many instances, determine what emerges from that committee. The custom of seniority limits leaders' potential impact on committee assignments to sitting members who desire to change assignments or to new members. In the case of freshmen members and new assignments the leaders of both parties are generally disposed to exercise only minimal influence unless vital issues are at stake.

In changes made in the 1970's, however, the House party leaders have moved into a position to prevent individuals from becoming chairmen or ranking minority members if they can persuade a majority of the party that such individuals are undesirable for those jobs.

In 1971 the Republican conference agreed to allow the conference to vote individually by secret ballot on the representatives nominated by the Committee on Committees to be ranking minority members. If the Republicans should again become the majority party in the House the same procedure would presumably apply to chairmanships. No successful challenges to seniority appointments have been made under the new procedure, although several unsuccessful attempts were made.

In 1971, 1973, and 1975 the House Democrats progressively opened the process of selecting chairmen. Both the caucus and aggressive leaders were thus given more leverage over these critical assignments. The 1971 change was similar to that made by the Republicans. Committee on Committee recommendations came to the caucus one committee at a time and, if requested by ten members, nominations could be debated and voted on—not just for chairmanships but for any position on any committee. If a nomination was rejected, then the Committee on Committees would submit another nomination. In 1971 an unsuccessful challenge was mounted against reappointment of the chairman of the Committee on the District of Columbia on the implied grounds that he did not reflect the majority Democratic opinion about committee business, that he was an arbitrary chairman, and that he pursued racist (anti-black) policies.

In 1973 the Democrats extended their procedure by making it necessary for chairman to obtain a majority vote in the caucus. Twenty percent of the members could demand a secret ballot. In 1973 all chairmen were voted on by secret ballot and all won by very large margins. For the Congress convening in 1975, however, three chairmen were deposed.

In 1975 the procedure on secret ballots on chairmanships was altered so as to make them automatic. Chairpersons of appropriations subcommittees were also made subject to caucus confirmation. The committee assignment power was transferred from the Ways and Means Committee to the Steering and Policy Committee. The Speaker was given the power to name Democratic members of the Rules Committee.

In short, both parties in the House have the machinery for rejecting an unacceptable product of the seniority system in the top spot of any standing committee. And the Democrats have used that machinery. The Republican conference members and Democratic caucus members could, of course, ignore the preferences of the formal party leaders either to retain or reject a chairman or ranking minority member.

But it seems likely that members who have come to those positions through seniority will not be deposed if they have the strong support of the party leaders. And, if the party leaders should ever agree on the necessity of rejecting a nomination for a top position based on seniority, they would probably stand a reasonably good chance of carrying either the caucus or the conference with them.

A second major point of interaction between party leaders and the committee system involves the scheduling of floor activity that, of necessity, has implications for the scheduling of committee business. If the party leaders of the majority party have an overall program in mind (and this is particularly likely to be the case if their party also controls the White House) they are going to need to spread the program out over a Congress. They cannot afford to have all of the important legislation come to the floor in the last two months of a session or, worse yet, the last two months of a Congress. Thus the leaders consult with chairmen about the major items on the agenda both to get some reading on when reports might be expected and to make some requests either to speed up or, less frequently, slow down committee consideration and action.

Similarly, committee chairmen have their own agenda to consider. Therefore, they make timing requests of the leaders for floor consideration on specific dates.

A third point of interaction between party leaders and committees involves the substance of legislative proposals. Party leaders may well be too busy with scheduling matters for the floor and working for their passage (or defeat) to have preferences on the substantive details of legislation. If they are working together with representatives of the White House or individual executive departments or agencies, however, they may have detailed requests on some matters. And some leaders have strong personal interests that they pursue. For example, when Sam Rayburn (D-Tex.) was Speaker he followed the work of the Ways and Means Committee on trade (he wanted fewer restrictions) and the oil depletion allowance (he wanted it preserved unchanged) and did not hesitate to intervene if he felt it necessary.

Leaders in the last few decades have tended to keep their intervention in the work of standing committees to a minimum. They have been much more likely to allow the committee to produce its substantive product by whatever natural processes exist in the committee and then work with the senior members of the committee for the passage (or defeat or amendment) of the committee's handiwork.

A rule adopted in 1973 by the House Democratic caucus increases the likelihood of more substantive input by the leaders into the work of committees. This rule allows fifty or more members of the party to bring to the caucus any amendment proposed to a committee-reported bill if the Rules Committee is requesting a closed rule. If the proposed amendment is supported by a majority of the caucus then the Rules Committee Democrats will be instructed to write the rule for floor consideration so that that specific amendment could be considered on the floor. In effect, this will prevent closed rules on bills if a majority present at a Democratic caucus opposes such a rule. The leeway for leadership intervention is again present here if the Speaker and/or majority leader and/or majority whip should decide to side with the members who want to force floor consideration of a specific amendment not favored by the committee (including at least some of the Democrats on the committee).

The Impact of Leader-Committee Interaction. The nature of the interaction between leaders and standing committees is particularly critical to the performance by Congress of its lawmaking function. In general, the nature of the interaction can be viewed along a spectrum ranging from virtual committee autonomy at one end to leader activism at the other. In a situation of committee autonomy the central party leaders rarely intervene in such matters as committee assignments, the scheduling and timing of committee business, and the substance of matters before committees. In a situation in which leader activism is predominant there is a considerable amount of such intervention. There are, of course, a number of mixed patterns along the spectrum.

Some facets of lawmaking for domestic policy and the domestic aspects of foreign policy (for example, defense procurement, or "buy American" or "ship American" provisions in foreign aid legislation) are different than for the non-domestic aspects of foreign policy. What is the same, however, is that the committee autonomy pattern leaves the congressional party leaders out of an important substantive role in policy of either kind.

When domestic policy is at stake (and also the domestic aspects of foreign policy) the existence of committee autonomy promotes the dominance of subgovernments. Leader activism, on the other hand, promotes increased influence not just for the leaders but also for the president and presidency when the leaders are in accord with presidential policies and for rank-and-file senators and representatives. This increased influence does not eliminate the influence of the subgovernments, but it puts some restraints on it. The subgovernments may or may not produce good or reasonable policy decisions but, in any event, they cannot be expected to consult more than a narrow range of interests in making their decisions. The increased influence for non-subgovernment members that is facilitated by leader activism allows for a broader range of interests to be articulated and consulted.

Another value that can best be served by the leadership activism pattern of interaction is coherence of the legislative program. This simply means that some order is apparent in the welter of proposals presented to Congress—both in terms of substance and in terms of timing. The leadership activism pattern leaves room for an activist president, but in no way does it place Congress in a subordinate position to the president. It simultaneously affords maximum influence for the party leaders and all members. In addition, it puts some restrictions on the influence of the members of the issue-specific subgovernments. If the program is set—both in substance and in timing—by these subgovernments, then little relationship will be seen between programs that are in fact competing for scarce resources or have other logical ties. In the leader activism pattern the centralizing forces can spell out those relationships so that the decisions can be made on the basis of more rather than less information and there is a chance for greater coherence of all legislative results considered together.

The major difference between the situation just described and the situation when non-domestic aspects of foreign policy are at stake is the enormous impact of the president and institutional presidency. Presidential influence over Congress is no longer as much of a problem for the president except on those occasions when he needs a treaty ratified or a new program approved. He may have more problems in relation to appropriations requests. Another major difference is that interest groups play only a very limited role. Thus the chief actors in this policy arena are the president and institutional presidency, the foreign policy bureaucracy, key committee members on the Senate Foreign Relations, House Foreign Affairs, and the two Appropriations Committees, the party leaders, and the individual members of the House and Senate.

An alliance between members of the foreign policy bureaucracy and senior committee members may have considerable influence on the routine aspects of foreign policy, particularly when a pattern of committee autonomy exists. Such an alliance may even limit presidential influence on such matters, although it seems as if the alliance is much less close between the foreign policy bureaucrats and committees and subcommittees than it is in many domestic areas (including the domestic aspects of foreign policy). The major subgovernment in foreign policy may, in fact, consist of the presidency and foreign policy bureaucracy with all congressional elements, including the key committee and subcommittee members as well as the party leaders, relegated to relatively minor roles.

In a pattern of leader activism the leaders increase their potential for influence in the foreign policy arena and can also enhance the potential for influence on the part of members of the two chambers not on the specific committees dealing with central foreign policy issues by serving as their spokesmen and by helping them aggregate their positions. It also seems likely that in the event of a major disagreement between a committee and the president, the committee itself will have a stronger hand if backed by at least some of the central party leaders —especially if the leaders are from both parties. Thus leader activism does not necessarily diminish the potential for influence on the part of committees, except perhaps in some of the routine matters that are left mostly to the interaction of committees and subcommittees and the foreign policy bureaucracy. The difference is that in domestic policy and the domestic aspects of foreign policy these routine matters, when aggregated, constitute the bulk of policy both in amount and importance. But in the foreign policy arena routine matters are not as important.

*　　*　　*　　*

If Congress is assessed in terms of its potential for important and swift policy action, the party leaders necessarily play a critical role. On those occasions when Congress has been at its most active the party leaders have usually been aggressive—both in their own right and in responding to an aggressive president. When the leaders are the most constrained in their actions, either of their own volition or by virtue of matters over which they have little control, Congress is most likely to be proceeding on a "normal" course of handling most matters in a disaggregated and incremental fashion. Thus the performance of the leaders offers an index to the overall mood and performance of Congress. And, since the leaders can help shape the environment in which they work, the choices they make on how they use their resources, what techniques they employ, and how they perform their functions can help determine the nature of congressional influence on public policy.

CHAPTER 7

OTHER INTERNAL INFLUENCES: STATE DELEGATIONS, GROUPS, STAFF, AND SUPPORT AGENCIES

MEMBERS OF THE HOUSE AND SENATE RECEIVE A CONSTANT BARRAGE of advice—both solicited and unsolicited—on which policies to support from their standing committee colleagues and from the party leaders. The committees and leaders are the most consistently important forces internal to Congress that shape public policy. There are, however, other forces inside Congress that also serve as important sources of advice and direction for individual members as they seek to cope with a staggering workload in a limited amount of time. State delegations, regional blocs, ideological groups, staff members working both for individual members and for committees, and four central support agencies all perform this function. The relative sizes of the two houses dictate that state delegations and ideological groups have particular importance in the House and that staff members have particular importance in the Senate.

STATE DELEGATIONS AND REGIONAL BLOCS

Throughout the American political system the states have always been important objects of loyalty. The federal scheme of the Constitution springs in part from such loyalty. Our national parties are more properly thought of as confederations of fifty state parties. State loyalties are also extremely important inside Congress, particularly in the House of Representatives (which, in a way, is ironic given that senators are explicitly thought to be the representatives of states). In the House, state loyalty is made operational through the functioning of the state delegations, usually divided on a partisan basis. These clusters of members can help each other by the sharing of useful and timely information and by aiding each other to maximize their ability to achieve desired ends such as attractive committee assignments and a "fair share" of federal program money and installations for their individual districts.

Sometimes state delegations meet on a bipartisan basis. Occasionally senators from the same state will be included, regardless of party. But these bipartisan, bicameral meetings are relatively rare and involve only questions relating to direct federal benefits for the state or region in which the state is included. Ordinarily, the state delegations that are important in the flow of information and benefits are the party delegations from the House alone. These delegations will be the focus of the following section.[1]

State Party Delegations in the House

Types of Delegations. State party delegations vary greatly in the frequency of their meetings, the extent to which they help socialize new members, the amount of interaction they have outside of meetings, the topics they discuss in their meetings, and whether they seek unity in voting on the floor of the House. In short, they vary greatly in cohesion.

State delegations can be grouped into four broad types.[2] The first type rarely meets, discusses only local issues (for example, new federal installations or the performance of federal programs in the state) at meetings, and explicitly does not seek unity in voting on the floor. The second type also meets rarely, but discusses national as well as local issues, and does seek floor unity. The third type meets often, discusses national and local issues, and seeks floor unity. The fourth type meets often, discusses only national issues, and does not seek floor unity. About half of the delegations in both parties seek unity and about half do not.

Two conditions seem to promote state delegation cohesion: stable membership and a relatively high proportion of members desiring to make their careers in the House.[3] Socioeconomic homogeneity of districts is not necessary for cohesion—defined in terms of interaction,

---

1. In addition to the material cited in footnotes 2–12 on state delegations see also Charles L. Clapp, *The Congressman* (Washington, D.C.: Brookings, 1963): 41–45; John H. Kessel, "The Washington Congressional Delegation," *Midwest Journal of Political Science* 8 (1964): 1–21; Leo M. Snowiss, "Congressional Recruitment and Representation," *American Political Science Review* 60 (1966): 627–639; and Richard Born, "Cue-Taking within State Party Delegations in the U.S. House of Representatives," *Journal of Politics* 38 (1976): 71–94.
2. Randall B. Ripley, *Party Leaders in the House of Representatives* (Washington: Brookings, 1967): 169–175.
3. Barbara Deckard, "State Party Delegations in the U.S. House of Representatives: A Comparative Study of Group Cohesion," *Journal of Politics* 34 (1972): 199–222.

information flow, and socialization—to be high. Such homogeneity, however, may be necessary for unified bloc voting to occur. Likewise, homogeneity of ideology or positions on public policy questions is not necessary for a delegation to function effectively to help members attain a variety of goals such as achieving good committee assignments, promoting the flow of federal benefits to the state, and creating a reliable set of informants on a variety of substantive questions.[4]

Delegations in the Communications Network. Most members of the House constantly seek information on the substance of the great number of matters they have to consider, on the procedure by which those matters are considered, and on the preferences and intentions of others both in the House and outside of it. Given the vast workload, the complexity of the rules, and the large number of policy actors, members value time-saving devices that can provide them with reliable information.

State party delegations are a means of providing a lot of information to members quickly. Members do in fact look to their state delegations for much advice concerning both procedure and substance, particularly on matters coming from the standing committees on which those other members sit.[5] A large delegation is likely to have members on many or most of the most important committees in the House and a representative from such a delegation is in a good position to minimize the amount of time he needs to spend in collecting information about bills emerging from the committee structure.

Delegations also communicate voting cues to members on the floor of the House. These cues may be worked out ahead of time in a meeting of the delegation when the preferred voting position for members is discussed and decided. The cues may also be transmitted at the last minute on the floor, perhaps by word of mouth or perhaps simply by members observing and imitating the vote of a key figure.

There are several motives for members to accept the cues. One is simply that they respect the opinion of the individual in the delegation to whom they turn for the cue in any given situation. A second is that if all of the members of a state party delegation vote the same way they protect themselves from criticism at home. They can offer each other a

---

4. Barbara Deckard, "State Party Delegations in the United States House of Representatives—An Analysis of Group Action," *Polity* 5 (1973): 311–334.

5. See Arthur G. Stevens, Jr., "Informal Groups and Decision-Making in the U.S. House of Representatives," (Ph.D. dissertation, University of Michigan, 1970); and Alan Fiellin, "The Function of Informal Groups in Legislative Institutions," *Journal of Politics* 24 (1962): 72–91. See also Fiellin, "The Group Life of a State Delegation in the House of Representatives," *Western Political Quarterly* 23 (1970): 305–320.

protective coloration by sticking together. Third, they are aware that they enhance their bargaining potential within the House if they maintain an alliance. If they can deliver a predictable number of votes, for example, on a given measure important to some other group or set of individuals in the House then they are in a position to ask for reciprocal action on something of particular importance to them (for example, an amendment to a public works bill adding a project in their state).

In addition to transmitting information on substance, procedure, and voting, state party delegations also serve as agents of socialization. In the discussions between more senior delegation members and more junior members the norms and traditions of life in the House are passed on, with any particular twists appropriate to the delegation involved. The delegations, especially those that are cohesive, also offer some relief from the normal frustrations of being a junior member of the House.[6] In general, members of delegations that interact a great deal both socially and substantively—delegations in recent years such as the Democrats from Illinois, Massachusetts, and Texas—seem to enjoy life in the House and are generally more highly House career-oriented than members of delegations with low cohesion, such as both the Democrats and Republicans from New York in recent years.

Delegations and the Distribution of Benefits. State delegations work to channel the benefits distributed to individual members of the House and to states, regions, and districts. For the individual representative one of the most important benefits is committee assignments. Delegations that have members serving on important committees strive to ensure that their seat on that committee is retained within the delegation whenever it becomes open. About two out of every five committee seats in the House are, in fact, reserved for members from specific states, regardless of turnover of individuals.[7] For example, New York Democrats always hold a seat on Banking, Finance, and Urban Affairs, no doubt because of the importance of the financial community in New York City. The member from the Virginia congressional district that includes part of the greater Norfolk area has consistently held a seat on the Merchant Marine and Fisheries Committee because of the importance of shipping, fishing, and other maritime pursuits to his district. In practice, since World War II this tradition of inheritance has protected medium and small Democratic delegations' seats on com-

6. See Deckard, "State Party Delegations . . . A Comparative Study . . .", 222.
7. Charles S. Bullock III, "Influence of State Party Delegations on House Committee Assignments," *Midwest Journal of Political Science* 15 (1971): 525–546.

mittees and has not allowed a takeover by the large states. In the Republican case, however, the norm of same state occupancy of key seats works in favor of the large delegations. Regionally, the norm works to the advantage of southern Democratic delegations; there is no such regional bias in the Republican party.

Delegations work to gain support for projects important to their states and regions. The bargaining power of a united delegation is considerable. For example, dependable support for the policy positions of the party leadership and Democratic presidents through the years on the part of Illinois Democrats is certainly related to the favored treatment Chicago has received in many federal programs during Democratic administrations.

Delegations also work for programmatic amendments that have broader impact. In 1964, for example, the North Carolina Democrats extracted a promise that a given federal official they disliked would not be employed in the proposed poverty program before they agreed to vote for the program on the House floor. Also in 1964, the California Democrats obtained a promise from the leaders that they would work to raise the amount of the pay increase for congressmen in a pending pay bill from $7,500 to $10,000.[8]

Delegations can use their important committee positions in bargaining both with other members and delegations and with the House party leaders. They also can use a high degree of unity in floor voting as a bargaining tool—a united delegation can deliver a sizable impact on a given House vote. Ample empirical evidence shows that delegations do in fact tend to vote together.[9] The fact of being from a given state (and party) accounts for some cohesion in roll call votes that cannot be explained by party combined separately with type of constituency, region, or ideology of members.[10]

The conclusion reached by a recent study is that the influence of state delegations is strong enough "to warrant attention to state party as a 'standard' predictor in the analysis of congressional voting behavior." [11]

---

8. For additional information about these and other examples see Lewis A. Froman and Randall B. Ripley, "Conditions for Party Leadership: The Case of the House Democrats," *American Political Science Review* 59 (1965): 62–63.

9. David B. Truman, "The State Delegation and the Structure of Voting in the United States House of Representatives," *American Political Science Review* 50 (1956): 1023–1045; Truman, *The Congressional Party* (New York: Wiley, 1959): 249–269; Stevens, "Informal Groups and Decision-Making"; and Aage R. Clausen, "State Party Influence on Congressional Party Decisions," *Midwest Journal of Political Science* 16 (1972): 77–101.

10. Stevens, "Informal Groups and Decision-Making," 135–136.

11. Clausen, "State Party Influence on Congressional Policy Decisions," 100.

Regional Party Delegations in the House

Although region is often used as a category for analyzing roll call votes in the House, this does not mean that regional groups actually interact very often. In general, such interaction is limited. Western Democrats from the mountain states have met with some regularity in some Congresses to discuss matters of common interest: reclamation, grazing policy, timbering policy, mining policy.

A group of conservative southern Democrats has also met with some regularity since the end of World War II in order to generate both discussion and positions on a wide variety of legislation. This group, called the "Boll Weevils" by the press, has had a fluctuating and uncertain membership. In the 1960s about thirty to thirty-five members usually attended meetings. The Democratic leaders in the House basically have been unwilling to deal with the "Weevils," most of whom are seen as uncompromisingly conservative. Occasionally the leaders will attempt to mute the "Weevils' " thrust, however. In 1963, for example, the most conservative Democratic member of the Ways and Means Committee (who was not a member of the "Boll Weevils") met with the "Weevils" at the request of the party leaders and Chairman Wilbur Mills to convince them that a Republican recommittal motion represented phony economy. His initiative met with some success; enough of the group voted against the Republican motion to insure that the leaders' and president's position would win on the floor. In 1972 the Democratic Research Organization (discussed below) was formed and has replaced the "Weevils."

Another recent regional development involved the New England states. Using money supplied principally by a regional business organization, New Englanders in 1973 established two Washington offices—the New England Congressional Caucus and an Economic Research Office. In theory, the Caucus office is to supply information and help frame agendas for action on the part of all of the senators and representatives from both parties in the region. The focus is on the economic problems of New England—high unemployment, tariffs, fuel oil imports, and bankrupt regional railroads. And one "thrust will be to see that New England gets what's coming to it." [12]

In late 1976 a new regional group was formed in Congress—The Northeast-Midwest Economic Advancement Coalition. It is composed of all 216 House members from sixteen northeastern and midwestern

---

12. John L. Moore, "Washington Pressures/Business Forms Economic Study Unit to Support Bipartisan New England Caucus," *National Journal* (February 17, 1973): 226–233. The quotation is from Representative Silvio Conte, Massachusetts Republican, and appears on p. 230.

states. Basically its purpose is to fight for federal dollars, especially through getting formulas in legislation favorable to the areas they represent. It hired a small staff to buttress its efforts in contesting with the "Sunbelt" states over federal largesse. The Northeast-Midwest Coalition claimed that federal formulas discriminated against their states and in favor of southern and western states.

State and Regional Delegations in the Senate

Senators from the same state and same party tend to vote together because they share both party ideology and face the same constituency needs and demands. Senators from the same state but different parties may vote very differently although they may well cooperate on pork barrel matters of interest to the state. They cooperate only sporadically with House members on the same kind of matters.

Region has also been used as an analytical category for studying roll call voting in the Senate. But actual interaction of regional groupings of senators, with the possible exception of southern Democrats until the last few years, has been sporadic. In general, it can be said that the Senate is small enough to do without many intermediate groups between individual senators and the standing committees.

OTHER GROUPS IN THE HOUSE

The membership of the House has always been addicted to forming clubs and groups. After World War II the Republicans took the lead in forming a variety of clubs that were based on a mixture of social congeniality, geography, committee assignment, and year of entry into the House. Some of these clubs—such as the Chowder and Marching Society, the S.O.S., and the Acorns have survived for a number of years. They perform primarily social functions but also serve as locations for the transmission of information and the discussion of policy. Even less formal groups, such as regular combinations of paddle ball players in the House gym, serve both social (and athletic) and discussion functions. Most of these social groups are only occasionally and marginally important in the development and passage of public policy in the House. There is no evidence, for example, that these largely social groupings have enough standing or members to bargain with party or committee leaders over policy.

The organization of freshman Democrats in the Ninety-fourth Congress (1975–1976) was unusual in that it was both very large (seventy-five members) and quite homogeneous ideologically. Thus it organized more formally than most "class" clubs (it even had its own whip organization), sought unity on a number of issues with considerable success, and did engage in bargaining with the leaders, both private and public, including one well publicized meeting with Speaker Albert. This group was particularly important in helping generate the changes in party organization in late 1974 (just after they had been elected) and early 1975.

Beginning in the late 1950s and then increasingly in the 1960s and 1970s various groupings of House members began to form a variety of caucuses and organizations that are specifically designed to influence public policy and to generate group unity behind specific positions and views.[13] These groups explicitly desire to help shape policy and to bargain with the leaders, committees, and other groups in the House. Some of them have been relatively successful.

By the late 1970s three major types of issue-oriented groups existed: what might be called programmatic or ideological groups (those that took positions on a broad range of issues), issue groups (those that focused only on one restricted and specific set of questions), and ethnic groups (those focusing on issues believed to be particularly important to a specific ethnic group).

Programmatic Groups

In the late 1970s four programmatic or ideological groups functioned in the House: the Democratic Study Group, the Democratic Research Organization, the Republican Study Committee, and the Republican Wednesday Group.

The Democratic Study Group.[14] The DSG began in 1957 as a loose alliance of liberal Democrats. It immediately set up a whip organization, which functioned sporadically until 1959 when the DSG was formally established. The group has developed into a sturdy institution with an elected chairman, a full-time staff of about 25, a budget

---

13. For a good survey of the group situation in the House as the 95th Congress opened in early 1977 see Michael J. Malbin, "Where There's a Cause There's a Caucus on Capitol Hill," *National Journal* (January 8, 1977): 56–58.

14. On the Democratic Study Group, see Mark F. Ferber, "The Formation of the Democratic Study Group," in Nelson W. Polsby (ed.), *Congressional Behavior* (New York: Random House, 1971): 249–267; Kenneth Kofmehl, "The Institution-alization of a Voting Bloc," *Western Political Quarterly* 17 (1964): 256–272; and Arthur G. Stevens, Jr., Arthur H. Miller, and Thomas E. Mann, "Mobilization of Liberal Strength in the House, 1955–1970: The Democratic Study Group," *American Political Science Review* 68 (1974): 667–681.

of about $300,000 in 1976 (contributed by members from their staff allowances), and an effective whip organization. Its membership has fluctuated, but basically has grown over time. Forty members attended the formal organizational meeting in 1959. During the Ninety-fourth Congress (1975–76) there were about 225 dues paying members. The DSG attempts to bring all liberal Democrats (including those from the South) into its membership and has been largely successful. Some Democrats who do not formally belong subscribe to its informational services.

The DSG members themselves form task forces and issue reports on various subject matter areas. The DSG staff produces five different kinds of documents. There is a weekly *Legislative Report* that summarizes legislative activity projected for the week. There are "Fact Sheets" that are detailed analyses of major bills and include summaries of both sides of major issues. There are also "Special Reports" that focus on broad topics that are not necessarily immediately before the House in the form of bills but are on the congressional agenda in a broader sense. There are also weekly "Staff Bulletins" and monthly roll call analyses.

The DSG whip organization performs much as the regular party whip organizations perform. Its main task is to get a good DSG turnout on the floor when critical votes are being taken.

In the 1964 congressional campaign the DSG moved into a new area of endeavor when it gave financial aid to the campaigns of 105 liberal Democratic candidates, 79 of whom won. Total spending in 1964 was $38,250, with between $250 and $1,250 going to each individual selected to receive aid (these were both incumbents and non-incumbents). In 1970 DSG campaign spending had increased to $120,000 and the size of contributions for individuals had also increased both because more money was available and fewer candidates were aided. Support was provided that year by the DSG for 68 candidates (26 incumbents and 42 non-incumbents), 46 of whom won (24 incumbents and 22 non-incumbents). By 1976 DSG campaign contributions had grown to $150,000, divided between about 100 candidates (roughly half incumbents and half non-incumbents).

DSG members vote together on the floor. For example a study by the DSG staff of voting in the Ninetieth Congress (1967–1968) concluded that DSG members voted together 91 percent of the time in support of Democratic programs and policies. An academic study also reached the conclusion that DSG members voted quite cohesively.[15] This is hardly surprising since ideological agreement is the basis for

---

15. Stevens and others, "Mobilization of Liberal Strength . . ."

self-selected membership. Because of its size and increasing skill in working in the House the DSG has come to be an important force on a variety of issues.

Democratic Research Organization. At the end of 1972 five conservative southern Democrats formed the DRO as a counterweight to the DSG. By 1976 it had about sixty-five to seventy members and a staff of four full-time persons and three part-time persons. As with the DSG, contributions by members from their office staff allowances supported the staff. The principal output of the staff is the DRO equivalent of DSG "Fact Sheets," which analyze major upcoming bills. The DRO also sponsors some meetings with speakers from outside the House who take and explain a conservative position.

Republican Study Committee. The RSC was formed in 1973 to promote conservative Republican views. By 1976 it had about sixty members and a staff of eleven. Its primary written output is "Fact Sheets."

Wednesday Group. Liberal Republicans, not very numerous in the House, formed this group in the Eighty-eighth Congress (1963–64). The group has expanded its ideological horizons a bit to include some moderates and had grown slowly from its initial fourteen members to thirty-six in 1976. The staff of four produces background papers on issues. The group meets weekly (appropriately on Wednesday) and is small enough that the members consider these meetings useful and important. Given its small minority status within the Republican Party, the group has little bargaining weight with the leadership, which is conservatively oriented.

Issue Groups

In 1977 there were at least seven different groups operating in the House (one included senators too) that focused on specific issues or sets of related issues. The Members of Congress for Peace through Law, founded in 1966, included thirty-five senators and 137 House members in 1976. The members come from both parties. It sponsors briefings and staff research. It grew basically as a home for "doves" during the period of the Vietnam War.

In 1976 another group in the national security area, the National Security Research Group, was formed to provide more "hawkish" or conservative alternatives to the Peace through Law group. The organizational meeting was attended by twenty-five members, about equally divided between Democrats and Republicans.

The Environmental Study Conference was formed in 1975. In 1976 it had 170 House members and thirty Senate members from both parties. It has a staff of seven, publishes a weekly bulletin, and sponsors briefings on environmental questions.

The Congressional Rural Caucus, formed in 1973, claimed 100 members by 1976. Its two-person staff attempts to follow principal issues dealing with rural development (defined more broadly than just agriculture).

The Congressional Clearinghouse on Women's Rights was formed in 1975 with fourteen members. The main product coming from the staff is a weekly newsletter.

The Congressional Clearinghouse on the Future, with a staff of one, began to put out a monthly newsletter in 1976 and scheduled seminars on projecting various aspects of the future for 1977.

In 1977 a new group was formed that might best be called a "blue collar" caucus. Its thirteen members were House members who had come to the House from full-time blue collar jobs. Their announced goal is to protect the rights of the workingman and to analyze legislation from the blue collar point of view.[16]

Ethnic Groups

There are two ethnic groups in the House. One is made up of the five members with Spanish surnames—the Congressional Hispanic Caucus. It was formed in very late 1976 and, given its small numbers, has not emerged as much of a force in the House.

The other ethnic group—the Congressional Black Caucus—is older, larger, better developed, and more of a force in the House.[17] It was formally organized in 1971 with the twelve members then sitting (the D.C. delegate joined shortly thereafter). In 1977 there were sixteen members. By definition its membership is limited to black members of the House (and the Delegate from the District of Columbia). A white representative applied for membership in 1975 but was turned down specifically on the grounds of race. Inside the House the staff of seven and the members follow legislative concerns the members feel

16. Martin Tolchin, "Congressmen Form a Caucus to Work for 'Little Guy'," *New York Times,* June 25, 1977.

17. On the Congressional Black Caucus see Marguerite Ross Barnett, "The Congressional Black Caucus," in Harvey C. Mansfield, Sr. (ed.), *Congress against the President,* Volume 32, No. 1, of *Proceedings of the Academy of Political Science:* 34–50; Charles P. Henry, "Legitimizing Race in Congressional Politics," *American Politics Quarterly* 5 (1977): 149–176; a special issue of *Focus,* vol. 5, no. 8 (August-September, 1977); and Alan Ehrenhalt, "Black Caucus: A Wary Carter Ally," *Congressional Quarterly Weekly Report* (May 21, 1977): 967–972.

are particularly important to blacks. Caucus unity on issues is almost always unbroken, not just because the members are all black but because they are also liberal Democrats. The Caucus is in some ways more important outside Congress than inside. It has sought, with considerable success, to be recognized as a leading national black organization that is legitimate in speaking for the concerns of black persons in a general sense. The Caucus has a $100,000 budget with which to support its work.

CONGRESSIONAL STAFFS

Staffing for Congress grew slowly until very recently. Then in the 1970s the numbers of both personal and committee staff members expanded rapidly. Every member of both houses now has a sizable personal staff and most members have committee staff members that are specially responsible to them personally or at least to a relatively small subcommittee on which they sit. Only since World War II has Congress shown consistent concern for developing professional staff—both for individual members and for committees. Since that time the "congressional bureaucracy" has grown from a few hundred to over 13,000 in number. These staff members are essential in managing the extremely heavy workload of Congress. Without them neither the individual members nor the committees could perform adequately. The presence of adequate staff does not guarantee good congressional performance, but without adequate staff Congress would certainly lose much of its capacity to be consistently important in shaping public policy.[18]

Personal Staff

Congress began to provide money for individual senators and representatives to hire personal staff members for their Washington offices in the late nineteenth century. Since that time there has been a steady increase in the funds allocated for this purpose.

The amount of money senators receive for their staffs varies accord-

---

18. For the most recent and most comprehensive treatment of congressional staff see Harrison W. Fox, Jr., and Susan Webb Hammond, *Congressional Staff: The Invisible Force in American Lawmaking* (New York: Free Press, 1977). On the place of staff in the functioning of Congress see Warren H. Butler, "Administering Congress: The Role of Staff," *Public Administration Review* 26 (1966): 3–13. For a more recent study of staff in the Senate alone, which concludes that staff is "ubiquitous and important in the policy process," see Norman J. Ornstein and David Rohde, "Resource Usage, Information and Policymaking in the Senate," in a compilation of papers prepared for the Commission on the Operation of the Senate, *Senators: Offices, Ethics, and Pressures* (Washington: U.S. Government Printing Office, 1977): 37–46.

ing to the size of the state the senator represents. In 1975 the range of the annual staff allowance to each senator was from $413,082 for states with fewer than two million people to $844,608 for states with more than twenty-one million people. There are no limits on the number of people who can be hired with this money. In 1975 junior senators were instrumental in amending the rules of the Senate to provide over $100,000 additional for each senator to hire three more staff members explicitly designated to help them with their committee work. These staff members are formally on committee staffs but, in effect, work as personal staff members.

In 1976 there were about 3,250 personal staff members working for senators. Virtually all senators had year-round offices in their states (most had more than one such office) and employed over one-fourth of all their staff members in those offices. State offices have expanded greatly in size in recent years. In 1972, for example, only about 15 percent of Senate personal staff members worked in the states.

Two examples of staff size and geographical location in 1977 serve to suggest the range in the Senate. In that year a California Democratic senator, Alan Cranston, employed fifty-four individuals—forty-three in Washington, four in a year-round office in Los Angeles, six in a year-round office in San Francisco, and one in a year-round office in San Diego. Senator Malcolm Wallop, a Wyoming Republican, employed a staff of eighteen, thirteen in Washington, two in a year-round office in Casper, two in a year-round office in Cheyenne, and one in a year-round office in Sheridan.

In 1975 each House member received a staff allowance of $238,584

Table 7–1
Number of Personal Staff Members in Congress,
Selected Years, 1930–1976

Year	Senate	House
1930	280	870
1935	424	870
1947	590	1440
1957	1115	2441
1967	1749	4055
1972	2426	5280
1976	3251	6939

Source: Harrison W. Fox, Jr. and Susan Webb Hammond, Congressional Staffs: The Invisible Force in American Lawmaking *(New York: Free Press, 1977): 171.*

and could hire up to eighteen staff members with that allowance. Only about one-third of the members hired eighteen; most hired fewer and paid them more. House rules also permit the use of staff money to hire persons who are then assigned to groups such as the Democratic Study Group and the Republican Study Committee. (Senate rules do not allow such pooling of resources.) In 1976 House members had hired a total of almost 7,000 personal staff members. About one-third of these members were assigned to district offices (and about half of the House members had more than one district office) and the rest were in the Washington offices.

Party leaders in both houses were also given extra staff members to work in their leadership offices.

Table 7–1 summarizes the growth of personal staff in the House and Senate from 1930 through 1976. Table 7–2 summarizes the very distinct trend in the last two decades for House members (and the trend has been the same in the Senate) to assign an increasing proportion of their staff to district offices and to establish more than one district office.

The Job of Personal Staff Members. Personal staff members are asked to undertake a great variety of jobs. In general, three kinds of skills are represented in the typical office: clerical-bureaucratic support skills, technical-professional legislative skills, and political skills. Clerical-bureaucratic work dominates what goes on in a member's office. The mail must be answered, constituent casework pursued, visitors received, files kept, and phones answered. The substance of proposed legislation and other legislative matters also need staff attention but since the same individuals are usually required to perform in all three areas, the demands of clerical-bureaucratic support work often leave little time for legislative problems. On the political front, members need some staff people who know the political situation in their state

Table 7–2
The Growth of District Offices for House Members

	1960	1967	1974
Percentage of total personal staff members assigned to district offices	14	26	34
Percentage of House members with more than one District office	4	18	47

Source: Morris P. Fiorina, Congress: Keystone of the Washington Establishment *(New Haven: Yale University Press, 1977): 58.*

or district and who can advise and work for successful re-election campaigns. Preparing for re-election is virtually a continual process, particularly in the House. Members of both chambers also need staff members who know the political situation inside both Congress and segments of the bureaucracy so that the member can maximize his impact on policy issues important to him.

A study of congressional workloads in the mid-1960s provides evidence that the staff, at least for House members, is unable to provide much legislative help.[19] Table 7-3 summarizes the results of that study. Only 14 percent of staff time was spent directly on legislative matters. A study that included a survey of the activities of professional personal staff in senatorial offices revealed the same situation.[20] A sample of 188 such staff members reported engaging in "legislative research,

Table 7-3
Average Staff Work Week for the Office of a United States Representative.

Activity	Percent of Staff Time Spent
Legislative Support	14.2
With member in committee	
With lobbyists and special interest groups	
Writing speech drafts, floor remarks	
On legislative research, bill drafting	
Constituency Service	24.7
Constituency casework	
Visiting with constituents in Washington	
Correspondence	40.9
On pressure and opinion mail	
On opinion ballots	
On requests for information	
On letters of congratulation, condolence	
On other correspondence	
Education and Publicity	10.3
On press work, radio, television	
Mailing government publications	
Other	9.9
Total	100.00

Source: Adapted from John S. Saloma III, Congress and the New Politics, *(Boston: Little, Brown, 1969): 185.*

19. John S. Saloma III, *Congress and the New Politics* (Boston: Little, Brown, 1969).

20. Harrison W. Fox, Jr., and Susan Webb Hammond, "The Growth of Congressional Staffs," in Harvey C. Mansfield, Sr. (ed.), *Congress against President,* Volume 32, No. 1, of *Proceedings of Academy of Political Science* (1975): 119. For other material on the work of personal staffs in the Senate see Kenneth Kofmehl, *Professional Staffs of Congress,* 3rd ed. (West Lafayette, Indiana: Purdue University Press, 1977): Chapter 11; and Randall B. Ripley, *Power in the Senate* (New York: St. Martin's, 1969): Chapter 8.

bill drafting, and reading and analyzing bills" much less frequently than they dealt with correspondence, with requests for information, and with lobbyists and representatives of special interest groups.

The Organization of Personal Staffs. Senators and representatives organize their offices in a variety of ways. Some have all of their top assistants report directly to them; others have a more hierarchically structured office. House offices tend to have a single top aide who combines skills in bureaucratic, legislative, and political areas. The others on the office staff are likely to be more exclusively concerned with bureaucratic-clerical matters.

Most Senate offices are organized functionally; duties are more clearly divided and defined than in House offices (largely because senators have much larger staffs). Typically, there are one or more professionals in charge of public relations, casework, legislation, political affairs, and office administration. The professionals are, of course, aided by a number of clerical employees.

One central purpose for any pattern of organization, either in the House or the Senate, is to handle routine matters expeditiously so that the members and their top staff aides have time to deal with more important matters involving the substance of policy. Sometimes, however, the pressure of the routine consumes virtually all of the time of the staff member and perhaps of the member too. The items in Table 7–3 under Constituency Service, Correspondence, and Education and Publicity dominate staff time.

The Legislative Impact of Personal Staff. Staff members in the offices of individual senators and representatives can and do have substantial legislative impact, despite the limited time available for legislative work.[21] This is particularly true of the top assistants to senators. For the most part, the average senator is not the genuine legislative expert that many House members are, given their limited and specialized responsibilities. Senators are fewer in number than House members and have a larger number of committee and subcommittee assignments. As a result they must spread themselves much thinner in terms of substantive expertise. Also, senators usually have more ex-

---

21. For general material on the legislative importance of personal staff members (and there is also some material on committee staff members too) see Michael J. Malbin, "Congressional Committee Staffs: Who's in Charge Here?," *The Public Interest*, No. 47 (Spring, 1977): 16–40; Michael Andrew Scully, "Reflections of a Senate Aide," *The Public Interest*, No. 46 (Spring, 1977): 41–48; Spencer Rich, "Senate Aides Play Key Role in Defense, Diplomacy Battles," *Washington Post*, June 2, 1975; and Spencer Rich, "An Invisible Network of Hill Power," *Washington Post*, March 20, 1977.

ternal demands on their time in terms of requests for speeches, television and radio appearances, newspaper interviews, and other such activities that do not as often involve the average representative. The typical senator therefore needs help, especially in the areas about which he knows very little and has little time to learn. For this help, he frequently turns to his staff members.

Case literature provides a great deal of evidence of the legislative importance of senatorial aides. For example, in the passage of the Clean Air Act of 1963 three assistants to individual senators were critical figures in making the final compromises that went into the statute.[22] They, working with one committee staff member, reached agreements that received only cursory scrutiny from the senators who were involved before final action was taken. Another example is provided by the legislative assistant for Senator Harrison Williams (D-N.J.) in the development of the bargains and compromises that led to the passage of the Mass Transportation Act of 1964.[23]

A close study of Oklahoma Democrat Mike Monroney's staff concluded that it "is designed to play many of the roles of a United States senator with a minimum of personal intervention." [24] One man in particular became a specialist on water resources and reclamation questions and was so effective that he was sometimes called "the third Senator from Oklahoma". Because of the confidence Monroney placed in him he was free to make many decisions about important matters on his own.

In 1976 and 1977 an experienced Senate aide to Senator Adlai Stevenson (D-Ill.) was the critical figure in designing and then working for the passage of the Senate's reorganization of its committee system.[25]

Senator Mark Hatfield (R-Ore.) summarized the general situation in the Senate from his point of view in 1977: "There is a growing dependency on staff, almost to the point of [an aide] saying, 'I think you should vote this way.' " [26]

---

22. See Randall B. Ripley, "Congress Supports Clean Air, 1963," in Frederic N. Cleaveland and associates, *Congress and Urban Problems* (Washington, D.C.: Brookings, 1969).

23. See Royce Hanson, "Congress Catches the Subway: Urban Mass Transit Legislation, 1960–1964," in Cleaveland, *Congress and Urban Problems.*

24. John F. Bibby and Roger H. Davidson, *On Capitol Hill* (New York: Holt, Rinehart and Winston, 1967): 94–112. For additional material on the behavior of specific staffs see Bibby and Davidson, *On Capitol Hill* (Hinsdale, Ill.: Dryden, 1972, 2nd ed.): 95–96, 111–114.

25. Martin Tolchin, "Aides in Congress, The Shadow Government," *New York Times,* September 25, 1977.

26. Quoted in *ibid.*

Staff members can increase their legislative impact if they are aggressive in advising the individual for whom they work and in challenging the views of that individual at least some of the time. They can also enhance their influence if they have a sense of exactly the proper time to release critical information or a point of view to a member. One Republican staff member in the Senate put it well: "At the point when a senator gets to a committee meeting, particularly the executive sessions, and at the point when he goes to the floor to listen to the last few chords of debate and cast a vote, there an assistant who is either well read or at least well prepared and is able to pick out the salient points and say which does what to whom, when and how can make a big difference in the final decision of the senator." [27]

Members become particularly reliant on personal staff for legislative assistance on new problems they have not faced before and on matters on which they have not become expert themselves. Junior members are more likely to rely heavily on personal staff for legislative help than senior members both because they are less experienced and expert personally and because they have less access to committee staff. Minority party members are also more likely to rely heavily on personal staff than majority party members because they have less access to committee staff.

Staff members for members from states with small populations (in the case of the Senate) or for members from states and districts geographically distant from Washington are most likely to be important legislatively. Senate staffs for members from large states are beseiged by an unusual amount of mail, casework, and personal visits that makes it difficult to free any time for legislative work. Staffs in either house whose member's state or district is relatively close to Washington have an inordinate amount of time eaten up by calls from constituents.

Committee Staff

In the mid-nineteenth century congressional committees gradually began to hire clerks to help them with their work, but formal professional staffs were slow to develop.[28] By the time of World War II only

27. Quoted in Ripley, *Power in the Senate:* 197.
28. On committee staff see Clapp, *The Congressman,* 256–264; James D. Cochrane, "Partisan Aspects of Congressional Committee Staffing," *Western Political Quarterly* 17 (1964): 338–348; *Congressional Quarterly's Guide to the Congress of the United States:* 160–164; George Goodwin, Jr., *The Little Legislatures* (Amherst: University of Massachusetts Press, 1970): 142–152; Kofmehl, *Professional Staffs of Congress;* John F. Manley, "Congressional Staff and Public Policy-Making: The Joint Committee on Internal Revenue Taxation," *Journal of Politics* 30 (1968):

the two Appropriations Committees and the Joint Committee on Internal Revenue Taxation had well-developed professional staffs. A provision of the Legislative Reorganization Act passed in 1946 made clear the intention of Congress that professional staffs be developed for all committees—it provided for four professional staff members and six clerical staff members for each committee and allowed the size of committee staffs to expand beyond that number. In 1970 Congress increased the formal allotment of professional members to six. In 1974 the House expanded the basic allotment for each standing committee (except Appropriations and Budget) to eighteen professional staff members and twelve clerical staff members. Senators provided up to 300 new committee staff members for themselves (three under the control of each senator) in 1975.

Shortly after the passage of the 1946 Reorganization Act, House committees had 193 staff members and Senate committees had 290 staff members. Those numbers had both increased to over 1,500 in each house by 1976. Table 7–4 summarizes the growth of committee staff between 1947 and 1976.

Staffing of committees reflects the partisan nature of Congress. On virtually all committees, majority and minority party members have separate staff. Formal authority for selecting committee staff members

Table 7–4
Number of Committee Members in Congress,
Selected Years, 1947–1976

Year	Senate Committees	House Committees
1930	163	112
1935	172	122
1947	290	193
1957	558	375
1967	621	589
1972	918	783
1976	1534	1548

Source: Harrison W. Fox, Jr., and Susan Webb Hammond, Congressional Staffs: The Invisible Force in American Lawmaking (New York: Free Press, 1977): 171.

1046–1067; Samuel C. Patterson, "The Professional Staffs of Congressional Committees," *Administrative Science Quarterly* 15 (1970): 22–37; David E. Price, "Professionals and 'Entrepreneurs': Staff Orientations and Policy-Making on Three Senate Committees," *Journal of Politics* 33 (1971): 316–336; Ripley, *Power in the Senate:* 200–212; and Michael J. Malbin, "Congressional Staffs—Growing Fast, But in Different Directions," *National Journal* (July 10, 1976): 958–965.

rests in part with the chairperson (it used to rest exclusively with him). In part subcommittee chairpersons and ranking minority members of both full committees and subcommittees also have the power to hire and fire committee staff members. In the Senate every senator has at least three committee staff members spread across his assignments personally responsible to him. Those with the power of appointment in both houses naturally want their staff to be personally loyal and responsible to them. Partially as a result of this method of selection, the distinction between personal staff and committee staff—particularly in the Senate—is blurred. Consequently, committee staff members often perform what amount to non-committee chores for individual senators and, to a lesser extent, representatives. These chores may include working on constituency matters or even re-election campaigns.[29]

Committee staff positions are generally well regarded on Capitol Hill and throughout the executive branch. Many committee staff members have had experience either in the executive branch or on the personal staff of one or more senators or representatives. There has been growing stability in the personnel on committee staffs. As is the case with the legislators they serve, seniority among committee staff members helps them develop influence in their jobs.

The Job of Committee Staff Members. Committee staff perform a variety of duties related to the work of the committee. For example, they may organize the hearings that the committee conducts. They may personally conduct research on topics relevant to committee investigations. They may draft bills and amendments, and prepare the language of committee reports. They may help legislators prepare for floor debate either by distributing materials to all members or by briefing the members of the committee who are primarily responsible for conducting the debate. They may participate in the preparation for meetings of conference committees and in the writing of conference reports. Committee staff members also serve as the committee's principal liaison agents with both the executive branch and interest groups.

A survey of committee professional staff members in 1974 (126 in the Senate and 130 in the House) revealed that the most important activities in which they engaged were acting on requests for informa-

---

29. See eight articles collectively called "The Capitol Game" by Stephen Isaacs and Mary Russell (the first seven are by Isaacs on the Senate and the last is by Russell on the House) in the *Washington Post* on February 16, 17, 18, 19, 20, 21, 23, and 24, 1975. See also Cochrane, "Partisan Aspects of Congressional Committee Staffing," 346–347.

tion; legislative research, bill drafting, and reading and analyzing bills; and engaging in investigation and oversight.[30] The first activity was dominant in the reported use of time by House committee members. The three activities were more nearly equally important in the Senate. This again suggests an important House-Senate difference: House members become personally more genuinely expert in their committee work than senators.

As indicated above, committee members also perform some tasks not related to the business of the committee. These tasks are performed for their patrons—that is, those who are responsible for their appointments. Use of committee staff on extra-committee work is accepted by the staff members themselves because of the highly personal nature of their appointments, and by other committee members because of the partisan nature of staff appointments.

The job of committee staff members has been described in terms of four principal functions they perform: intelligence, integration, innovation, and influence.[31] In performing the intelligence function committee staff members collect and filter a great deal of information before passing it on to committee members.

Committee staffers perform an integration function in several senses. Most committee staffs are harmonious internally. They also generally work closely with staff members from the committee or committees in the other chamber that have the same jurisdiction. This helps bridge the bicameral gap. It also means that conference meetings usually go smoothly. Staff members also help promote integration between committees and the related pieces of the executive branch. They work closely with staff members in the bureaucracy and may well have served there before coming to Congress.

Some committee staff members innovate by seeking out new problems for attention or by proposing new solutions to problems already identified. The more highly bureaucratized (that is, specialized) a committee staff is the more likely are its members to be innovative in dealing with policy.[32]

Committee staff members are influential both because of the vital tasks they perform and because of the trust they build up in their relationships with members of the House and Senate.

In performing their tasks and functions, committee staff members interact with a number of individuals. Primarily they are responsible

30. Fox and Hammond, "The Growth of Congressional Staffs," 119.

31. See Patterson, "The Professional Staffs of Congressional Committees," 26–29.

32. Eugene Eidenberg, "The Congressional Bureaucracy," (Ph.D. dissertation, Northwestern University, 1966).

to their appointing authority—which, in the case of the majority party's staff on House committees, means that they are primarily loyal to the chairman of the committee or of the subcommittee. The minority party's staff in the House, usually very small, is loyal and responsible principally to the ranking minority member. Senior members of House committees are, therefore, likely to have the most access to committee staffs. Junior members of committees tend to be distrustful of committee staffs and rely more heavily on their personal staffs for legislative help. In general, the typical member of the House does not rely heavily on committee staff members. For example, a survey of 158 House members in the Eighty-ninth Congress (1965–1966) produced the findings that in three categories of legislative activity committee staffs were relatively unimportant.[33] These members said that only 11 percent of their legislative research was done by committee staff (in contrast to 30 percent done by themselves and 45 percent done by their own staff); that only 21 percent of their preparation for committee meetings and hearings was done by committee staff (compared to 61 percent done by themselves); finally, that only 9 percent of their preparation for floor debate was done by committee staff (compared to 28 percent by their own staff and 60 percent by themselves).

Since 1975 senators have had more access to committee staff because, in effect, even the most junior senator has one committee staff member personally responsible to him on every committee. The general statements about dominance of committee staff by senior members applicable to the House would also have been applicable to the Senate until 1975. Since then the situation has changed somewhat: senior senators still have many more staff members at their disposal, but all senators have substantial help at the personal level. The most influential staff members are, however, still most likely to be responsible to the more senior senators.

Committee staff members also work closely with both executive branch officials and lobbyists. When asked about the best contacts on Capitol Hill, 25 percent of a sample of Washington lobbyists named committee staff members.[34] This was the single largest category—closely followed by 24 percent naming staffs of executive agencies and 23 percent naming members of Congress. When asked to name the second best contact another 29 percent named committee staffs, compared to 19 percent naming staffs of executive agencies and 15 percent

33. Donald G. Tacheron and Morris K. Udall, *The Job of the Congressman* (Indianapolis: Bobbs-Merrill, 1966): 285.
34. The findings in this paragraph were reported in Lester W. Milbrath, *The Washington Lobbyists* (New York: Rand McNally, 1963): 266, 268.

naming members of Congress. When asked about the best and second-best sources of "unofficial information" 29 percent named committee staffs as the best source (compared to 20 percent naming members and 14 percent naming executive agency staffs) and 25 percent named committee staffs second (compared to 15 percent naming members and 16 percent naming executive agency staff members).

Committee staff members, like senators and representatives, operate within the constraints of relatively well-developed norms as they perform their jobs. Although the norms vary from committee to committee both for members and for staff members, six norms are widespread.[35] These norms include: limited advocacy (the staff person is expected to restrain himself in advocating his own policies, conclusions and proposals), loyalty to chairmen, deference to congressmen, anonymity, specialization (committee staff are expected to become experts in a particular subject), and limited partisanship (the majority of the work of most committees is non-partisan, and the general expectation is that the committee's work will be conducted with limited partisanship). No norm is inviolable, however; the limited partisanship norm is particularly likely to be ignored on occasion.

Committee staffs are organized in a variety of ways, but three patterns predominate.[36] One pattern has a single staff director who is in charge of both the professional staff and the clerical staff and who reports to the chairman. A second pattern has two staff directors (one for the professional staff and one for the clerical staff) who each report to the chairman. In the third pattern, a staff director for the clerical staff reports to the chairman; each of the professional staff members also report directly to the chairman.

Partisanship and Committee Staff Members. For policy-related committee staff positions chairmen usually hire individuals from their own party who share their general policy orientation. Ranking minority members appoint members who share their party and political orientation. As suggested above, partisanship is muted on many committees. Committees that regularly deal with divisive partisan issues, (for example, House Education and Labor) however, are likely to have staffs with definite partisan orientations, simply because the appointing authorities on those committees are likely to be strong partisans.

Even though hiring is on a partisan basis, retention of professional staff members may be non-partisan. For example, a large number of

35. See Patterson, "The Professional Staffs of Congressional Committees," 29–31.
36. Ibid., 32–33.

staff members survived the party turnovers in Congress in 1947 (from Democrat to Republican), 1949 (from Republican to Democrat), 1953 (from Democrat to Republican), and 1955 (from Republican to Democrat). Nor is there a necessary conflict between a partisan staff and a professional staff. Individuals whose hiring and tasks are imbued with partisanship may simultaneously be first-rate professionals. In general, congressional staffs have become increasingly professional although they may well have remained at about the same level of partisanship.

In recent years, Republican members of the House and Senate, seemingly condemned to perpetual minority status, have become increasingly concerned about the small numbers of committee staff members assigned to the minority. In 1962, for example, out of a total of 504 staff persons for all House Committees (both standing and select) only 43 were assigned to the minority. The joint committees had only 2 out of 72 assigned to the minority.[37]

The 1970 Legislative Reorganization Act provided for at least three minority employees on most committees. The Republican capture of the White House for eight years beginning in early 1969 resulted in more access to executive branch staff for Republicans and thus lessened somewhat their drive for more minority staff. However, their concern did not disappear and again became stronger in 1977 with the return of the White House to the Democrats. In late 1974 and early 1975 the House came close to earmarking some special money for minority staffing (one-third of specially authorized staff funds) but the new Democratic majority after the 1974 election changed its mind and the provision was rescinded. In 1977 the Senate adopted a broad resolution affecting committees. One provision required that the staff of each committee reflect the size of the majority and minority contingents of senators on the committee and that, if the minority members requested it, at least one-third of the staff of the committee would be placed under minority control (except those members designated by the chairperson and ranking minority member as working for the whole committee). This provision, coupled with the 1975 provision giving all senators three committee staffers spread among their assignments, has the potential of significantly improving the access of the minority party to committee staff in the Senate.

The Legislative Impact of Committee Staff. Committee staff members, like personal staff members, may have considerable independent

37. Cochrane, "Partisan Aspects of Congressional Committee Staffing," 341–342.

impact on the shape of legislation. This impact varies from committee to committee. One study of staff behavior on three different Senate committees (Finance, Labor and Public Welfare, and Commerce) concludes that two kinds of behavior can be observed among equally competent staff members on different committees.[38] "Policy entrepreneurs" dominated the Labor and Public Welfare and Commerce Committee staffs. These individuals were not shy about consulting both their own policy preferences and political considerations as they carried out their jobs. Much of the time they did not pretend to be neutral. On the other hand the staff of the Finance Committee was dominated by "professionals" who valued neutral expertise most highly and who downplayed both their own preferences and politics.

A study of the staff of the Joint Committee on Internal Revenue Taxation concluded that it is "powerful," but that its power is largely based on the adroitness with which the staff members take cues from the members of the committee itself.[39]

Committee staff members cannot initiate public policy without regard to the wishes of their nominal and actual superiors. On the other hand, they can have considerable impact, at least on some committees and on some specific bills. Staff members with more seniority are likely to have more independent substantive impact than staff members with less seniority. Likewise, those who are closest personally to the chairman of a subcommittee or committee are more likely to be important. Staff members on subcommittees are in a particularly favorable position to develop influence because they work with only a few members on a limited agenda. Those working on technical matters that are hard for the members themselves to understand are likely to be independently important.

The Place of Congressional Staff in the National Government

Congressional staffs are a permanent feature of the governmental landscape in Washington. And, given the demands on the time of the elected members of the House and Senate, they inevitably will develop some independent influence. There is considerable sentiment for continuing to expand the staffs of Congress as a major way of seeking to offset the superior numbers and superior informational base of the executive branch. There has also been some opposition simply to continuing the expansion of numbers. Worries about such expan-

---

38. Price, "Professional and 'Entrepreneurs'," 335.
39. Manley, "Congressional Staff and Public Policy-making."

sion have been expressed on several grounds.[40] First, large staffs have the potential of becoming uncontrollable bureaucracies. Second, as staffs get larger there is probably a greater likelihood that staffers will simply perform chores for individual members that have little or no relation to the legitimate business of the committee—that is, every committee member will want his "man" on the committee. Senators have now achieved this goal. Third, it is impossible for the size of congressional staffs ever to match the size of the executive bureaucracy with which they interact. Rather than simply expanding the size of congressional staffs, then, attention should be directed toward improving their training and skills and increasing the resources available to them.

Thoughtful members and staff members alike express concern about the development of independent influence on the part of staffers. Staff members are, of course, not elected but speak in the name of individuals who are. And their views are usually accepted as those of the elected officials by other participants in the political system, including representatives of the media. (This problem is, of course, even more prevalent in the executive branch where bureaucrats and presidential appointees in top positions often presume to speak in the name of the president.)

Perhaps the most serious threat is that professional staff members in Congress may join with civil servants in the executive branch and representatives of interest groups to dominate policy in a variety of specialized areas. None of these individuals directly represents any segment of the electorate. All may be highly professional and highly competent, but the complexity of modern government means that they may in fact carry out large portions of government business without any meaningful intervention from elected representatives— either the president or the members of the Senate and House. Bad policy may not necessarily result (nor would good policy necessarily result from a greater intervention on the part of the elected officials) but a growing bureaucratization of Congress may reduce its repre-

---

40. On the various normative concerns with congressional staffing see Arthur Macmahon, "Congressional Oversight of Administration: The Power of the Purse," in Theodore J. Lowi (ed.), *Legislative Politics U.S.A.*, 2nd ed. (Boston: Little, Brown, 1965): 185–196; a number of working papers published by the House Select Committee on Committees in the summer of 1973: Kenneth Kofmehl, "Three Major Aspects of House Committee Staffing"; Walter Kravitz, "Improving Some Skills of Committee Staff"; Samuel C. Patterson, "Staffing House Committees"; James A. Robinson, "Statement on Committee Staffing"; and John S. Saloma III, "Proposals for Meeting Congressional Staff Needs"; Malbin, "Congressional Committee Staffs: Who's in Charge Here?"; and Scully, "Reflections of a Senate Aide."

sentative character. Both the genius of Congress and its greatest weakness may be that it contains large numbers of amateurs and semiprofessionals in the policy business who may ask questions and reach decisions that bureaucrats, operating on strict grounds of efficiency, would not reach. The bureaucratization of Congress could also result in an erosion of both its political character and its representative character. Such a result is certainly not foreordained but it is an inherent problem with large-scale professional staffing.

Support Agencies

In just the last few years staffing for Congress has expanded considerably through the upgrading of staff and redefinition of mission by two old agencies—the General Accounting Office and what is now called the Congressional Research Service of the Library of Congress—and through the creation of two new agencies—the Office of Technology Assessment in 1972 and the Congressional Budget Office in 1974. Collectively, these four agencies have come to be called congressional support agencies.[41]

General Accounting Office [42]

The General Accounting Office was created in 1921. Over the years its functions have expanded. In broad terms it simultaneously tried to remain independent of both Congress and the executive branch in order to conduct audits, investigations, and program analyses while also serving Congress directly. Trying to maintain both stances has often plunged GAO into the midst of controversy. Depending on the content of its reports, it has been criticized both as not very useful to Congress or as too responsive to political pressures emanating from Congress. Reflecting its dual purpose, GAO has power to initiate its own studies as well as being expected to respond to congressional requests.

GAO performs five major functions: it conducts independent audits and reviews of executive branch agencies and programs (some of these ask evaluative questions about the effectiveness of programs); it sets government-wide accounting standards; it gives a variety of legal

---

41. On all four agencies see Ernest S. Griffith, "Four Agency Comparative Study," in a compilation of papers prepared for The Commission on the Operation of the Senate, *Congressional Support Agencies* (Washington: U.S. Government Printing Office, 1976): 95–148.

42. See Joseph Pois, "The General Accounting Office as a Congressional Resource," in *Congressional Support Agencies*: 31–54.

opinions; it settles claims against the government; and it conducts studies in direct response to congressional requests (and those requests may come from Congress as a whole through statutes or from individual committees or individual members of the House or Senate).

The total staff of GAO is over 5,000. In Fiscal 1976 it was estimated that almost 1,650 person-years were devoted to work for Congress. Almost 100 individuals were working directly with congressional committees on loan from GAO. The use of GAO products in Congress varies a great deal from committee to committee. Some routinely rely on GAO findings in helping them make evaluative decisions about the future of programs. Others seem more inclined routinely to ignore GAO reports. Over the years, however, GAO has gained a larger clientele in Congress and has consequently had a larger impact on congressional decisions.

Congressional Research Service [43]

The predecessor agency of the Congressional Research Service, the Legislative Reference Service, was created in 1914, primarily to provide traditional reference library services (short-run, limited factual statements and bibliographic searches) to members of Congress. There was some expansion of the size and responsibilities of the LRS before 1970, but until the Legislative Reorganization Act of 1970 it performed mainly in this mode. Then in 1970 Congress mandated a new emphasis on broader-scale policy research done by the newly named Congressional Research Service, especially for committees.

Beginning in 1970 the CRS began to grow—both in size and in terms of its workload. It had 323 staff members in 1970; by 1977 it had 809 positions authorized. It was responding to about 300,000 congressional inquiries a year and was also conducting a number of major research projects for committees. It does not have investigative capacity or power but must rely on published materials and on file materials (including its own extensive files). It must also be careful not to appear to be advocating positions; since it is equally responsible to all members of Congress, neutrality and objectivity must be apparent to the members of Congress as they peruse the work of the CRS.

The CRS has the staff capacity to do research in almost any area. Its central problem is the tension between the short-run demands of members of Congress who want immediate help with a speech or with

---

43. See James D. Carroll, "Policy Analysis for Congress: A Review of the Congressional Research Service," in *Congressional Support Agencies:* 4–30; and Michael J. Malbin, "CRS—The Congressional Agency That Just Can't Say 'No'," *National Journal* (February 19, 1977): 284–289.

answering the request of a constituent and the more time-consuming demands of genuine policy-relevant research. In many ways the incentives are all loaded in favor of serving the short-run interests first —because they do have short deadlines and also because the members' own interests are oriented more toward short-range help than toward long-range analysis. The newly appointed director of CRS in 1977 was a former member of Congress who stressed that the organization had to meet the short-run demands of Congress above all.

Congressional Budget Office [44]

The Congressional Budget Office was created in 1974 as an integral part of the new congressional budget process (see chapter 11). It was to be a highly qualified staff working in the areas of economic forecasting, fiscal policy analysis, and cost projections. In effect, its domain was the economic aspects of all federal policies and programs—a vast domain indeed. Its staff was to work closely with the two budget committees created by the same act (one in each house) and was also to be particularly responsive to the revenue (Ways and Means and Finance) and appropriations committees. Other committees and members could also request information and special studies, although their requests for special studies would necessarily take a lower priority than those coming from the primary constituents.

The director of CBO is appointed for four years by the Speaker and President pro tempore of the Senate, although in fact the recommending power of the two budget committees is paramount. The director can be removed by a resolution of either house at any time. After considerable debate and political maneuvering the first director named was Alice Rivlin, an experienced economist with admirable professional credentials.

The CBO staff quickly was filled to its 193-person limit. The office began issuing a number of different kinds of reports soon after its establishment. Many of these reports get considerable attention. In general, there is agreement that the staff of CBO is highly competent.

Given its policy domain and given also the aggressive stance taken by Rivlin, it is not surprising that CBO is visible and sometimes controversial. During the Ford presidency some congressional Republicans felt that CBO's criticisms of the president's proposals were partisan. But early in the Carter presidency the president's energy program

---

44. See William M. Capron, "The Congressional Budget Office," in *Congressional Support Agencies*: 75–94; and Donald Smith, "Congressional Budget Office: Under Fire," *Congressional Quarterly Weekly Report* (June 5, 1976): 1430–1432. See also Chapter 11, below, for a discussion of the congressional budget process.

was the subject of a highly critical CBO report that said that his projected savings were far overstated. Speaker O'Neill was known to be upset by this report. Thus it seems that CBO is trying to be objective and let the fallout from its analyses descend on proposals without regard for their origin. By nature it is likely to remain a visible and controversial support agency, despite its relatively small size.

Office of Technology Assessment [45]

The Office of Technology Assessment was created by a 1972 statute and began operations in early 1974. Its primary function according to the statute is "to provide early indications of the probable beneficial and adverse impacts of the applications of technology and to develop other coordinate information which may assist the Congress."

Broad policy decisions for OTA are made by the Technology Assessment Board, which is made up of six senators, six representatives, and the Director of the agency. The Director is appointed by the Board for a six-year term and the congressional members are equally split between the parties. The chairmanship of the board rotates between the House and Senate contingents. The statute also specifies a Technical Assistance Advisory Council, which thus far has not had much importance.

Issues come to OTA through requests from congressional committees or from the Board or from the Director after consulting with the Board. OTA is thus set up to be primarily and directly responsible to congressional committees and especially to those members of the Board who choose to be active.

The professional staff of OTA by 1977 had reached about 150, although cuts were threatened. The Policy Board had established seven broad areas for organizing its work: energy, food, health, materials, oceans, transportation, and technology and world trade. In general, despite completion of some reports, most members of Congress were not aware of OTA and of its actual or potential utility.

In 1977 political conflict involving OTA broke out. A Republican representative charged that the agency had become a political adjunct to Senator Edward Kennedy (D-Mass.) and others took up her charge. Whether the agency can survive this political uproar and establish its objectivity and utility in the minds of members remains an open

---

45. See E.B. Skolnikoff, "The Office of Technology Assessment," in *Congressional Support Agencies*: 55–73; and Thomas P. Southwick, "Hill Technology Assessment Office Hit by Controversy, Future Role is Threatened," *Congressional Quarterly Weekly Report* (June 18, 1977): 1202–1203.

question. By late 1977 it had not built the kind of constituency it probably would need to sustain it over a long period of time.

INFORMATION AND POLITICS

In a broad sense all of the topics discussed in this chapter revolve around the need of members of the House and Senate to mingle adequate information with their political judgments as they make up their minds on an intimidating array of substantive matters. Information is not neutral in most situations. In Congress, which is by definition centrally and perpetually political, information is never neutral. Thus, whoever controls what kinds of information and the timing of its provision helps shape outputs. This is not to say that members do not seek "facts" as they make up their minds, but "facts" are always colored by a whole range of other factors, such as guesses about constituency attitudes, political ideologies, and personal ambitions.

Over the years individual members and committees of Congress have constructed the range of institutions and practices detailed in this chapter. Members have sought the company and views of other members from their state or region. Like-minded groups of members have created formal organizations such as the Democratic Study Group that mingle information, research, and ideology. Both personal and committee staff have proliferated at a rapid pace in recent years. And additional support agencies have also grown and prospered.

In some ways the demand for information is insatiable. Given the agenda of the federal government—which is, by definition, also the agenda of Congress—the members can never know everything that is relevant to their work. It seems reasonable to assert that at present sufficient staff resources have been given to Congress by itself in a variety of forms. The important questions now come in terms of organizing the resources to focus on those aspects of policies and programs most useful to decision-making. Policy decisions will never be made on apolitical grounds. And, given the representative nature of Congress, attempts to make decision-making "technocratic" are bound to fail and are misguided besides. To put the same point in another way: attempts to remove politics from congressional decision-making are counter to the spirit of the institution; fortunately, they have no hope of success. This is not to say that pointed, relevant information and analysis are useless. Many members genuinely seek and use expert analysis. But, ultimately, the decision-making calculus of any member includes many factors other than such analysis, no matter how expert.

Some perhaps hope that more and better information and analysis provided to Congress will help overcome its natural tendency to policy fragmentation. Perhaps some marginal integration can be achieved if the sources providing information and analysis are themselves more integrated and coordinated. However, by necessity many of those sources will remain tied to fragmented patrons—state or regional groups, ideological groups, committees, and subcommittees—and so will perhaps intensify policy fragmentation rather than alleviate it.

PART III

THE EXTERNAL ENVIRONMENT FOR CONGRESSIONAL POLICY-MAKING

CHAPTER 8

CONGRESS, INTEREST GROUPS, AND CONSTITUENTS

GIVEN THE CONCERN—BOTH APPARENT AND REAL—OF MEMBERS OF Congress with representation and the fact that there are various groups eager to influence the shape of the public agenda and policy results, it is important to examine the interaction of members with both constituents (organized and unorganized) and organized interest groups. Both are important—constituents often because the member anticipates their reactions to his actions and their views, and interest groups usually because they articulate their direct concerns with reasonable clarity and considerable persistence.

Interest groups have a number of channels of communicating both directly and indirectly with members. They do not necessarily dominate the resolution of issues in Congress, but they help set the agenda on which Congress acts. Constituencies and constituents also claim considerable congressional attention (some of it primarily rhetorical). Sometimes they enhance their access and influence by working with an interest group. Sometimes they simply go directly to the member. Much of the time they do not have to take an active stance because members anticipate and care about their needs and desires, or at least the member calculates that unless he takes their assumed wishes and interests into account his or her political future could be jeopardized.[1]

---

1. Constituents almost never have the alternative of communicating with their members through local political parties. These parties usually pay attention to the offices of senator and representative only for purposes of nominating candidates (and sometimes not even for that purpose). Once elected, a member almost never hears from his state or local parties. Thus both the member and those seeking to influence him must use other channels. This fact also enhances the potential impact of interest groups.

MEMBERS AND INTEREST GROUPS

Interest groups enter the policy-making process through their lobbying activities. These activities, however, are more subtle than popular opinion usually portrays. To reach a balanced conclusion about the effectiveness of lobbying, one needs to consider the setting in which interaction between lobbyists and legislators occurs (particularly the systematic bias that characterizes the interaction), the variety of lobbying participants, the patterns and techniques that characterize lobbying, the defensive nature of much lobbying, and the range of impact that lobbying can have.

The Setting for Interaction

Whom do interest groups represent? At the most general level the interest group system in the United States has a distinct bias favoring upper class and predominantly business interests. E.E. Schattschneider, a leading scholar of interest groups, has estimated that 90 percent of the adult population cannot get into the "pressure system" (his label for the phenomenon of organized groups pursuing special or private interests in the political arena).[2] Most of the active organized groups that lobby in the government represent very narrow segments of the polity with highly focused interests. The few groups that represent more general interests tend to have memberships that encompass only a small portion of their theoretically potential constituencies.

In short, the lobbying arena is loaded in favor of special interests. And those special interests are almost all working on behalf of the relatively privileged strata of society. One scholar has put the problem very succinctly:

> One of the most serious problems of a system of decentralized political units in a liberal society is the consequent uneven sharing in power. Some segments of the population are excluded from effective participation in the benefits of the political process because, as Madison observed, small units have less diversity than large units; they thus allow greater opportunities for the oppression of those who are already weak.[3]

---

2. E. E. Schattschneider, *The Semisovereign People* (New York: Holt, Rinehart and Winston, 1960).

3. Grant McConnell, *Private Power and American Democracy* (New York: Knopf, 1966).

There are two parties involved in every legislative lobbying activity —the lobbyist and the legislator—and they interact, usually to their mutual benefit. The relationship that is often portrayed of vulture-like lobbyists preying on helpless legislators is distorted. Lobbyists, to be sure, seek favors and assistance for their particular interests. But they are required to register and publicly identify themselves as lobbyists so their identity and affiliations are not secret. Also, legislators seek out lobbyists for the information on substance, on bureaucratic intent, and (less often) on constituency preferences that they can provide. The exchange of mere information for influential favors may at first seem an uneven trade, for legislators are in a position to do so much more than the lobbyist in terms of magnitude of favors granted. But the congressional system values the acquisition of a great deal of accurate information and this necessity balances out the exchange of favors for knowledge. At any rate, interest groups continue to flourish and their major offering continues to be information.

The interest groups are not always the initiators of action. Legislators will often take the lead in promoting a certain kind of action and will be joined later by lobbyists. For example, in 1973 when Congress debated at length the issue of whether to approve an oil pipeline across Alaska a senator from that state was the first individual to conceive of the possibility and necessity, from his point of view, of suspending some of the provisions of the National Environmental Policy Act to facilitate construction of the pipeline. Only after he had gathered about one-third or more of the senators as supporters of his amendment did the lobbyists for both the oil companies and the administration become active in its behalf.

Members in general view themselves as being free to act on the basis of their own judgment despite lobbying from interest groups. They feel pressure but also think they can withstand it. Occasionally they say there is no lobbying activity even on an important bill.[4] They often attribute influence on the part of lobbies in relation to other members, since most members do not willingly damage their self-image of independence. In general, it probably is accurate to say that lobbies rarely dominate a vote but there are at least usually a few members particularly concerned with enhancing their relation with one or more lobbies.

Generally, very few members question the legitimacy of interest groups and lobbying. In fact, a large proportion work actively to facilitate the interests of specific groups. Only a few think it necessary

---

4. Charles L. Clapp, *The Congressman* (Washington: Brookings, 1963): 163, 182.

to state that their position is to resist the requests of groups.[5] And, of course, even these members may in fact sometimes be helpful to a lobby supporting ideas they favor.

Types of Interest Groups and Lobbyists

There are many different types of interest groups—ranging from the large and well-financed to the miniscule and impoverished. There are also many types of lobbyists—ranging from full-time professionals to part-time amateurs.

Under the rubric "interest group" the large national associations (composed of both individual and organizational members) come to mind first—groups such as the National Association of Manufacturers, the U.S. Chamber of Commerce, and the American Federation of Labor-Congress of Industrial Organizations. There are also a number of industries that have their own national groups that engage in lobbying activities, for example, the American Petroleum Institute, the Manufacturing Chemists Association, and the National Coal Association. Some individual corporations, to some extent, constitute interest groups by themselves. When aerospace companies for example, compete for major contracts, they actively lobby on their own behalf.

Interest groups do not represent only industry, commerce, and labor. There are groups that represent smaller units of government: the National Association of Counties, the National League of Cities, and the U.S. Conference of Mayors, for example. A number of states, counties, and cities maintain their own representatives in Washington too.[6] Some national groups represent professions and act as inter-

---

5. Roger H. Davidson, in *The Role of the Congressman* (New York: Pegasus, 1969) reports on the attitudes of eighty-seven members of the House toward interest groups in the Eighty-eighth Congress (1963–64). He categorizes the members as facilitators, resistors, and neutrals. Facilitators are those members with a friendly attitude toward group activity and considerable knowledge about it. Resistors are those with a hostile attitude toward group activity and considerable knowledge about it. Neutrals are those who either had no strong attitude about groups or who had very little knowledge. Of his sample Davidson classed 29 percent as facilitators, 21 percent as resistors, and 49 percent as neutrals. Republican members were much more inclined to be facilitators (38 percent) than Democrats (24 percent) and much less inclined to be resistors (6 percent) than Democrats (31 percent). As Democrats became more senior they also became less likely to be facilitators and more likely to be resistors. Senior Republicans were more likely to be facilitators. Members from marginal districts tended to be resistors. Republicans from safe districts tended to be facilitators.

    As with most studies of self-perceived roles there is no empirical evidence about whether these differing attitudes resulted in differing patterns of behavior.

6. See John L. Moore "Washington Pressures/State-Local Lobbying Grows Despite Drive to Decentralize Government," *National Journal* (February 24, 1973): 262–270.

est groups when they become involved in the legislative process. The American Medical Association and American Bar Association fall in this category. Some professional or semi-professional groups specifically represent employees of other governmental units. For example, there is a National Association of State Aviation Officials, a National Association of Public Health Officials, and an Airport Operators Council (most airports are owned by a municipality).

There have always been interest groups that have asserted that they were working in the "public interest." Among older groups the League of Women Voters serves as a good example. In the 1970s two new organizations became highly visible and quite effective in representing what they claimed was the "public interest." One of these groups was Public Citizen and the other was Common Cause.[7] The former was an umbrella group or holding company for the various activities inspired by the leadership of Ralph Nader, who first became well known as a consumer advocate in the 1960s. By the mid-1970s it was estimated that Public Citizen was supported by contributions from about 175,000 people. Under the umbrella came various groups focusing on energy and consumer issues, tax issues, and health research. Considerable effort from Public Citizen went into lawsuits as well as into lobbying in Congress. Early successes of the Nader lobbyists included helping gain the repeal of the oil depletion allowance and helping gain approval for federal funding to aid consumers petitioning the Federal Trade Commission, a costly process not previously accessible to average consumers.

Common Cause was created in 1970 by John Gardner, a Republican who had served as Secretary of Health, Education, and Welfare under President Johnson. By the mid-1970s the group had about 250,000 members and an annual budget of $6 million. It had a paid staff of close to 100 in Washington and about fifty more scattered throughout the United States. The focus of Common Cause has been much more on process and structural issues than on substantive matters. Thus it was instrumental in helping achieve passage of the campaign finance law in 1974 and in helping create the mood that led to reform of seniority and opening many of the processes of Congress to public view. Common Cause successes in the publicity area have had demonstrable substantive results. For example, in late 1977 the House defeated a bill that would have specified that American-built and operated tankers would be guaranteed 9.5 percent of oil imports into

---

7. On Public Citizen and Common Cause see Al Gordon, "Public Interest Lobbies: Nader and Common Cause Become Permanent Fixtures," *Congressional Quarterly Weekly Report* (May 15, 1976): 1197–1205; and T. R. Reid, "Changing the Guard at Common Cause," Washington *Post*, May 15, 1977.

the United States. A major reason for the defeat of the bill was publicity by opponents of the bill of Common Cause press releases listing extensive campaign giving by maritime interests (both shippers and unions).[8]

The group of active lobbies is not static. As issues and social and economic conditions change, the configuration of active and influential groups also changes. A good example is provided by the emergence of effective lobbies for the elderly in recent years, a phenomenon primarily the result of the general aging of the U.S. population. On issues such as medicare, social security, and retirement age, organizations representing the elderly have proved to be very important. The largest group working in this area is the American Association of Retired Persons, whose membership grew from three million in 1971 to more than eleven million in 1977.[9]

"Membership" in an interest group is an elusive concept. All groups claim to represent the maximum number of members they can. In some groups the members are quite inactive. In others, like Common Cause, they tend to be quite active. And different groups also have different kinds of members. For example, when the eleven most important interest groups in the housing field alone were examined, they were found to be very different in size, in part because they had very different kinds of members—ranging from individuals to companies to other organizations. Table 8–1 summarizes this information. This diverse situation would be repeated in virtually any substantive area.

Table 8–2 summarizes the number and type of lobbying organizations registered with the Clerk of the House to lobby in Congress during the Ninety-first Congress (1969–70). This breakdown of groups indicates both the variety of lobbying groups and the predominance of business interests.

Interest groups often ally with one another for specific legislative battles. These alliances may be more or less permanent in some instances. For example, even before they merged their staffs in late 1969 the National League of Cities and the Conference of Mayors cooperated on virtually all issues. Other alliances may be formed over a single issue and may, in fact, unite groups that have fought each

---

8. On the role of Common Cause publicity in the cargo preference bill defeat see Ann Cooper, "House Sinks Cargo Preference Bill," *Congressional Quarterly Weekly Report* (October 22, 1977): 2223–2224, 2270; and George Lardner, Jr., "Cargo Preference for U.S. Tankers Scuttled by House," Washington *Post*, October 20, 1977.

9. Steven V. Roberts, " 'Gray Power' Getting Results in Congress," *New York Times*, October 24, 1977; and Roberts, "The Old-Age Lobby Has a Loud Voice in Washington," *New York Times*, October 30, 1977.

Table 8–1
Membership of Principal Interest Groups in Housing Field, 1973

Name of Group	Number of Members	Type of Members
American Bankers Association	13,500	Commercial banks
American Institute of Planners	6,000	Individual urban planners
Mortgage Bankers Association of America	2,200	Firms in mortgage banking
National Association of Home Builders	54,000	Builders and associates, individuals and firms
National Association of Housing and Redevelopment Officials	10,000	8,000 individuals and 2,000 organizations
National Association of Mutual Savings Banks	500	Mutual savings banks
National Association of Real Estate Boards	94,000	Individual realtors (in over 1,500 boards)
National Housing Conference	4,000	Individuals and organizations
National League of Cities	15,000	Municipalities and state municipal leagues
United States Conference of Mayors	500	Mayors of cities of more than 30,000 and state capitals
U.S. Savings and Loan League	4,814	Savings and Loan companies

other in the past and may do so in the future. For example, during the controversy over the SST in the early 1970s environmentalist groups such as the Sierra Club, Friends of the Earth, and the League of Conservation Voters opposed the efforts of the aerospace companies such as Boeing to gain congressional approval of the project. However, in 1973 the environmentalists were joined by a number of aerospace companies such as Boeing, Rohr Industries, and LTV in working for passage of a highway bill that allowed highway trust fund money to be used for mass transit. The environmentalists favored the bill as a way to reduce the polluting effects of the automobile and the environmental and aesthetic damage resulting from what they considered excessive roadbuilding. The companies favored the bill because the aerospace industry was in considerable economic trouble and a number of firms had turned to the manufacture of mass transit equipment such as subway cars in an effort to survive.[10]

In the effort to get support for the passage of the Alaska pipeline bill a consortium of interested companies was formed behind the leadership of the Alyeska Pipeline Service Company. These included the three oil companies that were the principal owners of the oil on the North Slope of Alaska. Cooperating with these companies were rep-

Table 8–2

Number and Type of Lobbying Organizations Registered during the 91st Congress.

Type of Group	Number of Registrations
Business Groups	223
Citizens Groups	96
Employee and Labor Groups	18
Farm Groups	6
Foreign Groups	8
Foundations	3
Individuals	5
Military and Veterans Groups	3
Professional Groups	11
Total	373

Source: Congressional Quarterly Almanac 1970: 1208.

10. "Busting the Highway Trust: An Unlikely Alliance," *Congressional Quarterly Weekly Report* (March 24, 1973): 643–644.

resentatives of the Alaska State government, the Department of the Interior and the AFL-CIO, particularly the maritime Unions, which were eager for jobs in the shipping business that the pipeline would create.[11]

When the Nixon administration suspended or terminated most housing programs aimed at helping low income families in early 1973, a National Ad Hoc Housing Coalition was quickly formed behind the leadership of the National Association of Housing and Redevelopment Officials. Although much of the work of the coalition was performed principally by NAHRO, the alliance was symbolically important because of the more than one hundred interest groups represented.

In 1977, in the struggle over the cargo preference bill mentioned above, two unusual coalitions emerged. Pushing for the bill was an alliance of unions (including both maritime and non-maritime unions and the AFL-CIO itself) and maritime business interests. The coalition opposed to the bill included oil companies, a Nader organization (Congress Watch), The League of Women Voters, the American Farm Bureau Federation, and the U.S. Chamber of Commerce. On both sides the groups often opposed each other on other issues but on this one issue they found common ground and could unite.

The largest interest groups maintain substantial Washington offices with a number of full-time lobbyists. Some even have their own buildings, usually located close to government offices. Small groups maintain a minimal Washington office—a staff of one professional lobbyist, one secretary, and a mimeograph machine is typical of a number of operations. Some groups and companies prefer not to maintain an office of their own but, instead, hire a "Washington lawyer" to represent their interests. These individuals specialize in lobbying and do very little legal work in the narrow sense. Some law firms in Washington are wholly devoted to this kind of work; others have some individuals specializing in it while others pursue more usual legal work. Some "Washington lawyers" are former government figures themselves (ex-senators and ex-secretaries of departments, for example). One of this breed of lobbyist may have a number of clients whose interests literally range from soup to nuts.

Others who serve as full-time lobbyists for an association, corporation, or union are retired military officers, ex-employees of the bureaucracy, and former congressional staff members. Perhaps the most prized catch for an interest group is an ex-senator or ex-representative.

---

11. Richard Corrigan and Claude E. Barfield "Energy Report/Pipeline Lobby Uses Its Political Muscle to Bypass Environmental Law," *National Journal* (August 11, 1973): 1172–1178.

These men are particularly valuable because of their personal and professional contacts on Capitol Hill. They probably also have a number of potentially useful contacts in the executive branch. There are few of this type of lobbyist—only nine former members of Congress or their law firms registered to lobby in 1970, for example. More common are retired high-ranking public officials other than members of Congress—sixty-six were listed as reigstered lobbyists in 1970.[12]

Patterns and Techniques of Lobbying Activity

There are several general features that characterize almost all lobbying activity. First, it should be stressed that the lobbyists' major task is mobilization of those who already believe rather than conversion of the infidels.[13] Lobbyists do not, by and large, concentrate on changing congressmen's minds. Rather they seek out persons whom they have identified as supporters and work to reinforce their views, providing them ammunition to use in pursuing the cause in which they both believe. Interest groups can accomplish nothing without creating and maintaining good relations with at least a few members of Congress.

Second, Washington lobbyists have a broader job than simply soliciting tangible actions—legislation, appointments, investigations—from members of the House and Senate. The lobbyists's principal goals are to use Congress to influence the administrative branch, to get information, or to achieve favorable publicity for an organization.[14] The typical request from the lobbyist to the legislator seeks help for personal, business, or professional problems; Lewis Dexter calls the handling of such requests by legislators "casework." [15] Most of these casework requests and not something the legislator can directly solve; usually the best he can do is to intercede with a bureau in the executive branch.[16] Such intercession can take many forms—ranging from one perfunctory telephone call by a congressional staff member that results in nothing to repeated personal requests from a member that are likely to result in the desired bureaucratic response.

12. *Congressional Quarterly Almanac 1970*: 1208–1213.
13. See Raymond A. Bauer, Ithiel de Sola Pool, and Lewis A. Dexter, *American Business and Public Policy* (New York: Atherton, 1963); and Randall B. Ripley, "Congress Champions Aid to Airports, 1958–59," and "Congress and Clean Air: The Issue of Enforcement, 1963" in Frederic N. Cleaveland and associates, *Congress and Urban Problems* (Washington, D.C.: Brookings, 1969).
14. Lewis A. Dexter, *How Organizations Are Represented in Washington* (Indianapolis: Bobbs-Merrill, 1969): 80.
15. Ibid., 81.
16. Ibid., 84.

Lobbying itself—that is, asking for explicit congressional action rather than information or indirect intervention in the bureaucracy—occurs principally when there is the occasion and some likelihood that Congress can and will act, when the interested lobbies have enough resources (mostly manpower) to spend on the enterprise, and when the bad effects of lobbying (indignant opponents, for example) are not likely to outweigh the good effects.[17] Unless an interest group takes these factors into account it is probably wasting its resources and perhaps harming its own cause.

The specific techniques that lobbyists employ as they pursue favors and information in Congress are numerous.[18] They make personal contacts with members of the House and Senate and staff members who work for individual representatives and senators and committees. On relatively noncontroversial issues they focus on contacts with staff members and on influencing substantive outcomes in committees. On more controversial issues they are more eager to contact members personally and shift their attention to influencing outcomes on the floors of the House and Senate.[19]

Communications with members and staff members can be made in person or by phone. Personal efforts may well involve a social aspect—such as the lobbyist taking the staff member out for lunch or a drink. Lobbyists can also work indirectly through other individuals thought to be important to or influential with specific congressmen—key constituents (for example, an important publisher or campaign contributor), representatives of allied interest groups, key bureaucrats, or, most important, other members of the House and Senate. These latter are the most persuasive "lobbyists" of all.

Lobbyists provide useful information to members and can often package this information in directly usable ways—as, for example, by preparing a speech for the member to deliver that espouses the interest group's viewpoint, thereby saving the time of the member and his staff. Lobbyists also testify before congressional committees that are holding hearings on bills. They prepare their testimony and distribute it widely in written form both before and after delivering it. They also

---

17. Ibid., 56.
18. For discussions of these techniques see Clapp: chapter 4; Harmon Zeigler, *Interest Groups in American Society* (Englewood Cliffs, N.J.: Prentice-Hall, 1964); Dexter, *How Organizations Are Represented in Washington;* David B. Truman, *The Governmental Process* (New York: Knopf, 1951); and Lester W. Milbrath, *The Washington Lobbyists* (Chicago: Rand McNally, 1963).
19. John M. Bacheller, "Lobbyists and the Legislative Process: The Impact of Environmental Constraints," *American Political Science Review* 71 (1977): 252–263.

respond to questioning, often in colloquies that are prearranged with sympathetic members of the committee. Their prepared testimony and the oral interchanges are also printed in the record of the hearings issued by the committee.

Lobbyists and their employers often attempt to influence critical assignments to committees that handle legislation of importance to them. They may make representations to the members of the relevant committee on committees about which members, or at least which type of member, would be satisfactory. They may work to get specific committees to conduct hearings they think would highlight information favorable to their positions.

Lobbyists try to stimulate mail supporting their position. This can be done on a selective basis (for example, for a few corporation presidents or union leaders) or it can be a mass campaign (for example, from as many members of a union or a chamber of commerce as possible). In general, the selective mailing is likely to attract more attention from the senators and representatives than the mass mailing. Mass mailings are generally obviously that and usually require minimal effort on the part of the individual mailer. Thus members often ignore or at least downplay them.

Interest groups may be particularly useful to members of Congress at election time by helping provide the large amount of funds necessary either to gain or retain a seat. In the 1972 congressional elections, for example, four different political action groups representing the milk industry costributed over $1.3 million to candidates for the House and Senate; the political arm of the American Medical Association contributed over $850,000; a banking group contributed almost $200,000; the political agency of the National Association of Manufacturers contributed over $440,000; the political arm of the AFL-CIO contributed almost $1.2 million; and the United Auto Workers contributed over $500,000.

One of the last milk contributions is particularly interesting. Near the end of the campaign the milk industry gave $462,000 to unidentified congressional campaigns through the House and Senate Republican and Democratic Campaign Committees. They simply trusted the party officials to give the money to the friends of the milk interests. A spokesman for the group said that the allocations were made on the basis of offering support for "friends of dairy farmers and supporters of agricultural legislation. We try to keep our friends in office and elect those who are our friends." Spokesmen for the congressional campaign committees say the money was given without explicit instructions on who should receive it. All parties in this arrangement indicated satisfaction that the "proper" individuals benefited. Subsequent disclosures have showed the milk industry to have been heavy financial backers of Richard Nixon's 1972 presidential campaign and allegations were made that those contributions facilitated favorable action by Nixon and the Department of Agriculture in considering a substantial increase in the support price for milk. Leading members of both parties (Nixon being the most prominent Republican and Johnson, Humphrey, and Mills being the most prominent Democrats) have received major campaign help from the milk interests for a number of years.[20]

In 1974 interest groups gave $12.5 million to congressional campaigns, and in 1976 they gave $22.5 million. In the latter year the largest givers were in the medical area ($1.8 million), in the dairy area (over $1.3 million), and in organized labor (almost $1 million each from the AFL-CIO and from the maritime unions).[21]

The provision of money for campaigns is the most important election-time service rendered by the interest groups. They can also be helpful by conducting voter registration drives and by providing campaign workers and campaign literature.

It should be noted that not all interest groups are equally skillful in using the techniques identified above. Even the most effective lobbyists can be rebuffed or make mistakes. Among the commonest errors committed by lobbyists are the misidentification of potential friends, sympathizers, and opponents; inattention to important stages in the legislative process; and the use of tactics that aggravate potential supporters. Interest groups—particularly the large ones—can also be rendered impotent by conflicts within their own membership.[22] For example, different individual unions may take opposing views, thus making it impossible for the AFL-CIO to take a strong position. An inept lobbyist can alienate even a natural ally. Groups are at their most effective when their representatives are, in fact, "reinforcing, providing ammunition for, and serving their sympathizers in the Congress." [23]

20. "Milk Group Gave $462,000 Just Before the Election," *Congressional Quarterly Weekly Report* (March 17, 1973): 568–588. The spending figures in the preceding paragraph are all calculated from data reported in this article.

21. The 1974 and 1976 figures were tabulated by Common Cause and were published in summary form in *Congressional Quarterly Weekly Report* (April 16, 1977): 710.

22. For examples of interest group mistakes see Ripley, "Congress Champions Aid to Airports, 1958–59," and "Congress and Clean Air: The Issue of Enforcement, 1963"; also the story on the Alaska pipeline in the *National Journal* (August 11, 1973), cited above in footnote 11.

23. Dexter, *How Organizations Are Represented in Washington*: 72.

Conditions for Interest Group Influence

Although interest groups do not dominate congressional decision-making or policy responses emanating from Congress, they are often important. A number of specific conditions can be identified that enhance their potential influence.[24]

In many cases there may not be two competing groups or coalitions of groups on an issue. Only one point of view may be presented in lobbying. Under such conditions that group or coalition is likely to get much of what it wants.

If the groups on one side of a controversy are unified and coordinated on the major issues they want to push or if they can cover up any disagreements, they will enhance their chances of success. When a single group or a few groups acting in concert can demonstrate the primacy of their interest in a particular area, they gain both visibility and effectiveness. For example, the walnut growers are represented by a single highly organized group. They are likely to get what they want legislatively. By contrast, chicken farmers are dispersed over the entire nation and have no effective single group to speak for them. Therefore they have difficulty in achieving their legislative ends.[25]

If there are key members of the House and Senate (for example, a subcommittee chairman) who actively believe in the interest group's position, the chances of success are greatly enhanced. The same is true when a lobbying effort is made in a field where the power of Congress vis-à-vis the executive branch is unusually strong. Former Assistant Secretary of the Treasury Stanley S. Surrey makes this point in relation to tax legislation:

> The Congress regards the shaping of a revenue bill as very much its prerogative. It will seek the views of the executive. . . . But control over the legislation itself, both as to broad policies and as to details, rests with the Congress. Hence a congressman, and especially a member of the tax committees, is in a position to make the tax laws bend in favor of a particular individual or group despite strong objection from the executive branch. Under such a governmental system the importance to the tax structure of the institutional factors that influence a congressman's decision is obvious.[26]

---

24. See Michael T. Hayes, "The Semi-Sovereign Pressure Groups: A Critique of Current Theory and an Alternative Typology," *Journal of Politics* 40 (1978): 134–161.

25. On these two groups in the Eighty-sixth Congress (1959–60) see Clem Miller, *Member of the House* (New York: Scribner's, 1962): 137–140.

26. Stanley S. Surrey, "How Special Tax Provisions Get Enacted," in Randall B. Ripley (ed.), *Public Policies and Their Politics* (New York: Norton, 1966): 53.

The visibility of the issues for which groups lobby is another very important factor affecting their impact. On issues regarded as routine by Congress without much wide public visibility, interest groups become entrenched in the decision-making system in Congress and the executive branch; subgovernments prosper. In these relatively invisible areas interest groups are likely to have maximum impact. Their impact is also likely to be high when they seek single, discrete amendments to bills as opposed to advocating a large legislative package. As the visibility of issues increases and public attention to issue areas grows the impact of interest groups tends to diminish. In 1977 the visibility given the cargo preference bill is what caused its defeat.

Another factor that works in favor of an interest group is support for or, at least, no opposition to its aims from the relevant executive branch agency in its representations to Congress.

Groups sometimes state views on matters remote from their primary interests. But an interest group is likely to have greatest impact on issues that coincide with the interests the group purports to represent. Thus the AFL-CIO may be very influential in advising on matters concerning the working conditions of factory workers, but they receive less attention from legislators when they advocate a higher tariff for tung nut imports or when they make a broad pronouncement on foreign policy.

Interest groups are likely to be most consistently important on issues defined either as distributive or as regulatory with the potential of being converted to self-regulatory (which turns out to be another form of distribution in most ways). They are less influential on redistributive issues.

Interest groups will usually have a greater impact on amendments than on entire pieces of legislation. This is because amendments are generally technical and thus less widely understood and salient to only a few people.

On such issues conflict can usually be limited. As the field of conflict widens, more participants enter the fray and any single participant is likely to be less influential. The fewer the participants, the greater their influence.[27]

The Defensive Nature of Lobbying

Much lobbying is defensive—that is, aimed at preventing changes in the existing situation. In many policy areas there are well-established patterns of special privilege and entrenched interests that will resist

---

27. See Schattschneider, *The Semisovereign People,* for an elaboration of this notion.

any change not to their benefit. Given the complexity of the decision process in Congress and the executive branch, those taking a negative position, rather than those urging something new to be done, have an advantage.[28]

A good example of successful defensive lobbying occurred in 1977, with the defeat in the House of the common site picketing bill.[29] Organized labor had long sought an amendment to the labor laws of the country that would allow one union to close down an entire construction site by picketing one subcontractor (a 1951 Supreme Court decision had held that such picketing was illegal). The building trades unions were particularly eager to have the bill pass.

When the Ninety-fifth Congress opened in early 1977, it seemed likely that the common site bill would pass easily, and President Carter had indicated he would sign it. The bill had passed in the less heavily Democratic Ninety-fourth Congress but had been successfully vetoed by President Ford.

However, those opposed to the bill put together a strong lobbying campaign aimed particularly at Republicans, southern Democrats, and freshmen of both parties who had probably not taken a public position before. A large variety of organizations cooperated to oppose the bill and to generate "grass roots" feeling. These included associations representing contractors, home builders, and construction suppliers; individual large companies such as Pittsburgh Plate Glass and Dow Chemical; the three largest general business lobbying organizations (the U.S. Chamber of Commerce, the National Association of Manufacturers, and the Business Roundtable); and the House Republican Campaign Committee. The last named group used its list of 300,000 campaign contributors to solicit letters to representatives (the House was scheduled to consider the bill first). The Association of General Contractors distributed postcards with paychecks that resulted in thousands of union members sending correspondence to House members that took a position in opposition to their union leaders.

When the final vote came on the House floor, the opponents of the organized labor position had won, 217 to 205. They put together 129 Republican votes (out of 143 voting) with sixty-five southern Democratic votes (out of eighty-five voting) and twenty-three critical northern Democratic votes (out of 194 voting) to achieve their victory.

---

28. See Dexter, *How Organizations Are Represented*: 62; and Truman, *The Governmental Process*: 391–392.

29. Mary E. Eccles, "House Rejects Labor-backed Picketing Bill," *Congressional Quarterly Weekly Report* (March 26, 1977): 521–524; and Mary Russell, "How Minority GOP Beat Labor's Bill," *Washington Post*, March 30, 1977.

The history of attempts to pass federal strip-mining legislation, finally successful in 1977, affords a good example of defensive lobbying that prevented a bill for a number of years and then succeeded in obtaining some key weakening amendments when passage did come.[30] Congressional consideration of federal regulation of strip-mining began in 1968, when a Senate committee first held hearings. By 1972 the House passed a bill but the Senate did not act. In 1974 President Ford pocket-vetoed a bill that Congress had passed (that is, he vetoed it after Congress had adjourned and so it had no chance to override the veto). In 1975 Congress passed another bill, which Ford vetoed, and an override attempt in the House failed by three votes. In 1976 the House Rules Committee twice prevented bills from reaching the floor (they would have been vetoed had they passed). Throughout this period a coalition of mining interests, led by coal, prevailed.

When success finally came in the form of legislation that passed Congress and was signed by President Carter in 1977, the years of successful opposition had resulted in some key changes in the legislation. For example, the bill addressed only coal mining and left other types of mining alone (although other mining, such as that for copper, also uses stripping techniques). This was a move to reduce the political weight of the opponents of the bill by concentrating only on coal. And even in the provisions dealing with coal mining, several provisions were weaker than House proponents in particular would have liked because of the persistent opposition and arguments of the coal interests. For example, the provision relating to strip-mining on alluvial valley floors in the West was weakened so that such mining was not banned but only somewhat restricted. Similarly, relatively small operators were given a temporary exemption from the environmental provisions of the act.

No-fault insurance (whereby persons injured in automobile accidents could simply collect from insurance companies without having to go to court in most cases) has been successfully opposed thus far (through 1977). It was narrowly defeated in the Senate in 1972 and 1976 and failed because of House inaction in 1974. The most potent defensive lobbying group in this case has been the Association of Trial Lawyers of America, whose members probably make $1 billion or more in fees for handling lawsuits resulting from automobile acci-

---

30. For background on the struggle over strip mining legislation see Randall B. Ripley and Grace A. Franklin, *Congress, the Bureaucracy, and Public Policy* (Homewood, Ill.: Dorsey, 1976): 98–103. For the 1977 Act see James R. Wagner, "Congress Clears Strip Mining Control Bill," *Congressional Quarterly Weekly Report* (July 23, 1977): 1495–1500.

dents. As a new struggle over the issue began to take shape for 1978, a pro-no-fault lobby took the field and could alter the outcome. Prior to 1977–78 the ATLA faced little concentrated lobbying opposition.[31] In general, successful defensive lobbying in one year does not necessarily remove an item from the congressional agenda for future years. Legislation in a given area may eventually be forthcoming, but skillful defensive lobbying can postpone it and probably produce some amendments that weaken a measure when it finally passes. For example, in 1972 defensive lobbying was credited with defeating a number of major initiatives: no-fault insurance, extended minimum wage coverage and a higher minimum wage figure, the establishment of a consumer protection agency, the opening of the highway trust fund for mass transit purposes, the inclusion of small businesses in a new occupational safety law, strip-mining regulation, and gun control.[32] Five years later, at the end of 1977, only a few of these seven initiatives had become law, usually in weakened form. A higher minimum wage figure was achieved in 1977, but coverage was not expanded, the highway trust fund was opened to mass transit uses in 1973, and strip-mining legislation with important limits was passed in 1977. No-fault insurance, a consumer protection agency, inclusion of small businesses under occupational safety, and gun control were still meeting successful opposition.

The Impact of Interest Groups on Congressional Decision-Making: An Assessment

In the final analysis, the impact of interest groups "depends more on the harmony of values between the groups and the legislators than it does on the ability of a group to wield its 'power' either through skillful techniques or presumed electoral influence." [33] For example, the Welfare Rights Organization facing a predominantly conservative Congress will make much less headway on issues important to it than it will under a predominantly liberal Congress.

What are the implications of interests groups' activity for representative government? A measure of skepticism and distrust is not entirely misplaced. Much national public policy reflects the special interests represented by the various groups. And competing groups may all

31. Linda E. Demkovich, "It's Time for Another Battle on No-Fault Insurance," *National Journal* (October 8, 1977): 1572–1573; and Spencer Rich, "High-Stakes Lobbying Battle Shaping Up over No-Fault," Washington *Post*, July 26, 1977.
32. "Opponents of Major Legislation Score Success," *Congressional Quarterly Almanac* (1972): 1074–1080.
33. Zeigler, *Interest Groups in American Society*: 274.

get part of their preferences written into statutes, even if that results in "irrational" public policy—that is, policies that contain built-in contradictions and simultaneously aim at opposing ends.[34] Unchecked, interest groups present some dangers. They participate in cozy subgovernment arrangements that essentially make policy in many areas without benefit or hindrance from other sources. They provide a large amount of issue-related information to legislators that naturally tends to be biased. Their very existence usually works for the maintenance of the status quo; they play an important role in keeping the agenda of Congress looking pretty much the same from year to year. They buttress Congress's preference for familiar, nonthreatening solutions to familiar issues.

Any system of government that is truly representative must allow interest groups to have their say, although participants must realize that the groups do not necessarily represent all legitimate interests. And there are checks on untrammeled influence on the part of interest groups. Congressmen may receive information that is biased, but they often are exposed to adverse views from competing lobbyists. It may not be possible to eliminate the coziness of subgovernment arrangements in many policy areas, but the entry of new people into a subgovernment helps new ideas to emerge. In addition, a watchful press can be very important in checking the activities of interest groups both in their subgovernments and as they lobby in Congress. The extensive role of the milk producers in financing both presidential and congressional campaigns, for example, was revealed by enterprising journalists. Journalists have also been aggressive in reporting on tax advantages engineered by and for special interests. Those stung by such revelations often brand the journalists as irresponsible "muckrakers," but the revelations may cause the lobbyists to abandon or curtail at least the most questionable of their practices.

Congress itself made a presumably comprehensive attempt to regulate lobbying in Title III of the Legislative Reorganization Act of 1946. In fact, this act is based on the assumption that simple collection and publication of information about the identification of lobbyists and spending for lobbying activities will be sufficient to keep the activities within reasonable (although undefined) bounds. There is no particular evidence supporting the accuracy of this assumption. In addition, the act requires the filing of data only when a group is engaged in spending *principally* for the purpose of influencing legislation. This means that many groups that may spend considerable sums and hire a number of representatives for legislative purposes but can interpret their

---

34. Truman, *The Governmental Process*: 393.

principal activities to be for other purposes do not file the required reports. In short, the information collected is only partial, is simply presented in raw form, and seems to have little effect on lobbying (although it should also be added that the drafters of this statute had no particularly clear desired effect at the time of its enactment). A major revision of the lobby disclosure provisions failed to pass in 1976. New efforts began in 1977.

MEMBERS AND CONSTITUENTS

In addition to dealing with groups, some of which purport to represent consituent interests, members of the House and Senate must also deal directly with constituents. Members view their constituents in a variety of ways. They sometimes see them through the filter of interest groups. For example, a House member might think of his district having 5,000 members of the United Auto Workers, 10,000 members of railway unions, 3,000 members of civil service unions, 1,000 members of the National Farmers Organization, 2,000 members of the American Farm Bureau Federation, seven corporate members of the National Association of Manufacturers, 4,000 members of the Sons of Italy, 3,000 members of the National Rifle Association, and 2,000 members of the Sierra Club. Or he might see them as being affiliated with the major economic institutions of the district: 15,000 employees of the Burlington Northern, 5,000 employees of John Deere, 2,000 employees of Swift and Company, 14,000 employees of the federal government, and 5,000 employees of the state government.

Members might also think in terms of the general socioeconomic characteristics of their districts: highly urban or highly rural, large or small ethnic and black populations, well-educated or poorly educated, well-paid or poorly paid, predominantly Protestant or predominantly Catholic, highly identified with the Republican party or the Democratic party. They may not realize that they are using analytical categories but in fact they instinctively do so. Interviews with members include statements such as the following: "My people are mostly poor Czechs and Germans." "I've got a lot of blacks and poor white Appalachians." "Most of my folks own their own farms or own their own businesses in small towns. They have all lived in those counties a long time."

They might also think of at least a few of their constituents as individuals: the editor of the district's largest newspaper, the party county chairmen, the managers of the largest plants, the presidents of the largest unions, and other such local notables are likely to be known as individuals by a member.

A study based on close observation of seventeen House members from 1970 through 1976 concluded that members see four different kinds of constituencies when they think about their districts.[35] First they see a geographical constituency, consisting of all of their constituents, and they also see some basic differentiations. They are generally aware of whether their district is fairly homogeneous in terms of population characteristics or whether it is quite heterogeneous. Second, members see a re-election constituency made up of the people the member thinks vote for him. Third, members identify a primary constituency, those supporters among the re-election constituency who are viewed as being the most reliable, active, and strongest. Finally, members have a personal constituency, those strong supporters who interact often with the member on a personal basis.

Regardless of the filter he uses, the member of Congress is sure to be thinking of his constituents in one way or another almost all of the time. "This bill has important benefits for the folks back home and I have to work for its passage." "How will my vote on this controversial roll call be received at home?" "What are the responses from the questionnaire I sent home last week looking like?" "Will I have time to get home this month for some speaking and unofficial campaigning?" Constituency is important to members for a variety of reasons, but the most elemental, of course, is that it is constituents who elect and re-elect members to Congress. In this section we will look at the interaction between the congressman and his constituency and at the impact that constituency can have on congressional behavior.

Interaction between Constituents and Members

Members of the House and Senate have a number of methods of communicating with their constituents. They can appear on radio and television shows (in the Eighty-ninth Congress the average House member made eight radio appearances and four television appearances per month).[36] They can send newsletters to their constituents and can solicit opinions through mailed questionnaires. Other means by which the member informs his constituents include: promoting newspaper coverage of his activities; writing reports or columns for newspapers; sending committee reports and government publications; establishing

35. Richard F. Fenno, Jr., "U.S. House Members in Their Constituencies: An Exploration," *American Political Science Review* 71 (1977): 883–917. See also Fenno, *Home Style: House Members in Their Districts* (Boston: Little, Brown, 1978).

36. John S. Saloma III, *Congress and the New Politics* (Boston: Little, Brown, 1969): 174–175. See also Donald G. Tacheron and Morris K. Udall, *The Job of the Congressman* (Indianapolis: Bobbs-Merrill, 1966): 280–288.

film and record libraries on government activities and programs; speaking at public functions such as service club meetings and high school graduations; acting personally as a host for visitors from the constituency; and responding to constituent mail. There are other communications that don't contain information about legislation but that help the member to enhance his image: for example, most members write letters of congratulation and condolence and send such useful items as free seeds and booklets on baby care to constituents.[37]

Members receive information from their constituents through a number of sources, including: letters, telegrams, phone calls, personal visits to members and their staffs, and appearances before committees. The mail, however, is the most important vehicle for transmitting constituents' opinions to members. Organized letter-writing campaigns from constituencies, often generated by an interest group, are considered less important by congressmen than letters from individual constituents. An organized campaign is usually recognizable by the set phraseology or standard form of the letters.[38]

On a number of important issues there is little mail from constituents to their representatives. Constituents are generally uninformed about the procedural and substantive details of congressional life, their level of issue-specific information varies from issue to issue. In fact, well-formed constituent opinion does not exist on most matters; even that opinion transmitted to members of Congress is likely to be somewhat vague and poorly expressed. This means that much of the time the member does not have any empirical indications of constituency opinion to guide his behavior.

Even when constituent opinion is expressed, two distortions accompany it. First, it tends to come from individuals who already agree with the position of their representative or senator. Second, members tend to interpret what they hear as being supportive of views they already hold. This is relatively easy since many communications from constituents are unclear and ambiguous. In short, members tend not to be heavily influenced by constituency opinion, except that which agrees with what they already feel or believe. Thus a member generally represents his image of his district or state, and that image is largely of his own shaping and creation.[39]

Some members of Congress let the expressed opinions of a few individual constituents speak for the opinion of the entire constituency.

---

37. See Clapp, *The Congressman*: Chapter 2 on all of these activities.
38. See Lewis A. Dexter, "What Do Congressmen Hear?" in Nelson W. Polsby (ed.), *Congressional Behavior* (New York: Random House, 1971).
39. Lewis A. Dexter, *The Sociology and Politics of Congress* (Chicago: Rand McNally, 1969): Chapter 8.

These are people the congressman trusts and considers to be representative. Although they may transmit no opinion other than their own, the important point is that the congressman values those opinions, accepts them as representative, and probably interprets them as endorsements of positions he already holds.[40] The identity of these individuals varies widely from case to case. They may include prominent industrialists, editors, union leaders, local politicans, or rather obscure people who just happen to be old friends and confidants.

Congressional Workloads and Constituency Service

There is conflicting evidence on how much of their time and resources congressmen allocate to constituency service, broadly defined. In fact, different members proceed very differently in their constituencies. A pioneering study by Richard Fenno concluded that each member of Congress has a "home style" and that each home style is at least partially unique. Three aspects of home style seemed to vary: how the member allocated both his personal resources and those of his office, how the member presented himself at home, and how the member explained his personal activities and those of congress in Washington at home.[41] Constituencies are important to virtually all members but they proceed differently.

Discussions with members of the House in 1959 led Charles Clapp to assert that legislators spent most of their time dealing with constituency-related aspects of their jobs:

A congressman is administrator, educator, and errand boy, as well as legislator. In each of these roles he is mindful of his constituents. He organizes his office with them, rather than his legislative responsibilities, in mind. Though he considers his work in behalf of individuals as less fundamental to his job than work on legislation, he nonetheless gives it precedence. He both derives satisfaction from it and is dismayed by it. It often is an onerous chore, but it meets a real need, brings him valuable information, and is the activity most likely to "pay off" at the polls. He resents the time it takes, but he will not slight it.[42]

More systematic surveys have found that members claim legislative work to be more time-consuming than constituency service. In Roger

---

40. For a discussion of this phenomenon at the state level, see George R. Boynton and others, "The Missing Links in Legislative Politics: Attentive Constituents," *Journal of Politics* 31 (1969): 700–721.

41. Fenno, "U.S. House Members," and *Home Style*.

42. Clapp, *The Congressman*: 103; see also 50–53.

Davidson's study, only 16 percent of the legislators listed constituency service as their primary activity (although 59 percent listed it as their secondary activity); 77 percent claimed legislative work to be their primary activity. Constituency service was less important to senior members than to junior members because senior members felt less need to strive for electoral safety (which they had already achieved) but junior members were still building it.[43]

An elaborate survey of workloads in the Eighty-ninth Congress showed that the average member spent only 28 percent of his time on constituency service; legislative work consumed 65 percent of his time.[44]

The House Commission on Administrative Review in 1977 published data based on a survey of House members conducted in mid-1977 on how members spent their time. They presented their data in terms of an "average" day of eleven hours and twenty-six minutes of work in Washington. When those figures are converted to percentages, the Commission reported that the average Representative spent 39 percent of his or her time on the floor of the House and in committee and subcommittee and conference committee work, 29 percent of the time in his or her office, 18 percent of the time at other locations in Washington, and the remaining time (14 percent) in miscellaneous other activities. Except for the first category, much of the time was spent on constituent business. And, of course, a number of days were spent in the district devoted wholly to constituent business. The Commission's observation on these data is more important than the exact figures: "Members are extraordinarily busy people. An average day for legislators is so filled with diverse activities that little time is available for concentrated attention on any single issue. Legislators have exhaustive schedules that keep them running back and forth from their offices to floor sessions, committee meetings, or receptions and events in various parts of Washington. Legislators, too, are regularly flying or driving back and forth between Washington and their congressional districts." [45]

If the work of the representative or senator is divided between legislative work and constituency support, the job of congressional staff is much less divided—staff work is principally devoted to constituency service. A survey of congressional staff in the Eighty-ninth Congress showed the average office spent 25 percent of its time in direct

---

43. Davidson, *The Role of the Congressman*: 99; Clapp, *The Congressman*: 52.

44. Saloma, *Congress and the New Politics*: 184.

45. Commission on Administrative Review, *Administrative Reorganization and Legislative Management*, House Document No. 95–232, Vol. 2 (September 28, 1977). The data are from pages 17–19. The quotation is from page 17.

constituency service, 41 percent of its time answering the mail, 10 percent of its time on education and publicity, and only 14 percent of its time on legislative support.[46]

Constituency Impact on Member Behavior

Constituency impact on the behavior of members of the House and Senate falls into three broad categories. First, there are those instances in which the economic interests of the district (or, more likely, a few specific individual or corporate constituents) push a member into a given stance. For example, in 1977 members of the House from sixteen northeastern and midwestern states (the "frostbelt") formed a coalition to work for changing federal aid formulas they felt were discriminatory against their area in favor of the "sunbelt" states of the South and West.[47] One study found a relationship between federal spending for agriculture, education, and space to be related to roll call voting patterns in the Senate—senators coming from states receiving high benefits in these areas would only rarely vote against bills containing such benefits.[48]

At the individual level there are innumerable examples of members sponsoring legislation aimed at benefiting primarily their own districts or a few constituents in those districts. For example, in April, 1977, an Arkansas senator and a Maine senator sponsored a bill that would have no impact except on two chicken processing plants in Arkansas and Maine. The bill involved tax relief for these two firms and passed in the Senate, after some ineffective protest, 85–12.[49] The size of the vote reflects the fact that most senators would want similar support for similar kinds of legislation in the future and thus were reluctant to vote against anyone else's special request.

Second, there are a few issues on which enough constituents are so concerned that a major wrong move by a member could cost him his seat. If in the 1940s or 1950s a southern member had come out in favor of strong civil rights legislation, he almost surely would have been defeated. If a member from a strongly unionized district came out in favor of the Taft-Hartley Act in 1947, he might have been defeated in 1948. If a member from a middle-class suburban area came out in

---

46. Saloma, *Congress and the New Politics,* 185.
47. Joel Havemann and Rochelle L. Stanfield, "A Year Later, the Frostbelt Strikes Back," *National Journal* (July 2, 1977): 1028–1037.
48. Lance T. LeLoup, "The Impact of Domestic Spending Patterns on Senate Support: An Examination of Three Policy Areas," *American Politics Quarterly* 5 (1977): 219–236.
49. Spencer Rich, "Senate Votes Poultry Processors Tax Relief," Washington *Post,* April 29, 1977.

favor of massive busing to achieve school integration with an adjacent metropolitan area, even now he might be defeated. If a member from a sparsely populated western state vigorously espoused the cause of gun control, he might well lose his seat. But this kind of issue is relatively rare. On most issues the member has a great deal of freedom to maneuver because most of his constituents are uninformed or unconcerned about the issue. But there is good evidence that members try to anticipate issues that may cause them problems in their constituencies and they try to avoid trouble in voting by guessing the safe route to take.[50]

The third kind of constituency impact occurs principally in the mind of the senator or representative himself. He thinks that representing constituents is important and therefore attempts, usually by intuition rather than by gathering data, to reflect the opinion of the constituency on a given issue or to hypothesize what the constituency would favor if it were asked to voice an opinion. In making these calculations a number of subtle processes occur. Most members seek information that confirms them in their previously held beliefs. They can distort information they receive or simply rely, almost unconsciously, on a previously held image of constituency opinion. But this still does not mean that constituency opinion is not a very real phenomenon in the minds of members. It is a factor that concerns them constantly.

And, of course, members are aware of the voting habits of their constituents—both for Congress and in general. Typical statements from members might include the following: "Registration in my district is two to one Democratic but a smart Republican can still carry it." "The district is competitive. My constituents always split their tickets and elect some candidates from both parties." "My people don't much like political parties. You are better off not harping on party."

As members internalize all of these various understandings and pressures, both perceived and real, they tend to lean toward one of two poles in terms of how they articulate the effect of constituency on their behavior. At the one pole are members who perceive themselves to be "delegates"—that is, individuals who are simply instructed in one way or another by their constituents how to behave and how to vote and who willingly do it. At the other pole are members who perceive themselves to be "trustees"—that is, they consider constituency opinion and make-up as they understand it but they take final responsibility for

50. Morris P. Fiorina, *Representatives, Roll Calls, and Constituencies* (Lexington, Mass.: Lexington Books, 1974).

reaching decisions, on the grounds that they hold the welfare of their constituency in trust and should do what is best for the constituency regardless of the constituents' own perceptions or misperceptions.[51] Most members generally operate on the basis of some middle position and the categories of "delegate" and "trustee" are not very useful empirically except to indicate that members have a wide range of choice both about what they perceive and how those perceptions influence them. There is nothing fixed about the outcome of this transaction; what is fixed is that members are concerned with representing constituencies well according to their own individual lights.

External events and conditions can also change the way in which members think about the importance of constituency opinion. For example, there is evidence that southern Democrats and eastern Republicans increased their rate of defection from their respective dominant party positions in House roll calls in the 1960s because the tumultuous events of the 1960s—especially violence surrounding civil rights and anti-Vietnam war activities—made politics more salient to their constituents, and thus members tried to be more responsive to what they thought was dominant opinion in their constituencies on a number of issues.[52]

Unfortunately, students of Congress have not found definitive ways of measuring the impact of constituency using the general considerations above. Rather they have focused on making inferences about the impact of constituency—both in terms of opinion and in terms of socioeconomic and partisan categories—by examining roll call votes. There are some limits to the use of roll calls in this way but, if the issues selected are fair tests of congressional behavior, roll calls can provide evidence about variations in the impact of constituency.

Constituency attitudes vary in impact from issue to issue and can be reflected in members' behavior on roll call votes in several ways. Figure 8–1 provides an overall scheme. The critical variables are the member's own attitude, the way he perceives the constituency's attitude, and his willingness to deviate from that perception in his behavior. After investigating roll call votes in three issue areas—civil rights, social welfare, and foreign involvement—Warren Miller and Donald Stokes concluded that the local constituency does have a measure of control over member behavior. The pattern of constituency-

51. On representational roles see Roger H. Davidson, *The Role of the Congressman*, Chapter 4.

52. Barbara Sinclair Deckard, "Political Upheaval and Congressional Voting: The Effects of the 1960s on Voting Patterns in the House of Representatives," *Journal of Politics* 38 (1976): 326–345.

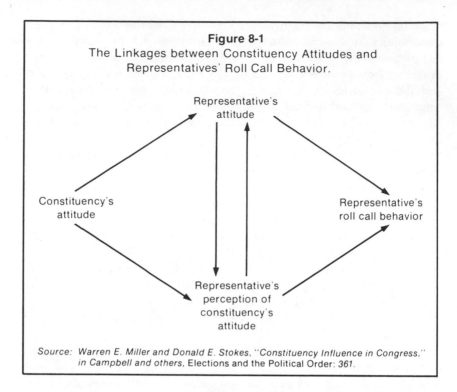

Figure 8-1

The Linkages between Constituency Attitudes and
Representatives' Roll Call Behavior.

Representative's attitude

Constituency's attitude

Representative's roll call behavior

Representative's perception of constituency's attitude

Source: Warren E. Miller and Donald E. Stokes, "Constituency Influence in Congress,"
in Campbell and others, Elections and the Political Order: 361.

representative relations varied from issue to issue: in the civil rights issue domain the correspondence between roll call behavior and constituency attitudes was greatest (and quite high), in the area of foreign affairs it was least (and quite low), and if fell into a middle ground in the area of social welfare.[53]

Another way to attempt to explore the impact of constituents is to try to sort out the groups that tended to vote for a member and to see if that member is particularly responsive to the presumed interests of those groups. An analysis using this method studied the voting of senators in 1963–64 and found that senators indeed seemed to be particularly responsive to the interests of individuals voting for them. The party affiliation of the senators was also highly important.[54]

Still another—and the most common—way to explore the impact of constituents is to aggregate their characteristics by district and then examine the difference that variations in these characteristics seem

53. Warren E. Miller and Donald E. Stokes, "Constituency Influence in Congress," in Angus Campbell and others, Elections and the Political Order (New York: Wiley, 1966).
54. Gregory B. Markus, "Electoral Coalitions and Senate Roll Call Behavior: An Ecological Analysis," American Journal of Political Science 18 (1974): 595–607.

to make in the behavior of the members. A number of such studies have been done—always with roll call voting as the measure of member behavior—and some conflicting findings have emerged.[55] But there are areas of agreement.

First, certain kinds of constituencies tend to elect Democratic members and others tend to effect Republican members. In general, districts represented by Democrats are poorer and more urban than districts represented by Republicans. They also have a larger proportion of non-white population. There is an important regional variation that should be noted, however: southern Republican districts are more urban than southern Democratic districts. They remain "whiter" than Democratic districts but there is virtually no difference in the percent of owner-occupied housing units. Table 8–3 summarizes data from the Ninety-second Congress (1971–72) to support these generalizations.

Table 8–3

Comparison Between Democratic and Republican Districts, by Region, 92nd Congress (1971–72)

	Democratic Districts			Republican Districts		
	All *(N = 255)*	*Northern and Western (N = 176)*	*Southern (N = 79)*	*All* *(N = 180)*	*Northern and Western (N = 153)*	*Southern (N = 27)*
% Urban	75	81	61	70	70	68
% Non-White	18	15	23	7	5	17
% Owner-Occupied Housing Units	59	57	65	68	69	65

Percent owner-occupied housing units is used as a measure of both wealth and social class. A family able to buy a house—even if it is not particularly imposing—is likely to be relatively well-off financially and think of itself as solidly in the middle class whereas a family that rents is more likely to be less well-off financially and is also less likely to have a middle class image of itself. The other measures in the table are self-explanatory.

Source: Calculated from Congressional District Data Sheets prepared by the Census Bureau.

---

55. See, for example, Thomas A. Flinn and Harold L. Wolman, "Constituency and Roll Call Voting: the Case of the Southern Democratic Congressmen," *Midwest Journal of Political Science* 10 (1966): 192–199; Lewis A. Froman, *Congressmen and their Constituencies* (Chicago: Rand McNally, 1963); Julius Turner and Edward V. Schneier, Jr., *Party and Constituency: Pressures in Congress* (Baltimore: Johns Hopkins, 1970); W. Wayne Shannon, *Party, Constituency and Congressional Voting* (Baton Rouge: Louisiana State University Press, 1968); Duncan MacRae, Jr., *Dimensions of Congressional Voting* (Berkeley: University of California Press, 1958); Aage R. Clausen, *How Congressmen Decide* (New York: St. Martin's, 1973); and Fiorina, *Representatives, Roll Calls, and Constituencies.*

Table 8–4 portrays some differences in the *distribution* (*averages* are reported in Table 8–3) of constituency characteristics among all Democratic and Republican representatives in the Eighty-eighth Congress (1963–64). This shows that Democrats were more likely to come from poorer, more urban districts with a relatively large non-white population and Republicans were more likely to come from richer, more suburban districts with a relatively small non-white population. It also shows, however, that there is not an absolute cleavage between the parties: there are Republicans from districts with basically Democratic characteristics and there are Democrats from districts with basically Republican characteristics.

A second conclusion of most studies is that constituency characteristics are wedded to ideological differences among congressmen. Democrats and Republicans generally differ in their views, particularly on domestic policy, with the Democrats being generally more liberal and

Table 8–4

Selected Constituency Characteristics, by Party for
The House of Representatives, 88th Congress.

Type of Constituency Characteristic	% of All Democratic Seats (N = 256)	% of All Republican Seats (N = 178)
Median Income in District		
Under $4000	25	2
$4000–6999	70	76
$7000 and over	6	21
Percent Owner-Occupied Housing Units in District		
Under 50.0	20	3
50–69.0	62	55
70.0 and over	19	43
Percent Non-White Population in District		
Under 10.0	51	91
10–19.9	14	8
20.0 and over	34	1
Urbanness of District		
Urban	38	20
Suburban	12	21
Rural	50	60

Source: Data on the first three characteristics are calculated from the Congressional District Data Book *for the 88th Congress. The urban-suburban-rural classification comes from* Congressional Quarterly Almanac 1963: 1170–83.

the Republicans generally more conservative. Within the parties, however, differences between the districts represented by individuals are not always systematically predictive of which party members will be the more liberal or more conservative or more or less loyal to the party.[56] A few variables are more predictive of ideological differences than others. For example, among urban southern Democrats (N=36) in the Eighty-eighth Congress the percent urban population in the district was highly correlated with party unity, support for a larger Federal role, and support for President John Kennedy's programs. That is, among this subset of congressmen those from the more urban districts were the more liberal, loyal Democrats. Among rural southern Democrats (N=42) the percentage of black population in the district was negatively correlated with party unity, support for a larger federal role, and support for the president's programs. That is, the rural southern Democrat with the greatest proportion of blacks in his district tended to be the most conservative and least loyal to his party's legislative positions.[57] The whites in the districts with the largest number of blacks have reacted to that "threat" in part with conservative politics.

Finally, when constituency characteristics are weighed against the influence of party affiliation, party generally emerges as the stronger force. One classic study specifically found party differences to be more explanatory than differences in urbanness or ethnic or racial composition of districts.[58]

A recent study presented more differentiated findings. When the impact of party and constituency were compared on five policy dimensions, constituency was found to be relatively potent on questions of international involvement and civil liberties but party was found to be more important on questions of agricultural assistance, social welfare, and government management.[59]

It may be that the "dispute" in the roll call literature between party influence and constituent influence is ultimately pointless since the type of district helps determine the party of the congressman. Thus it seems reasonable to argue that in most cases party influence and constituent influence as measured by aggregate constituency characteristics such as race, home-owning patterns, income, urbanization, and so

---

56. Ripley, *Party Leaders in the House of Representatives,* 157–158, 211–212.

57. See Flinn and Wolman for these data and a discussion of them.

58. Turner and Schneier, *Party and Constituency.* See also Demetrios Caraley, "Congressional Politics and Urban Aid," *Political Science Quarterly* 91 (1976): 19–43, for findings that party affiliation is more important than constituency characteristics in explaining voting on urban aid measures.

59. Clausen, *How Congressmen Decide.*

on push in the same direction. Given the four levels of constituency Fenno has found members to perceive, it is also inaccurate to talk about "constituency" as if it can be measured adequately by aggregate characteristics. Such measures may capture one meaning of constituency, but the other three are ignored. Constituency interests are obviously important but they are very hard to measure in the ways that have usually been used.

AN OVERVIEW OF INTEREST GROUP AND CONSTITUENT IMPACT ON CONGRESS

Neither interest groups nor constituents set the agenda for Congress, although they influence it. Likewise, neither of them determine policy outcomes, although they can influence them. They both help set the bounds within which Congress operates. Their presence is tangible and real in a variety of ways. Skillful lobbyists can achieve at least part of their aims. Constituent interests—whether explicitly articulated by constituency spokespersons or operating in the imagination of the member—usually find eager supporters in the House and Senate.

It is also quite clear that members have the latitude, if they have the will, to use interest groups and lobbyists for their own ends and to lead constituency opinion much of the time rather than just following it. Thus, to portray members generally as captives of interest groups or constituencies is inaccurate. Some may lean in that direction. Some lean in the other direction. But the choice is theirs.

To the extent that members pay attention to the policy preferences of interest groups and constituents, those preferences, because they are numerous and diverse, push in the direction of greater policy fragmentation rather than greater policy integration. This is inevitably and necessarily so. In a sense, the integrating forces in Congress are permanently in a state of tension with interest groups and constituency interests.

CHAPTER 9

CONGRESS,
THE PRESIDENT,
AND THE PRESIDENCY

O N 8 AUGUST 1974, RICHARD NIXON ANNOUNCED HIS RESIGNATION AS president of the United States to the American people. That unique event in American history helps put the power of Congress in relation to that of the president in perspective in two ways. In an immediate sense individuals and committees in Congress helped build the case against Nixon and his subordinates that led to resignation as an alternative preferable to impeachment by the House of Representatives and conviction by the Senate. The work of the Senate Watergate Committee and the House Judiciary Committee, when combined with the activities of the special prosecutor, the federal judiciary, and the press helped create the public sentiment that Nixon's misdeeds were so unprecedented as to warrant an unprecedented ouster of a president. Also, three leaders of Congress of the president's own party— Senators Barry Goldwater (the Republican presidential nominee in 1964) and Hugh Scott (the Republican floor leader in the Senate) and Congressman John Rhodes (the Republican floor leader in the House) —joined with the White House staff chief Alexander Haig and Secretary of State Henry Kissinger in advising the president that there was no way he could remain in office and that the national interest demanded that he resign.[1]

The political demise of Richard Nixon also affords a broader perspective on the place of Congress in contemporary American society.

---

1. For the story of how these five individuals broached the subject of resignation with Nixon, see the column by Rowland Evans and Robert Novak in the *Washington Post,* August 10, 1974, and the comments by Senator Scott as reported in the same newspaper, August 12, 1974.

In many ways the twentieth century has been a century of presidential domination of the national government. Congress has been consistently more important than is generally recognized, but it is true that on the greatest issues facing the American people the role of Congress has seemed to pale in comparison to that of the president. However, with the growing unpopularity of the Vietnam War in the late 1960s and early 1970s and the revelations of presidential abuse of power under Nixon, the will in Congress to be more assertive was strengthened. A war powers act passed in 1973 and a budget reform act passed in 1974 were designed to give Congress more power on the major issues of war and peace and governmental impact on the economy. Watergate and its aftermath do not spell an automatic and dramatic reversal in the state of congressional power in relation to the executive branch in the late 1970's and early 1980's, but those events both afford an opportunity for Congress to assert itself vigorously on major policy questions and may well help prolong the will to make such assertions evidenced by the war powers and budget acts.

At the end of the first year of the presidency of Jimmy Carter a number of members of Congress, including the leaders, expressed a great deal of satisfaction that the balance between president and Congress had been restored to a healthier level for Congress than in the "imperial presidency" of a few years before. Speaker O'Neill said, "Congress is asserting its legitimate powers. I don't think there's any question about the fact that there was an erosion of power in Congress that started in the last years of Sam Rayburn's life. That erosion has been reversed." House Majority Leader James Wright observed that measures such as the new budget process and the War Powers Act had improved the congressional position: "This was a relatively major shift back toward the direction of power-sharing. We define the stream banks through which executive power may flow." The Republican floor leader in the House, John Rhodes, agreed: "Congress has gotten used to kicking Presidents around, and they don't care whose President it is." [2]

Despite this optimism and the unquestioned increasing aggressiveness of Congress since 1973, the president has not been dramatically reduced in power. Symbolic reductions are more prevalent than real reductions. The president still is, in many ways, the legislative leader. The president and Congress are still not equal at some points in the policy process, particularly the development of coherent policy state-

---

2. All quotations in this paragraph come from Martin Tolchin, "Power Balance Tips to Congress from President," *New York Times*, October 9, 1977.

ments.[3] A single individual with considerable formal power can inevitably declare a position and follow through on it more skillfully and rapidly than a multi-headed body like Congress. An example from 1973 is worth describing at some length to make this point.

In 1973 the Democratic majority in Congress was anxious to prepare its own program of wage and price controls rather than simply extending their delegation of that power to the president for another year, the course favored by President Nixon. Yet, despite overwhelming party sentiment for such congressional initiative, Congress ultimately passed, with a great many Democratic votes, the exact extension desired by the president.

The reasons for the Democratic failure on this issue are several and are particularly apparent in the House. The central problem was that the Democrats could not agree on a single strategy. In the Banking and Currency Committee, which first considered the bill, different points of view among the Democratic members were never resolved; instead a variety of amendments were added to the bill. A number of relatively stringent provisions on prices were added by liberal Democrats even though there was considerable feeling that they went too far for the whole House to accept. In the Rules Committee, which next had to consider the bill, it was found necessary to send the bill to the floor with a provision against points of order, a provision that offended many House members, including Democrats. By the time the bill finally reached the floor, it was an unpassable product, despite the numerous special allowances, regulations, and exceptions designed to satisfy particular interests and gain their support.

The Democratic leaders in the House tried to produce some order out of the chaos. According to then Majority Leader O'Neill, "The speaker called in members of the Banking and Currency Committee and the House leaders on three different occasions, to try to iron things out." The leadership effort in the Banking Committee failed and this left the leaders without a defensible position on the House floor. They openly sought a winning formula during the floor debate as a large number of amendments, many of them dealing with the date a price freeze would take effect, were debated and voted on. But their quest for compromise, which might have been successful had it been done quietly and in advance, only added to the image of confusion and ineptness because of its hurried and visible nature.

---

3. For a good review of the literature on the president as a legislative leader see John F. Manley, "The Presidency, Congress and National Policy-Making," in Cornelius P. Cotter (ed.) *Political Science Annual, Volume 5* (Indianapolis: Bobbs-Merrill, 1974): 227–273.

Adding to the Democrats' woes was an unusually effective effort in support of the president by a great variety of lobbies, including those for the Chamber of Commerce, retailers, food chains, realtors, bankers, farmers, and cattlemen. Only some labor unions gave much effective support to the Democrats.

Ultimately, the House decided that it could not legislate in this complex area and had no choice but to acquiesce to the president's wishes, even though the majority did not agree with his position. Several members underscored the basic problem in post-debacle comments. Morris Udall, an Arizona Democrat, said "It's the difference between an organization headed by one powerful man and a many-headed organization." Sam Gibbons, a Florida Democrat, said, "I don't think this expresses our support for Nixon's handling of the economy but Congress can't administer the country. We are 535 people with no administrative authority at all. Some people do Congress a disservice by overstating the amount of authority we have." [4]

But once the congressional disadvantage in initiation is acknowledged, then the president and Congress face similar kinds of tensions as they ponder how to deal with each other. Both must decide on the level of activism they will adopt as their basic legislative stance, and to what extent they will cooperate with some other branch. Some presidents and some Congresses are relatively restrained in the legislative tasks they set for themselves and in the energy they display in working toward the achievement of those tasks. Other presidents and Congresses set goals and expend much energy in the pursuit of them. And, of course, the minority parties in Congress might take very different stances from each other.

The decision about relative activism or relative restraint is much more conscious and explicit for the president than it is for Congress, simply because one person can decide something with greater clarity than 535 people. But leaders of different Congresses also express different attitudes toward the legislative task; their statements offer a fairly accurate guide to the level of activism likely to be espoused by the Congress. For example, in the Eighty-ninth Congress (1965–1966) the leaders of the majority party made it clear that they were eager to have Congress cooperate with President Johnson in working on a

---

4. This discussion of the House action on wage and price controls is based on "House Backs Nixon on Economic Controls Extension," *Congressional Quarterly Weekly Report* (April 21, 1973): 938–941; and Daniel J. Balz, "Economic Report/ Mismanagement, Lobbying Imperil Democrats' Attempts to Impose Tough Controls," *National Journal* (April 28, 1973): 611–615. The quotations from Udall and Gibbons come from the first article. The quotation from O'Neill is taken from "O'Neill: Watergate May Help Free Republican Votes," *Congressional Quarterly Weekly Report* (May 19, 1973): 1210.

very full legislative agenda. But those same leaders in the Ninetieth Congress (1967–1968) were equally clear in their position that Congress should proceed at a more deliberate pace, thus helping the government and the nation digest the new programs that had been created in the preceding Congress.

THE PRESIDENTIAL SIDE

Presidential access to Congress depends on a number of variables, the most important of which are the president's view of his legislative role, his skill at implementing his vision of the role both personally and through the institutional presidency, the willingness and ability of the leaders of the president's party to transmit and obtain his legislative wishes from the standing committees and the rank-and-file members on the floor, and the president's direct access to the leaders of his party, the other party, the committees, and the rank-and-file members. In short, presidential will, style, and institutions are all important elements affecting the outcome of the policy process, but they are balanced against a variety of congressional wills, styles, and institutions. Success is never guaranteed to a president, even when a sizable majority of his party controls both the House and Senate.

Presidents' backgrounds help explain some of the variations in personal relationships between them and the members of Congress. Presidents who have served for a long time in Congress and who have risen to positions of leadership in the House or Senate seem more likely both to enjoy working with members of Congress on a personal basis and to have a good "feel" for how to deal with members in the most efficacious way. Thus, for example, Lyndon Johnson, a formidable leader in the Senate before becoming president, was praised by many as an authentic genius in interacting with key members of the House and Senate so as to get desired results (until the Vietnam escalation soured his relations with Congress.) His performance in 1964 and 1965 contrasts with those of this predecessor, John Kennedy, and his successor, Richard Nixon. Kennedy and Nixon had served in both the House and Senate but neither had risen to leadership positions and neither seemed to enjoy legislative life very much. Both were reluctant to deal personally with members after they became president and neither possessed a great deal of skill at it. In his last year in office Nixon's relations with most members of Congress simply ceased.

President Ford did not have the flair or reputation for leadership in Congress during his long service in the House that Johnson did during his period of Senate leadership. Nevertheless, he was clearly a career congressman until he was nominated to be vice-president by

Nixon after Spiro Agnew resigned in the autumn of 1973. He began his presidency indicating that he expected close and cordial relations with individual members of Congress even though he knew there would be policy disagreements. In his first address to Congress, just three days after becoming president following Nixon's resignation, he expressed admiration both for Congress as an institution and for congressmen as individuals. Given the values inculcated by twenty-five years of service in the House, Ford felt little discomfort in dealing with members of Congress, even though the majority often did not agree with his policy stances.

In his first year in office President Carter exhibited considerable tentativeness in dealing with Congress. This was not surprising, in part because he had had no experience with Congress either as a member or in any other way. He had problems both with setting clear priorities and in following through with actions designed to enhance the chances of success for his initiatives.

Presidential Techniques for Dealing with Congress

If a president decides on an aggressive approach to Congress on legislative matters he has a number of techniques at his command.

First, he can set much of the agenda for Congress by making a series of specific proposals. Presidents have always submitted some preferences. In the last few decades the "program of the president" has emerged as the largest part of the legislative agenda for Congress, even in those cases in which Congress and the White House are controlled by different parties. Since the early 1930s all presidents have routinely assumed they would submit a large program to Congress. The only partial exception occurred in 1953 when President Eisenhower was unsure of the wisdom of doing so. But his advisers, especially those in the Bureau of the Budget (the forerunner of the Office of Management and Budget), convinced him that he must submit a large program and he did so in 1954.

Presidential proposals are contained in the annual state of the union message (or multiple messages, as President Nixon used in 1973), the annual budget message, the annual economic message, and a great variety of special messages. The use of this technique is now virtually automatic and represents the minimum effort any president is likely to make. Congress has become dependent on these messages. In 1969, for example, the Democratic leaders of the House and Senate became publicly restless when President Nixon was, in their view, slow in putting forth a program. In effect, they complained that Congress could not really function until the president had set the most important parts of the agenda.

Second, the president can seek to garner popular support for his proposals by making public statements in support of them. Presumably, if popular support develops it will be transmitted in one way or another to the members of Congress and increase their willingness to support the proposals. All presidents make appeals to the public but vary a great deal in the frequency with which they use this method. Franklin Roosevelt, for example, sought popular support for a great variety of programs, especially through the medium of his "fireside chats" on radio. Presidents Truman and Eisenhower were considerably more restrained than Roosevelt. John Kennedy was selective in his addresses to the people, focusing on a few issues like medical care for the aged and economic policy. Lyndon Johnson returned to a more Rooseveltian posture, speaking often and with great force on a wide variety of issues, notably aid to education and civil rights early in his presidency and in defense of his policies in Southeast Asia late in his presidency. President Nixon did not make public statements on every issue but concentrated on a few, such as Southeast Asia policy, revenue-sharing, and economy in government. In his first year in office President Carter made a major continuing appeal to the public on his energy program. He labeled it the "moral equivalent of war" and criticized the level of profits of the oil companies in the course of seeking support for his program.

Presidents can also seek to magnify their public appeal by having other respected and well-known citizens openly endorse their views. On critical matters of foreign policy, for example, recent presidents have sought and received the public support of living ex-presidents. Business leaders, labor leaders, and other such individuals are also approached by presidents for their public support. A president often finds it particularly useful to seek endorsement for a proposal from a well-known national figure from the opposition party. President Kennedy and Johnson used this technique often in trying to build support for foreign aid proposals, for example. President Carter enlisted the support of leading Republicans, including former president Ford and former secretary of state Kissinger in working for ratification of the Panama Canal treaties.

Third, the president can take a hand in allocating projects and patronage to encourage Congress to back his proposals. The executive branch has many resources at its disposal: jobs, post offices, courthouses, dams, federal contracts, and other tangible rewards. Because of civil service laws the president's power over the dispensation of federal jobs (the "spoils system") has been reduced. But he and his departmental secretaries still have about 6,700 positions at their disposal. These include about 3,500 top jobs throughout the executive branch exempt from civil service, White House employees, 140 ambassadors to foreign countries, 523 federal judgeships, 93 U.S. attorneys, 94 U.S. marshals, and about 2,100 part-time positions on commissions and boards. Even if the last category is deleted the president is or can be the effective appointing authority for 4,600 highly desirable positions. The Senate must ratify many of the president's nominations for these positions. President Carter in his first year was reluctant to use his control over jobs ("patronage") to further party and policy ends.[5]

Fourth, the president can give personal attention to members of the House and Senate. By inviting members to meals at the White House, having them conspicuously present at bill signing ceremonies, calling them on the phone, writing complimentary letters that are released for publication, sending them autographed pictures, and boosting their egos in a number of other ways a president can enhance his chances of legislative success. President Johnson was particularly skillful in using this technique, especially in the first years of his incumbency. President Carter's White House barbecues were aimed at establishing "folksy" rapport with members of Congress.

Fifth, a president can get personally involved in the inevitable compromise and bargaining process that takes place once a presidential proposal has arrived on Capitol Hill. By making critical compromises at just the right time the president can help to insure the success of most of the initiative. Presidents Kennedy and Johnson used this technique extensively especially in courting the support of Senate Minority Leader Everett Dirksen on matters such as civil rights, foreign aid, the nuclear test ban treaty, and support for United Nations bonds.

Sixth, a president can give direct campaign help to particularly helpful members of the House and Senate from his own party by campaigning for them personally or by channeling campaign funds to them. He can give indirect campaign help to members of the opposition party by refraining from any activity on behalf of their opponents.

Seventh, the president has the power to veto (disapprove) legislation coming to him from Congress. This power is defensive, however, and is not a good basis upon which to build presidential legislative influence in a positive sense. It is most often resorted to by presidents

---

5. The figures on jobs come from *National Journal* (April 6, 1974): 503. On Carter and patronage see Martin Tolchin, "Carter Has Acted as if Patronage Doesn't Count," *New York Times*, May 22, 1977.

Table 9–1
Public Bill Vetoes and Overrides, 1945–1977

President and Years	Total Number of Public Bills Vetoed	Non-Pocket Vetoes		
		Number	Number Overridden	Percentage Overridden
Truman, 1945–53	83	54	11	20
Eisenhower, 1953–61	81	36	2	6
Kennedy, 1961–63	9	4	0	0
Johnson, 1963–69	13	6	0	0
Nixon, 1969–1974	40	24	5	21
Ford, 1974–77	61	45	12	27
Carter, 1977	2	2	0	0

Source: Congressional Quarterly's Guide to Congress *(Washington: Congressional Quarterly, 1976, 2nd edition): 628; and* Congressional Quarterly Almanac, 1976: 28.

whose party is in the minority in Congress. Before the presidency of Abraham Lincoln the power was used only sparingly. Since then it has been used much more frequently, and as of the end of 1977 close to 2,400 bills had been vetoed. Less than 4 percent of all vetoes had been overridden by Congress. The most important vetoes are those on public bills. And the real test of whether Congress can override a veto comes only when Congress is still in session. (Those vetoes that occur after Congress has adjourned and therefore cannot vote on override attempts are called pocket vetoes.) Table 9–1 reports data on the number of vetoes from 1945 through 1977 and the number and percentage of overrides of non-pocket vetoes. Even presidents like Nixon and Ford, faced with a Congress containing a large majority of the opposition party, are usually successful in having their vetoes sustained. Presidents with large majorities of their own party—like Kennedy, Johnson, and Carter—generally veto very few bills and, in these cases, those few vetoes were never overridden. In his first year in office President Carter found only two occasions to veto a bill coming to him. He talked of vetoing several more but reached compromises with Congress in close consultation with Speaker O'Neill before use of the veto became a real question.[6] The two vetoes were on relatively minor matters; no attempt was made to override either one.

6. For some analysis of the conditions under which vetoes are most likely to occur see Jong R. Lee, "Presidential Vetoes from Washington to Nixon," *Journal of Politics* 37 (1975): 522–546.

Institutional Support for
Presidential Relations with Congress

The president is a powerful individual in dealing with Congress. But he lacks the time to pursue his congressional relations single-handedly, and the volume of work and the scope of subjects prevents him from having a personal grasp of all that is going on. Over the years, two parts of the institituional presidency—the White House congressional liaison office and the Office of Management and Budget—have become important presidential agents in seeking congressional support for the president's program.

The White House Liaison Operation. A central part of the relations between the presidency and Congress involves extensive personal contact. The liaison office in the White House is basically in business to provide such contact. The liaison staff spends a great deal of time in communication with members and staff members of the House and Senate. In 1977 the White House had a staff of about fifteen handling liaison (this included about half a dozen clerical persons). The chief of White House liaison also was supposed to coordinate a large network of department agency liaison offices scattered throughout the bureaucracy, but many of them proceeded with considerable autonomy.

Presidents Franklin Roosevelt and Harry Truman both used assistants in the White House in dealing with Congress but neither routinized much of the job. Under President Eisenhower, however, the liaison staff was expanded: more individuals were added and duties were divided. Different individuals were responsible for the Senate and for various regional groupings in the House. The whole operation was overseen by a close and trusted adviser to the president, Bryce Harlow.

President Kennedy appointed Lawrence O'Brien as his chief liaison officer. O'Brien expanded and centralized the operation inherited from Harlow. The basic innovation was to require the legislative liaison offices in all departments and agencies to report on Monday to O'Brien's office on their activities completed during the past week and projected for the coming week. O'Brien's staff digested these reports and briefed Kennedy before his weekly Tuesday breakfast with the Democratic leaders of the House and Senate. Thus the president was kept informed, and liaison activities were coordinated so that not too many messages were being sent to the Hill simultaneously and so that there would be no contradictory message sent, although there was some confusion in the early months of the operation. This arrangement also allowed the president to give the leaders of his party the sense of helping control the flow of information to the House and Senate.[7]

Subsequent presidents kept the essentials of the Kennedy-O'Brien operation, although, of course, the personnel changed.

At the beginning of 1973 the Nixon liaison operation underwent several changes. The liaison staff in the White House was given responsibility for dealing with interest groups as well as for dealing with Congress. This underscored formally the White House strategy of trying to orchestrate interest group campaigns in ways favorable to its own policy ends. A greater degree of control over departmental liaison personnel and operations was also asserted by the president and the White House liaison staff by making these individuals presidential appointees who would be supervised directly by the White House. This change was intended to increase the coordination of executive branch lobbying and counteract the centrifugal forces in the bureaucracy that sometimes set departmental objectives that differ from presidential objectives. Nixon planned to increase the frequency of his meetings with the Republican leaders of Congress. He also planned to invite the Democratic leaders for more ad hoc meetings. During early 1973 these meetings did, in fact, increase. But the breaking of the Watergate scandal in mid-1973 and the aftermath that led eventually to Nixon's resignation resulted in reduced contact during his last year in office.

President Ford was on friendlier terms with Congress personally than Nixon and also paid more attention to his White House liaison operation. Thus the operation resumed its less hierarchical and more informal aspect of pre-Nixon days. The Carter liaison office had some early problems in relating smoothly to members, and the president continued to seek to remove the "bugs" into his second year in office.

The Office of Management and Budget. OMB was created in 1970 as the successor to the Bureau of the Budget, which had been created in the Treasury Department in 1921 and was moved to the newly organized Executive Office of the President in 1939. OMB plays a

7. For details on White House liaison, especially in the Kennedy years, see Abraham Holtzman, *Legislative Liaison* (Chicago: Rand McNally, 1970). On Nixon's liaison operation see Dom Bonafede, "White House Report/Administration Realigns Hill Liaison to Gain Tighter Grip on Federal Policy," *National Journal* (January 13, 1973): 35–43. On Ford's operation see Dom Bonafede, "White House Report/ Ford's Lobbyists Expect Democrats to Revise Tactics," *National Journal* (June 21, 1975): 923–927. On Carter's operation see Dom Bonafede, "Carter's Relationship with Congress—Making a Mountain out of a 'Moorehill'," *National Journal* (March 26, 1977): 456–463.

number of management and substantive roles for the president. In relating to Congress it is in constant contact on the details not only of the budget and appropriations bills but also on the details of a broad range of substantive legislative questions.

Any agency that wants to submit proposed legislation to Congress must first clear it with OMB.[8] If OMB decides that the proposal of the agency is "not in accord with the program of the president" then the agency cannot formally submit its proposal, although a member of Congress in favor of the proposal may still submit it on his own. The White House feels free to intervene in the OMB legislative clearance process to assemble and pursue its own legislative priorities.

OMB also gets heavily involved, along with the White House and relevant agencies, in generating the ideas that eventually are packaged annually as the program of the president.[9] In many ways virtually all of the professional staff members of OMB get involved in the development of the legislative program. The total OMB (BOB) staff was about stable in size between 450 and 525 under Eisenhower, Kennedy, and Johnson but grew considerably under Nixon to over 700. By 1977 it had shrunk a little to under 700.

Constraints on Presidential Legislative Activity

Despite the power and resources he commands and despite his substantial institutional support, the president still faces a number of practical limits as he seeks to influence the course of legislation in Congress. He is limited, for example, by the complexity of the government in which he must operate. The size of the enterprise alone is awesome. The president presides over roughly two and a half to three million civilian employees, another three million people in the armed services, eleven major departments, more than forty independent agencies and regulatory commissions, and an elaborate set of institutions collectively called the presidency. He also has to interact with two other elaborate sets of institutions, namely, Congress and the judiciary.

The president is the most visible individual in a large and complex government. Given the problems posed by the vastness of the government, the range of issue areas being dealt with, and the monitoring of

---

8. See Richard E. Neustadt, "Presidency and Legislation: The Growth of Central Clearance," *American Political Science Review* 48 (1954): 641–671; and Robert S. Gilmour, "Central Legislative Clearance: A Revised Perspective," *Public Administration Review* 31 (1971): 150–158.

9. See Richard E. Neustadt, "Presidency and Legislation: Planning the President's Program," *American Political Science Review* 49 (1955): 980–1021.

information, the president faces constant difficulties as he attempts to overcome the ever-present problems of communication and bureaucratic inertia within the government.

Furthermore, a president cannot be too imperious in setting forth his program. He must request and persuade; he cannot demand and command. A president and his advisers who get the reputation for being too demanding must be prepared to suffer a negative reaction. For example, President Nixon and his closest White House advisers had poor relations with Congress much of the time. Congress felt it was being pushed around and/or ignored as Nixon tried to accomplish his policy goals. Thus when the Watergate scandal broke, congressional opinion was that now Congress could and would recoup both lost prestige and power. The Watergate affair provided the opportunity for Congress to reassert itself, but such a move would have occurred even without Watergate, for many members of Congress indicated that President Nixon and the White House staff had gone too far in trying to legislate without Congress. Senate Majority Leader Mike Mansfield described the situation:

> It's my belief that before Watergate broke, the Congress was really on the ropes; that our influence was diminishing and that the influence of the men around the President was increasing.
>
> However, they pushed too far with their espousement of executive privilege, claiming it was applicable to all 2.8 million government employees; too far in the area of impoundment; too far in vetoing legislation and too far in lack of consultation with the Congress.
>
> So when the Watergate thing really broke open, I would assume it had a part in pushing ahead a movement that was already under way.

Senate Minority Leader Hugh Scott also expressed his displeasure with the way in which the White House had consulted with him and other members of the Republican leadership in Congress. "They never invite me for the take-offs, but they damned well want me there for the crash landings."

Still another Republican senator, one thought of as a supporter of Nixon programs, complained that top White House staff members such as John Ehrlichman and H. R. Haldeman "had the attitude that Congress was more fun and games than reality. So when Watergate broke, there was less room for maneuver by the White House because of the alienation process which had preceded it." [10]

---

10. The quotations from Mansfield, Scott, and the unnamed Republican senator come from Andrew J. Glass, "Congress Report/Watergate Diminishes Nixon's Leverage, Forces Series of Legislative Compromises," *National Journal* (July 21, 1973): 1049–1056.

The Watergate scandal and related problems of the Nixon administration certainly made members of Congress more aware of a desire to limit the presidency. But the basic fact of the president being in a position of asking rather than commanding has always been true. Had Watergate not intervened it is probably accurate to argue that the reaction to Nixon's presidential style would not have been as extreme and he probably could have achieved some of the centralization and some of the bypassing of Congress he desired. But Watergate underscored limits already present, and transformed some of them from potential to actual. The practical limits on the presidency grew because of Watergate, but they were not invented at that time. (What was, perhaps, "invented" because of Watergate was a willingness on the part of liberal Democratic intellectuals to criticize the power of the presidency in principle—a criticism rarely made by them for the preceding forty years.) From the congressional point of view the presidency had become bloated and arrogant under Nixon. Several moves were made to add language to legislation reducing the White House and Office of Management and Budget expenditures, staff sizes, and number of high-paying jobs. None of these measures became law but one of the first things President Ford did upon assuming office was to make some changes in these two staffs that went a long way toward meeting congressional criticism. Had the Nixon administration somehow managed to finish its term such restrictions might well have been put into statutory form.

President Carter began his term in 1977 as an "outsider" to Washington. He had, in fact, made a virtue of his status in the campaign in 1976. In his first year in office many members of Congress saw him as aloof and self-righteous in making legislative "demands."

The president and the institutional presidency are virtually excluded from many policy areas because of the close-knit relationships within the numerous low-profile subgovernments. The more routinized a policy area becomes, the less the possibility that the president will have much impact on it. Less routine matters generally break out of these subgovernments and a wider range of participants becomes involved. Only then is there much opportunity for presidential access and leverage. But any president is likely to have minimal impact on such items as allocation of sugar quotas to foreign nations, the details of defense procurement, or the interpretation and application of patent policy.

Policies and programs tend to change very slowly and by small increments or decrements. In the very complex world of American public policy both the necessity for compromise among many actors and the technical nature of many policies make marginal change from an existing situation the most likely (but not an inevitable) outcome of any policy debate. The incremental nature of policy change means that under normal conditions the president cannot hope to alter dramatically a large number of policies simultaneously and quickly. He usually must choose to stress only a few areas and, even then, efforts to achieve dramatic change will meet with resistance. Of course, innovative congressmen meet this same resistance when they attempt to initiate substantial policy change.

THE CONGRESSIONAL SIDE

The constraints the president faces when dealing with Congress are offset by constraints on Congress. The absence of a unified legislative program to counterbalance the annual program of the president is the major limitation. Because Congress is a multi-headed organization, it cannot organize and develop a unified program, although in the past the party caucuses have sometimes performed this function. Further, there is no single spokesman for Congress on controversial issues. Congressmen are likely to espouse quite different views on the same issue, often regardless of party lines. Moreover, even when there are forceful policy statements by leading members of Congress there is no assurance that the press will always transmit these views to the public whereas press coverage for presidential policy is much more assured.

The Critical Role of the Majority Party and Its Leaders

The relationship between the presidency and party leaders in Congress is critical in helping determine the policy-making role of Congress at any given time. Particularly important is the relationship between the majority party and its leaders on the one hand and the president and presidency on the other. Even if the majority party suffers from internal dissension, it still has the potential for dominating congressional performance. And although the leaders cannot dictate outcomes in Congress, they play a mediating role between the presidency and the rank-and-file members of Congress and, occasionally, the standing committees and subcommittees, thus setting the tone for congressional response to presidential wishes.[11]

The importance of the majority party leader-presidential relationship was underscored in 1977 by the relations between President Carter and Speaker O'Neill and Senate Majority Leader Byrd. The

---

11. See James L. Sundquist, "Congress and the President: Enemies or Partners," in Henry Owen and Charles L. Schultze (eds.), *Setting National Priorities: The Next Ten Years* (Washington: Brookings, 1976): 583–618.

Carter-O'Neill relationship developed into a close one, and the Speaker helped initiate the President into the most productive ways of doing business with the House, often running interference for him and preventing mistakes on his part. In June, 1977, Carter autographed a picture of himself for O'Neill: "To my friend Tip O'Neill—thanks for another lesson in good politics." The relationship between the two led to successes in getting the president's energy program through the House nearly intact, in reaching an agreeable compromise with the House over water projects (proving that presidents can at least make a dent in pork barrels), and in reaching a mutually agreeable compromise over the level of funding for the Department of Health, Education, and Welfare, and the Department of Labor (a compromise that avoided what would have been a politically destructive veto and override attempt in which the Democrats could only have looked bad no matter what happened).[12]

By contrast, Carter did not have such a relationship with Robert Byrd in the Senate. Thus as the year wore on he took his legislative lumps in that body without the wise counsel and reliable support of the key figure in it. The lack of a close, supportive relationship helps explain why the Senate proceeded to gut the president's energy program, with the president apparently helpless and the majority leader showing little leadership.

The Types of Relationship between Presidents and Majority Parties and Their Leaders

There are some important regularities in the relations between presidents and majority parties and their leaders. Three different types of majority party—a presidential majority, a congressional majority, and a truncated majority—recur in Congress. Illustrations of each kind of majority scattered throughout the twentieth century support some general statements about the policy impact of the relationship under different conditions.[13]

The Presidential Majority. In a presidential majority the president and the majorities of both houses are of the same party; the president, viewing himself as the single most significant legislative leader, actively attempts to have Congress enact his legislative preferences into law.

---

12. For a good story on the Carter-O'Neill Relationship see Martin Tolchin, "An Old Pol Takes on the New President," *New York Times Magazine,* July 24, 1977.
13. For much more detail on the examples used in the following pages see Randall B. Ripley, *Majority Party Leadership in Congress* (Boston: Little, Brown, 1969).

Leader-president relations in a presidential majority in twentieth century Congresses have been characterized by a trend of increasing cooperation on the part of congressional leaders. The more recent leaders in the presidential majority situation, faced with an active and demanding legislator in the White House, have come to see themselves almost unquestioningly as lieutenants of their president. Their fellow senators and representatives, the press, and the interested part of the general public have also begun to see the role of loyal lieutenant as the natural one for a congressional leader of the president's party.

The cooperative relationship that develops in a presidential majority underscores the importance of bargaining in a productive Congress. A presidential majority usually produces considerable legislation that follows the outlines of what the president wants. But that legislation may contain many modifications and concessions designed to avoid potential roadblocks in Congress. The president makes some of these concessions personally and authorizes others to be made on his behalf by White House officials and congressional leaders both on the floor and in committee. When compromise cannot be reached or is not sought, failure may result. Three examples scattered throughout this century illustrate how differing presidential majorities have functioned.

In the Sixty-third Congress (1913–1915) President Woodrow Wilson worked with able Democratic leaders and solid Democratic majorities in both houses. A major legislative agenda was set by Wilson and he and the leaders were successful in achieving a great part of it. Together they passed a new tariff, the Federal Reserve Act, the Clayton Antitrust Act, and the Federal Trade Commission Act. Other successes included: a ship registration and insurance bill, a war revenue bill, a bill to regulate cotton exchanges, and a bill providing a government railroad in Alaska. Wilson was also successful in gaining the repeal of the tolls exemption for American coastwise ships using the Panama Canal, even though the House leader opposed this measure and some of the Senate leaders were lukewarm. Only a few major disappointments marred the record of the Sixty-third Congress from the Democratic point of view: a ship purchase bill was buried in the Senate and two conservation measures and a Philippines autonomy bill never came to a vote.

But even with this highly successful legislative record a number of concessions and changes had to be made and bargains had to be struck to ensure final passage. For example, in the House Wilson promised progressives that a future antitrust bill would contain a provision outlawing interlocking back directorates in order to gain their support for the more conservative Federal Reserve bill. In working on a tariff bill Wilson bargained on details with the chairman of the Ways and Means Committee in the House, who was also the majority leader. In order to get the bill through the Senate Wilson submitted to the progressive Democrats' demand that the maximum surtax on large incomes contained in the House bill be doubled. Only in working for the ship purchase bill did Wilson reveal a streak of imperiousness and unwillingness to compromise, with the result that he failed to get any kind of bill at all.

In the Seventy-third Congress (1933–1934) President Franklin Roosevelt worked with very large Democratic majorities and pliant Democratic leaders in the House and Senate. The sickening spectacle of the Depression made both the country and the Congress eager for a dynamic president bent on righting an upturned economy. In this two-year period Congress enacted a great volume of major laws. Major administration-leadership successes were scored in the areas of farm, welfare, banking, securities, conservation, industrial aid, public works, and trade legislation. The president and his congressional leaders also received some setbacks: the passage of civil service pay restoration over a presidential veto; the delay or defeat of bills concerned with pure food and drugs, labor disputes, the administration of oil resources, unemployment insurance, and old-age pensions; and the refusal to add desired amendments to laws already passed on agriculture and banking.

Even a dynamic president like Roosevelt in a crisis situation such as the Depression had to make important concessions in order to gain his ends. For example, the tax provisions of the industrial recovery bill were liberalized to appease congressional Democrats concerned about proposed rates for lower tax brackets. In order to pass the economy bill (which proposed major cuts in government spending, including salaries of employees) in 1933 Roosevelt had to agree to a compromise that restored about $100 million (a lot of money in 1933, even for the government!) of desired cuts.

In the Eighty-eighth Congress (1963–1964) both Presidents Kennedy and Johnson worked with sizable Democratic majorities and sympathetic Democratic leaders in pursuit of a number of legislative goals. The major legislation passed by the Eighty-eighth Congress provided a tax cut, an agency and program designed to fight poverty, increased civil rights guarantees, aid to hospitals, manpower training programs, a national wilderness system, aid for mass transit in urban areas, and a land conservation fund. From the Democratic perspective major failures were in the area of medical care for the aged and special aid for Appalachia.

In the effort to pass the antipoverty bill the president agreed that a specific official considered too liberal by the North Carolina Democrats in the House would not be appointed to a position in the program. This was the price for their support on the floor. In laboring for a tax cut President Kennedy promised the chairman of the Ways and Means Committee that he would seek to tighten controls on federal spending in return for cooperation on the measure. President Johnson had to promise the chairman of the Senate Finance Committee specific economies in the federal budget in order to get his support on the same bill. In seeking approval of the mass transit bill, spokesmen for the president agreed to a "buy American" provision, a 25 percent cut in the cost of the program, and a specific amendment proposed by some labor unions. Thus the president simultaneously sought to appease Republicans, conservatives in both parties, and liberals principally in his own party.

Thus Wilson, Roosevelt, Kennedy, and Johnson all had reasonable legislative success. Critical to this success were the good relations with their respective party leaders who maintained presidential-congressional contact. They also took part in the bargaining process personally, as well as directing the involvement of subordinates.

The Congressional Majority. In a congressional majority the president and the majorities in both houses share the same party, but the president is willing to let Congress take more of a lead in legislative matters. He does not consider himself the most significant legislative leader. Although he may still make some recommendations to Congress, the volume is smaller and the advocacy is less vigorous than in presidential majorities. The congressional leaders themselves can state legislative preferences that are in part different from, or at least independent of, those of the president and they can expect to get action on them. They can also anticipate more control over the details of scheduling and tactics.

Much of the time in a congressional majority the basic relationship between the president and the majority party leaders is one of unsupported initiation. Each will state some preferences but neither will rally to support the preferences of the other.[14]

This relationship underscores the necessity of presidential-congres-

---

14. There are four possible variations to this relationship of unsupported initiation. First, initiation can come from the president but be ignored by Congress. Second, both the president and the congressional leaders can initiate on the same issues, without ever supporting (or opposing directly) each other's initiatives. This variation is, of course, closely related to a relationship of opposition. Third, both the president and congressional leaders can be inactive and allow initiation to come from other sources. Fourth, the congressional leaders can initiate and the president can remain largely inactive.

sional cooperation in order to achieve policy of major importance. Same party control of Congress and the White House alone is not sufficient to insure a very imposing legislative product. In a congressional majority the majority party leaders don't take the president very seriously as a legislative figure. Even when he becomes active legislatively nothing very much may happen. And, typically, the leaders are not in a position to generate much action on their own either. Again, examples taken from three congressional majorities in this century lend support to these generalizations.

In the Sixty-seventh Congress (1921–1923) President Warren Harding and the Republicans controlled both houses by large margins. Harding obtained much of what he and the leaders of his party had agreed on concerning an emergency tariff, a permanent tariff revision, a revenue act, a packers and stockyards act, and a grant-in-aid program for road building. The farm bloc in Congress was successful in initiating and passing a number of bills, many of which were opposed by Harding and the regular Republican congressional leaders. These measures included an act to protect farm co-ops from antitrust laws and an agricultural credits act.

Harding had several major confrontations with Congress and was defeated in most of them. He did not get the pro-business tax legislation he wanted. His position favoring the reduction of surtax rates on high incomes was ignored. His proposal for a ship subsidy did not pass. His foreign debt refunding bill finally passed, but considerably altered. He won one battle, barely, when the Senate upheld his veto of a veterans' bonus.

In some of his dealings with Congress Harding simply acquiesced to what Congress wanted. In some he made proposals but got little support from his party's leaders. In others he was opposed by them. Only sporadically did he really try to mobilize the resources of his office to achieve what he wanted, and then he usually failed. The congressional leaders did not routinely look to him for leadership—in fact, they were surprised when it came—but they could not put together a legislative program of their own either.

In the Sixty-ninth Congress (1925–1927) Calvin Coolidge was president and had moderately large majorities in both houses. Even more emphatically than Harding, Coolidge showed little desire to be a legislative leader. The legislative product of the Sixth-ninth Congress, mutually pleasing to the president and the Republican congressional leaders, was not large. The Senate passed a World Court bill. Administration forces were also successful in getting legislation on cooperative marketing, tax reduction, additional assistant secretaries for aviation in three federal departments, foreign debts, banking, control of radio, and railway labor disputes.

Several legislative developments displeased the Republican leaders and Coolidge. In the area of agricultural legislation both houses passed the McNary-Haugen bill, which proposed governmental purchase of some U.S. crops at the world market price plus whatever the tariff would bring. The government would then sell the crops abroad and assess a small fee on the participating farmers if it lost money. The purpose was to keep domestic crop prices relatively constant. A Coolidge veto stood without being tested. However, the major administration farm bill, designed to quiet demands for McNary-Haugen, was defeated. Coolidge suffered the humiliation of having his nominee for Attorney General rejected by the Senate. A filibuster at the end of the second session left a number of important bills dangling without final action. These bills included: a deficiency appropriations bill, a public buildings bill, a bill on Muscle Shoals (a large government-owned dam and factory on the Tennessee River that later became a key part of the Tennessee Valley Authority, created during Franklin Roosevelt's presidency), an alien property bill, and a postal rate bill.

Coolidge typically let Congress initiate what it wanted, but not much was forthcoming. Only on matters of economy did he exhort Congress forcefully. The danger of such lethargy for the president was that when a controversial matter did arise—such as McNary-Haugen, which Coolidge opposed vigorously—he could not offer his leaders in Congress much support, and his past performance had not given them any feeling of responsibility to him and the administration.

In the Eighty-third Congress (1953–1954) Dwight Eisenhower was president and both houses were narrowly Republican. Eisenhower was more active than either Harding or Coolidge but had a number of doubts about how aggressive he should be as a legislative leader. His popularity was such that it would have supported activism but he voluntarily exercised self-restraint.

The Eighty-third Congress did not produce a large volume of major legislation. It moved slowly and its performance generally satisfied neither the president nor the congressional leaders sympathetic to presidential policies.

Congress allowed the president a free hand in his reorganization plans for the executive branch. It passed legislation restoring control of tidelands and the oil underneath to the states. It passed tax bills satisfactory to the president. The Senate defeated, by one vote, a version of the Bricker amendment to tie the hands of the president in making treaties and executive agreements. Congress also passed bills establishing the St. Lawrence Seaway, liberalizing social security benefits and unemployment compensation, and extending the reciprocal trade agreements program.

Other measures sought by the president and at least formally supported by the leaders were not passed. These included: a bill increasing the debt limit, a bill increasing postal rates, statehood for Hawaii, amendments to the Taft-Hartley Act, health insurance, and aid to education. Congressional revisions of immigration bills, mutual security bills, and the reciprocal trade bills were displeasing to the administration. The president was forced to use his veto power often, even with a Congress of his own party. He vetoed fifty-two bills, including a federal pay raise bill, and no vetoes were overriden.

Eisenhower and the Republican leaders usually avoided direct clashes with one another. Only occasionally did they work together closely and enthusiastically. On some matters the leaders responded to the president's initiative apathetically, and the president then either turned directly to relevant committee personnel or gave up. In general, Eisenhower's sporadic leadership and the leaders' sporadic loyalty contributed to a legislative product that was not highly pleasing to any of them.

The Truncated Majority. A truncated majority is defined simply: the majority of at least one house of Congress is controlled by the party in opposition to the president.

In a truncated majority congressional leaders usually cooperate with the president on matters of foreign policy, but oppose him on domestic matters. Congressional leaders may announce their own legislative program, but to succeed with it, they must command the votes to override a potential veto, and must also be able to appeal to public opinion or at least have a president who is ineffective in mobilizing public opinion.

Frustrations seem inevitable for a truncated majority because once the leaders have announced a legislative program, that program immediately is divided among the various standing committees. Consequently, it is neither seen as a whole nor thought of as a single program. The president's program is also split in this way, but he has the advantages of being able to call the program to the attention of the public by periodically submitting lists of "must" legislation and reminding the public of the nature and scope of his program. Reminders of this nature by congressional leaders are not often made and receive minimum attention when they are.

In general, not much legislation is produced in truncated majorities, particularly on domestic matters. What domestic legislation does pass is likely to be bland and inconsequential. If, somehow, controversial and far-reaching matters in the domestic area do get passed by a truncated majority they will continue to be intensely debated in the future, for truncated majorities rarely settle major issues of public policy in the domestic area for very long periods of time. Foreign policy legislation passed by truncated majorities can still be important. Examples taken from three truncated majorities in this century underscore the above general points.

In the Sixty-second Congress (1911–1913) William Howard Taft, a Republican, was president but the House was controlled by a solid Democratic majority. The Senate was nominally Republican but, in fact, the critical votes on many issues were in the hands of insurgent progressive Republicans. Without their support the regular Republicans fell short of a majority as did, of course, the Democrats.

Taft concentrated on obtaining approval of reciprocal trade with Canada and reforms in antitrust laws. He obtained his first objective, failed in his second, and was forced to veto a number of bills with which he disagreed.

The legislative output of the Sixty-second Congress was small. Passed and signed by the president were: a bill ratifying a Canadian reciprocity treaty, a bill forbidding the shipment of liquor into states that prohibited its sale, a bill creating a place for the Labor Department in the cabinet, a bill granting free passage to American coastwise ships using the Panama Canal, and a bill providing for an eight-hour day on work done under government contract. Arizona and New Mexico were admitted as states after Taft had vetoed one bill on the subject.

Taft vetoed Democratic tariff bills, including ones on wool, cotton, metal, and the free list. Congress overrode none of the vetoes. He also vetoed an immigration bill because of a literacy test provision.

The Democrats, in addition to their largely successful attempt to embarrass Taft, also used their control of the House to hold a number of investigations and hearings focused on the money trust, the American Sugar Refining Company, campaign expenditures, the tariff, and the currency.

In the Eightieth Congress (1947–1948) Harry Truman, a Democrat, faced a Congress controlled by moderate-sized Republican majorities. Truman had succeeded to the presidency in April 1945.

The president and Republican leaders did cooperate in the area of foreign policy. The Marshall Plan, Greek-Turkish aid, and the consolidation of the different armed services into the Defense Department were the leading achievemnts.

The president won some relatively minor and temporary victories on domestic policies, including a few changes in farm policy, highway aid, and the school lunch program. On matters such as civil rights, social security, universal military training, old age and survivors insurance, aid to education, labor laws, and federal health insurance, his recommendations were ignored or defeated.

The Republicans in Congress were basically successful in the following areas: labor (with the Taft-Hartley Act completely rewriting the basic labor-management relations legislation and another act that covered portal-to-portal pay), reciprocal trade agreements, rent control, and tax reduction. Truman persuaded the Senate to pass major housing and aid to education bills but the House refused to go along.

In general, then, both parties to the conflict got something but a large number of major policy areas in which proposals were made saw no legislation passed. In the 1948 presidential campaign Truman explicitly ran against the record of what he called the "do-nothing Eightieth Congress," not a totally fair characterization but one that proved to be politically effective.

In the Eighty-sixth Congress (1959–1960) Eisenhower faced a House and Senate overwhelmingly Democratic. His primary initiative was to fight for economy. Democratic leaders developed a number of their own domestic proposals.

The major legislative products of the Eighty-sixth Congress were a labor bill that was unsatisfactory to the Democrats and a civil rights bill that contained little substance. Bills that were desired by the Democratic leaders but that failed either in Congress or because of a veto included: a large-scale housing bill, a substantial increase in federal aid to airports, aid for depressed areas, federally insured medical care for the aged, an increase in the minimum wage, and federal aid for school construction. Eisenhower took a basically negative stance in the Eighty-sixth Congress: he asked for little and except for two vetoes that were overridden he got what he wanted. His few positive recommendations received little attention. In addition, he suffered the humiliation of having one of his cabinet nominees rejected by the Senate.

PRESIDENTIAL IMPACT ON CONGRESSIONAL POLICY-MAKING: AN ASSESSMENT

Various aggregate measures have been used to examine variations in the magnitude of presidential impact on congressional policy-making. One of these, which was devised and used by *Congressional Quarterly* from 1954 through 1975, is simply the percentage of presidential requests passed by Congress. This measure is, of course, approximate. Many presidential requests may be passed in form but altered dramatically in substance by the congressional amending process. Even

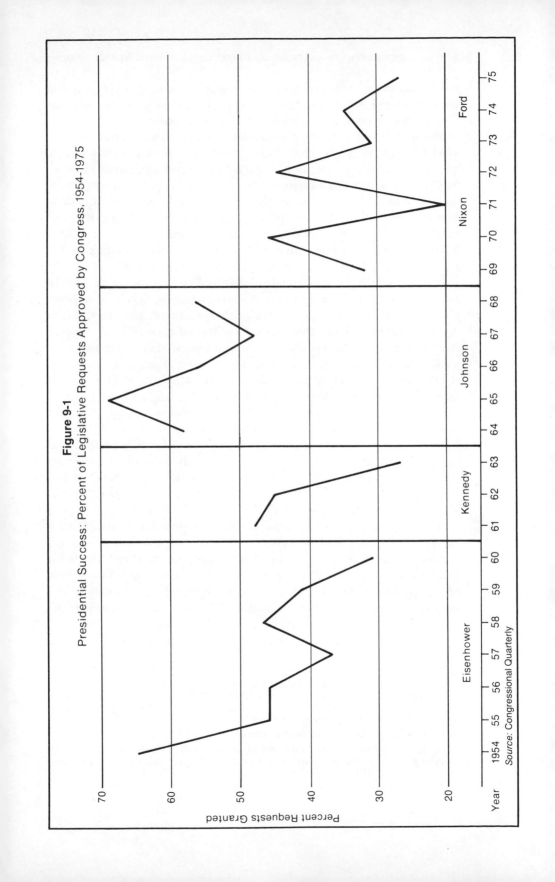

Figure 9-1

Presidential Success: Percent of Legislative Requests Approved by Congress, 1954-1975

Percent Requests Granted

70 · 60 · 50 · 40 · 30 · 20

Year: 1954 55 56 57 58 59 60 61 62 63 64 65 66 67 68 69 70 71 72 73 74 75

Eisenhower · Kennedy · Johnson · Nixon · Ford

Source: Congressional Quarterly

more important, the percentage of requests granted does not take account of the extent of those requests or their content or whether they represent intelligent responses to national needs.

Figure 9-1 summarizes the percentage of requests enacted from 1954 through 1975. The only years in which a president was able to get more than 50 percent of his proposals enacted were in 1954, when Eisenhower still had a Congress controlled by his party to work with, and in four of the five years that Lyndon Johnson was president. Eisenhower, Kennedy, and Johnson all suffered declines in their ability to get what they wanted as their terms wore on. Nixon did not have any notable success with the Democratic Congress he faced; 1971 represented the least success of any president in the period.

Presidential impact on congressional policy behavior can also be analyzed in terms of congressional voting—that is, levels of support for the president and shifts in favor of the president's proposals. There is considerable evidence that many members of Congress will support the foreign policy initiatives of the president if they share the same party label even though they might well oppose those same initiatives if the president belonged to the other party. Thus, for example, a fair number of southern Democrats inclined to be skeptical of such programs as foreign aid under Republican presidents will support such programs under Democratic presidents. Likewise, a substantial number of midwestern Republicans inclined to oppose such programs as foreign aid under Democratic presidents will support them under Republican presidents.[15] On the other hand, the president does not seem to have this same kind of pull on domestic issues.[16] There is also evidence that support for presidential proposals increases as individual members of Congress perceive his popularity to be strong among their electoral supporters.[17]

Another measure, also developed by *Congressional Quarterly,* is the success rate of the president on votes on the House and Senate floor on which he has taken a clear position. Figure 9-2 summarizes this success measure from 1953 through 1977. Although the figures are higher than the box score reported in Figure 9-1, the patterns are generally the same (with the exception of President Kennedy—who got

15. See Aage R. Clausen, *How Congressmen Decide* (New York: St. Martin's, 1973); and Mark Kesselman, "Presidential Leadership in Congress on Foreign Policy," *Midwest Journal of Political Science* 5 (1961): 284–289, and "Presidential Leadership in Congress on Foreign Policy: A Replication of A Hypothesis," *Midwest Journal of Political Science* 9 (1965): 401–406.

16. Clausen, *How Congressmen Decide*: Chapter 8.

17. George C. Edwards, III, "Presidential Influence in the House: Presidential Prestige as a Source of Presidential Power," *American Political Science Review* 70 (1976): 101–113.

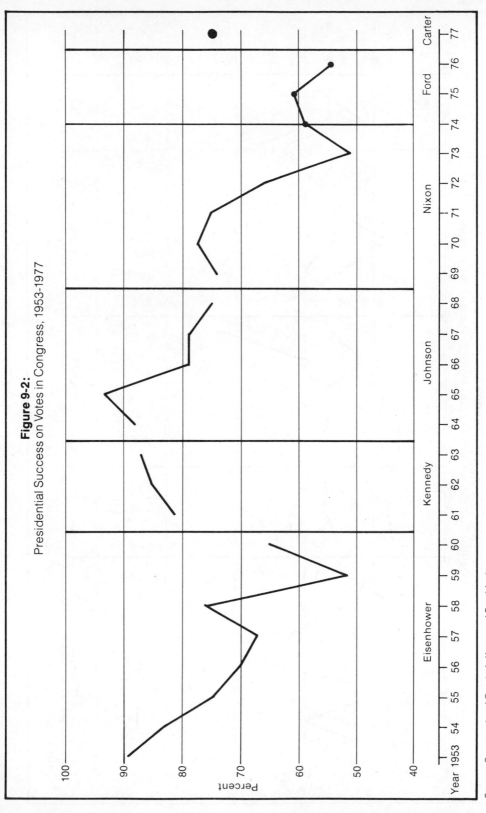

Figure 9-2:
Presidential Success on Votes in Congress, 1953-1977

Source: Congressional Quarterly Years and Presidents

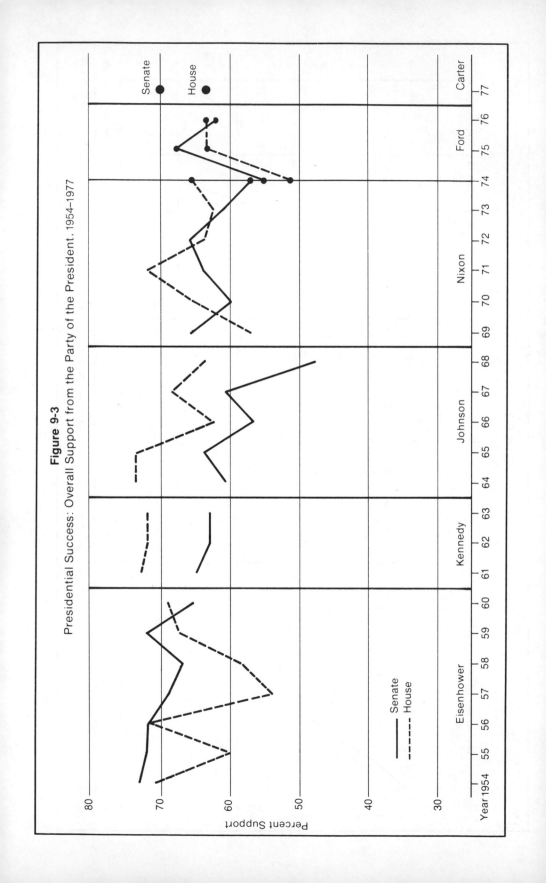

Figure 9-3

Presidential Success: Overall Support from the Party of the President, 1954–1977

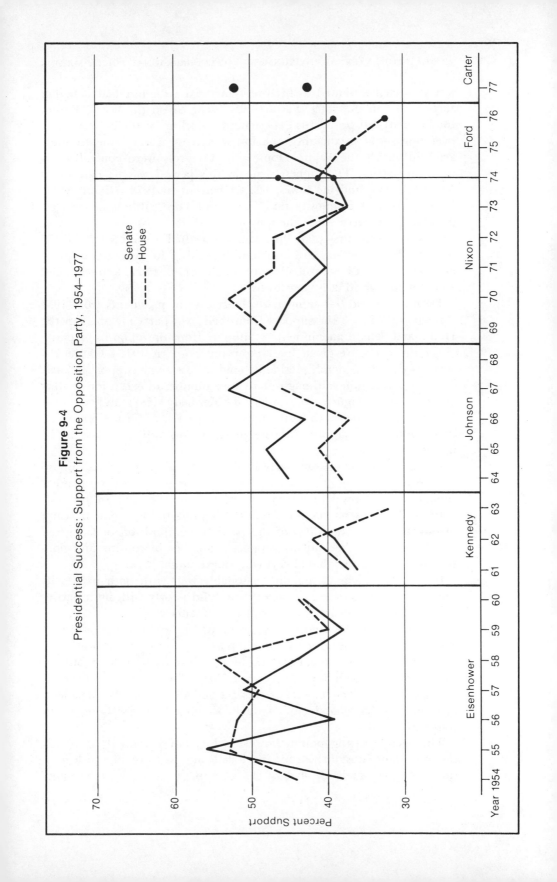

Figure 9-4

Presidential Success: Support from the Opposition Party, 1954–1977

less of what he wanted as his presidency wore on but had a higher success rate on the votes that actually occurred on the floor). Except for Kennedy, all presidents experienced a decline in their success rate over time. And predictably, the lowest success scores came in those years in which the White House and Congress were controlled by different parties. The highest score in this period was 93 percent in 1965 (Johnson) and the lowest was 51 percent in 1973 (Nixon). (The 1974 figure is a composite for Nixon and Ford, although their individual scores were about the same.)

In 1977, in his first year, President Carter had a success score of 75 percent. This was not an auspicious beginning for a first-year president with Congress controlled by his party. Eisenhower, Kennedy, and Johnson all started at higher levels.

Figures 9–3 and 9–4 summarize the success of presidents from 1954 through 1977 in getting support from their own party members in the House and Senate and in getting support from the opposition party. (Separate scores are given for Nixon and Ford in 1974.) Figure 9–3 suggests that, in general, presidents tend to lose some support in their own party over time, although there are a number of exceptions to this generalization. Figure 9–4 shows the Kennedy years and the late Nixon and Ford years to be the most highly partisan in the sense that opposition party support for the president on roll calls was at its lowest.

However, no opposition party is absolutely adamant in its opposition. Even in the most partisan years the average opposition member supported the president around 40 percent of the time in roll call voting. This suggests that any president is going to have some measure of success almost regardless of the partisan composition of Congress, largely because all presidents support a number of routine and noncontroversial matters that always win congressional backing.

In 1977 President Carter did reasonably well with both parties in the Senate on this aggregate measure and did poorly with both parties in the House when compared to other presidents.

The impact of the president is not limited to empirical measures of success and support, however. One important substantive impact is his contribution to the content of legislation. Primarily he sets the bulk of the legislative agenda for Congress with his various annual and special messages. Thus, even before specific actions are taken, the president, in effect, decides what is and is not most important for Congress to consider.

The agenda-setting power, however, does not necessarily diminish the important substantive contributions Congress can make to legislation. Congress and its leaders can still be creative in approving, amending, and criticizing the proposals of even a very active president. And limited initiation, even though difficult, is not impossible. A recent empirical study of the relative substantive inputs of president and Congress to a broad range of legislation concluded that the congressional contribution was very large.[18]

As indicated in Chapter 1, the image of a fixed sum of "power" or "influence" for which the Congress and president compete is misleading. This implies that both cannot be "strong" or "weak" together, whereas in fact they can. It also implies that there are no other competitors for legislative influence, whereas there are—especially the bureaucracy and interest groups.

The president has certainly become a more visible policy-maker in this century. But Congress has in many ways also become more important simultaneously, simply because the range of matters with which the federal government deals has increased both in scope and in importance. The "seesaw" image of relative influence is simply false. Experience in this century suggests that active, influential legislative leaders in Congress can co-exist successfully with an active, influential legislative leader in the White House. Legislative creativity may be present simultaneously within both the White House and the Capitol.

It should also be noted that some of the least active and effective congressional leaders in this century appeared on the scene when some of the least active and effective presidents were in office, suggesting that congressional leaders do not necessarily become "strong" when there is a "weak" President but rather that legislative weakness in the White House may breed legislative weakness in Congress.

The president is one of the primary forces working on Congress that can help bring some integration to congressional policy deliberations. However, he can only achieve a limited amount in pushing in the direction of integration. The forces of fragmentation are strong and presidents are under severe constraints as they deal with Congress. This chapter has portrayed the most important of these constraints. Above all, it should be reiterated that a greal deal of public policy is not subject to much presidential influence or even to much congressional influence above the committee or subcommittee level. Subgovernments make policy in many substantive areas regardless of the policy positions or activities of the president or the congressional leaders.

---

18. Ronald C. Moe and Steven C. Teel, "Congress as Policy-Maker: A Necessary Reappraisal," *Political Science Quarterly* 85 (1970): 443–470.

CHAPTER 10

CONGRESS
AND THE BUREAUCRACY

AMONG MODERN NATIONS A LARGE BUREAUCRACY IS AN IMPORTANT feature of the central government. The United States is no exception. There are almost three million civilian employees and over two million uniformed military personnel directing and operating programs costing almost $500 billion a year and affecting the lives of all citizens in many ways. Just as individual citizens have had to accommodate to the reality of such a bureaucracy, so has Congress. The basic congressional response to the fact of a large, expert bureaucracy administering hundreds of programs has been to seek influence by cooperating with the bureaucracy most of the time and challenging it only now and then. Congress might well be overwhelmed in a situation of perpetual conflict. Conflict occurs, but cooperation is a more common characteristic. In the recesses of the thousands of relationships between the congressional members and their staff and the bureaucrats a great deal of American public policy that actually impinges on citizens is decided.

So much emphasis is usually placed on presidential-congressional relations that the role of the bureaucracy is often shortchanged, both in journalistic accounts of the workings of American government and in more analytic treatments. But the bureaucracy is, in fact, at the heart of what American government can and does achieve. It limits both the president and Congress and is, at the same time, limited (although not always directed) by them.

CONGRESS, THE BUREAUCRACY, AND SUBGOVERNMENTS

A very large proportion of the interaction between Congress and the bureaucracy represents the ongoing activities of subgovernments (clusters of individuals with shared policy interests and easy and frequent access to each other that make most routine policy decisions). Subgovernments dominate distributive policy decisions, whether domestic or involving foreign policy and national defense issues. They also dominate competitive regulatory policy. They play a moderately important role in protective regulatory policy and are at least sporadically important in framing policy in redistributive areas. Given that there is also a natural tendency for all domestic issues and even many foreign policy and defense issues to be defined or redefined as distributive if possible, the importance of subgovernments is enhanced even more.[1]

The basic institutional units in typical subgovernment interactions are standing subcommittees (occasionally a full committee) from the House and Senate and various administrative units below the departmental level in the executive branch such as bureaus, agencies, services, and administrations. Much of the detailed business of the government is carried on between these units, sometimes with the participation of interest group representatives. Larger units (for example, the entire House or Senate, the White House, or the office of a departmental secretary) get involved in details much less frequently. In general, only highly visible and politically sensitive issues are likely to receive attention from the larger units; relatively less visible matters are often handled completely by a bureau speaking for the entire executive branch and a subcommittee speaking for the entire House and Senate. Individual members of the House and Senate and their staff members also get involved with the bureaucracy, usually because of a pending "case" involving a constituent.

Not only do subgovernments exist in fact but most individuals both in Congress and in the bureaucracy believe that they should exist. They also generally believe that a high degree of interest group access to both Congress and the bureaucracy is appropriate. Thus the belief system of the individuals who make policy sustains the legitimacy and predominance of subgovernments.[2]

A classic case of a subgovernment is described by Douglass Cater:

. . . consider the tight little subgovernment which rules the nation's sugar economy. Since the early 1930's, this agricultural commodity

1. For considerable empirical evidence supporting the generalizations in this paragraph, see Randall B. Ripley and Grace A. Franklin, *Congress, the Bureaucracy, and Public Policy* (Homewood, Ill.: Dorsey, 1976).

2. For important and creative work that provides the evidence for the statements in this paragraph see Joel D. Aberbach and Bert A. Rockman, "The Overlapping Worlds of American Federal Executives and Congressmen," *British Journal of Political Science* 7 (1977): 23–47; and Aberbach and Rockman, "Bureaucrats and Clientele Groups: A View from Capitol Hill," unpublished paper.

has been subjected to a cartel arrangement sponsored by the government. By specific prescription, the sugar market is divided to the last spoonful. . . .

Political power within the sugar subgovernment is largely vested in the chairman of the House Agricultural Committee who works out the schedule of quotas. It is shared by a veteran civil servant, the Director of the Sugar Division in the U.S. Department of Agriculture, who provides the necessary "expert" advice for such a complex marketing arrangement. Further advice is provided by Washington representatives of the . . . producers.[3]

Richard Neustadt adds the necessary caveat that this system of subgovernments does not cover areas in which there are "jurisdictional entanglements" and "mingled programs" involving several agencies in the bureaucracy. In these areas congressional participation may be much more sporadic.[4]

The occasions for contact between Congress and the bureaucracy are many. The principal formal point of contact involves subcommittee or committee appropriations hearings that are, in most cases, held annually for given agencies and programs. These hearings are taken very seriously both in Congress and in the bureaucracy. Considerable preparation for them goes on in both institutions. Authorization hearings for executive programs are usually less frequent than appropriations hearings, but they are also regarded by participants as very important. In addition to the hearings there are also numerous year-round contacts in the form of lunches, phone calls, and personal visits between personnel from the agencies and members and staff members in the House and Senate.

One relatively recent development affecting contact between Congress and the bureaucracy has been the proliferation of formal liaison units throughout the executive branch.[5] A few agencies had legislative liaison units in the 1920s and 1930s. But the White House and most of the executive departments did not begin developing formal

---

3. Douglass Cater, *Power in Washington* (New York: Random House, 1964): 17–18. For a discussion of subgovernments and ways in which their influence might be reduced, see Roger H. Davidson, "Breaking up Those 'Cozy Triangles': An Impossible Dream?," in Susan Welch and John G. Peters (eds.), *Legislative Reform and Public Policy* (New York: Praeger, 1977): 30–53. On the nature of relations between Congress and the bureaucracy also see Morris P. Fiorina, *Congress: Keystone of the Washington Establishment* (New Haven: Yale University Press, 1977).

4. Richard E. Neustadt, "Politicians and Bureaucrats," in David B. Truman (ed.), *The Congress and America's Future* (Englewood Cliffs, N.J.: Prentice-Hall, 1965): 108.

5. On this topic in general see Abraham Holtzman, *Legislative Liaison* (New York: Rand McNally, 1970).

liaison apparatus until after World War II. White House liaison became a "big-time" operation during the Eisenhower presidency. Every department had a formal liaison staff early in the Kennedy administration. By fiscal 1963 the ten departments then in existence employed 500 liaison employees, almost half of them in the Defense Department. No department employed fewer than 13. The independent agencies (those not in a departmental hierarchy) employed an additional 233 liaison employees.[6] White House and departmental liaison officials typically work with the leaders of their party in Congress to achieve overall goals on the floor. Their intervention at the committee or subcommittee level is far less frequent. Liaison at the agency or bureau level has also grown. Some departments, such as HEW, have formal liaison units for each of their principal administrative subdivisions. Sub-departmental units in other departments may not have a formal liaison staff but some of their officials will, in fact, spend time engaged in liaison activities.

RESOURCES FOR INTERACTION

Members of Congress and the bureaucracy each possess resources the other values. When relations are going well and smoothly a continuous trading of these resources goes on. When disagreements arise withholding or punitive use of resources can occur. Typically, the advantages of smooth relations far outweigh any advantages to be gained in conflict and so the incentives to strive for smooth relations are great.

Congressional Resources [7]

In most instances it is Congress that determines whether a program will live or die. A few small programs can be established by executive order of the president if there is vague statutory authority from some time in the past. But most programs require explicit congressional authorization and virtually all programs—certainly those of any size or permanence—require congressional action in terms of appropriations. Not only can Congress say either yes or no to a program at the time of its establishment, it also holds the power of life or death in the most elemental terms throughout the existence of any program. Inertia is powerful, of course; once a program is established it is not

---

6. G. Russell Pipe, "Congressional Liaison: The Executive Branch Consolidates Its Relations with Congress," *Public Administration Review* 26 (1966): 17.

7. For a detailed review of congressional resources see Chapter 12 of William J. Keefe and Morris S. Ogul, *The American Legislative Process*, 4th ed. (Englewood Cliffs, N.J.: Prentice-Hall, 1977).

lightly terminated by Congress. But the power to terminate, either by refusal to renew authorization or the refusal to appropriate funds, is firmly lodged in Congress and nowhere else. Congress has discussed the possibility of automatic termination of programs ("Sunset" provisions) in recent years as a way of reducing inertia and increasing Congressional control.

The allocation of money to all federal agencies, usually through the appropriations process but also through the creation of trust funds and methods of funding other than appropriations, is controlled by Congress. This is undoubtedly the single most important resource Congress has in its dealings with the bureaucracy.

Congress can also, both by statute and by informal means, help shape the content of programs administered by the bureaucracy. Specific actions can be prohibited; others can be encouraged. In recent years Congress has been aggressive in seeking new ways of assuring itself of this continued power even in the face of a vast proliferation of executive agencies and personnel.[8] Two means have been particularly effective—the requirement in many cases that programs be authorized annually (virtually all programs also receive annual appropriations) and the requirement for a number of programs that formal committee agreement be solicited and received before specific actions can be taken by the bureaucracy (this is the so-called "legislative veto" or "committee clearance"). The requirement for annual authorizations means that some agencies and programs are subject to four separate congressional reviews each year—those by the relevant House and Senate authorizing committees and those by the relevant House and Senate appropriations subcommittees.

The legislative veto can take several forms. Statutory provisions in an increasing number of fields may contain one of the following requirements:

1. That an agency report proposed administrative actions in advance to a committee.

2. That an agency "come into agreement" with a committee before a given action is undertaken.

3. That an executive proposal lie before Congress for a fixed period of time before it can be implemented. If Congress, or part of it, (the provisions can vary) disapproves of the specific proposal then the executive is prevented from going forward with its plans. A variation of this requirement does not specifically provide for explicit congressional disapproval, but rather assumes that if Congress

---

8. Neustadt, "Politicians and Bureaucrats," 105–106.

does not like a particular executive proposal positive action will be taken to circumvent it rather than vetoing it. This technique is used, for example, in relation to the closing of military facilities.

4. That Congress or some part of it (provisions vary) must give positive approval before the executive can proceed with a planned action.

In the mid-1970s two developments in relation to the legislative veto occurred. First, Congress, particularly the House, became much more aggressive in seeking to add legislative veto provisions to new legislation, and in 1976 the House almost passed a bill that would have created a legislative veto over all regulations issued by bureaucratic agencies. Second, court challenges to the one-house veto alleged it to be unconstitutional. Lower federal courts had upheld the practice (it exists in about 300 provisions of about 200 laws that have been passed since the mid-1920s) as of mid-1977 and it seemed likely that the Supreme Court would eventually rule on it.[9]

Congress often approves what the executive proposes, but it is also capable of exercising its power of denial. For example, between 1946 and 1968 Congress rejected twenty-two plans offered by four different presidents for reorganizing parts of the executive branch. One example of the results of its negative actions was that Congress thus preserved the status quo in its relationships with a number of regulatory commissions that handle distributive matters particularly salient to members of Congress.

In addition to these techniques for shaping content, Congress can, of course, simply write specific statutory details in authorization or even appropriations legislation. Such language is theoretically forbidden in appropriations bills, but the practice occurs nonetheless. Informal continuing contact between members of the House and Senate and their staff members and bureaucrats also affords numerous opportunities for substantive congressional input in shaping programs.

Congress also has power over the structure of the bureaucracy. Not only do the House and Senate have veto power over reorganization plans offered by the president, they can also write specific organizational provisions into statutes. Thus they have considerable control over where in the bureaucracy a given program or agency is lodged. It was congressional pressure and activity, for example, that kept the

---

9. "Veto Over Agency Rules Pressed in Congress," *Congressional Quarterly Almanac 1976* (Washington: Congressional Quarterly, 1976): 508–510; Thomas P. Southwick, "Legislative Veto Issue May Go to Supreme Court," *Congressional Quarterly Weekly Report* (May 28, 1977): 1052; and Morton Mintz, "Court Backs One-House Veto by Hill," Washington *Post*, May 23, 1977.

bureaucratic responsibility for air and water pollution in motion for a decade. The responsibility was located in at least four different bureaus for short periods.

In this case Congress was trying to instill some aggressiveness into the bureaucracy in the area of abatement enforcement. Congress can also have considerable impact on the internal structure of individual bureaus or agencies. Personnel within the executive branch, both at an aggregate and an individual level, are subject to congressional influence. At the aggregate level, Congress provides the money for salaries. Congress also often sets limits on the number of slots open for an agency's top-level executives such as assistant secretaries and "supergrade" civil servants.

At the individual level Congress will sometimes specify the status of a specific job. For example, when the Department of Housing and Urban Development was created Congress stipulated that one of the five assistant secretary positions allocated to the Department be filled by the Federal Housing Commissioner. This signaled congressional devotion to the FHA program because it routinely provided visible benefits for middle class citizens eager to own homes and also accustomed to voting and warned the new HUD secretary that he should not try to downgrade it.

Also at the individual level, members of Congress support specific persons for specific open jobs in the bureaucracy. They concentrate their attention on top jobs, not on postmasterships and relatively unimportant jobs.

The Senate has to ratify a number of presidential appointments. The Constitution, in Article II, section 2, speaks of the "Advice and Consent" of the Senate as necessary for a number of positions—both those specified in the Constitution and those later established by law with a ratification provision. How much "advice" the President seeks varies, but the "consent" in the form of a majority vote is necessary. The Senate now considers well over 100,000 nominations every two years, but many of these are military officers and are handled routinely. Few presidential nominations are rejected outright on the floor of the Senate, but a larger number are killed in committee. In other cases a nomination will cause so much controversy that the president will withdraw it. And some nominations are never confirmed simply because the Senate adjourns with some still pending.

The most important offices requiring Senate ratification include cabinet and subcabinet secretaryships, ambassadorships, and federal judicial officials, including Supreme Court justices, district and appeals court judges, and U.S. marshals and attorneys. High officials who serve on an interim basis before confirmation must proceed very cautiously in making decisions. Rejection of an important nominee is embarrassing to the administration and may also frustrate the achievement of some policy goals.

Over time the Senate has been relatively active in defeating or forcing the withdrawal of Supreme Court nominations—over 20 percent of all presidential nominations have failed in one way or another. It has been much more reluctant to intervene in presidents' choices of cabinet members, and since the Civil War only four cabinet nominations have been defeated on the Senate floor. However, at the subcabinet level the Senate has been more active. For example, in 1975 the Senate did not defeat any presidential nominees on the floor but did defeat three in committee and returned two to the president without committee action. The president also chose to withdraw a few nominations. In 1976 the Senate again followed the same pattern of not rejecting any on the floor but of killing some in committee, leaving some in limbo by virtue of taking no action, and, in effect, forcing presidential withdrawal of others.

Finally, Congress has the power to investigate the activities of bureaus, both through normal authorization and appropriation hearings and also through specific hearings on individual programs or even individual changes in personnel. For example, a subcommittee of the Senate Commerce Committee held hearings to investigate the firing of a Civil Aeronautics Administration official during the Eisenhower years. Just as important, Congress can also deliberately refrain from conducting a thorough probe of the activities of an agency.

Bureaucratic Resources

The projects and activities that a bureau administers are important to members, either because of their views regarding the importance and utility of particular programs or because they perceive that their constituents' interests are affected by a bureau's activities.

The decisions that bureaus make about the physical locations of their projects and activities are important to senators and representatives, who are generally anxious to increase the number of federal projects and activities in their respective districts and states. Occasionally, they may want to make sure that a controversial project or activity, such as a Job Corps camp, is *not* located in their constituency.

Bureaus are responsible for the handling of individual "cases"— that is, instances in which some person or persons disentangle themselves from the aggregate mass of bureau clients and beneficiaries to demand special, personalized attention. These cases are constituents of some representatives and senators and are, therefore, potentially important to him or her.

Bureaus possess vast amounts of program information that is useful to members of the House and Senate in many ways. This information can be used by a member to increase his knowledge about programs, aid in his decision-making, and improve his performance as a committee member. An adroit use of information can increase a member's intellectual reputation and therefore enhance his status with fellow members. The member's reputation for knowledgeability and responsibility among his constituents is improved if he commands information well.

Departmental legislative liaison personnel help the bureaucracy in the use of these resources but they are not a substitute for direct contact between the bureaus and committees. Neither do they get involved in the appropriations process, perhaps the single most important area of congressional-executive interaction. The best study of legislative liaison in the executive branch concludes that liaison personnel are important because they help congressmen meet their own perceived self-interest and needs. Specifically, liaison personnel can provide access to the secretary of a department for a congressman who needs it; they can help provide individual members with a substantive point of view about programs; they provide "collaborators" for congressmen who are legislative activists; and they can help congressmen meet constituent needs.[10]

THE JOINT SHAPING OF PUBLIC POLICY: INITIATION AND SUPPORT

Much public policy is jointly shaped by interaction between the bureaucracy and members of Congress. Even if one branch dominates the development of legislation in a given area there are still many occasions for intimate interaction as that area is administered. And, in many cases, the basic statutes themselves are jointly developed. For most fields, there are three areas where shared policy development is possible: 1) in the development of substantive legislation; 2) in the development of appropriations legislation; and 3) in the development of projects, rules, regulations, procedures, and the other details of day-to-day administration. Many of the conditions for shared influence vary

---

10. Holtzman, *Legislative Liaison*: 51–53. See chapters 7 and 8 for a lengthy discussion of the strategies and tactics used by liaison officers.

in each of these fields. In general, however, the partisan situation cuts across all three areas: the chances of relatively smooth relations and shared influence between Congress and the bureaucracy are enhanced if the majority of both houses and the White House are controlled by the same party; the chances are diminished if there is split control.

Authorizing Legislation

One of the classic questions in the scanty literature on bureaucratic-congressional relations is: who initiates? For some reason the answer to this question has been viewed as highly significant, although the significance is usually never analyzed except in terms of either applauding or bemoaning the supposed demise of Congress. Also, much of this literature seems to assume that it is only in the initiation of authorizing legislation that Congress can have a significant impact on the shape of national policy.

The "who initiates" question is important only if the answer indicates that over time one branch or the other is effectively shut out of any role in shaping authorizing legislation. The best evidence seems to indicate that regardless of the source of initiation, the other branch—whether it be Congress responding to bureaucratic initiative or the bureaucracy responding to congressional initiative—ordinarily makes some important changes.

Instances both of congressional initiation of authorizing legislation and of major congressional impact on executive branch initiatives are numerous. For example, a study of ninety major laws between 1890 and 1940 attributed major initiative to Congress in about 40 percent of the cases, to the president in about 20 percent, to both jointly in about 30 percent, and to interest groups in about 10 percent.[11] An updating of this study for the years from 1940 through 1967, using the same impressionistic standards, arrrived at the same basic conclusion: that Congress was still extremely important in the development of authorizing legislation. In the words of the authors, "Our conclusion challenges the conventional wisdom that the president has come to enjoy an increasingly preponderant role in national policy-making. . . . The evidence suggests that Congress continues to be an active innovator and very much in the legislative business."[12]

---

11. Lawrence H. Chamberlain, *The President, Congress and Legislation* (New York: Columbia University Press, 1946).
12. Ronald C. Moe and Steven C. Teel, "Congress as Policy-Maker: A Necessary Reappraisal," *Political Science Quarterly* 85 (1970): 467–468.

An impressionistic review in 1975 by a journalist assigned to cover Congress for the Washington *Post* credited Congress with initiation in a number of policy areas: Medicare, Social Security disability insurance, pension reform, the eighteen-year-old vote, political campaign reform, air pollution (including that from automobiles), reduction and cessation of the U.S. role in Indochina, chemical additives in food, the creation of a consumer protection agency, mandatory automobile safety standards, food programs for the poor, and increases in the minimum wage.[13] He also added references to major investigations initiated by Congress, including those of the drug industry, multinational corporations, organized crime, and labor racketeering.

Instances of joint collaboration between parts of Congress and parts of the bureaucracy on specific authorization bills are legion. A few illustrations will have to suffice.[14]

In the housing field in recent years much of the bill drafting was done jointly by staff members from the General Counsel's office in the Department of Housing and Urban Development and its predecessor, the Housing and Home Finance Agency, who collaborated with the staff director of the Housing Subcommittee of the House Committee on Banking and Currency.[15]

In the consumer protection area the same kind of relationship between bureaucrats and congressional staff members developed. "There has been a great deal of staff contact between Senator Nelson's subcommittee investigating prescription drugs and the Food and Drug Administration. The Commerce Committee staff worked with the Federal Power Commission on gas pipeline safety. There has been a whole range of these ad hoc contacts . . ." [16] In this field the ad hoc contacts also tend to vanish once the issue is off the congressional agenda. This is probably because consumer protection is a relatively new field and there are jurisdictional instabilities in both the executive and legislative branches. In other fields, where jurisdictions are clearer and more well established, contacts are also likely to be more permanent.

In the air pollution field, even though Congress has taken the initiative, there has been informal cooperation from the executive branch

---

13. Spencer Rich, "Congress Has Lead in Major Programs," Washington *Post*, February 14, 1975.
14. For a number of additional examples see chapters 4–7 of Ripley and Franklin, *Congress, the Bureaucracy, and Public Policy.* See also Gary Orfield, *Congressional Power: Congress and Social Change* (New York: Harcourt Brace Jovanovich, 1975).
15. Harold Wolman, *Politics of Federal Housing* (New York: Dodd, Mead, 1971): 107.
16. Mark V. Nadel, *The Politics of Consumer Protection* (Indianapolis: Bobbs-Merrill, 1971): 115.

staff. This cooperation has come despite formal bureaucratic positions that often ran counter to congressional initiatives. For example, in 1962 legislative and technical experts from the Public Health Service and the General Counsel's office in the Department of Health, Education, and Welfare worked with a representative of the United States Conference of Mayors (an interest group representing roughly the 100 largest cities in the country), and a few senators and representatives and their staffs to produce draft legislation even though the Public Health Service formally was opposed to some of the provisions they were drafting.[17]

Appropriations

Both agencies and subcommittees approach the matter of appropriations in such a way that general patterns of behavior can be discerned and described. Executive officials, above all, seek to reduce uncertainty in the process. They want to know as early as they can how much money they have to spend and they want to be able to predict how much they will have in the future so they can plan ahead. Typically, officials seek to reduce uncertainty by seeking the confidence of the appropriations subcommittee members to whom they are responsible. In seeking confidence they are especially careful in preparing for the hearings of their subcommittees so that they appear to be "on top" of their job. They also are assiduous in maintaining personal contacts outside of the formal hearings.

The members of the appropriations subcommittees, especially in the House, start with the view that all budgets can be cut. Their basic suspicion of bureaus and bureaucrats is overcome when they gain a level of confidence in particular individuals. They are particularly rigorous in investigating proposed increases, proposed new programs, and programs with little client support. Well-established programs with a satisfied and politically potent clientele do not receive such rigorous scrutiny. Thus the foreign aid agency budget and the Office of Economic Opportunity budget regularly get cut heavily whereas the Soil Conservation Service or the Federal Bureau of Investigation get about what they ask for. The members are eager to keep the relationship strictly between themselves and responsible bureau officials. For that

---

17. Randall B. Ripley, "Congress and Clean Air: The Issue of Enforcement," in Frederic N. Cleaveland and associates, *Congress and Urban Problems* (Washington: Brookings, 1969): 224–278. See also Charles O. Jones, *Clean Air: The Policies and Politics of Pollution Control* (Pittsburgh: University of Pittsburgh Press, 1975).

reason they bar departmental liaison officials from participation and limit the number of witnesses outside the government. In 1963, for example, government witnesses at House appropriations hearings out-numbered non-government witnesses by two to one; in only two sub-committees of twelve was the number of outside witnesses greater than the number of government witnesses. The Senate Appropriations Com-mittee differs from the House Appropriations Committee principally because its deliberations always follow those of the House chronologi-cally and senators are used to serving as an appeals court in which the executive officials who feel that the House was too severe can make their case. The Senate Committee is less likely to cut requests than the House Committee.[18]

Not all subcommittees and agencies interact as described above. Ira Sharkansky has shown how both the agency and the committee can behave otherwise in examining the interaction between one House appropriations subcommittee and four of the agencies for which it is responsible over a period of a dozen years. He summarizes the be-havior of the subcommittee as follows:

> Evidently, the legislators vary their oversight activity among agen-cies. They devote more than the average amount of supervisory and control efforts to the agencies that spend the most money, whose re-quests have increased the most rapidly, and whose behavior toward the subcommittee has deviated most frequently from subcommittee desires. In a sense, they allocate their time and staff assistance to agencies most "in need" of supervision and control.[19]

Writing from the perspective of the agencies, Sharkansky concluded that agencies vary in the level of assertiveness with which they ap-proach appropriations subcommittees; that those agencies with greater public and administration support are more assertive; and that ad-ministrators are not totally guided to their levels of assertiveness by subcommittee attitudes and behavior, which usually appear fuzzy anyway.[20]

18. The preceding two paragraphs are based primarily on the meticulous work of Richard F. Fenno, Jr., *The Power of the Purse* (Boston: Little, Brown, 1966), especially parts of Chapters 6, 7, and 11. See also Robert D. Thomas and Roger B. Handberg, "Congressional Budgeting for Eight Agencies, 1947–1972," *American Journal of Political Science* 18 (1974): 179–187.

19. Ira Sharkansky, "An Appropriations Subcommittee and Its Client Agencies: A Comparative Study of Supervision and Control," *American Political Science Review* 59 (1965): 628.

20. Ira Sharkansky, "Four Agencies and an Appropriations Subcommittee: A Com-parative Study of Budget Strategies," *Midwest Journal of Political Science* 9 (1965): 254–281.

Day-to-Day Administration

Congressional influence on the bureaucracy does not end once authorization and appropriations statutes have been passed. Interaction continues on a daily basis as agencies administer their programs. Some examples can provide the flavor of the interaction. The following discussion of the Office of Education is illustrative:

> Perhaps more important than formal amendments, however, congressional influence on administrative behavior is manifest in the nature of questions put to officials in hearings; in subcommittee requests for information; in press statements and in public speeches attacking or questioning existing practices within an agency; in letters or telephone calls to the Commissioner or to the Secretary of HEW. Agencies live by congressional favor, and congressional power is variable. For this reason, the views, opinions, and attitudes of key legislators (especially committee and subcommittee chairmen and their immediate staffs) are powerful influences on administrative behavior. Francis Keppel (the Commissioner of Education) spent agonizing months trying to fill top level vacancies because Congressman Adam Clayton Powell insisted upon a number of Negro appointees. A great deal of time of top officials is taken up in the laborious and often harrowing processes of meeting both the legitimate and illegitimate calls of Congress for program review.[21]

When a subgovernment is firmly entrenched there is likely to be intimate congressional involvement in administration. Theodore Lowi describes the situation in the agricultural field, where he identifies ten different "self-governing systems" dealing with different sets of programs:

> Each of the ten systems has become a powerful political instrumentality. The self-governing local units become one important force in a system that administers a program and maintains the autonomy of that program against political forces emanating from other agricultural programs, from antagonistic farm and nonfarm interests, from Congress, from the Secretary of Agriculture, and from the President. To many a farmer, the local outpost of one or another of these systems *is* the government.

> The politics within each system is built upon a triangular trading pattern involving the central agency, a Congressional committee or

21. Stephen K. Bailey and Edith K. Mosher, *ESEA: The Office of Education Administers a Law* (Syracuse: Syracuse University Press, 1968): 185.

sub-committee, and the local district farmer committees (usually federated in some national or regional organization).[22]

Sometimes bureaucrats who disagree with the policies of a president and his appointees can use their ties with Congress to protest. Alternatively, members of Congress who disagree with the presidential policies can seek out dissident bureaucrats. The lack of interest of the Nixon administration in pursuing civil rights in a number of fields spurred congressional-bureaucratic cooperation highly critical of the administration. For example, in 1969 a Senate subcommittee in effect conspired with pro-civil rights bureaucrats in the Equal Employment Opportunity Commission to harass the administration on its handling of a discrimination case involving three large textile companies in the south. A similar kind of alliance was formed with regard to job discrimination policy in the Department of Transportation and succeeded in getting some equal opportunities actions taken that otherwise would not have been forthcoming.[23]

Several empirical studies lead to some general statements about when a congressional committee is more or less likely to pursue its oversight of an agency's daily activities vigorously.[24] Oversight is promoted by the existence of autonomous subcommittees; ample committee staffs; perceptions of partisan advantage on the part of the majority party members; and perceptions that service to constituents can be enhanced by such activity. Oversight is also most likely on the part of committees that are highly prestigious and oriented toward a relatively large amount of legislative output. Oversight is most vigorously pursued when a committee is considering major revisions in policy. Thus, for example, congressional oversight in the housing field has been heavy for several decades because most of the above conditions were met. Oversight over enforcement of civil rights laws has been made more sporadic because a number of the above conditions have not been met.

Vigorous oversight is discouraged if there are close, mutually reward-

---

22. Theodore J. Lowi, "How the Farmers Get What They Want," in Theodore J. Lowi and Randall B. Ripley (eds.), *Legislative Politics U.S.A.*, 3rd ed. (Boston: Little, Brown, 1973): 188.

23. Orfield, *Congressional Power*: 82–84.

24. See John F. Bibby, "Committee Characteristics and Legislative Oversight of Administration," *Midwest Journal of Political Science* 10 (1966): 78–97; and Seymour Scher, "Conditions for Legislative Control," *Journal of Politics* 25 (1963): 526–551. On oversight in general see Morris S. Ogul, *Congress Oversees the Bureaucracy: Studies in Legislative Supervision* (Pittsburgh: University of Pittsburgh Press, 1976); and Ogul, "Congressional Oversight: Structures and Incentives," in Lawrence C. Dodd and Bruce I. Oppenheimer (eds.), *Congress Reconsidered* (New York: Praeger, 1977): 207–221.

ing contacts between members and agency officials that might be disrupted by such activity. Aggressive oversight is also to be avoided if it seems to members that a great deal of negative reaction from interest groups, important to them and part of an existing subgovernment, is likely.

CONFLICT OVER PUBLIC POLICY

Much of the time, most members of Congress have strong incentives to get along with the various parts of the federal bureaucracy. Thus in most policy areas congressional-bureaucratic relations proceed relatively smoothly and inconspicuously.

But conflict does occur. When congressmen—particularly members of relevant committees and subcommittees—perceive their interests to be threatened they will react by seeking to bring agency policy into line with their preferences. The motivation for the conflict may be programmatic or political, but the effect is the same: Congress and the executive branch engage in conflict over substantive policy statements and actions. Either side may prevail in these conflicts. The bureaucracy has considerable resources with which to pursue its point of view. But in cases where congressional feeling is intense Congress usually prevails, at least in symbolic ways that mollify the protesting members.

In a conflict situation those congressmen (again usually organized in committees or subcommittees) who are involved use all of the resources available to them in order to prevail. A number of examples illustrate how conflicts can be resolved.

The harshest punishment Congress can administer in settling a conflict is to kill an existing program. Congress administered that fatal stroke to the Area Redevelopment Administration in 1963, even though it had only been created in 1961. The principal reason for this action was that a number of members had become convinced that, despite clear provisions in the law, the ARA was encouraging industries to relocate in redevelopment areas. In the eyes of those congressmen and their constituents from districts losing such industries, the ARA was engaging in "piracy." [25] After being assured by the administration that such abuses would not occur in the future, Congress reestablished the ARA program in 1965 under a different name—the Economic Development Administration.

Congress can demand and obtain major programmatic concessions

25. See Randall B. Ripley, *The Politics of Economic and Human Resource Development* (Indianapolis: Bobbs-Merrill, 1972): Chapter 2, and the literature cited therein.

in exchange for extending the life of a program. For example, in dealing with a small juvenile delinquency program during the Kennedy administration, Edith Green, chairman of the House subcommittee with jurisdiction over the program extracted the following concessions to put the program more in line with her vision of it in return for extending the program in 1963: [26]

1. The extension was changed from three years to two years and was, by informal agreement, considered the terminal extension.

2. Funds were authorized for only one year, which meant that annual justification of the program before Congress would be necessary.

3. New projects would not be comprehensive in scope but rather would be limited demonstration projects. The director of the Office of Juvenile Delinquency provided a written statement for Green to read into the record to make this agreement explicit.

4. A special amendment was added to the bill requiring, in effect, that a project be started in the District of Columbia.

Congress can redefine the jurisdictional authority of a regulatory agency so that it no longer has the power to make decisions in a particular area. This was the case when the Federal Trade Commission first sought to move against cigarette advertising. An irate Congress simply removed the FTC's jurisdiction that would have allowed it to accomplish what it wanted to do. It was not until several years later that a weakened version of the original FTC position was allowed to be implemented.[27]

Congress can determine what standards a program will be allowed or required to use in evaluating its operation. Then the Army Corps of Engineers wanted to implement new, more accurate cost-benefit standards for determining which water projects it should undertake, Congress passed an amendment to the Transportation Act of 1966 prohibiting the implementation of more rigid standards and preserving the standards that would maximize the number of Corps projects throughout the country, despite the dubious economic validity of some of them.[28]

---

26. John E. Moore, "Controlling Delinquency: Executive, Congressional and Juvenile, 1961–1964," in Cleaveland et al., *Congress and Urban Problems*: 166–67. Interestingly, one thing that had offended Green was that the program sought to put a project in her home district before the local officials had submitted what she considered to be a good plan. She refused to play politics with the program, even though it meant losing some federal money at home.

27. See Lee A. Fritschler, *Smoking and Politics* (New York: Appleton-Century-Crofts, 1969).

28. Robert Haveman and Paula Stephan, "The Domestic Program Congress Won't Cut," in Raymond E. Wolfinger (ed.), *Readings on Congress* (Englewood Cliffs, N.J.: Prentice-Hall, 1971): 367–370.

Congress can reverse an organizational edict issued by an agency if it feels pressure to do so. In 1968 HEW sought to decentralize programs authorized under the Elementary and Secondary Education Act of 1965. This decentralization would have spread responsibility for the programs to HEW field establishments and would have diminished the power of the Office of Education officials in Washington. The move was opposed by "the education lobby." Wilbur Cohen, Secretary of HEW at the time, told how the chairman of the relevant Senate appropriations subcommittee reversed the HEW decision:

> When we went up to Senate Appropriations, the committee reduced the Office of Education's budget by about $2.4 million. So I paid a visit to Sen. (Lister) Hill (D.-Ala.), and I said, 'What goes?' And he replied, 'The National Education Association doesn't want that program decentralized.' I said, 'If I rescind that order, will you give me that money back?' And he said, 'Yeah.' So I rescinded that order and I doubt whether to this day it's been reissued.[29]

Congress can use the threat of investigative hearings to influence the policy decisions of an agency. Only the threat of negative publicity from hearings in both the House and Senate seems to have moved the Food and Drug Administration to refuse certification in 1969 for a drug called Panalba manufactured by a major pharmaceutical company. Until the impact of that threat was considered, the FDA seemed disposed to go along with the company and the representative from the company's district.[30]

Congressional-Bureaucratic Relations: A Summary Assessment

The analysis in this chapter may to some extent suggest that conflict is unimportant in the policy-making process of the national government. This is clearly not the case. But there is a great amount of cooperation between Congress and the bureaucracy and it is in good measure based on mutual self-interest. There is nothing insidious about this cooperation; most prolonged human relationships are characterized by the desire for relative harmony and calm. Harmony and calm may produce either beneficial or useless public policy. However, the same may be said for conflict.

Occasional conflict has the merit of raising questions about the status quo in any given policy area. The resolution of the conflict

---

29. *National Journal* (December 16, 1972): 1932–1933.
30. Nadel, *The Politics of Consumer Protection*: 77–78.

may ultimately result in little movement away from that status quo, but at least its content is examined. And, occasionally, substantial departures from the status quo follow major conflict. Thus, for example, a number of the policy innovations of the mid-1960s (the New Frontier and Great Society measures such as basic federal aid to elementary and secondary education, medical care for the aged, and several poverty programs) came after extended periods of conflict over similar or related proposals for the preceding years.

A superficial consideration of congressional-bureaucratic relations tends to suggest that Congress dominates the bureaucracy. This is not the case. Congressional influence is substantial but in many areas the powerful members choose not to exercise it. In addition, even in those cases in which a few members or subcommittees do seek to exercise their influence they may win some skirmishes or battles only to lose the war of overall policy direction. This can happen when the president and presidency lend the full weight of their support to a particular part of the bureaucracy under attack. This kind of support by the presidency occurs infrequently, but when it is used it is often effective because the weapons are very powerful: the impounding of large amounts of money that Congress has appropriated for specific purposes, the withholding of vital information from Congress under the claim of "executive privilege," and the taking of initiatives while Congress is out of session.

At root, the predominance of incentives for both bureaucrats and members of Congress to maintain good relations with each other so that the trading of valued resources is not disrupted also loads the legislative process in favor of the status quo. Habits and patterns of personal interaction and thought about public policy develop and become firmly entrenched. Participants hesitate to stray very far from policies that are known to command widespread support, regardless of their true value, their shortcomings, or the nature of their impact on American society. Disruptive forces such as visionary or aggressive presidents or major party upheavals can and do alter this situation, but they are the exception and not the rule. Not all policy change is minute or slow-moving, but most of it is. This situation may result in either "good" or "bad" policy; it certainly results in familiar policy.

Despite considerable talk in Congress about increased oversight of executive branch activities and bureaucratic performance, the dice are still loaded against sustained oversight. There is little political payoff either in Washington or at home for senators and representatives in being aggressive overseers. And there may be negative outcomes in the form of a less cooperative bureaucracy when the member is pursuing interests particularly close to his or her heart. In addition to the political disincentives for vigorous pursuit of oversight by Congress there is also the fact that the very broad delegations of power Congress has given the bureaucracy over the years, particularly beginning in the 1930s, makes oversight very difficult because there are often no standards in the legislation against which to measure performance, even in a rough sense.[31] Likewise, in the 1970s the especially complicated implementation patterns that go with general and special revenue sharing programs (which now account for tens of billions of dollars of expenditures of federal money each year) make meaningful oversight extremely difficult to achieve, even if will is present. Even where abuses have become publicly evident, as in the case of the intelligence agencies in the 1970s, it takes Congress considerable time to decide it wants to get involved in oversight.[32]

In short, oversight by Congress is not a natural activity. Coordinated oversight might, in theory, provide some policy integration. The much more natural stance for Congress is either nonexistent or sporadic and disjointed oversight, which in turn contributes to sustaining policy fragmentation.

---

31. Peter Woll, *American Bureaucracy,* 2nd ed. (New York: Norton, 1977).
32. See John T. Elliff, "Congress and the Intelligence Community," in Dodd and Oppenheimer, *Congress Reconsidered*: 193–206. See also Harry Howe Ransom, "Congress and the Intelligence Agencies," in Harvey C. Mansfield, Sr. (ed.), *Congress against the President,* Vol. 32, no. 1 of Proceedings of The Academy of Political Science (1975): 153–166.

PART IV

CONGRESSIONAL
INFLUENCE
OVER AMERICAN
PUBLIC POLICY

CONGRESSIONAL ACCESS
TO POLICY-MAKING

C ONGRESS WIELDS IMPORTANT INFLUENCE OVER AMERICAN PUBLIC POL-
icy. That fact cannot be doubted. However, the amount of influence and the substantive results of that influence both vary over time
and from instance to instance. In general, two central questions about
congressional policy influence are worth pursuing in some detail.
First, what explains variations in the amount of congressional influence? Second, what is the impact of influence wielded by Congress?
The first question will be the focus of the present chapter. The second
question will be treated in the succeeding chapter.

In broad terms, the amount of congressional influence over policy-
making is a function of the nature of congressional access to policy and
program decisions. Congress does not have equal potential for developing influence in all cases because congressional access varies, depending on the type of policy under consideration and at different
points in the sequence of policy-making. Fortunately, there are patterns to the variance of congressional access. This chapter focuses on
the patterns of access in relation to the stages of policy-making, the
types of policy, the *internal* distribution of influence in Congress, and
the character of relations with the executive branch.

ACCESS AND THE STAGES OF POLICY-MAKING

There are many ways to try to comprehend a phenomenon as complex as the policy process in the American national government. A
short discussion of stages in that process is introduced here in order
to pinpoint those activities in which Congress is likely to have the
most access.

Three different broad stages of policy activity lead to broadly defined policy products. The first stage in the process is one of *agenda-setting*. Those topics to which the government gives its attention can be said to be on the agenda of government. This is the stage of problem identification. Since even a government as large and active as that of the United States cannot pay attention to all potential problems, there is constant definition and redefinition of what is on the agenda. There is also constant shifting of priorities of what problems should receive how much attention from which actors and institutions. The policy product emerging from this stage of the process is the agenda of government.

In the agenda-setting stage no one institution or actor or group of actors is dominant. There is relatively open competition for getting the attention of the decision-makers and inducing them to take a problem seriously enough to contemplate action. Congress as an institution, given its fragmented and multi-headed nature, rarely speaks with one voice about new items that should be added to the governmental agenda. However, active and visible individual members and groups of members of both houses participate in the complex and often confusing process by which issues emerge somehow "certified" as being on the agenda, regardless of the relative weight of the individual problems. Thus, for example, in the mid-1970s members of Congress added their voices to the chorus in helping identify a number of aspects of energy as being a central problem requiring concerted attention. A number of members of Congress also helped call attention—through publicity—to the newly discovered national problem of child pornography in 1977. It is probably accurate to say that no major item comes onto the agenda of the United States government, at least in the domestic sphere, without congressional participation of some sort in adding it.

The second major stage in the policy process is that of policy formulation and legitimation. Once an item is on the agenda, then presumably there will be pressures from both inside and outside of government to do something about it. Policy formulation is the development of a proposed alternative for what should be done. Legitimation involves the ratification and possible amendment of that choice in its details. The products of these activities are policy statements. Congress is a major participant in the policy formulation and legitimation process. The passage of any major statute is the culmination of formulation and legitimation activities. Constitutionally, Congress as a collectivity has to participate in a major way in the decisions leading up to such passage. At the individual level, members, and especially subcommittees, make many of the critical decisions.

There are a number of specific activities that go on during the formulation and legitimation of policy statements. The access of Congress to formulation and legitimation overall is better thought of as varying degrees of access to those specific activities. The activities that occur are (1) the collection, analysis, and dissemination of information; (2) the development and selection of policy alternatives; (3) advocacy of the most widely supported alternative or alternatives; and (4) final formal decisions (in statutory form). Table 11–1 summarizes the potential access of the principal institutional actors to these four activities. The table suggests that the bureaucracy is particularly important in information collection, analysis, and dissemination activities and thus helps narrow the range of what is considered possible even before formal alternative development and selection begins. All of the major institutional actors play a role in both alternative development and selection and in advocacy, with the president playing a particularly important advocacy role when he chooses. It needs to be stressed, of course, that the president cannot possibly take a position on all of the issues facing the government and so may abdicate his advocacy potential much of the time. The formal decision stage, since it ultimately involves action on statutes or amendments to statutes, necessarily creates major access for both Congress and the president.

The third stage is program implementation. Once a policy statement has been made, then numerous decisions about the details of what should be done to implement it have to be made. The products of this stage are policy actions. Implementation is enormously important in the overall transmission of policies to intended beneficiaries. However, it need not detain us long here because it is basically the

Table 11–1
Potential Access of Principal Institutional Actors
to Policy Formulation and Legitimation Activities

	Institutional Actor			
Activity	*Congress*	*Presidency*	*Bureaucracy*	*Interest Groups*
Information Collection, Analysis, and Dissemination	X	X	XXX	X
Alternative Development and Selection	XX	XX	XX	X
Advocacy	XX	XXX	XX	XX
Formal Decisions	XXX	XXX	—	—

XXX = primary access
XX = considerable access
X = some access
— = little or no access

province of bureaucracies (including many state and local bureaucracies). Congressional participation in implementation is minimal and sporadic and usually consists of isolated interventions by individual members or, occasionally, subcommittees.

A secondary product of implementation—or, put another way, a product of the policy actions—is the impact of the policies on society. Theoretically, both the program implementation itself and the impact of that implementation on target groups and on society in general should be evaluated in order that informed decisions can be made about the future. In principle, Congress should play a major role in that evaluation. In fact, very little systematic evaluation of either implementation or impact occurs with congressional participation. Congressional incentives, as indicated earlier, do not work in favor of oversight. And if oversight is used to encompass the notion of evaluation, the same disincentives for systematic program evaluation exist. Thus, at least to date, congressional "evaluation" tends to consist of judgments based on political considerations, anecdotes about the benefits conferred by programs or individuals ("Minnie Jones' hearing was saved by medicare."), and gut feelings and intuitions. Some have argued this is inevitably the case, given the incentive structure in Congress. Others have argued that more systematic evaluation by Congress is possible.[1]

Figure 11–1 summarizes the principal policy stages and policy products in the American national government and also indicates the general nature of congressional access to each stage. The arrows indicate the usual flow of activity. The "decisions about the future" stage is simply a way of indicating that the cycle can be re-entered at earlier stages. Like any graphic presentation of a messy process, this all appears quite tidy. Reality is, of course, considerably less structured.

ACCESS AND TYPES OF POLICY

In Chapter 1 it was argued that one of the major policy consequences of fragmentation in Congress was that most domestic issues tended to be defined as distributive—that is, providing primarily sub-

---

1. For a number of treatments of this question see the articles by James A. Thurber, Allen Shick, Robert H. Haveman, Charles O. Jones, Alton Frye, Andrew S. Carron, and Roger H. Davidson in *Policy Analysis* 2 (1976): 197–323; the articles by Randall B. Ripley, Charles O. Jones, Frederick O'R. Hayes, and Richard Royce in *Policymaking Role of Leadership in the Senate,* a compilation of papers prepared for the Commission on the Operation of the Senate (Washington: U.S. Government Printing Office, 1976); and Daniel A, Dreyfus, "The Limitations of Policy Research in Congressional Decisionmaking," *Policy Studies Journal* 4 (1976): 269–274.

Figure 11-1:
Congressional Access to Policy Stages and Policy Products

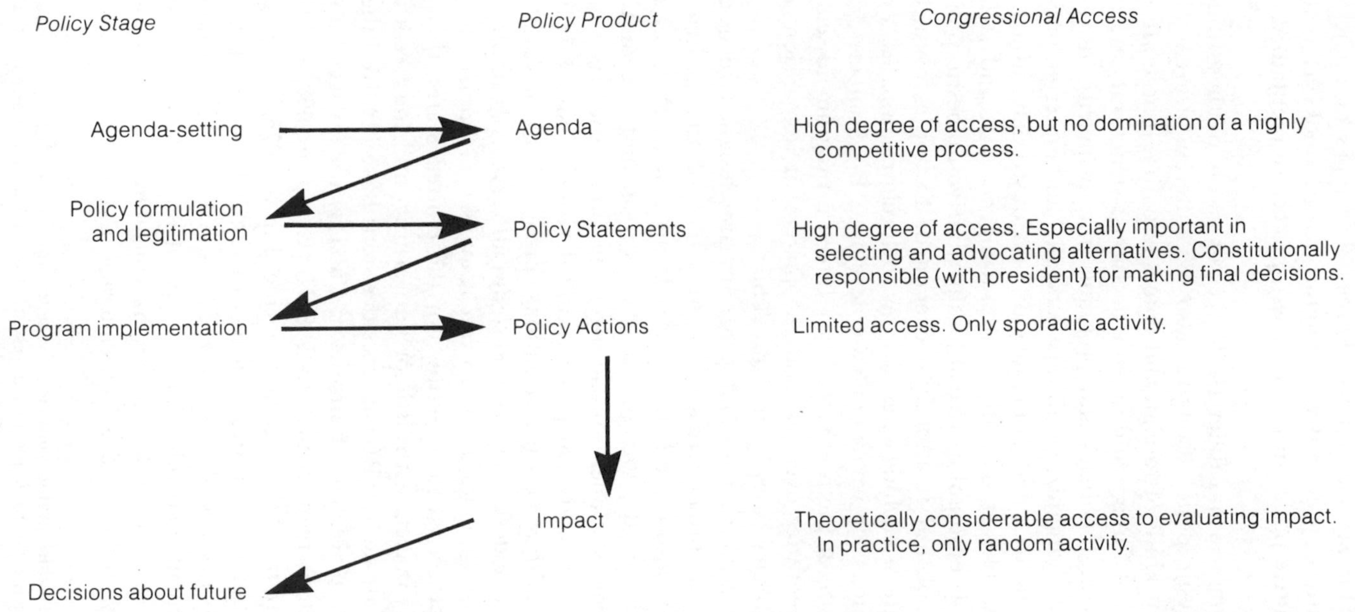

Policy Stage	*Policy Product*	*Congressional Access*
Agenda-setting	Agenda	High degree of access, but no domination of a highly competitive process.
Policy formulation and legitimation	Policy Statements	High degree of access. Especially important in selecting and advocating alternatives. Constitutionally responsible (with president) for making final decisions.
Program implementation	Policy Actions	Limited access. Only sporadic activity.
	Impact	Theoretically considerable access to evaluating impact. In practice, only random activity.
Decisions about future		

sidy for private activity. Three other types of domestic policy were identified: competitive regulatory (which looks a great deal like distributive policy in many senses), protective regulatory, and redistributive.

Congress has different degrees of access to these different kinds of domestic policy. Congress also has different degrees of access to different kinds of foreign and domestic policy. There are three principal types of foreign and defense decisions: structural, strategic, and crisis. Structural policies and programs aim primarily at procuring, locating, and organizing military personnel and materiel, presumably within the confines and guidelines of previously determined strategic decisions. This is basically a subsidizing activity, and structural foreign and defense policy resembles distributive domestic policy in terms of the political relationships generated. Examples of such policies and programs include sales of arms to foreign countries, weapons systems decisions (do we or don't we develop a B-1 bomber?), decisions about the size of the reserve military forces, a program to send surplus farm commodities overseas, and the placement, expansion, or contraction of military bases in the United States.

Strategic policies and programs are designed to assert and implement in broad terms the basic stance of the United States toward other nations, both in military terms and in terms of foreign policy. Foreign trade, foreign aid, the location and size of U.S. troop contingents stationed abroad, decisions about the basic mix of military forces, immigration policies, and decisions about involvement in specific military-political situations abroad (Vietnam, Cambodia, the Mideast, Rhodesia, Angola, and so on) all serve as examples.

Crisis policies are short-run responses to immediate problems that are perceived to be serious for the United States, that have burst on policy-makers with little or no warning, and that seem to demand immediate action. Recent crisis decisions have involved the U.S. reaction to the placement of missiles in Cuba by the Soviet Union in 1962, the North Korean seizure of a U.S. Navy ship in 1968, and the Cambodian seizure of a U.S. merchant marine ship in 1975.

Different institutional actors in the policy-making process have different degrees of access to the formulation and legitimation of policy statements depending on the type of policy under consideration.[2] The principal contending actors are considered to be the president, presidency, and centralized bureaucracy (that is, the Office of Management

---

2. For considerable empirical evidence supporting this general statement and the specific points made in the rest of this section, see Randall B. Ripley and Grace A. Franklin, *Congress, the Bureaucracy, and Public Policy* (Homewood, Illinois: Dorsey, 1976), especially pp. 16–20 and chapters 4–8.

Table 11–2
Decision-Making Patterns for Different Types of Policy Statements

	Relative Access of:					
Policy Type	President, presidency, and centralized bureaucracy	Bureaus	Congress	Subcommittees	Private Sector	Most Important Relationship in Determining Decisions
Distributive (domestic)	Low	High	Low (supports subcommittees)	High	High (the subsidized)	Subgovernment of subcommittee-bureau-interest groups representing the subsidized
Competitive regulatory (domestic)	Low	High	Low (supports subcommittees)	High	High (the competitors for regulated benefits)	Subgovernment, as above
Protective regulatory (domestic)	Moderately high	Moderate	Moderately high	Moderate	Moderately high (the regulated interests)	Presidency-Congress-regulated interests
Redistributive (domestic)	High	Moderately Low	High	Moderately low	High (peak associations representing clusters of interest groups)	Presidency-Congress-Peak associations
Structural (foreign and defense)	Low	High	Low (supports subcommittees)	High	High (the subsidized) Moderate	Subgovernment, as above
Strategic (foreign and defense)	High	Low	High	Low	(interest groups, corporations) Moderate	Presidency-Congress
Crisis (foreign and defense)	High	Low	Low	Low	Low	Internal to the presidency

and Budget and presidential appointees scattered throughout the executive branch); bureaus and other subunits in the executive branch; Congress as a whole (symbolized by decision-making on the floor of the House and Senate); the subcommittees of Congress is a disaggregated sense; and relevant portions of the private sector (the definition of which varies from policy type to policy type). Table 11–2 summarizes the relative degree of access for each of these five sets of actors to each of the seven types of policy (four domestic and three foreign and defense). The last column indicates the most important multi-actor relationship in making policy determinations for each type of policy.

Several general statements emerge from an inspection of Table 11–2. First, three patterns are identical—those for distributive domestic policy, competitive regulatory policy, and structural foreign and defense policy. Second, no one actor or combination of actors completely dominates decision-making leading to policy statements. Third, the private sector in various incarnations is important in all policy areas except crisis, which supports a modest view of the "authoritative" nature of governmental action. Most policy is, in fact, made with significant input from and usually at least grudging acquiesence of the most directly affected portions of the private sector. And in those three policy areas in which the classic triangular subgovernments dominate, the private sector is generally enthusiastic about supporting government policies and programs that emerge.

Short examples follow of policy formulation and legitimation in six of the seven policy areas (competitive regulatory is omitted because it looks so much like distributive). Obviously, single cases of each type do not "prove" the generalizations that have been offered, but they are illustrative of the kinds of relationships that are present.

Distributive Policy: Rivers and Harbors Legislation [3]

The treatment of the projects of the Army Corps of Engineers by Congress and the close relations between subcommittee decision-makers, Corps officials both in Washington and in the field, and interest groups (especially local interests seeking federal projects) provide a classic instance of a subgovernment working in a distributive field. Attempts to place decision-making about water projects undertaken

---

3. In general, see John A. Ferejohn, *Pork Barrel Politics: Rivers and Harbors Legislation, 1947–1968* (Stanford, Calif.: Stanford University Press, 1974); Arthur Maass, *Muddy Waters* (Cambridge, Mass.: Harvard University Press, 1951); and Elizabeth B. Drew, "Dam Outrage: the Story of the Army Engineers," *Atlantic*, April, 1970.

by the Corps on something other than a largely political basis have failed.

In the decision-making about specific projects there is a bubble-up process at work. Projects originate at the local level and work their way up through some screening by Corps professionals. Some projects are removed during this process but many survive. The surviving proposals go to the House and Senate Public Works Committees, which authorize some for funding and construction. Subcommittees of both the House and Senate Appropriations committees provide monies for feasibility studies and for the actual construction of authorized projects.

When an outsider, such as the president, tries to intrude in the elaborate decision-making norms and customs that have developed over the years, and especially if he tries to cut a project important to a key legislative actor, that outsider usually comes up on the short end of the decision. For example, early in 1977 when President Carter sought to cut thirty water projects from the federal budget for future years, one item on his "hit list" was the Tennessee-Tombigbee project in Mississippi and Alabama, a $1.5 billion endeavor. Senator John Stennis of Mississippi, a member of the Senate for thirty years and chairman of the Appropriations Committee, hardly agreed with the presidential judgment and set out to reverse it. In doing so he used his seniority and position to gain access to the decision process in four different major ways. First, he appeared before the Mississippi state legislature and asked that they put up a symbolic amount of state money to support the project (the Mississippi legislature responded with $40 million; Alabama also contributed $30 million dollars, the two sums combined representing only a few percent of the federal contribution). Second, he talked to the president directly and told him how important Tenn-Tom was to him personally. He hardly needed to remind the president of his general importance as Appropriations Chairman to many administration plans and hopes. Third, he lined up mutual support with his fellow legislators whereby in exchange for their backing of Tenn-Tom he would back some of their threatened projects. Finally, he arranged for hearings in Columbus, Mississippi, a town in the heart of the area to be enriched by the federal largesse. A carefully orchestrated procession of local folks endorsed Tenn-Tom. Almost needless to say, Tenn-Tom was restored to the budget.[4]

A detailed study of rivers and harbors decisions involving Corps projects for twenty years (1947–1968) arrived at the conclusion that

---

4. Wendell Rawls, Jr., "Tenn-Tom and Senator Stennis," *New York Times Magazine* (May 8, 1977): 46.

Congress gave favored treatment to both the program and the budget of the Corps.[5] In return, the Corps made decisions that gave favored treatment to members of the public works committees of both the House and Senate and members of the public works subcommittees of the Appropriations committees in both houses. Within those groups the senior members from the majority party and particularly those on the appropriations subcommittees got the most favored treatment of all.

Protective Regulatory Policy: Strip Mining, 1975 [6]

A short history of federal strip-mining legislation was included in Chapter 8 and need not be repeated here. Basically, there was a ten-year struggle (from 1968 through 1977) to create a federal law in the field. At every point in the process, in accord with the expectations portrayed in Table 11–2, all of the actors got involved, but final decisions were not left to the nexus of bureaus, subcommittees, and private interests. Rather two general coalitions were formed—one supporting relatively restrictive federal legislation and one supporting either no legislation or, at worst, permissive legislation. Whichever coalition lost at the subcommittee level in Congress appealed to the full House and/or Senate. And during much of the controversy the president was also an important actor.

In 1974 President Ford pocket-vetoed a bill Congress passed. When the new Congress convened in early 1975—with a much increased Democratic majority as a result of the 1974 congressional elections—it appeared that passage of a bill similar to the 1974 bill would be relatively easy, even over a veto if necessary. In early 1975 the Ford Administration proposed eight specific changes in the 1974 bill that had been vetoed and indicated that these changes, if adopted by Congress, would make the bill acceptable to the President. The subcommittees writing the legislation acceded to parts of some of the administration requests but still reported bills to the two houses that were more restrictive than Ford wished. These bills were passed overwhelmingly in both houses—84–13 in the Senate and 333–86 in the House. Both margins were well over the two-thirds needed to override a veto.

However, beginning with the passage of the bills on the floor in March, 1975, a massive and well-coordinated lobbying campaign aimed at sustaining what promised to be a sure Ford veto was begun. There

---

5. Ferejohn, *Pork Barrel Politics.*
6. See *Congressional Quarterly Almanac, 1975*: 177–190.

were three major elements in the coalition: the coal industry, the utilities, and the president and his lobbyists. The administration and the coal industry used the line of argument that, because of overly severe restrictions, jobs would be lost in the coal mining industry if the bill were passed. The utilities relied primarily on the argument that they would be forced to raise prices to consumers because coal used to generate electricity would become more expensive. Ford also used personal ties with Republicans in the House from his days as minority leader to appeal for support.

This presidentially regulated interest lobby focused on the House floor. Some impact was observable by early May when the House passed the conference report 293 to 115, a considerably reduced margin from the initial passage in March. Then the payoff came after a presidential veto in late May. When the House sought to override the veto in early June, the effort failed 278 to 143. Critically, 24 Republicans who had voted aye on the conference report now voted with the president and the coal and utility positions. Thus, as indicated in Table 11–2, the critical relationship in arriving at a final decision on strip-mining legislation in 1975 was that between the presidency, Congress as a whole (specifically, the entire House), and the regulated interests (in this case, interests that would be regulated directly or affected indirectly in the future if the legislation were passed).

Redistributive Policy: Legal Services Corporation [7]

The Office of Economic Opportunity and the "War on Poverty" were created by statute in 1964. By the early 1970s it was evident that the war was over, not because it was won but because the political situation simply made its continuance either programmatically or organizationally highly unlikely. Thus those who supported the initial redistributive thrust of some of the poverty programs operated both by OEO and by other federal agencies had to look for ways in which to save residues of the effort.

One of the efforts to save a program that tended to be redistributive centered around the creation of a Legal Services Corporation for the poor. Congress first passed a bill in 1971 creating such an autonomous Corporation, but President Nixon vetoed it. A variety of discussions and legislative maneuvers took place in 1972 but no bill emerged. In 1973 Nixon sent a proposal to Congress for a Corporation along lines he would find acceptable. In 1973 and 1974 two coalitions of indi-

---

7. See *Congressional Quarterly Almanac, 1973*: 581–585; *Congressional Quarterly Almanac, 1974*: 498–495; and Ripley and Franklin, *Congress, the Bureaucracy, and Public Policy*: 125–126.

viduals and interests—one "liberal," the other "conservative"—formed around the question of how the Corporation shold be structured and what it should be allowed to do. In the conservative coalition were the President and members of his administration concerned with legal matters, a variety of members of both the House and Senate (not limited to the relevant committees and subcommittees), and conservative members of the legal profession. In the liberal coalition were liberal members of the House and Senate with allies from among the liberal segment of the legal profession. The American Bar Association, the most powerful group representing lawyers in the country, did not take an overall position although it reacted negatively to any specific provision it felt threatened to establish a "socialized legal system" for more than just the indigent.

Given the power of the presidential veto and the inability of the liberals in Congress to count on mustering enough votes to override a veto, a compromise was worked out between the president and Congress (with the passive blessing of the ABA) that sharply reduced the amount of redistribution represented by the new Corporation but did allow it to be created. Critically, at the last minute the conferees in Congress agreed to delete a provision in the bill providing for backup research centers. The liberals estimated this was essential to avoiding a veto and therefore the price that had to be paid for having a Legal Services Corporation at all.

The liberals also had to pay other prices to produce a bill Nixon would sign. They agreed to give the president the power to appoint all of the directors of the corporation (the lack of such a provision had been the reason for the 1971 veto). They severely restricted the political activities of corporation attorneys, even on their own time. Provisions were included prohibiting lawsuits aimed at desegregation or obtaining abortions for other than therapeutic reasons. Corporation lawyers were prohibited from becoming involved in either criminal cases or cases involving the Selective Service System.

Structural Foreign and Defense Policy: Reserve Forces [8]

Since World War II, questions concerning the size, status, and compensation for the reserve military forces of the United States have been decided by a classic subgovernment. Regular officers in the three military branches holding relevant bureaucratic positions, key members of the Armed Services Committees in the House and Senate, and

---

8. See William F. Levantrosser, *Congress and the Citizen-Soldier* (Columbus: Ohio State University Press, 1967).

Reserve Officers Association lobbyists have united on almost every issue. Their aims have been to create and retain a large reserve force and to pay reservists generously both with salary and with benefits. For more than thirty years now these aims have been achieved.

This policy can be considered as structural—or, in effect, the same as distributive—because the security of the country is not really at issue. What is at issue is the distribution of government largesse. Thus a self-serving subgovernment using the rhetoric of national security has been able to withstand occasional challenges by "outsiders" such as the Secretary of Defense. The Reserve Officers Association is particularly active in this instance. It initiates legislation and its representatives participate personally in committee decision-making sessions.

Strategic Foreign and Defense Policy: Turkish Military Aid [9]

In 1974–75 the long-standing feud between Cypriots of Greek extraction and those of Turkish extraction spilled over into decision-making in the strategic foreign and defense arena in the United States. The issue involved controversy and, ultimately, compromise between the president and secretary of state on the one hand and a variety of members of the House and Senate on the other hand. Interest groups representing Americans of Greek extraction also played a part in generating the issue and prolonging the negotiations that led to the final compromise.

In July, 1974, Turkey invaded Cyprus in support of what it felt was repression (and pending genocide) of the minority Turkish community on the island. The Turks were armed, in part, with weapons they had received through the military portion of the United States foreign aid program. This seemed to be in violation of United States law, which prohibits the use of such weapons for other than defensive purposes. Immediately, Greek-American organizations began calling for American action against the Turks (and there was no countervailing force in the form of Turkish-American organizations, because there are very few persons of Turkish extraction in the United States). In response to these pleas Congress made a decision to suspend military aid to Turkey. The president and other foreign policy officials opposed this decision, but to no avail in the first instance.

Elaborate parliamentary manuevering took place throughout the

---

9. See *Congressional Quarterly Almanac, 1975*: 327–331; and Ripley and Franklin, *Congress, the Bureaucracy, and Public Policy*: 156–158.

fall of 1974 and early 1975 that was aimed at arriving at an agreement that would allow Congress to appear to be responsive to its Greek-American constituents (and the law) and would also allow the administration to have the flexibility it felt necessary to deal with Turkey. Congress was ambivalent in its actions in late 1974 and through mid-1975. On the one hand, it wanted to preserve some latitude for the administration. On the other hand, it did not want to appear to be abdicating its role to the executive branch, despite executive claims that this was a matter involving strategic considerations of U.S. security, principally the good relations with NATO ally and militarily important Turkey. The Turks themselves entered the fray in mid-1975 by ordering American bases in Turkey closed in response to what they considered to be unwarranted American meddling in their affairs.

In October, 1975, the final symbolic compromise was reached that allowed all sides to escape the impasse without losing face. Congress agreed to a partial lifting of the arms embargo in order to give the president the weapon he needed to persuade the Turks not to make the base closings permanent. Reporting requirements on subsequent use of American weapons by the Turks and on the status of Greek-Turkish negotiations over Cyprus (including periodic certifications that "progress" was being made) were passed. With this compromise the issue receded from view, bases were reopened, and military aid resumed. Congress had flexed its muscles (or, more to the point, it had transferred the pressure it received from the Greek-American community) and had intruded into a strategic area (a common occurrence), but had hesitatingly and with some strings acquiesced to continued presidential insistence on a more flexible course of action.

Crisis: The Good Ship Mayaguez [10]

Despite the passage of the War Powers Act over presidential veto in late 1973, crisis situations in the international domain are still basically the province of the president and those few individuals he chooses to involve. Some of those individuals may be members of the House or Senate in any given case, but that is the decision of the president, not of the members themselves. The most visible crisis of a short-term (although probably relatively minor) character since the passage of the War Powers Act was the seizure of an American mer-

---

10. See *Congressional Quarterly Almanac, 1975:* 310–311; and Roy Rowan, *The Four Days of Mayaguez* (New York: Norton, 1975).

chant ship, the *Mayaguez,* by military forces of the government of Cambodia in May, 1975.

The major provisions of the War Powers Act are that the president must report combat commitments of U.S. troops overseas to Congress within forty-eight hours of such commitment. He must cease combat after sixty days unless Congress specifically approves continuation (although he is also given a thirty-day extension privilege if he feels American troops would be endangered by a more hasty withdrawal). And, in general, the Act provides that the president should "in every instance possible . . . consult with Congress" before taking steps that either involve or risk military hostilities.

Despite these provisions, when news of the seizure of the *Mayaguez* reached President Ford, he consulted with officials from the White House, State Department, and Defense Department before *informing* a few members of Congress of his decision to use force to recover the ship (the force involved U.S. Marine seizure of the ship and rescue of the crew from an island, coupled with Air Force bombing of selected targets on the Cambodian mainland). No *consultation* took place. Senator Mansfield, then majority leader of the Senate and a leading member of the Foreign Relations Committee, accurately described the procedure: "I was not consulted. I was notified after the fact about what the administration had already decided to do. . . . I did not give my approval or disapproval because the decision had already been made."

ACCESS AND THE INTERNAL DISTRIBUTION OF INFLUENCE

Congress strives to achieve two objectives: a responsiveness to national problems, and the maintenance of a central role in policy-making. The way influence is distributed in the House and Senate has a profound effect on the degree to which these goals can be met. Ideally, the internal distribution of influence should promote the following conditions, all of which are important to a strong congressional policy-making role: ready access for members to the most important points in the legislative process, efficient procedures that allow a relatively steady stream of output, and a moderately high degree of institutional stability.

These conditions in turn affect a set of values that influence congressional responsiveness to public needs; thoroughness, representativeness, and responsibility. *Thoroughness* is present in congressional actions if the major aspects of a problem are identified and appraised and the major alternative solutions to the problem are also identified and

appraised. *Representativeness* is present if the main contending interests are heard and weighed during the decision-making process. *Responsibility* is present if the agents who have the most influence in
making decisions are readily visible. Where responsibility is lacking,
arbitrary action is more likely to be invisible and undetected.

The distribution of influence in the House and Senate involves a
variety of traditions and units within the institution: party leaders,
committees, committee chairmen, prevailing norms, and socialization
patterns. It is the members of Congress as individuals that finally determine how Congress will operate. The distribution of influence is not
the result of any single individual's efforts; it is, however, affected by
the behavior and decisions of a variety of individuals. For example,
a committee chairman who takes an aggressive role in running his
committee or party leaders who work diligently to achieve party unity
on roll call voting help shape broader and longer lasting patterns of
influence distribution.

The distribution of influence in the House and Senate is subject
to varying degrees of centralization. In a centralized distribution control is exercised by influential and aggressive central party leaders
and committee chairmen who are loyal to those leaders and who have
considerable authority in their respective committees and use that authority to pursue outcomes desired by the leaders. Individual senators
and representatives are oriented toward their party and possess only
limited personal influence.

In a decentralized distribution party leaders are at most only moderately aggressive and influential, while standing committee chairmen
and subcommittee chairmen are largely independent from party leaders
and tend to be relatively influential in their own committees in pursuit
of outcomes defined with little concern for what the party leaders want.
Individual members, especially the more senior ones, are also influential within the specific committees and subcommittees on which they
sit.

A classic case of centralized distribution existed in the period during
the first few years of Woodrow Wilson's presidency (1913 and 1914).
The majority leaders in both houses—Oscar W. Underwood in the
House and John W. Kern in the Senate—guided their respective caucuses in making sure that the most important bills emerging from the
standing committees had their approval and the support of the majority of Democrats. Committee chairmen worked closely with these
leaders in shaping details of bills so that they would be true to the
general policy positions taken by the leaders and by the caucuses.
Individual members had their major policy impact through their participation in the party caucus, through loyal support of the positions

that emerged from the caucus, and through bills that came from the standing committees that were in accord with caucus directions.

In many ways a very strong pattern of decentralization was dominant in both houses during much of the 1940s and 1950s (with the partial exception of the two Republican-controlled Congresses in 1947–48 and 1953–54). Despite the presence of Sam Rayburn as Speaker of the House during the entire period and Lyndon Johnson as majority leader of the Senate during the latter part of the period only some committee chairmen were consistently concerned with the policy preferences of those energetic and resourceful leaders. In a way Rayburn and Johnson seemed so resourceful because they had to exercise considerable wile to have any substantive impact on the products that emerged from the standing committees. And, regularly, conservative-dominated committees ignored their preferences and produced legislation unacceptable to the leaders but—given the number of Republicans and conservative southern Democrats in Congress at the time—that often passed both in committee and on the floor.

A high degree of decentralization is probably the "natural" state of Congress in that the structure and norms of both houses seem to emphasize independent action on the part of individual members that often gets translated into support for "strong" committees and "weak" leaders. However, there is nothing inevitable about the dominance of decentralization. Some members argue that there is more genuine independence in working with aggressive central party leaders than in working more immediately under both the thumb and gaze of domineering committee or subcommittee chairmen. There is constant ferment in Congress about the proper ratio of powers that should be allocated to and exercised by party leaders, caucuses, and standing committees. Judging by the last seventy years it seems safest to predict that the forces favoring increased centralization will lose more than they will win; but it is not accurate to say that that has been a uniform outcome during the seventy years or that it will be a uniform outcome in the future.

Different values are served by differing distributions of influence. *Thoroughness* of consideration seems to be most likely at the decentralized end of the spectrum and least likely at the centralized end. As decentralization increases, more members of the House and Senate increase both their substantive expertise and their degree of specialization. This means that virtually all members of the Senate and most members of the House have the potential of becoming expert on some legislative matter. They are aided by a relatively large number of knowledgeable and independently important staff members. There is more chance that thorough examination will take place under such conditions than when the committees are merely doing the bidding of the party leaders, without independent contributions from individual members or staff members.

Representativeness of the greatest number of interests is also most likely to occur in a situation of decentralization of influence and least likely to occur in a situation in which influence is centralized. With influence highly fragmented many interests have a chance to ally themselves with a key subcommittee or individual senator or representative or staff member, and thus become effectively represented. In a highly centralized situation the interests that are close to the party leaders are represented, but competing interests may not be.

If *representativeness* is considered in a second sense, however—that of weighing competing interests—it may be facilitated more by a centralized distribution of influence than by a decentralized distribution. Since political parties have to agree to compromises between interests in order to attract broad electoral support, the centralized situation may lead to a weighing of competing interests before matters reach the Senate and House floors. Similarly, since an important subcommittee chairman does not necessarily have to weigh competing interests and because his judgment, in the form of a bill, usually passes on the floor, only one interest may dominate a specific, relatively small area of public policy. Perhaps, in the matter of representativeness, when both number of interests and the weighing of competing interests are considered responsiveness to national problems is best promoted by a situation in which the standing committees dominate their subcommittees, thus preventing the subcommittees from becoming autonomous satrapies.

Responsibility is most likely in a highly centralized situation and least likely in a highly decentralized one. In the former situation the party leader or leaders, along with the president, can be held responsible for what the Senate and House do legislatively. These leaders may be arbitrary, but the arbitrariness is highly visible. When decentralization is the norm, however, it is often impossible to assign responsibility in any meaningful sense.

In short, no single distribution of influence maximizes all of the values of *thoroughness, representativeness* in both senses, and *responsibility* simultaneously. High decentralization seems most likely to provide thorough consideration and action. High centralization seems most likely to provide responsible consideration and action. And some mid-point between the two extremes seems most likely to provide representative consideration and action.

Access and the Character of Relations with the Executive

The way Congress shapes its relations with the executive determines in large part not only how effective it will be in day-to-day duties, but also its effectiveness in policy-making in general and its responsiveness to broad public needs. A variety of factors help determine the level of cooperation between Congress and the president. These include: the party label of the president and majority parties in the House and the Senate; how leadership is defined by the president and congressional leaders; personal styles of the people in both institutions; the skill with which resources are used; and the willingness to compromise.

Relations with the Executive and Performance of Basic Congressional Functions

Alternative Institutional Goals for Congress. Congress is, of course, composed of a large and diverse group of individuals, and most of the time these individuals, alone and in groups, differ in their goals for Congress. It is possible, however, for a sizeable majority of the members to articulate and pursue (with varying degree of consciousness) broad institutional goals. Pursuit of these broad goals enables Congress to have specific kinds of impact on the substance of public policy.

Three alternative goals seem particularly relevant in affecting the substance of public policy. The first is to *maximize support for the substantive program of the president.* The second is to *maximize the independent influence of Congress on positive policy actions by the government.* The third is *to maximize ability of Congress to limit governmental innovation and to restrain the increase in governmental activity.*

Among the most articulate advocates of these three goals are James MacGregor Burns, who has written in support of maximum congressional support for the program of the president,[11] Theodore J. Lowi, who would like to see Congress exert its independent influence,[12] and

---

11. James MacGregor Burns, *Congress on Trial* (New York: Harper, 1949) and *The Deadlock of Democracy* (Englewood Cliffs, N.J.: Prentice-Hall, 1963).

12. Theodore J. Lowi, "Congressional Reform: A New Time, Place and Manner," in Lowi and Ripley (eds.), *Legislative Politics U.S.A.* (Boston: Little, Brown, 1973, 3rd ed.).

James Burnham, who has argued that Congress should take the lead in curtailing governmental activity.[13]

Most public debate on the proper role of Congress focuses on the conflict between the Burns position and the Burnham position, and the seeming radical contradiction between them. Little public attention has thus far been given the Lowi or "independent influence" position.

The Burns and Burnham positions do, to be sure, conflict. They are, as stated by their proponents, wedded to differing ideologies—the Burns position to a liberal ideology and the Burnham position to a conservative ideology. In an important sense both Burns and Burnham would make Congress dependent on adherence to rather rigid ideological considerations rather than promoting flexibility and adaptability in the institution. This dependent position for Congress would vary with changes in presidents and changes in the status quo within the bureaucracy. When Burns initially stated his position, for example, his ideal was congressional subservience to a strong, liberal Democrat as president. He would be unlikely to espouse similar subservience to Richard Nixon but would instead insist on continuing single-minded pursuit of outcomes in line with his own liberal ideology. When Burnham initially stated his position he could probably think comfortably of Congress working well with many of the bureaus and their programs in the executive branch because many of them were quite limited and conservative in their goals. Those that appeared too aggressive, large, or threatening to his conservative vision of government should be challenged by Congress until they too had adopted the proper perspective. During a period of relatively expansionist, liberal bureaucracy—such as that during the 1964–66 era—Burnham would no doubt favor a more assertive Congress seeking to impose its ideological vision on the executive branch.

Congressional Performance of Functions to Attain Different Goals. The way in which Congress performs its functions of lawmaking, oversight of administration, education of the public, and representation will help determine which goal or goals are in fact being sought. If, as is often the case, Congress consciously chooses no single goal and no single mode of performing its functions then bits and pieces of all three goals will in fact be pursued simultaneously.

To achieve maximum *support for the program of the president,* Congress should perform its lawmaking functioning by enacting whatever legislative proposals the president submits or supports. It should

---

13. James Burnham, *Congress and the American Tradition* (Chicago: Regnery, 1959).

perform its oversight function very generally, if at all, in the cases of agencies and programs that appear to have presidential approval. If, for example, the president seems satisfied with the activities of the Department of Defense, then the uncritical stance of a Mendel Rivers or of an F. Edward Hebert (recent chairmen of the House Armed Services Committee) is quite appropriate. The president may, however, be concerned about the activities of some of the agencies and programs theoretically under his control and might welcome careful congressional scrutiny to help him influence matters that otherwise might be independent of any real checks. In these cases the president can make clear to various congressional committees those programs and agencies that he wants overseen and Congress can assist him in this way.

Congress should perform its public education function by propagandizing in favor of presidential proposals before enactment and on behalf of presidential performance after enactment. It should perform its representation function by concentrating on narrow activities (casework for individuals and corporations and division of federal "goodies") in order to avoid conflict with the executive branch on broader questions—except in those few cases in which the president might view such conflict as beneficial to his program.

To achieve maximum *independent influence on positive policy positions,* Congress should perform its lawmaking function by including explicit standards for administering new programs in all legislation it enacts. Congress can demand that the executive branch include such standards in draft legislation, it can add such standards amending bills coming from the executive branch, and it can include them in bills initiated in Congress. Placing a termination date on all legislation would also help propel Congress toward the goal of maximum independent influence.

Congress should perform its oversight function by examining the role of specific federal agencies and programs in meeting or not meeting broad national needs. This form of oversight can uncover new areas and problems in which legislation is needed. Oversight to meet the goal of maximizing independent congressional impact should insist on rigorous adherence by executive branch agencies to the standards of performance included in the statutes authorizing the programs administered by those agencies. This form of oversight should also insist that agencies develop their own rigorous standards for evaluating performance and relative degrees of success or failure. Congressional committee members and staff members could themselves help in the development of such standards.

Congress should perform its public education function by selecting specific substantive areas in which efforts to stimulate public attention and support should be concentrated. Congress has little impact as a collectivity when it tries to educate the public on every side of every issue simultaneously. But if there is some genuine consensus, either bipartisan or at least on the part of the majority party in Congress, on which issues need special and constant attention, then Congress— through its most visible members—can educate at least the attentive part of the public.

Finally, Congress should perform its representation function by concentrating considerable attention on questions of national concern such as the total federal responsibility in relation to racial equality or environmental quality. For maximum impact such activity should be limited to only a few subject areas. If virtually every issue is claimed to involve matters of profound principle and the national good, the impact of the claim becomes diluted. Naturally, Congress would also continue the narrower kinds of representation (casework for individuals and corporations and division of federal largesse) and these are perfectly proper activities as long as they do not conflict with a focus on a limited number of broad-based proposals and questions reflecting the central problems of American society.

To achieve *limited governmental innovation and to restrain the increase in governmental activity,* Congress should perform its lawmaking function very sparingly, restricting the number of new laws enacted. Those that are enacted should contain "legislative veto" provisions guaranteeing continued tight congressional control. Similar provisions should be added to existing legislation. It should perform its oversight function by constantly involving itself in the details of the administration of all programs. Representative Edith Green's proprietary attitude toward some juvenile delinquency and education programs mentioned in Chapter 10 would become the model for congressional behavior. Given the seniority system there are always new proprietors in training when established ones leave Congress. Relationships with key bureaucrats and interest group representatives for purposes of maintaining the status quo in a wide range of programs should be cultivated and maintained.

Congress should perform its public education function by warning about asserted dangers of big government such as invasion of privacy or too much spending. Simultaneously, selective public education efforts should be undertaken to support existing specific programs (for example, coalitions might emerge to stress the benefits of existing cotton price supports, the Department of Defense relations with the aerospace industry or with specific companies within it, and the Appalachian development program). Finally, Congress should perform its *representation* function by concentrating exclusively on casework and the division of federal benefits.

Three central points should stand out following the discussion in this chapter. First, Congress has the capacity for being influential over policy decisions because it has generally good access to the processes by which decisions are made. Second, that access is not undifferentiated —it is predictably greater under some conditions and it is predictably less under other conditions. Third, Congress as an institution has considerable choice about how it chooses to use the access it undoubtedly has. Neither the institution nor the individual members are caught in a situation in which their behavior is simply determined by outside influences. They have considerable latitude for determining their own potential for impact on policy despite important pressures and constraints built into the normal way of doing business in both Congress and American government and society more broadly considered.

CHAPTER 12

———

CONGRESSIONAL IMPACT
ON POLICY

I N THE PREVIOUS CHAPTER WE SAW THAT, DESPITE THE FRAGMENTATION of the institution, Congress has a number of major points of access to policy decisions. The present chapter explores some aspects of how Congress uses that access. It first underscores the policy consequences of the dominance of fragmentation in Congress. Second, it covers briefly and with broad strokes the contemporary record of Congress in a number of major policy areas. Third, it looks at the popular standing of Congress as one measure of impact. Finally, it considers "reform"—both actual and proposed—and its relation to congressional impact.

THE CONSEQUENCES OF FRAGMENTATION

In Chapter 1 the general consequences of fragmentation and of integration in Congress were spelled out. In subsequent chapters Congress has emerged as an institution that is usually more fragmented than integrated. The various consequences of that state of affairs have been portrayed in some detail in this volume. Here it seems useful to summarize the three major consequences that have been observed, because they have a great deal to do with the nature of congressional impact on public policy.

The first major consequence of fragmentation is stable policy. That simply means that significant changes in ongoing policies and programs are difficult to achieve. The structure of Congress itself leads to the expectation that only small changes will occur in policies at any given time. Congress is imbedded in a policy system that most of the time is weighted toward some close variant of the existing situation.

This situation should not be overstated or misunderstood. It does not mean that all policy is "conservative" in the sense of favoring only economically privileged interests. It is conservative in the sense of favoring entrenched interests regardless of their economic or social status. Thus if less privileged interests measured in terms of economic and social status become entrenched, as they sometimes do, then the conservatism of the system also serves to protect them from change. For example, labor unions, which at least initially represented some less well off people, have a protected position in much legislation that would be difficult to change quickly. However, it is hardly surprising that the more privileged elements in society also tend to be more entrenched.

Nor does this "normal" situation mean that Congress is powerless. It is, after all, a mark of considerable power that Congress can much of the time play a pivotal role in helping prevent major change, even when there are strong forces pushing for that change.

Finally, the "normal" situation is neither universal nor inevitable. In the next section we will review briefly some of the substantive impacts of Congress on policy in the last several decades. In some areas, usually where some elements of centralization have been present at least temporarily, Congress has been innovative and has promoted substantial policy change.

A second major consequence of a high degree of fragmentation is that most domestic policy is either initially defined as distributive or, even if the initial definition places it in some other category, it is re- defined over time as distributive. There is a parallel trend with foreign and defense policy that leads to some considerable straining to view policies as structural rather than strategic (the crisis category is not as malleable and a crisis, when it happens, is usually perceived as such by everyone involved). Thus we have seen that some policies that started life as redistributive, such as Model Cities, have become rede- fined as distributive. Successful protective regulatory initiatives, such as that on strip-mining, are weakened during the course of passage. Other protective regulatory initiatives—such as land use legislation or consumer protection legislation—have very long gestation periods that may, given the absence of results so far, turn out to be false preg- nancies. The major congressional action that transformed potentially redistributive programs into much more distributive programs was the move in the 1970s to both general and special revenue sharing and block grant programs.

A third major consequence of fragmentation in Congress is that there is only minimal and sporadic concern with overseeing bureau- cratic performance. In those policy areas (the majority) in which subgovernments are dominant, "oversight" simply means talking with like-minded people in the bureaucracy on a routine basis to make sure that no major deviations are occurring in policies and programs that the members of the subgovernment have long since ratified. Simultaneously, the members of the subgovernment worry about the possible intrusion of outsiders such as the president or central bureaucracy or a party leader in Congress or a public interest group. They seek to prevent or offset such intrusions. When such activities are the focus of interaction between Congress and the bureaucracy, oversight in the sense of monitoring or evaluation of government programs is obviously beside the point.

THE CONTEMPORARY POLICY RECORD

In Chapter 1 four models of congressional involvement in policy-making were presented: executive dominance, joint program development, congressional dominance, and stalemate. Table 1–3 summarized those models comparatively. In this section congressional action in a number of (but not all) major policy areas over the last few decades will be reviewed in summary fashion. This review will serve two purposes. First, it will be aimed at giving a general sense of the applicability of different models to different policy areas at different times. Second, it will provide additional concrete examples (to be added to those scattered throughout the book) of the substantive content of congressional policy activity over the last few decades in selected major fields.

Economic Policy [1]

Congress is heavily involved in policy and program decisions affecting the domestic economy, the usual model being that of joint program development, whether the specific programs concern appropriations, taxation, or management of the public debt.

Despite its important role in individual programs, it is virtually impossible for Congress to develop and implement an overall economic policy of its own. Almost inevitably this task must fall to the president

---

1. See Ralph K. Huitt, "Congressional Organization and Operations in the Field of Money and Credit," in Commission on Money and Credit, *Fiscal and Debt Management Policies* (Englewood Cliffs, N.J.: Prentice-Hall, 1963): 399–495; and Harvey C. Mansfield, "The Congress and Economic Policy," in David B. Truman (ed.), *The Congress and America's Future* (Englewood Cliffs, N.J.: Prentice-Hall, 1965): 121–149.

and his top advisers, who set general economic goals and strategies in the annual budget message and economic report and monitor performance in light of those goals on a continual basis.

Congress also contributes to the more general debate through the work of two joint committees: the Joint Economic Committee and the Joint Committee on Internal Revenue Taxation. But these committees cannot perform a consolidating function in lieu of presidential activity. As one student of this policy area has concluded:

> The experience of the Joint Economic Committee testifies that it is possible to organize a unit in Congress that can open up national perspectives on the economy and draw on the most advanced techniques of economic analysis to make prescriptions. But it is not conceivable that the JEC could acquire the power to enact them; it is a teacher, not a governor.
>
> The experience of the Joint Committee on Internal Revenue Taxation testifies that it is possible to organize a unit in Congress sufficiently powerful to control the use of the taxing power. But it is not conceivable that the taxing committees, in doing so, will apply the prescriptions, or even adopt the perspectives of the JEC.[2]

A specific example of an economic policy issue that moved from a stalemate model to joint program development model is provided by what became the Area Redevelopment Act.[3] In the 1950s Senator Paul Douglas, an Illinois Democrat, began to build a coalition in favor of giving special federal aid to economically depressed areas of the country. Gradually that coalition became a majority in Congress, and Douglas' bill passed. President Eisenhower, however, vetoed the bill containing the program and Congress did not override the veto (stalemate). When a Democrat became president the new administration and the congressional supporters reached agreement on details and the bill passed (joint development). After the administrators of the original program had committed some fatal blunders a new liaison effort between congressional supporters and the executive branch produced a revised program and a renamed agency (joint development).

An example of an economic measure that began with congressional initiative and then became a matter of joint development is provided

2. Mansfield, "The Congress and Economic Policy," 148.

3. See Ripley, *The Politics of Economic and Human Resource Development:* Chapter 2; Roger Davidson, *Coalition-Building for Depressed Area Bills: 1955–1965,* Inter-University Case Program no. 103 (Indianapolis: Bobbs-Merrill, 1966); and Sar A. Levitan, *Federal Aid to Depressed Areas* (Baltimore: Johns Hopkins, 1964).

by the Humphrey-Hawkins full employment bill (named for Senator Hubert H. Humphrey, Minnesota Democrat, and Representative Augustus F. Hawkins, California Democrat, its primary sponsors). The bill was introduced in 1974 and called for mandatory measures to reduce unemployment to 3 percent within eighteen months. The bill made no headway while Republicans Nixon and Ford were still president. However, in late 1977 President Carter worked out a compromise with congressional sponsors and they jointly endorsed a new version that set a 4 percent unemployment goal within five years. The compromise bill authorized new programs but did not require their use in reaching the goal. As watered down, it seems likely that the bill will be merely symbolic and have little programmatic reality. Thus joint development also helped produce a general statement of aspirations that may or may not bear fruit.

Human Resource Development Policy [4]

In the 1960s and 1970s the federal government became increasingly involved in efforts to alleviate the effects of poverty and to develop human resources. This involvement has taken many different specific forms. Some of the programs have been generated in a fashion much like the model of executive dominance. This was true of the development and passage of the Economic Opportunity Act of 1964 as well as the Model Cities program. Other parts of the specific programs, however, were generated in accord with a joint policy development model. The Appalachia program of 1964 is an example of such development. It also involved state and local officials as initiators.

But even in programs like EOA and Model Cities, in which the immediate initiative clearly came from the executive branch, there had been a prior history of at least sporadic (and unsuccessful) congressional initiative. For very different reasons, for example, both liberal and conservative critics of urban renewal had laid some of the groundwork for the Model Cities program. Likewise, Democrats in the 1950s had taken a variety of initiatives—for a Youth Conservation Corps, for example—that were absorbed by the executive branch in its fashioning of the Economic Opportunity Act.

In the Nixon-Ford years, stalemate on most aspects of human re-

---

4. See Ripley, *Politics of Economic and Human Resource Development,* Sar A. Levitan, *The Great Society's Poor Law* (Baltimore: Johns Hopkins, 1969); Sar. A. Levitan and Robert Taggart, *The Promise of Greatness* (Cambridge, Mass.: Harvard University Press, 1976); and Robert D. Plotnick and Felicity Skidmore, *Progress against Poverty: A Review of the 1964–1974 Decade* (New York: Academic Press, 1975).

source development policy developed, for the simple reason that the Republican presidents and the large majority of the Democrats in Congress disagreed about what was needed. The compromises that were reached were primarily in the form of parceling out monies for human resource development activities to states and localities. Presidents Nixon and Ford and congressional Republicans liked this solution because it was in accord with their general ideological preference for less federal government and more state and local autonomy. Congressional Democrats went along because it was the principal way to save some large chunks of tax revenue for use in human resource development activities, given the power of the presidential veto to thwart most of their initiatives.

Urban Problems

Congressional involvement has been critical to the successful establishment of programs in many urban problem areas, including air and water pollution control, juvenile delinquency, food stamps, aid to airports and to mass transit. The conclusion of a number of case studies of congressional impact in these areas was that in all except juvenile delinquency "Congress provided the leadership, the continuity, the persistence in formulating new policies and programs and guiding them through the political thicket of the legislative process to final decision." [5] Individuals from interest groups and the executive branch assisted in some of these initiatives but in other cases the executive branch was characterized by division and uncertainty. In a few cases the executive branch actively opposed the initiatives coming from Congress.

It should be underlined that the period covered included both the last half of the Eisenhower administration and the first term of Kennedy and Johnson. Thus the pattern that is found in this area cannot be attributed to the political differences between Eisenhower and a Democratic Congress. Congress often had to push the Democratic administration as well as the Republican administration.

In assessing the case studies in these areas only juvenile delinquency comes close to fitting the model of executive dominance. There was also an abortive effort to establish an Urban Affairs Department in 1961 and 1962 that fits the stalemate model. Food stamps, aid to airports and to mass transit best fit the model of joint program develop-

---

5. Frederic N. Cleaveland and associates, *Congress and Urban Problems* (Washington: Brookings, 1969): 355.

ment. Air and water pollution fit rather closely the model of congressional dominance.

As with human resource development policy, stalemate developed during the Nixon-Ford years between the president and Congress on many urban problems. For example, Nixon became increasingly hostile to a number of programs in the housing field initiated by Democrats over the years, and finally in 1973 he suspended virtually all of them. The best response that Congress could make was to compromise with him in producing the Housing and Community Development Act of 1974, which got around the stalemate problem by transferring most of the money and authority in the community development field to states and localities through a block grant program. In 1977, with a Democrat again in the White House, there were signs that the President and Congress would resume a joint development activity in the field of housing akin to that in the Kennedy-Johnson years.

"Urban policy," like "human resource development policy" or "science policy" or "foreign policy" or any other large-scale substantive category for policy is, of course, an artificial construct. "Urban policy" or any other broad policy is really an aggregate of many specific individual policies and programs. Thus, in some ways, the much publicized quest of the Carter administration in 1977 and 1978 to establish an "urban policy" was doomed to be fruitless, except at the symbolic level. Joint development of specific urban policies and programs with important congressional participation was a much more realistic hope.

Educational Policy

Between World War II and the present, Congress has enacted a great number of education laws. There is a popular misconception that, until the major educational legislation of the Johnson administration in the mid-1960s, which was impressive in both scope and magnitude, all federal aid to education proposals had been stalemated. This is true of general aid to elementary and secondary education but is untrue in other fields. In the pre-1965 period, for example, the federal government provided aid to higher education through various "G.I. bills" for ex-servicemen, subsidies for college dorms, and the National Defense Education Act. Elementary and secondary education also received aid from the NDEA as well as from an extensive program of aid to school districts that were considered to be "federally impacted" because the proximity of large federal installations increased the school age population. These various measures emerged in large part on the basis of the joint program development model. The major Johnson accomplishments—particularly the Elementary and Secondary Education Act of 1965—were also developed jointly.[6]

Science Policy [7]

As already indicated, science policy is really a collection of discrete policies. In the post-World War II period Congress has been sporadically important in some scientific areas. Some specific policies, as in the field of atomic energy, have been the product of joint development. Other policies and programs have essentially been executive branch programs in which there has been congressional input. The creation of the National Science Foundation serves as a good example here.

Examples of congressional leadership, sometimes verging on dominance, are afforded by some specific areas of health research and the space program.

Perhaps it is most accurate to say that science policy in some senses could be dominated by the executive in principle but in practice congressional input has been and is likely to be very important from time to time. The reasons for this are least threefold: the president is not always well staffed to deal with science policy across the board; Congress has some pockets of genuine staff expertise in scientific areas (and the Office of Technology Assessment is supposed to give Congress additional strength); and even where congressional expertise is lacking, members of Congress will not usually think of "science policy" as something either separate or sacred. Thus, if "science policy" has to do with the location of a costly government facility, such as an accelerator for atomic particles, members are likely to see the decision as another locational-distributive issue, not as a matter involving the treatment and development of something abstract called "science."

Energy Policy

Before the "energy crisis" of the early 1970s there seemed only occasional realization by anyone in either the executive branch or Congress that there should be some overall plans for coping with what, in retrospect, was an inevitable shortage of at least some forms of energy, especially that based on petroleum products.

---

6. See Eugene Eidenberg and Roy D. Morey, *An Act of Congress* (New York: Norton, 1969).
7. Sanford A. Lakoff, "Congress and National Science Policy," *Political Science Quarterly* 89 (1974): 589–611.

Once the realization broke on the country in the form of closed gas stations, a lowered speed-limit, soaring energy prices, and closed, unheated schools and factories, there was a flurry of activity in the executive branch and in Congress to deal with the problems.

By late 1977 no comprehensive energy policy had emerged. Presidents Nixon, Ford, and Carter had all made proposals (quite different from each other) and various individuals and committees in Congress also made proposals. There were certainly disagreements among various proposals from all sources and there were also congressional-presidential disagreements of a major character. But the whole period of ferment, despite its confused nature, can best be characterized as joint policy development. The jointness of the work does not, of course, mean that a coherent single policy will emerge. What it does mean is that the final package—no matter what its content—will bear both presidential and congressional imprints.

One of the most interesting institutional developments during the course of the debate over energy policy occurred in 1975 and showed what Congress could do when it proceeded in a more integrated fashion than usual. After President Ford proposed a comprehensive energy and economic recovery program in early 1975, the Democratic leaders in Congress decided that they would like to respond with their own program. The mechanisms for preparing such a response were not readily available; a number of committees in both houses were responsible for various aspects of energy policy. Thus both Speaker Albert and Senate Majority Leader Mansfield improvised. Albert had appointed a task force of the Democratic Steering and Policy Committee to design a Democratic economic program before the president's state of the union message containing his proposals. Albert announced the Democratic plan just before Ford's speech and then sent its pieces to a number of standing committees with instructions to report back within ninety days.

Mansfield appointed an ad hoc subcommittee of the Democratic Policy Committee to respond to Ford's proposals. The staff of the policy committee worked with other knowledgeable staff from the standing committees in developing specific proposals. At the same time Albert asked the task force that had already produced a Democratic economic proposal to undertake to respond to the president in the energy area too.

The president's speech had come in mid-January. By mid-February the two Democratic task forces began to meet jointly to look for common ground on which they could fashion a comprehensive Democratic proposal. They reached such agreement and confronted the president directly with their alternatives. In the end no comprehensive policy emerged at all, because of continuing disagreement between Ford and the Democratic leaders in Congress. The Democrats did, however, use their unity to force Ford to cancel one tariff increase on oil.[8]

Foreign Policy

One of the most common generalizations in both scholarly and popular literature on Congress is that the executive branch, especially the president, has completely overshadowed Congress in foreign policy matters and that the president takes all major initiatives in foreign affairs without any opposition.[9] Like most generalizations, this one fails to portray a complicated relationship very accurately.

In many ways the model of executive dominance may well have described a period from roughly 1955 to roughly 1965.[10] Before the mid-1950s Congress was heavily involved in the post-World War II foreign policy initiatives of the United States: the United Nations, the Marshall Plan and other foreign aid, and NATO. Members of the House and Senate were involved in the early planning of these initiatives and consideration of them by Congress was comprehensive. In recent years Congress has again become more assertive—particularly in reaction to Vietnam and the power of the president to wage an undeclared war—but also on other questions, such as foreign aid. For approximately ten years Congress did not raise major objections to the expansion of presidential influence. Congress was willing to pass resolutions that gave the president virtually a unilateral right to use American troops almost anywhere in the world if he deemed such action to be wise and in the national interest. The last resolution of this sort was

---

8. On the 1975 congressional initiatives in the energy field see John G. Stewart, "Central Policy Organs in Congress," in Harvey C. Mansfield, Sr. (ed.), *Congress against the President* (New York: Academy of Political Science, 1975): 21–22.

9. For statements of this position see Aaron Wildavsky, "The Two Presidencies," in Wildavsky (ed.), *The Presidency* (Boston, Little, Brown, 1969): 230–243; and James A. Robinson, *Congress and Foreign Policy-Making* (Homewood, Illinois: Dorsey, 1967, revised ed.).

10. For material supporting this thesis that congressional impotence in foreign affairs was mainly limited to one identifiable period of time in the late 1950s and early 1960s see Ronald C. Moe and Steven C. Teel, "Congress as Policy-Maker: A Necessary Reappraisal," in Moe (ed.), *Congress and the President* (New York: Goodyear, 1971); John F. Manley, "The Rise of Congress in Foreign Policy-Making," *Annals of the American Academy of Political and Social Science* 337 (1971): 60–70; Holbert N. Carroll, *The House of Representatives and Foreign Affairs* (Boston: Little, Brown, 1966); and Edward A. Kolodziej, "Congress and Foreign Policy: The Nixon Years," in Mansfield (ed.), *Congress against the President*: 167–179.

the now-repealed Gulf of Tonkin Resolution passed in 1964. Even in this period of congressional passivity, however, Congress had major influence in the creation of the Development Loan Fund in 1957 and the International Development Association in 1958.[11] These were new facets of the foreign aid program stressing loans and grants to underdeveloped nations for economic purposes only.

It is true that presidential influence on roll call voting in Congress is stronger in the area of "international involvement" than in any other. In fact, in four other areas: government management, social welfare, agricultural assistance, and civil liberties, his influence on roll call voting is virtually absent.[12]

A study concluding that the president predominates on foreign policy also reported a number of cases in which congressional influence was predominant and a few cases in which the initiative was congressional (six of twenty-two cases were found to have been initiated by Congress).[13] An even stronger position is taken in another study, based on a survey of a large number of cases. In many areas congressional participation was noted to be vigorous, although not dominant. This was true as regards the role of the Senate in treaty-making (the Japanese Peace Treaty of 1952, the North Atlantic Treaty, and the United Nations Charter are cited as examples) and the role of the House Appropriations Committee in a number of foreign policy areas. In addition, Congress was found to dominate "many areas of foreign policy which in themselves appear to be peripheral. Collectively, however, they constitute a major portion of U.S. foreign policy. For example, Congress is generally credited with dominant influence over decisions on economic aid policy, military assistance, agricultural surplus disposal, and the locations of facilities, to name only a few. In addition, immigration and tariff policies are generally considered part of foreign policy and there is considerable evidence to indicate that Congress remains a major actor in these fields." [14]

Congress became noticeably more aggressive and self-assertive on foreign policy matters during the Nixon and Ford years. This self-assertiveness continued into the Carter presidency and thus cannot be dismissed as mere Democratic-Republican hostility. Congress still

---

11. See David A. Baldwin, "Congressional Initiative in Foreign Policy," *Journal of Politics* 28 (1966): 754–773.
12. For an analysis of these patterns of presidential influence on voting on the five dimensions see Aage R. Clausen, *How Congressmen Decide* (New York: St. Martin's, 1973), especially Chapter 8.
13. Robinson, *Congress and Foreign Policy-Making*: 65.
14. Moe and Teel, "Congress as Policy-Maker," 49.

helped shape important parts of foreign aid policy, for example. The Senate took center stage in 1977 as it began to work toward exercising its constitutionally granted power to ratify or reject the Panama Canal treaties that had been negotiated and endorsed by the President. Congress also played an important role in slowing President Carter's attempt to be less automatic in support of Israel than previous presidents.

A balanced conclusion about the relative positions of the president and Congress in foreign policy-making must recognize that the participants have different capabilities that enable each to perform some things better than the other. The president has some natural advantages that allow him to dominate certain aspects of foreign policy. For example, his greater degree of mobility and his superior information sources are assets in diplomacy. Imagine, for instance, the likelihood of the multi-headed Congress arranging and successfully executing a re-opening of ties with China, an accomplishment that President Nixon and his foreign advisor, Henry Kissinger, managed with apparent ease in 1972. The enormous press coverage inherent in such foreign policy coups as the China thaw lends a great deal of support to the misconception of the president's ability to dominate all foreign affairs.

Foreign policy spectaculars such as the resumption of contact with China are rare events. Much policy-making in foreign affairs is without glamor and may receive little or no press coverage, which results in low public visibility, but it is no less important to the total foreign policy picture. And it is generally in these less visible areas that congressional involvement is likely to be high. For example, work on the details of trade policy, foreign aid, and immigration policy, though slow and tedious, is important to shaping overall U.S. policy toward much of the world. And Congress has considerable influence in these fields.

Defense Policy

Congress is often written off entirely in the defense field. But closer analysis reveals substantial congressional impact. As in the case of foreign policy a facile generalization about the total power of the executive is not accurate.

On the one hand, there is good evidence that particularly in the late 1950s and early 1960s individual members did not consider the broad aspects of defense policy when they were called on to make decisions about that policy. For example, the Armed Services Committees often were more concerned about "real estate" decisions (the location or closing of military facilities) than about defense policy writ large. Members in general felt technically incompetent to challenge the judgment of military personnel.[15] And, at the institutional level, it is true that Congress does not usually make major cuts in the overall defense budget proposed by the president.[16]

But a closer look at defense budgets in the 1960s shows that congressional impact was substantial. The key to understanding the nature of congressional impact is to disaggregate the budget into its component parts.[17] Although congressional impact on the overall budget figures for the Department of Defense appears to be limited, when the budget is split into four categories [18]—personnel; operations and maintenance; procurement; and research, development, testing, and evaluation—a more precise view of congressional impact is evident. Congress makes only small changes in the areas of personnel and operations and maintenance, and these areas account for over half of the budget. There is considerable congressional activity in the areas of procurement and research, development, testing, and evaluation. Table 12–1 summarizes the average congressional change in the president's budget by category for the eleven years between 1960 and 1970. The distinction between the two no-change categories and two substantial change categories becomes clear in this table.

A careful analysis of congressional action on the defense budget also supports the proposition that Congress was relatively acquiescent in

Table 12–1

Average (Mean) Congressional Change in the President's
Defense Budget, 1960–1970.

	Mean Change (%)
Total Department of Defense Budget	2.3
Personnel	1.1
Operations and Maintenance	1.2
Procurement	4.4
Research, Development,Testing and Evaluation	4.5

Source: Adapted from Arnold Kanter, "Congress and the Defense Budget: 1960–1970," American Political Science Review 66 (1972): 134.

---

15. Lewis A. Dexter, "Congressmen and the Making of Military Policy," in Raymond E. Wolfinger (ed.), *Readings on Congress*: 371–387.

16. See Douglas M. Fox, "Congress and U.S. Military Service Budgets in the Post-War Period: A Research Note," *Midwest Journal of Political Science* 15 (1971): 382–393.

17. What follows is drawn from Arnold Kanter, "Congress and the Defense Budget: 1960–1970," *American Political Science Review* 66 (1972): 129–143.

18. Construction is not included in the categories.

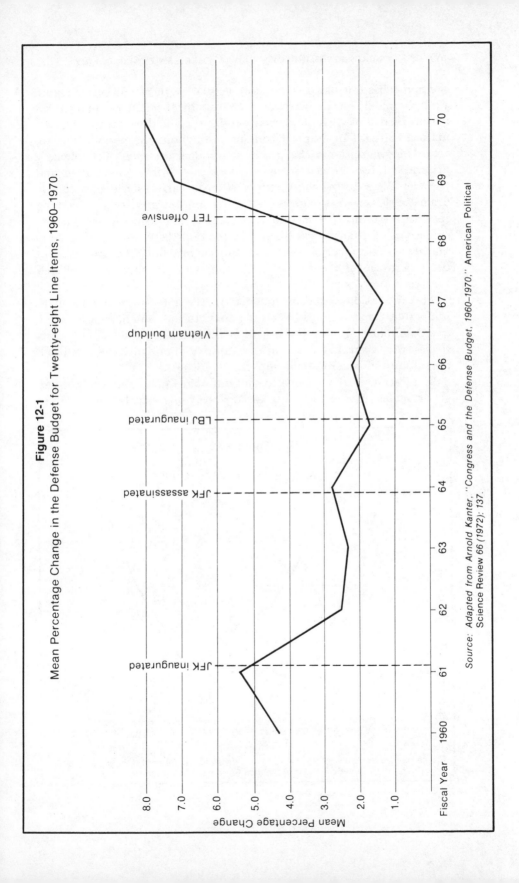

Figure 12-1

Mean Percentage Change in the Defense Budget for Twenty-eight Line Items, 1960–1970.

Source: Adapted from Arnold Kanter, "Congress and the Defense Budget, 1960–1970," American Political Science Review 66 (1972): 137.

the mid-1960s but has become more aggressive in recent years. Figure 12–1 shows the mean percentage change in the defense budget between 1960 and 1970 for twenty-eight specific line items that remained constant in terms of content throughout the period. The increase of congressional changes in the budget after the Tet offensive (a series of coordinated surprise attacks by North Vietnamese and the Viet Cong during the Vietnam War) in early 1968 is particularly dramatic. Likewise, Congress was much more aggressive in changing specific line items in 1969 and 1970 than it had been earlier. The incidence of no changes was highest in the mid-1960s. Figure 12–2 summarizes the distribution of change/no change outcomes in terms of the percentage of the twenty-eight line items that Congress altered each year.

This discussion of defense budgets in the 1960s does not mean to imply that Congress makes defense policy. In fact, the model of executive dominance applies to the field as a whole. But the example does suggest that even in a situation of executive dominance there is room for substantial congressional impact.

In addition to the systematic congressional impact on defense budgets revealed in the foregoing discussion, Congress also makes indi-

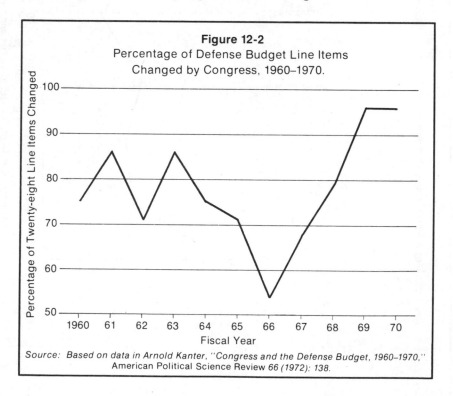

Figure 12-2
Percentage of Defense Budget Line Items
Changed by Congress, 1960–1970.

Source: Based on data in Arnold Kanter, "Congress and the Defense Budget, 1960–1970," American Political Science Review 66 (1972): 138.

vidual budget decisions about major defense items that are important. In recent years the most publicized was the decision by Congress in 1977 to go along with the scuttling of the proposed B-1 bomber announced by President Carter. This ended many years of struggle at least temporarily. Whether Congress would have voted negatively on this major new weapons system had President Carter decided to promote it is, of course, an open question. In a sense, however, Congress helped determine the ultimate outcome by stalling long enough to prevent President Ford from making the final decision (his administration firmly supported continued development and production of the B-1) and leaving the decision to Carter instead. A critical House vote shortly after Carter's announcement narrowly sided with the cancellation.[19]

The War Powers Act

A special instance of both foreign and defense policy was the passage of the War Powers Act over a Nixon veto in late 1973. At the time it was heralded as a major preventative against U.S. involvement in another situation like Vietnam. Looked at from the perspective of five years later, it appears to be primarily a symbol of congressional insistence that Congress has the ultimate power to declare war coupled with acquiescence to the practical realities of the modern world that suggests that a president may sometimes have to use force and commit troops without the opportunity for congressional action or even consultation with members of Congress.

There has been a great deal of constitutional and theoretical debate about the meaning of the Act. Perhaps more important, there has now been some experience with relatively small crises that show the vagueness of the statute and the power of the president to interpret the law as he sees fit. In a speech in April, 1977, former President Ford voiced his opposition to the Act and also discussed his experiences as president.[20] He identified six events during his presidency that might have come under the provisions of the War Powers Act: the evacuation of U.S. citizens from three locations in Indo-China in the spring of 1975; the rescue of the Mayaguez in May, 1975; and two evacuation operations in Lebanon in June, 1976. Ford asserted he did not believe the Act applied to any of these cases. Some congressional critics had thought otherwise at the time. But, in fact, as events unfold rapidly, the president clearly has the upper hand on what he does and does

19. Nicholas Wade, "Battle of the B-1 Bomber," Washington *Post,* July 31, 1977.
20. Gerald R. Ford, "The War Powers Resolution," speech delivered April 11, 1977, at the University of Kentucky and published by the American Enterprise Institute (Washington, D.C., 1977) as Reprint No. 69.

not do. Congressional criticism can be forthcoming afterward, and a president may pay a political price in terms of loss of support in Congress for differences of opinion. But there is very little Congress can do in the short run if the president and the majority opinion in Congress differ on the applicability of the Act in any given situation.

Ford also made it clear that even the consultation provisions in the Act (which simply urge consultation of congressional leaders by the President) were difficult to implement:

> Once the consultation process began, the inherent weakness of the War Powers Resolution from a practical standpoint was conclusively demonstrated.
>
> When the evacuation of DaNang [in South Vietnam] was forced upon us during the Congress's Easter recess, not one of the key bipartisan leaders of the Congress was in Washington.
>
> Without mentioning names, here is where we found the leaders of Congress: two were in Mexico, three were in Greece, one was in the Middle East, one was in Europe, and two were in the People's Republic of China. The rest we found in twelve widely scattered states of the Union.
>
> This, one might say, is an unfair example, since the Congress was in recess. But it must be remembered that critical world events, especially military operations, seldom wait for the Congress to meet. In fact, most of what goes on in the world happens in the middle of the night, Washington time.
>
> On June 18, 1976, we began the first evacuation of American citizens from the civil war in Lebanon. The Congress was not in recess, but it had adjourned for the day.
>
> As telephone calls were made, we discovered, among other things, that one member of Congress had an unlisted number which his press secretary refused to divulge. After trying and failing to reach another member of Congress, we were told by his assistant that the congressman did not need to be reached.
>
> We tried so hard to reach a third member of Congress that our resourceful White House operators had the local police leave a note on the congressman's beach cottage door: "Please call the White House."

Perhaps the most accurate conclusion about the War Powers Act—although hardly comforting—is that it remains an unclear and probably ineffective congressional attempt to control warmaking powers. Needless to say, there are no automatic formulas, given modern technology that allows mass destruction to be ordered and occur within minutes, that can preserve congressional power in all contingencies.

THE POPULAR STANDING OF CONGRESS:
ONE MEASURE OF IMPACT

When asked, people usually have an opinion about Congress. However, it is fair to say that often that opinion is not deeply held, because much of the time Congress is simply not salient to a lot of people.[21] There is not a great deal of news about Congress contained in most newspapers or on television news. This is especially true when one compares news about the president to news about Congress. Congress is an extremely complex institution (as readers of this volume should know by now!) and coverage of more than the most superficial aspects of it is rare in anything read or heard by the general public. The many-headedness of Congress militates against clear coverage.[22]

Regardless of the saliency of Congress, especially compared to the president, it is important to note that public opinion about congressional performance fluctuates a great deal. For example, between 1963 and 1977 both the Gallup and Harris organizations asked a sample of the general public almost every year (and several times in some years) about the kind of job Congress was doing.[23] During those years the favorable responses varied from a low of 21 percent (in early 1974) to a high of 64 percent (in late 1965). The unfavorable responses varied from a high of 69 percent to a low of 26 percent (the same two dates). Somewhere between 7 percent and 23 percent had no opinion, a substantial figure by public opinion poll standards (and a figure that offers some confirmation of the point about the relatively low salience of Congress for a number of people).

---

21. See Glenn R. Parker, "A Note on the Impact and Saliency of Congress," *American Politics Quarterly* 4 (1976): 413–421.

22. In addition to the Parker article just cited see Robert O. Blanchard (ed.), *Congress and the News Media* (New York: Hastings House, 1974); and Max M. Kampelman, "Congress, the Media, and the President," in Mansfield (ed.), *Congress against the President*: 85–97.

23. The Harris questions were worded: "How would you rate the job Congress is doing this year—excellent, pretty good, only fair, or poor?" The Gallup questions allowed only two choices: "Do you approve or disapprove of the way the U.S. Congress is handling its job?" In the text the term "favorable responses" refers to excellent and pretty good ratings combined in the Harris surveys and to answers of "approve" in the Gallup surveys. "The term "unfavorable responses" refers to fair and poor ratings combined in the Harris surveys and to answers of "disapprove" in the Gallup surveys. Both also had a residual category for people who did not have an opinion or were not sure. The percentage in that category was usually higher in the Gallup results than in the Harris results.

For a summary of Harris and Gallup data on congressional popularity since 1939 see Glenn R. Parker, "Some Themes in Congressional Unpopularity," *American Journal of Political Science* 21 (1977): 93–109.

Earlier figures from Gallup for scattered years between 1939 and 1958 suggest variation similar to that observed in the post-1963 data.

A poll taken just before the 1977 off-year elections by the New York *Times* and CBS News produced some interesting results. When asked, "Do you approve of the way Congress is handling its job?" 31 percent of a national sample said yes and 50 percent said no. When asked the same question about President Carter, 55 percent said yes and 27 percent said no. However, their evaluations of the two institutions—Congress and the presidency—were not uniformly skewed in favor of the president. On the question of honesty there was certainly strong preference for the president: 58 percent thought the president more honest than Congress while only 16 percent thought Congress was more honest than the president and 8 percent thought they were equal. However, when asked, "Which part of government generally makes better decisions?" 38 percent chose the president, 40 chose Congress, and 7 percent thought they were equal. Congress also held its own in terms of perceived responsiveness. In answering whether they thought the president or Congress "pays more attention to what people like you think," 42 percent chose Congress and 40 percent chose the president.[24]

Why does popular opinion of Congress fluctuate so much? Why does it seem to be generally low (the favorable ratings very rarely get above 50 percent and usually hover much lower)? One careful study [25] found that unpopularity of Congress is likely to increase as economic conditions decline and as active and aggressive presidents take center stage. The study also found the absence of international crises made Congress more vulnerable to increasing unpopularity. In times of crisis there seems to be a popular reaction of "rallying around the flag," which means in part supporting the major institutions of government, including Congress.

Another possibility is that popular estimates of Congress as an institution tend to vary as the productivity of Congress varies. Figure 12–3 makes the relationship between popular estimates of congressional performance and the legislative productivity of Congress for the years from 1963 through 1975 quite clear. From 1963 through 1971 these two items coincided in variation almost exactly. The line summarizing positive popular evaluation of congressional performance is based on the favorable responses to Harris poll questions (the Gallup Poll in

24. Adam Clymer, "Survey Finds Fewer Think Carter Can Restore Trust in Government," *New York Times,* November 2, 1977.

25. Parker, "Some Themes in Congressional Unpopularity."

1975). The line summarizing legislative productivity represents the annual "presidential box score" reported by *Congressional Quarterly* for the same years. This is simply the percentage of presidential requests enacted into law as calculated by *CQ*.

After 1971 the relationship between evaluation and productivity is less clear. The Harris Poll did not ask the question about the popular rating of Congress in 1972. The 1973 figure of 38 percent for the excellent and pretty good categories comes from a poll in February of that year, just before the Watergate scandal began to develop. By January 1974, the excellent and pretty good answers had dropped to 21 percent. Watergate and related matters had lowered the public's view of Congress as well as of most public institutions and officials. Another poll taken in July 1974, however, showed popular evaluation of Congress beginning to rise slightly—now the excellent and pretty good categories contained 29 percent of the respondents.

Congressional Quarterly quit calculating a presidential box score after 1975 and so we do not have comparable data for analyzing the last few years. However, it seems reasonable to assert that the general

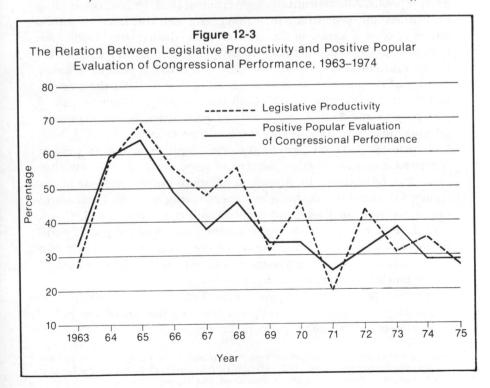

Figure 12-3

The Relation Between Legislative Productivity and Positive Popular Evaluation of Congressional Performance, 1963–1974

productivity of Congress has not been high in the 1976–78 period, and it is certainly accurate to report that the overall popular assessment of congressional performance has remained low.

This relationship between popular esteem and productivity suggests a dilemma for Congress: it is perceived in positive terms only when it reacts positively to presidential initiatives. Yet the leaders of Congress take a very understandable and reasonable position when they resist proceeding on an executive dominance model. At minimum it seems likely that joint policy development must be extensively used as a model. An aggressive group of members of Congress (particularly party leaders and committee chairmen) are not likely to acquiesce to executive dominance; likewise, an aggressive president and bureaucratic officials are not likely to acquiesce to a wide use of the congressional dominance model. The stalemate model, of course, is the most counterproductive of all in terms of popular reaction to Congress. Much of what transpired in 1963 and 1969–71 could fairly be called stalemate; these years also represent the low points of congressional popularity in the last decade.

Congress has not been alone in its decline in the estimation of the general public. All institutions of government (and, in fact, the leading institutions and professions in society) have also dwindled in public esteem. Political cynicism in general grew during the 1960s. For example, in 1964 78 percent of the population felt they could trust the government always or most of the time. Only 22 percent felt they could trust the government only some of the time. In 1968 these figures had changed to 62 percent with high trust in the goevrnment and 38 percent with low trust. By 1972 only 53 percent fell in the high trust category, and 47 percent fell in the low trust category. In 1973, with Watergate breaking, 34 percent registered high trust and 66 percent registered low trust. Similar patterns of response over the same time period can be observed in answers to questions about the waste of tax money, for whose benefit the government is run, whether government employees know their jobs, and whether politicians are crooked.[26]

In the long run, the most important implication of the public's estimation of Congress may be in terms of the kinds of individuals who are attracted to a career in Congress. The very best individuals might not be much interested in seeking membership in a body that is, over a long time period, held in low esteem. Year-to-year fluctuations are not so dangerous from this standpoint but long periods of low public evaluation of congressional performance are.

---

26. For a convenient summary of data on various aspects of public trust in government in selected years from 1958 through 1973 see Herbert B. Asher, *Presidential Elections and American Politics* (Homewood, Ill.: Dorsey, 1976): 8.

Congressional Performance and "Reform"

"Reform" of Congress is a favorite parlor game played by large numbers of people. Many who pay any attention to the institution at all feel they know what is wrong with it and have one or more quick fixes for the ailments they see. The standard criticisms of Congress revolve around charges that it is not responsive, not efficient, and does not uphold high ethical standards for behavior by its members. Usually one or more remedies are proposed. Most of these remedies turn out to be fairly mechanical and may or may not have any relationship to the problem toward which they are allegedly aimed.

Thus most outsiders promote reform packages that the proponents assert will cure the problems they allege to be rampant in Congress, whether they be problems of unresponsiveness, inefficiency, or dishonesty or some combination of such problems. Favorite prescriptions over the years have focused on such items as eliminating seniority for selecting committee chairpersons, disclosing personal financial worth and holdings of members, strengthening conflict of interest laws, setting a retirement age for members, increasing staff, installing computers to allow for greater storage and recovery of information, and changing specific rules of procedure such as that allowing filibusters in the Senate. Rarely are these prescriptions analyzed to see if they can reasonably be expected to cure the problems identified. And rarely are additional consequences projected and analyzed.[27]

The perspective on "reform" that is offered briefly here is not meant to deny the utility and necessity of some reforms. There are always aspects of congressional life and behavior that can profit by change; and the public does, in fact, stand to gain by some changes. But Congress is an extremely complex institution, and some changes billed as reforms may not have any effect at all on the problem that has been identified, and some may have unforeseen effects that are not necessarily desirable. While some changes do effectively address problems that have been identified, there is nothing automatic or easy about the matching of changes with problems.

Several additional specific points need to be made about reform or change in Congress. First, the same reform may be viewed very differ-

27. For thoughtful treatments of reform issues see Roger H. Davidson and Walter J. Oleszek, *Congress against Itself* (Bloomington, Indiana: Indiana University Press, 1977); Leroy N. Rieselbach, *Congressional Reform in the Seventies* (Morristown, N.J.: General Learning Press, 1977); chapters by Charles O. Jones, Richard F. Fenno, Jr., and Lawrence C. Dodd in Dodd and Bruce I. Oppenheimer (eds.), *Congress Reconsidered* (New York: Praeger, 1977); and chapters by Walter J. Oleszek, Charles O. Jones, and Roger H. Davidson in Susan Welch and John G. Peters (eds.), *Legislative Reform and Public Policy* (New York: Praeger, 1977).

ently by different individuals. For example, senior members and junior members may view changes in the seniority system quite differently, for the obvious reason that one group has something to lose and the other group presumably has something to gain. However, proposed changes in seniority are rarely debated in such straightforward self-interest terms. Instead the debate takes on a highly moralistic tone both in Congress and outside.

A lot of what is billed as reform primarily represents jockeying for position by individuals or by ideological blocks. Such reforms, if adopted, may have the desired impact in the short run. But in the long run they may be used in the service of interests and values quite distasteful to the original reformers. The classic case of changes used primarily in the service of values different from those originally served involves the position of the Speaker of the House. In 1910–11 the progressives in the House revolted against Speaker Joseph Cannon and stripped him (and succeeding Speakers) of many powers. These reforms were undertaken expressly to aid progressive legislative causes. But within a few years it became clear that the weakening of the Speakership fostered the development of virtually autonomous committee chairmen who, for the most part, came to use their power for relatively conservative purposes. By the 1960s and 1970s the liberals in Congress took the lead in restoring some powers to the Speaker so that he could effectively lead the liberal forces against the more conservatively oriented committee and subcommittee chairpersons.

Second, "reform movements" often embrace contradictory goals simultaneously. In the 1970s in the House, for example, the reformers simultaneously sought to strengthen the position of the subcommittees (and individual members on those subcommittees), the position of the Speaker, and the power of the Democratic Caucus. In many ways these institutions are competitors for power. They can work together, but the reforms did not really address the problem of how to promote cooperation. Rather the changes aimed at maximizing the potential impact and autonomy of each of them simultaneously.

Third, some matters are worth policing and changing for their own sake, although the precise nature of the most desirable state of affairs is not usually self-evident. The whole area of honesty and ethics is certainly one in which high standards should be set and upheld. However, there is legitimate debate over the specific measures designed to define and implement those standards. And, by and large, the impact of Congress on most public policy most of the time will not be affected by changes in standards, codes of ethics, limits on outside income, disclosure of personal financial information, and like measures. To be sure, the influence of a foreign government, such as that of the Republic of Korea, that seems willing to attempt to buy influence may be reduced. The most obvious conflicts of interest that are exposed may inhibit certain kinds of preferential legislative treatment for specific interests. But "better policy" is not likely to emerge overnight (or ever) solely because senators and representatives have to be honest in their personal financial dealings and report those publicly. Such requirements are simply good in themselves if properly drawn and at least may help lay the groundwork for more public acceptance of Congress as an institution populated by honest folk.

Fourth, the most important reforms and changes are those that increase or decrease the access of Congress institutionally to critical leverage points in the policy process and thus will, over the long run, increase or diminish the institution's capacity for making a substantive impact.

We need to realize, however, that Congress has only limited control over its own access to policy-making. In Chapter 1, in the discussion of supporting conditions for relatively high degrees of institutional integration and relatively high fragmentation, only two major conditions (out of twelve discussed) were identified as very manipulable by Congress itself: the nature of committee organization and the nature of party organization in Congress. The other conditions are largely givens with which Congress must work and to which Congress must adjust.

However, within the areas in which Congress does have room for maneuver, specifically in relation to committee, subcommittee, and party leadership organization and powers, changes can be very important in affecting the potential for institutional impact on policy. Thus an observer of Congress should be particularly alert to changes in those areas.[28] In recent years, strengthening the speakership, coupled with the election of O'Neill, seems to have given the House the potential for a more integrated impact on policy areas such as energy, for example.

In addition to the areas of committee organization and party leadership in which Congress has made changes in recent years (and these changes were discussed at length in earlier chapters) the most important reform Congress has made thus far in the 1970s involves the establishment of a new budget process and related institutions.[29]

---

28. For an excellent treatment of a reform process and outcomes involving committee organization in the House see Davidson and Oleszek, *Congress against Itself.*

29. On the congressional budget process and related institutions see Lance T. LeLoup, *Budgetary Politics* (Brunswick, Ohio: King's Court, 1977): Chapter 7 and pp. 233–235; John W. Ellwood and James A. Thurber, "The New Congressional Budget Process: The Hows and Whys of House-Senate Differences," in Dodd and Oppen-

All of the details of the new budget process need not be recounted here. The important institutions that were created were the budget committees in the two houses and the Congressional Budget office. The former were given adequate staffing and considerable formal powers that allowed them to engage in bargaining with other standing committees. The latter added important staff competence to the congressional institution, as discussed in Chapter 7.

Two new processes were set up. One dealt with the presidential power to impound (that is, not to spend) money appropriated by Congress. The procedures included in the 1974 law severely restrict that power and give Congress the final say on whether money will or will not be spent. The second process set up a new budget timetable and also made Congress adopt overall spending and revenue goals and then adjust specific spending measures within the limits of those goals. Table 12–2 summarizes the congressional budget timetable.

Table 12–2
Congressional Budget Timetable

Action to be completed	On or before
President submits current services budget to Congress	November 10
President submits annual budget message to Congress	15 days after Congress meets
Congressional committees make recommendations to budget committees	March 15
Congressional Budget Office reports to budget committees	April 1
Budget committees report first budget resolution	April 15
Congress passes first budget resolution	May 15
Legislative committees complete reporting of authorizing legislation	May 15
Congress passes all spending bills	Seven days after Labor Day
Congress passes second budget resolution	September 15
Congress passes budget reconciliation bill	September 25
Fiscal year begins	October 1

Source: Lance T. LeLoup, Budgetary Politics *(Brunswick, Ohio: King's Court, 1977): 130.*

---

heimer (eds.), *Congress Reconsidered*: 163–192; Ellwood and Thurber, "The New Congressional Budget Process: Its Causes, Consequences, and Possible Success," in Welch and Peters (eds.), *Legislative Reform and Public Policy*: 82–97; and three articles by Joel Havemann in the *National Journal* (September 25, 1976: 1346–1352; August 13, 1977: 1256–1260; and September 24, 1977: 1476–1479).

The new process and timetable have been used thus far for three fiscal years: 1976 (on an experimental basis), 1977, and 1978. They have had a surprising degree of impact, considering the dire prophesies of failure by many at the time of their enactment. In each of the three years they have resulted in some altered spending priorities and in a modest reduction in overall spending. There is good evidence that the targets set in the first resolution have actually influenced the nature of final budget outcomes. In 1975 (for fiscal 1976) the defense authorization bill was reduced because of Senate Budget Committee action. In 1976 both budget committees helped reduce the rate of growth of retirement benefits for federal employees. Again in 1977 budget committee decisions helped cut a billion or two dollars from the final defense appropriations.

Naturally, in other areas budget committee initiatives have been rebuffed. But, in general, Congress has lived with the guidelines (although, to some extent, the figures contained in those guidelines are based on predictions of what the appropriations process might produce anyway). Congress has also generally stayed on schedule with reference to the timetable with a few exceptions such as the inability to pass an appropriations bill for the Departments of Labor and Health, Education, and Welfare in 1977 because of a dispute between the two houses over the use of federal money to finance abortions.

The new process has had some perilous moments on the floor, particularly in the House, but survived even the defeat of the first budget resolution in the spring of 1977. The budget committee went back to work and produced a resolution acceptable to the majority the second time around.

Thus, at this point in the evolution of the budget process, it seems to continue to hold promise for increasing congressional impact on overall spending (and, to a lesser extent, taxing) priorities.

Fifth, "reform" in the classic sense (that is, focused around prescriptions about matters such as seniority, ethics, retirement age, and specific rules) is usually not central to the quality of congressional performance and the nature of congressional impact on policy. Much more central is the will of the members of the House and Senate. The machinery of Congress is not inherently deficient. The links with the public are not deficient. The electoral system is not deficient. The ties with the other organs of government are not deficient. What may be deficient is resolve on the part of a sufficient number of members to make the machinery, the ties to other publics and agencies, and the "system" work. It can work when that resolve is present. But the willingness to experiment consciously with internal structures and arrangements and the willingness to take stands that might at least temporarily be unpopular with a mass public, an elite public, or other officials are critical in determining potency.

In a general sense this book ends on a "reformist" note: a hope that members of the House and Senate will not relax with set patterns of thinking and doing but will instead seek new patterns, even within the confines of existing congressional institutions. The institutions allow for both stagnation and innovation; the critical question is how the people responsible for making the institutions function behave. There are no permanent solutions to making Congress a body that arrives at responsive and intelligent decisions about matters affecting the citizens of the nation. But in a dynamic setting such as that surrounding Congress, adjustments and changes to afford at least temporary solutions to perceived problems can be important in determining both the standing of the national legislature and the kind of policy it helps produce.

SELECTED BIBLIOGRAPHY

The amount of writing on Congress is vast. The following bibliography is selective and omits a great deal of good literature. It is intended as a guide for readers who want to explore further the topics treated in this volume. A number of items included are not cited in the footnotes. The bibliography is organized along the line of the book. Parts 1 through 8 correspond to the topics covered in Chapters 1 through 8. Part 9 of the bibliography encompasses the concerns of both Chapters 9 and 10. Part 10 of the bibliography covers both Chapters 11 and 12. Some of the items cited are useful for several purposes and the annotations indicate those cases. The bibliography does not include comprehensive textbooks or volumes composed of previously published material. Material on "reform" is included primarily in section 1.

1. THE NATURE OF CONGRESS

American Political Science Association, "Toward a More Responsible Two-Party System," *American Political Science Review* 44 (1950), supplement. A classic statement of the case for reform inside Congress in order to enhance "party responsibility." Written by a committee chaired by E.E. Schattschneider, a perceptive student of American politics.

Bibby, John F. and Roger H. Davidson, *On Capitol Hill* (Hinsdale, Ill.: Dryden, 1972, 2nd ed.). Original case studies of campaigns, workdays of members, party leadership, a committee, and legislative action.

Bolling, Richard, *House Out of Order* (New York: Dutton, 1965). A reformist analysis of the House by an important liberal Democrat from Missouri.

Burnham, James, *Congress and the American Tradition* (Chicago: Regnery, 1959). A conservative view of the proper role of Congress: i.e., to stop executive expansion of governmental activities.

Burns, James MacGregor, *The Deadlock of Democracy* (Englewood Cliffs, N.J.: Prentice-Hall, 1963). A liberal attack on Congress for being unresponsive to national needs, especially as interpreted by the president.

Cater, Douglass, *Power in Washington* (New York: Random House, 1964). Primarily a study of "subgovernments" in action.

Clapp, Charles L., *The Congressman* (Washington: Brookings, 1963). A report and commentary on interviews with and discussions by about fifty members of the House in 1959. Good material on relations with constituents and interest groups, the impact of party leadership, and the working of committees.

Clark, Joseph S., *Congress—The Sapless Branch* (New York: Harper, 1965, revised ed.). A reformist argument by a former Democratic Senator from Pennsylvania.

Congressional Quarterly. Publications of this Washington-based organization are indispensable for the student of the post-World War II Congress. Especially useful are the weekly reports it has issued since 1945, the yearly almanacs, its *Guide to the Congress of the United States* (1976, 2nd ed.), and *Congress and the Nation* (volume 1 covers politics and policy from 1945 through 1964; volume 2 covers 1965 through 1968; volume 3 covers 1969 through 1972; volume 4 covers 1973 through 1976).

Davidson, Roger H., David M. Kovenock, and Michael K. O'Leary, *Congress in Crisis: Politics and Congressional Reform* (Belmont, Calif.: Wadsworth, 1966). A study of how members feel about specific reform proposals.

Davidson, Roger H. and Walter J. Oleszek, *Congress against Itself* (Bloomington, Indiana: Indiana University Press, 1977). A careful analysis of the attempt by the House in 1973–1974 to restructure its committee system.

de Grazia, Alfred (ed.), *Congress: The First Branch of Government* (Garden City, N.Y,: Doubleday Anchor Books, 1967). Twelve original essays on topics such as oversight, decision-making, liaison, information systems, and congressional handling of the budget.

Dexter, Lewis A., *The Sociology and Politics of Congress* (Chicago: Rand McNally, 1969). A collection of essays by one of the most original students of Congress. Especially useful on elections and relations with constituents and interest groups.

Dodd, Lawrence C. and Bruce I. Oppenheimer (eds.), *Congress Reconsidered* (New York: Praeger, 1977). A volume of mostly original papers focusing on the changing Congress of the 1970s.

House Republican Task Force on Congressional Reform and Minority Staffing, *We Propose: A Modern Congress* (New York: McGraw-Hill, 1966). The views of a number of House Republicans on needed reforms.

Huitt, Ralph K. and Robert L. Peabody, *Congress: Two Decades of Analysis* (New York: Harper & Row, 1969). Part I of this book is a long and very useful essay by Peabody summarizing and evaluating the literature on Congress. Part II is a collection of articles by Huitt, one of the pioneers of modern congressional research. These articles include his classic studies of Lyndon Johnson as a Senate Majority Leader and William Proxmire as a maverick senator.

Mayhew, David R., *Congress: The Electoral Connection* (New Haven: Yale University Press, 1974). An insightful essay that links most congressional behavior to the single, central fact that the members are elected.

Miller, Clem, *Member of the House* (New York: Scribner's, 1962). Insightful letters from a California representative to his constituents. Good material on House procedure, the workload of a representative, the impact of party in the House, and relations with interest groups.

National Journal. This Washington-based publication comes out weekly and is focused on policy developments. Excellent material on executive-congressional relations. Some material on the internal workings of Congress.

Orfield, Gary, *Congressional Power: Congress and Social Change* (New York: Harcourt Brace Jovanovich, 1975). An argument that "Congress is more important and less conservative than is generally believed" in domestic policy.

Ornstein, Norman J., *Congress in Change: Evolution and Reform* (New York: Praeger, 1975). A collection of mostly original papers focusing on change in Congress both throughout its history and primarily in the early 1970s.

Rieselbach, Leroy N., *Congressional Reform in the Seventies* (Morristown, New Jersey: General Learning Press, 1977). An analysis of reform in Congress in the first half of the 1970s.

Saloma, John S. III, *Congress and the New Politics* (Boston: Little, Brown, 1969). An analysis of congressional capabilities and performance. Useful material on workload, relations with constituents, and relations with the executive branch.

Tacheron, Donald G. and Morris K. Udall, *The Job of the Congressman* (Indianapolis: Bobbs-Merrill, 1966). Intended as a manual for new representatives. Also contains much basic information useful to the student of the House.

Vogler, David J., *The Politics of Congress* (Boston: Allyn and Bacon, 1977, 2nd ed.). An evaluative interpretation of Congress.

2. CONGRESSIONAL DEVELOPMENT

Alexander, DeAlva S., *History and Procedure of the House of Representatives* (Boston: Houghton Mifflin, 1916). Still an important work on the House.

Baker, Richard A., *The United States Senate: A Historical Bibliography* (Washington: U.S. Government Printing Office, 1977). A comprehensive bibliography on the Senate, with special attention to historical materials, including biographies of senators.

Blaine, James G., *Twenty Years of Congress*, 2 vols., (Norwich, Conn.: Henry Bill Publishing Co., 1884–86). Memoirs of the period between 1800 and 1880 by an important Speaker of the House.

Chiu, Chang-wei, *The Speaker of the House of Representatives Since 1896* (New York: Columbia University Press, 1928). A standard work on the Speakership during a period of transition.

Clark, Champ, *My Quarter Century of American Politics*, 2 vols., (New York: Harper, 1920). Insightful memoirs of a long-time member who was a Speaker of the House.

Dunn, Arthur W., *From Harrison to Harding*, 2 vols., (New York: Putnam's,

1922). Memoirs of a journalist that contain much valuable material on Congress and congressional-executive relations during the period.

Farrand, Max, *The Framing of the Constitution of the United States* (New Haven: Yale University Press, 1913). Indispensable source for understanding the original vision of the role of Congress (and the alternative visions that were rejected).

Follett, Mary P., *The Speaker of the House of Representatives* (New York: Longmans, Green and Co., 1896). An excellent treatment of the speakership in the nineteenth century.

Galloway, George B., *History of the United States House of Representatives* (New York: Crowell, 1962). An "official" history of the House; brief, but useful. Also available as House Document No. 246, Eighty-seventh Congress, First Session (1962).

Gwinn, William R., *Uncle Joe Cannon, Archfoe of Insurgency* (New York: Bookman Associates, 1957). A useful biography of Speaker Cannon.

Hamilton, Alexander, John Jay, and James Madison, *The Federalist* (New York: Random House, n.d.). Contains a number of papers explaining the founders' notion of how Congress would function in the total political system.

Haynes, George H., *The Senate of the United States,* 2 vols., (Boston: Houghton Mifflin, 1938). A standard history of the Senate.

Huntington, Samuel P., "Congressional Responses to the Twentieth Century," in David B. Truman (ed.), *The Congress and America's Future* (Englewood Cliffs, N.J.: Prentice-Hall, 1973, 2nd ed.). A reformist analysis of House development.

MacNeil, Neil, *Forge of Democracy: The House of Representatives* (New York: McKay, 1963). Summarizes much of the anecdotal material on the House. Contains a good bibliography.

Patterson, James T., *Congressional Conservatism and the New Deal* (Lexington: University of Kentucky Press, 1968). A study of executive-legislative relations and internal congressional politics from 1933 to 1939. Explores the rise of the "conservative coalition" of Republicans and southern Democrats.

Polsby, Nelson W., "Institutionalization in the U.S. House of Representatives," *American Political Science Review* 62 (1968): 144–168. Explores and documents the growing stability of the House in the twentieth century.

Price, H. Douglas, "Congress and the Evolution of Legislative 'Professionalism'," in Norman J. Ornstein (ed.), *Congress in Change: Evolution and Reform* (New York: Praeger, 1975): 2–23. Examines various aspects of the "professionalization" of the congressional career.

Price, H. Douglas, "The Congressional Career—Then and Now," in Nelson W. Polsby (ed.), *Congressional Behavior* (New York: Random House, 1971). Contrasts the instability of nineteenth century congressional membership with the stability of twentieth century membership.

Rothman, David J., *Politics and Power in the United States Senate, 1869–1901* (Cambridge: Harvard University Press, 1966). An excellent account of the evolution of the Senate from chaos to party government.

Stephenson, Nathaniel W., *Nelson W. Aldrich: A Leader in American Politics* (New York: Scribner's, 1930). Fine biography of the most important Republican leader in the Senate in the late nineteenth and early twentieth centuries.

Wilson, Woodrow, *Congressional Government* (New York: Meridian, 1956). This classic interpretation of Congress was first published in 1885 and still contains many valid observations.

Young, James S., *The Washington Community, 1800–1828* (New York: Columbia University Press, 1966). A fascinating study of the national government in its youth. Rich material on Congress of the period.

3. Congressional Elections

Cover, Albert D. and David R. Mayhew, "Congressional Dynamics and the Decline of Competitive Congressional Elections," in Lawrence C. Dodd and Bruce I. Oppenheimer (eds.), *Congress Reconsidered* (New York: Praeger, 1977): 54–72. Documents declining competition for congressional seats and discusses some possible causes and consequences.

Cummings, Milton C., Jr., *Congressmen and the Electorate* (New York: Free Press, 1966). A study of the relationship between voting for president and voting for House members.

Erikson, Robert S., "Is There Such a Thing as a Safe Seat?," *Polity* 8 (1976): 623–632. Argues that incumbency is not such a strong protection against defeat in the modern Congress as is generally believed.

Fishel, Jeff, *Party and Opposition* (New York: McKay, 1973). A study of all the challengers for House seats in the 1964 election and of the subsequent six years in the careers of those who won.

Hacker, Andrew, *Congressional Districting* (Washington: Brookings, 1964, revised ed.). A brief, but thorough treatment of the subject.

Jones, Charles O., *Every Second Year* (Washington: Brookings, 1967). A study of the effect of the two-year term for House members and of the consequences of various alternative proposals.

Jones, Charles O., "The Role of the Campaign in Congressional Politics," in M. Kent Jennings and L. Harmon Zeigler (eds.), *The Electoral Process* (Englewood Cliffs, N.J.: Prentice-Hall, 1966). A useful overview of the limited importance of campaigns in influencing congressional behavior.

Leuthold, David A., *Electioneering in a Democracy* (New York: Wiley, 1968). A detailed study of the 1962 congressional campaigns in the San Francisco Bay area.

Mayhew, David R., "Congressional Elections: The Case of the Vanishing Marginals," *Polity* 6 (1974): 295–317. A treatment of declining competition for congressional seats from 1956 through 1972.

Price, H. Douglas, "The Electoral Arena," in David B. Truman (ed.), *The Congress and America's Future* (Englewood Cliffs, N.J.: Prentice-Hall, 1973, 2nd ed.). An examination of changing electoral patterns and practices in the twentieth century.

4. CONGRESSIONAL DECISION-MAKING

Clausen, Aage R., *How Congressmen Decide* (New York: St. Martin's, 1973). A study of five substantive dimensions of voting in the House and Senate.

Fenno, Richard F., Jr., "The Internal Distribution of Influence: The House," in David B. Truman (ed.), *The Congress and America's Future* (Englewood Cliffs, N.J.: Prentice-Hall, 1973, 2nd ed.). A summary assessment of how things get done in the House.

Froman, Lewis A., Jr., *The Congressional Process* (Boston: Little, Brown, 1967). A discussion of the use and impact of the rules in the House and Senate.

Huitt, Ralph K., "The Internal Distribution of Influence: The Senate," in David B. Truman (ed.), *The Congress and America's Future* (Englewood Cliffs, N.J.: Prentice-Hall, 1973, 2nd ed.). A summary assessment of how things get done in the Senate.

Kingdon, John W., *Congressmen's Voting Decisions* (New York: Harper and Row, 1973). An analysis, based largely on interviews, of how members of the House make up their minds on floor voting.

Matthews, Donald R., *U.S. Senators and Their World* (Chapel Hill: University of North Carolina Press, 1960). An analysis of decision-making in the Senate in the 1940s and 1950s.

Matthews, Donald R. and James A. Stimson, *Yeas and Nays: Normal Decision-Making in the U.S. House of Representatives* (New York: Wiley, 1975). A study of cue-giving and cue-taking in the House of Representatives as an explanation of decision-making.

Mayhew, David R., *Party Loyalty Among Congressmen* (Cambridge: Harvard University Press, 1966). A roll call study that shows that Democrats support each other's interests better than do Republicans.

Ripley, Randall B., *Power in the Senate* (New York: St. Martin's, 1969). Focused on decision-making in the Senate in the 1960s. Also has some material on Senate history.

Shannon, W. Wayne, *Party, Constituency and Congressional Voting* (Baton Rouge: Louisiana State University Press, 1968). An intensive roll call analysis for the period from 1959 through 1962 in the House. Compares the impact of party to the impact of constituency.

Turner, Julius and Edward V. Schneier, Jr., *Party and Constituency: Pressures on Congress* (Baltimore: The Johns Hopkins Press, 1970, revised ed.). A roll call analysis of the comparative importance of party and constituency for scattered congresses between 1921 and 1967.

5. COMMITTEES

Fenno, Richard F., Jr., *Congressmen in Committees* (Boston: Little, Brown, 1973). A comparative study of the workings of six House committees.

Fenno, Richard F., Jr., *The Power of the Purse* (Boston: Little, Brown, 1966). A long and valuable study of appropriations politics, focused primarily on the House Appropriations Committee.

Goodwin, George Jr., *The Little Legislatures* (Amherst: University of Massachusetts Press, 1970). A brief, but thorough treatment of committees.

Hinckley, Barbara, *The Seniority System in Congress* (Bloomington: Indiana University Press, 1971). A thorough analysis of seniority in Congress that concludes that its policy impact is quite limited.

McConachie, Lauros, *Congressional Committees* (New York: Crowell, 1898). A classic work on the development of standing committees.

McGown, Ada C., *The Congressional Conference Committee* (New York: Columbia University Press, 1927). An early and still useful treatment of conference committees.

Manley, John F., *The Politics of Finance* (Boston: Little, Brown, 1970). A perceptive study of the House Ways and Means Committee.

Masters, Nicholas A., "Committee Assignments in the House of Representatives," *American Political Science Review,* 55 (1961): 345–357. Still the best description of this process.

Matsunaga, Spark M. and Ping Chen, *Rulemakers of the House* (Urbana, Illinois: University of Illinois Press, 1976). A thorough study of the House Rules Committee.

Murphy, James T., "Political Parties and Porkbarrel: Party Conflict and Cooperation in House Public Works Committee Decision Making," *American Political Science Review* 68 (1974): 169–185. A study that focuses on the highly partisan nature of the House Public Works Committee.

Robinson, James A., *The House Rules Committee* (Indianapolis: Bobbs-Merrill, 1963). An examination of the functions and internal politics of this important committee.

Steiner, Gilbert Y., *The Congressional Conference Committee* (Urbana: University of Illinois Press, 1951). Analyzes conference committee behavior in the 1930s and 1940s.

Vogler, David J., *The Third House* (Evanston: Northwestern University Press, 1971). Analyzes conference committee behavior in the 1950s and 1960s.

6. PARTY LEADERSHIP

Bolling, Richard, *Power in the House* (New York: Dutton, 1968). A history of party leadership in the House with proposals for reform in the direction of responsible party government. Written by a representative from Missouri since 1949.

Brown, George R., *The Leadership of Congress* (Indianapolis: Bobbs-Merrill, 1922). A very perceptive account of party leadership in the first two decades of the twentieth century.

Evans, Rowland and Robert Novak, *Lyndon B. Johnson: The Exercise of Power* (New York: New American Library, 1966). Contains a long and perceptive account of Johnson as Democratic floor leader in the Senate.

Hasbrouck, Paul D., *Party Government in the House of Representatives* (New York: Macmillan, 1927). A first-rate study of the development of party leadership in the House.

Jones, Charles O., *The Minority Party in Congress* (Boston: Little, Brown,

1970). A perceptive analysis of the role of the minority party in Congress with special attention to party leadership.

Jones, Charles O., *Party and Policy-Making: The House Republican Policy Committee* (New Brunswick: Rutgers University Press, 1964). A detailed analysis of the operations and importance of this party committee from 1959 to 1964.

Nelson, Garrison, "Partisan Patterns of House Leadership Change, 1789–1977," *American Political Science Review* 71 (1977): 918–939. Concludes that "the two parties differ significantly in their patterns of House leadership change."

Peabody, Robert L., *Leadership in Congress* (Boston: Little, Brown, 1976). A study of leadership stability and change from 1955 through 1974.

Ripley, Randall B., *Majority Party Leadership in Congress* (Boston: Little, Brown, 1969). An analysis of party leadership and leader-president relations based on data from ten Congresses in the twentieth century.

Ripley, Randall B., *Party Leaders in the House of Representatives* (Washington: Brookings, 1967). An analysis that includes some attention to historical development and a focus on leadership in the early 1960s.

Stewart, John G., "Two Strategies of Leadership: Johnson and Mansfield," in Nelson W. Polsby (ed.), *Congressional Behavior* (New York: Random House, 1971). A comparison of the contrasting styles of these two Senate Democratic leaders.

Westefield, Louis P., "Majority Party Leadership and the Committee System in the House of Representatives," *American Political Science Review* 68 (1974): 1593–1604. Argues that party leaders increase their leverage in the House by increasing the size of committees, thus providing more desirable assignments for the members.

7. INTERNAL GROUPS AND CONGRESSIONAL STAFF

Born, Richard, "Cue-Taking within State Party Delegations in the U.S. House of Representatives," *Journal of Politics* 38 (1976): 71–94. An argument that the importance of state party cues have been exaggerated in other studies.

Butler, Warren H., "Administering Congress: The Role of the Staff," *Public Administration Review* 26 (1966): 3–12. A brief description of the place of congressional staff.

Clausen, Aage R., "State Party Influence on Congressional Party Decisions," *Midwest Journal of Political Science* 16 (1972): 77–101. A roll call analysis that shows the strong influence of state party delegations.

Deckard, Barbara, "State Party Delegations in the United States House of Representatives—An Analysis of Group Action," *Polity* 5 (1973): 311–334. An attempt to explain delegation cohesiveness and its relation to alliance behavior.

Deckard, Barbara, "State Party Delegations in the U.S. House of Representatives—A Comparative Study of Group Cohesion," *Journal of Politics* 34 1972): 199–222. An analysis based on interviews.

Ferber, Mark F., "The Formation of the Democratic Study Group," in Nelson

W. Polsby (ed.), *Congressional Behavior* (New York: Random House, 1971). An examination of the conditions that led to the creation of the DSG and its early functioning.

Fiellin, Alan, "The Functions of Informal Groups in Legislative Institutions," *Journal of Politics* 24 (1962): 72–91. A study of the New York Democrats in the House.

Fox, Harrison W., Jr., and Susan Webb Hammond, *Congressional Staffs: The Invisible Force in American Lawmaking* (New York: Free Press, 1977). A thorough analysis of the functioning and impact of congressional staff.

Henry, Charles P., "Legitimizing Race in Congressional Politics," *American Politics Quarterly* 5 (1977): 149–176. A study of the Congressional Black Caucus in the House of Representatives.

Kofmehl, Kenneth, *Professional Staffs of Congress* (West Lafayette, Indiana: Purdue University Press, 1977, 3rd ed.). A description of congressional staffs that omits only personal staffs for members of the House.

Manley, John F., "Congressional Staff and Public Policy-Making: The Joint Committee on Internal Revenue Taxation," *Journal of Politics* 30 (1968): 1046–1067. An excellent case study of the policy impact of one committee staff.

Patterson, Samuel C., "The Professional Staffs of Congressional Committees," *Administrative Science Quarterly* 15 (1970): 22–37. A concise, but thorough discussion of committee staffs.

Stevens, Arthur G., Jr., Arthur H. Miller, and Thomas E. Mann, "Mobilization of Liberal Strength in the House, 1955–1970: The Democratic Study Group," *American Political Science Review* 68 (1974): 667–681. A study of the origins and functioning of the Democratic Study Group in the House.

Truman, David B., "The State Delegation and the Structure of Voting in the United States House of Representatives," *American Political Science Review* 50 (1956): 1023–1045. An early roll call study that seeks to isolate the impact of state delegations.

8. RELATIONS WITH CONSTITUENTS AND INTEREST GROUPS

Bacheller, John M., "Lobbyists and the Legislative Process: The Impact of Environmental Constraints," *American Political Science Review* 71 (1977): 252–263. A study exploring the differences in the behavior of lobbyists in approaching Congress on different issues.

Bauer, Raymond A., Ithiel de Sola Pool, and Lewis A. Dexter, *American Business and Public Policy* (New York: Atherton, 1963). A case study of a decade of reciprocal legislation that concludes that interest groups and constituents had only limited influence.

Davidson, Roger H., *The Role of the Congressman* (New York: Pegasus, 1969). An analysis of the distribution of self-perceived roles, including those relating to representation of constituents and attitudes toward interest groups.

Dexter, Lewis A., *How Organizations Are Represented in Washington* (Indianapolis: Bobbs-Merrill, 1969). A rich source for understanding the subtleties of relations between lobbyists and Congress.

Fenno, Richard F., Jr., *Home Style: House Members in Their Districts* (Boston: Little, Brown, 1978). An insightful and provocative study of what House members do "back home."

Froman, Lewis A., Jr., *Congressmen and Their Constituencies* (Chicago: Rand McNally, 1963). A study based on election statistics and roll call votes.

Milbrath, Lester W., *The Washington Lobbyists* (Chicago: Rand McNally, 1963). A general study of Washington lobbyists that contains much material on their relations with Congress.

9. RELATIONS WITH THE PRESIDENT, PRESIDENCY, AND BUREAUCRACY

Aberbach, Joel D. and Bert A. Rockman, "The Overlapping Worlds of American Federal Executives and Congressmen," *British Journal of Political Science* 7 (1977): 23–47. A study that suggests that the belief systems of bureaucrats and members of Congress are not very different.

Chamberlain, Lawrence H., *The President, Congress and Legislation* (New York: Columbia University Press, 1946). Short studies of major legislation passed by Congress for over half a century. Assessments are made of the relative influence of Congress and the executive branch.

Cleaveland, Frederic N. and associates, *Congress and Urban Problems* (Washington: Brookings, 1969). Seven case studies from the 1950s and 1960s offer considerable material on executive-legislative relations in urban policy-making.

Davidson, Roger H., "Breaking Up Those 'Cozy Triangles': An Impossible Dream?," in Susan Welch and John G. Peters (eds.), *Legislative Reform and Public Policy* (New York: Praeger, 1977): 30–53. An exploratory essay on how the influence of subgovernments might be reduced.

Fiorina, Morris P., *Congress: Keystone of the Washington Establishment* (New Haven: Yale University Press, 1977). An argument that members of Congress help perpetuate their own tenure in office by publicly berating bureaucracy and privately cooperating with bureaucrats.

Holtzman, Abraham, *Legislative Liaison* (Chicago: Rand McNally, 1970). A study of White House and departmental liaison efforts. Especially strong on the Kennedy presidency.

Mansfield, Harvey C., Sr. (ed.), *Congress against the President,* Proceedings of the Academy of Political Science 32 (1975). A collection of original papers exploring a number of aspects of presidential-congressional relations.

Moe, Ronald C. and Steven C. Teel, "Congress as Policy-Maker: A Necessary Reappraisal," *Political Science Quarterly* 85 (1970): 443–470. An updating of Chamberlain's work that reaches the same conclusion: Congress is an influential partner in the policy process and is not subservient to the president and bureaucracy.

Neustadt, Richard E., "Politicians and Bureaucrats," in David B. Truman (ed.), *The Congress and America's Future* (Englewood Cliffs, N.J.: Prentice-Hall, 1973, 2nd ed.). An examination of the tripartite relationship between members of Congress, the president, and bureaucrats. Argues that the former two have common interests different from those of the bureaucrats.

Neustadt, Richard E., "Presidency and Legislation: The Growth of Central Clearance," *American Political Science Review* 48 (1954): 641–671. A discussion of growing control by the Executive Office of the President over legislative proposals coming from the bureaucracy.

Neustadt, Richard E., "Presidency and Legislation: Planning the President's Program," *American Political Science Review* 49 (1955): 980–1021. A discussion of the evolution of the "program of the president."

Ogul, Morris S., *Congress Oversees the Bureaucracy: Studies in Legislative Supervision* (Pittsburgh: University of Pittsburgh Press, 1976). A general consideration of oversight with some detailed case examples.

Pipe, G. Russell, "Congressional Liaison: The Executive Branch Consolidates Its Relations with Congress," *Public Administration Review* 26 (1966): 14–24. A description of the size and scope of departmental liaison efforts.

Ripley, Randall B., *Kennedy and Congress* (Morristown, N.J.: General Learning Press, 1972). A case study of congressional-presidential relations in 1961–1963.

Ripley, Randall B. and Grace A. Franklin, *Congress, the Bureaucracy, and Public Policy* (Homewood, Illinois: Dorsey, 1976). An analysis of the impact of congressional-bureaucratic relations on different types of policy.

Robinson, James A., *Congress and Foreign Policy Making* (Homewood, Ill.: Dorsey, 1967, revised ed.). An intensive study, based in part on interviews, of executive-legislative relations in the area of foreign policy.

Wildavsky, Aaron, *The Politics of the Budgetary Process* (Boston: Little, Brown, 1974, 2nd ed.). A general treatment of budgeting that contains rich material on relations between bureaus and appropriations subcommittees.

10. CONGRESS AND POLICY

Bailey, Stephen K., *Congress Makes a Law* (New York: Vintage, 1964). A classic case study of the passage of the Employment Act of 1946.

Carroll, Holbert N., "The Congress and National Security Policy," in David B. Truman (ed.), *The Congress and America's Future* (Englewood Cliffs, N.J.: Prentice-Hall, 1973, 2nd ed.). Updates Carroll's earlier work on the House and treats the growing aggressiveness of both houses in this area.

Carroll, Holbert N., *The House of Representatives and Foreign Affairs* (Boston: Little, Brown, 1966, revised ed.). A careful evaluation of the growing role of the House in foreign policy.

Clausen, Aage R. and Carl E. Van Horn, "The Congressional Response to a Decade of Change: 1963–1972," *Journal of Politics* 39 (1977): 624–666. A study that explores the conditions for change or stability in the policy orientations of individual members.

Dahl, Robert A., *Congress and Foreign Policy* (New York: Harcourt, Brace, 1950). A thoughtful early study of the foreign policy role of Congress.

Eidenberg, Eugene and Roy D. Morey, *An Act of Congress* (New York:

Norton, 1969). A case study of the passage of the Elementary and Secondary Education Act of 1965.

Ferejohn, John A., *Pork Barrel Politics: Rivers and Harbors Legislation, 1947–1968* (Stanford, California: Stanford University Press, 1974). A careful study of congressional handling of rivers and harbors legislation for 20 years, with some general explanation of how Congress handles distributive policies.

Huitt, Ralph K., "Congressional Organization and Operations in the Field of Money and Credit," in Commission on Money and Credit, *Fiscal and Debt Management Policies* (Englewood Cliffs, N.J.: Prentice-Hall, 1963). A perceptive study of congressional influence in this field in the 1950s and early 1960s.

Jewell, Malcolm, *Senatorial Politics and Foreign Policy* (Lexington: University of Kentucky Press, 1962). A detailed study of Senate activity in the foreign policy area.

Kanter, Arnold, "Congress and the Defense Budget: 1960–1970," *American Political Science Review* 66 (1972): 129–143. A study that shows that Congress has an important impact on defense budgets.

Kolodziej, Edward A., *The Uncommon Defense and Congress, 1945–1963* (Columbus: The Ohio State University Press, 1966). A detailed study of the congressional role in defense policy.

Mansfield, Harvey C., "The Congress and Economic Policy," in David B. Truman (ed.), *The Congress and America's Future* (Englewood Cliffs, N.J.: Prentice-Hall, 1973, 2nd ed.). A summary of congressional involvement in economic policy.

Morgan, Donald G., *Congress and the Constitution* (Cambridge: Harvard University Press, 1966). Includes ten case studies of congressional action on matters involving constitutional questions from 1818 through 1964. Urges that Congress not rely on the Supreme Court for constitutional wisdom but arrive at independent decisions instead.

Munger, Frank J. and Richard F. Fenno, Jr., *National Politics and Federal Aid to Education* (Syracuse: Syracuse University Press, 1962). A careful analysis of the congressional role in federal aid to education legislation—both successful and unsuccessful.

Parker, Glenn R., "Some Themes in Congressional Unpopularity," *American Journal of Political Science* 21 (1977): 93–109. A study that seeks to explain fluctuations in public opinion about Congress.

Redman, Eric, *The Dance of Legislation* (New York: Simon and Shuster, 1973). A well-told story of the passage of the Emergency Health Personnel Act of 1970.

Rosenthal, Alan, "The Effectiveness of Congress," in Gerald M. Pomper and others, *The Performance of American Government* (New York: Free Press, 1972). A positive summary evaluation of the policy-making capability and performance of Congress.

Sinclair, Barbara Deckard, "Party Realignment and the Transformation of the Political Agenda: The House of Representatives, 1925–1938," *American Political Science Review* 71 (1977): 940–953. An exploration of the changes in roll call voting patterns in the House before and after the coming of the New Deal.

Sundquist, James L., *Politics and Policy* (Washington: Brookings, 1968). A detailed study of domestic policy-making and the interaction between Congress and the executive branch from 1953 through 1966. Argues that most of the successful Democratic initiatives of the 1960s were developed in Congress in the 1950s during the Eisenhower administration.

INDEX

abortion financing, 395
accommodation, within Congress, 124–25, 131
activism, leadership, 224–26, 296, 313
Adams, John Quincy, 50
adjournment, 221
Administrative Review, Commission on (House), 284
aerospace industry and legislation, 264, 268, 285, 368, 377
agencies, federal, *see* bureaucracy, federal
agenda, *see* workload and agenda
agenda-setting, 348
Agnew, Spiro, 298
Agriculture, Department of, 144–45, 337
Agriculture, Nutrition, and Forestry Committee (Senate), 148, 155, 166
Agriculture Committee (House), 67, 144, 148, 155, 166, 173, 176
agriculture interests and legislation, 144–46, 148–49, 176, 201, 285, 312–13, 337–38
Alaska oil pipeline, 263, 268–69
Albert, Carl, 195, 208, 234, 378
alternatives, 349, 361–62
amendments, to bills, 140, 145, 172, 179, 181, 190–93, 220, 224, 246, 275–76
amendments, to the Constitution, 146
  fourteenth, 51

fifteenth, 51
seventeenth, 48, 79
see also Constitution
American Association of Retired Persons, 266
American Bar Association, 265, 358
American Farm Bureau Federation, 269
American Federation of Labor–Congress of Industrial Organizations, 264, 269, 272–73, 275
American Medical Association, 265, 272
Anderson, John B., 211
Angola, 352
Appalachia program, 368, 374
apportionment, 83–84
apprenticeship, of freshmen Congressmen, 125–29, 167, 177–78
appropriations bills, 48, 121, 140, 182, 201, 304, 326–29, 332, 335–36
Appropriations Committee (House), 67, 140, 155, 166, 168, 169, 174–175, 178, 182, 186–87, 191, 222, 225, 245, 336, 355
Appropriations Committee (Senate), 126, 155, 166, 178, 182, 225, 245, 336, 341, 355–56
Area Redevelopment Act, 373
Area Redevelopment Administration, 29, 339
area redevelopment legislation, 29–30, 35, 339, 373

Job Corps, 28, 331
job training legislation, *see* manpower
    development legislation
Johnson, Andrew, 49
Johnson, Lyndon B., 33, 111, 112, 120,
    126, 136–37, 162, 198–99, 210,
    217–18, 265, 273, 296, 297, 299–
    301, 304, 310–11, 318, 322, 363,
    375–77
joint committees, 157–58, 250
judiciary, 46–47, 84–87, 146, 300, 304
    see also Supreme Court
Judiciary Committee (House), 49–50,
    67, 155, 293
Judiciary Committee (Senate), 140,
    146–47, 155, 166
junior members, *see* freshmen in Con-
    gress
Juvenile Delinquency, Office of, 340
juvenile delinquency legislation, 340,
    368, 375

Kennedy, Edward, 256
Kennedy, John F., 24–25, 112, 120,
    136–37, 291, 297, 299–301, 302–3,
    304, 310–11, 318, 322, 327, 340,
    375–76
Keppel, Francis, 337
Kern, John W., 362
Kirkpatrick v. *Preisler,* 86
Kissinger, Henry, 293, 299, 381
Korea, 156, 205–6, 352, 392

Labor, Department of, 308, 315, 395
labor interests and legislation, 32, 91–
    92, 149, 176, 188, 264, 275–76, 285,
    296, 316, 334, 374
land use legislation, 371
leadership, *see* party leadership
League of Women Voters, 265, 269
Legal Services Corporation, 357–58
Legislative Reorganization Act (1946),
    245, 279
Legislative Reorganization Act (1970),
    250, 254
Legislative Research Service, 254
legislative veto, 328–29, 368
legitimation, 348–49
letter-writing campaigns, 282
liaison units, 302–3, 326–27, 332, 336
Library Joint Committee, 157

library services, 254
Lincoln, Abraham, 51, 301
lobbying, *see* interest groups
logrolling, 124–25
Long, Russell B., 173–74
loyalty, *see* institutional loyalties;
    party loyalties; state loyalties

McCarthy, Joseph, 124
McCormack, John, 196
McFall, John, 205–6
McGovern, George, 35
McKinley, William, 52, 71
McNary-Haugen bill, 313
Madison, James, 43–46
Magnuson, Warren, 27
majority leader:
    House, 69, 73, 196, 203, 205, 207,
        208, 211, 212, 217, 224
    Senate, 74, 195, 198–99, 203, 209–10,
        211
majority party, 205–6, 212–13, 220,
    307–16
    House, 68, 98, 103, 115, 180, 186,
        188, 215
    Senate, 64, 98, 104, 115, 146, 198, 215
    see also party control of Congress
Management and Budget, Office of,
    23, 201, 207, 298, 303–4, 306, 352,
    354
manpower development legislation,
    30, 32, 35, 185–86, 201, 310
Mansfield, Mike, 146, 198–99, 210, 217,
    305, 361, 378
maritime interests, 265–66, 269, 273
Marshall Plan, 315, 379
mass transit legislation, 183–84, 243,
    268, 278, 310–11, 375
Mass Transportation Act (1964), 243
Mayaguez, 360–61, 385
medical interests, 265, 272–73
medicare, 30, 38, 175–76, 188, 266, 334
Merchant Marine and Fisheries Com-
    mittee (House), 154, 155, 230
Michel, Robert H., 211
Mideast, 352, 381, 385
military legislation, *see* defense policy
    and legislation
Mills, Wilbur, 169, 172, 175–76, 193,
    232, 273
milk industry interests, 272–73, 279